Cultures of Inquiry

From Epistemology to Discourse in Sociohistorical Research 308

Cultures of Inquiry provides a unique overview of research methodologies in social scientific, historical, and cultural studies. Facing Kant's proposition that pure reason cannot contain social inquiry, John R. Hall uses a method of hermeneutic deconstruction to produce a "critique of impure reason," thereby charting a "Third Path" to knowledge. Inquiries conventionally allocated to science or interpretation, modern or postmodern, he argues, depend upon interconnected methodologies that transcend present-day disciplinary and interdisciplinary boundaries. *Cultures of Inquiry* identifies four formative discourses and eight methodological practices of inquiry, and explores new possibilities for translation between different types of knowledge. Its analysis neither exoticizes academic subcultures nor essentializes Culture as the spirit of Academe. Instead, it addresses workaday issues of research via a sociology of knowledge that speaks to controversies concerning how inquiry is and ought to be practiced under conditions of epistemological disjuncture.

JOHN R. HALL is Director of the Center for History, Society, and Culture and Professor of Sociology at the University of California, Davis. His publications include *Culture: Sociological Perspectives* (1993), with Mary Jo Neitz, and *Gone from the Promised Land: Jonestown in American Cultural History* (1987). He has also published widely on topics in sociological theory and sociohistorical research.

Cultures of Inquiry

From Epistemology to Discourse in Sociohistorical Research

John R. Hall

CAMBRIDGE
UNIVERSITY PRESS

PUBLISHED BY THE PRESS SYNDICATE OF THE UNIVERSITY OF CAMBRIDGE
The Pitt Building, Trumpington Street, Cambridge CB2 1RP, United Kingdom

CAMBRIDGE UNIVERSITY PRESS
The Edinburgh Building, Cambridge, CB2 2RU, United Kingdom
http://www.cup.cam.ac.uk
40 West 20th Street, New York, NY 10011-4211, USA   http://www.cup.org
10 Stamford Road, Oakleigh, Melbourne 3166, Australia

First published 1999

Printed in the United Kingdom at the University Press, Cambridge

Typeset in Plantin 10/12 pt. [wv]

A catalogue record for this book is available from the British Library

ISBN 0 521 64220 5 hardback
ISBN 0 521 65988 4 paperback

The fox knows many things, but the hedgehog knows one big thing.

Archilochus, quoted by Isaiah Berlin 1970: 1

Pragmatism, pending the final empirical ascertainment of just what the balance of union and disunion among things may be, must obviously range herself upon the pluralistic side. Some day, she admits, even total union, with one knower, one origin, and a universe consolidated in every conceivable way, may turn out to be the most acceptable of all hypotheses. Meanwhile the opposite hypothesis, of a world imperfectly unified still, and perhaps always to remain so, must be sincerely entertained. This latter hypothesis is pluralism's doctrine. Since absolute monism forbids its being even considered seriously, branding it as irrational from the start, it is clear that pragmatism must turn its back on absolute monism, and follow pluralism's more empirical path.

William Jones 1908: 161

Contents

Tables and figures

Acknowledgments

On the argument of the present book, foreshadowed in the prologue below, the analysis of cultures of sociohistorical inquiry contained herein can only be the product of a particular perspective. It is neither a view from nowhere nor objective truth: it is an account shaped by my own experiences. I grew up in an academic family. My interest in C. P. Snow's famous "two cultures" – science and the humanities – goes back to formative influences of my father, an embryologist, and my mother, a student of the relation between old French epics and medieval English literature. From the 1960s to the present, I have studied and worked under the institutional conditions of public and private universities in the United States.

Along the way, I received much in the way of useful directions, vital encouragement, thought-provoking criticisms, and important support. Among organizations, thanks go to the Graduate Research Council at the University of California–Davis for a graduate research fellowship; and to New College, Oxford University, and the Centre d'Analyse et d'Intervention Sociologique, Ecole des Hautes Etudes en Sciences Sociales, Paris – both for the opportunities for reflection they provided during a 1996–97 sabbatical year. I also wish to thank publishers for permission to reprint from two previously published essays which served as working papers for the present book. First, "Epistemology and sociohistorical inquiry," *Annual Review of Sociology* 16 (1990): 329–51, is reproduced, with permission, © 1990 by Annual Reviews, Inc.; revised portions of this essay were incorporated into chapters 1 and 2. Second, from "The problem of epistemology in the social action perspective," pp. 253–289 in Randall Collins, ed., *Sociological Theory 1984* (San Francisco: Jossey-Bass, 1984), revised portions were incorporated into chapter 4.

Important as organizational support has been, people have made the more crucial contributions. My appreciation of my parents, Edmund K. Hall and Marian Ross Hall, is beyond words. More directly, I am particularly grateful to Guenther Roth, H. Stith Bennett, Leonard Hochberg, and Doug Mitchell for inspiring and encouraging the project as a whole, and to William Brustein, Gary Hamilton, Michael Hechter, and Margaret Somers for timely counsel at important points along the way. As I completed drafts of the book's sections, I presented them at colloquia, seminars, and professional meetings, and asked people to read chapters. These activities have been immensely important to refining the analysis. In particular, I have benefited from the comments of Robert Alford, Ron Aminzade, Benjamin Bratton, Elaine Hoye, Edgar Kiser, Alan Sica, Charles Tilly, and Stephen Turner. I am especially grateful for the generosity of the anonymous reviewers and other individuals who commented on drafts of the entire manuscript – Richard Biernacki, Jenny Broome, Craig Calhoun, Jennifer Dunn, Steve Fuller, John Martin, Maureen Sullivan, and Ksenija Vidmar. At Cambridge University Press, the publishing of this book has been graced by the editorial wisdom of Catherine Max, whom I thank for her vision of the project and her efforts toward its fulfillment.

As anyone will understand who knows some of the people I thank, they are diverse in their thinking. It will be surprising if any of them agree with all of what follows. What I appreciate most is their willingness to engage me on issues of mutual interest. Yet for all the thanks that they richly deserve, responsibility for the shortcomings that seem inevitable to intellectual ambition is wholly my own. I dedicate this book to the woman who has led me to so much of value in life beyond it, Jenny Broome.

Prologue

A Third Path leads beyond modern and postmodern methodological debates in the social sciences, history, and the humanities. It turns out that choices between the routes of science and interpretation, history and theory, objectivism and relativism are more illusory than real. Even radically opposed methodologies for creating knowledge are only relatively autonomous of one another.

These are not conclusions I set out to reach when I first envisioned this book in the late 1980s. I began with an interest in bringing epistemology – the study of knowledge – into stronger relation with questions about the diverse styles of actual research. I wanted to explore the alternative cultural logics of what I will call "sociohistorical inquiry" – encompassing historical investigations, interpretive analyses, field research, and quantitative studies. The idea for how to do so came as I was completing a book on Jim Jones's Peoples Temple, *Gone from the Promised Land: Jonestown in American Cultural History* (Hall 1987). Reflecting on the methodological rationale of that study, I began to think more broadly about the relationships between what I call "forms of discourse" and "methodological practices of inquiry."

The more I read exemplars and the more I combed epistemological and methodological writings, the more I became convinced that virtually all kinds of inquiry about the social world are amalgams that combine the resources of four different kinds of discourse – value discourse, narrative, social theory, and explanation/interpretation. But despite my sense that these formative discourses are nearly ubiquitous, it became equally obvious that not all research combines the four discourses in the same way. For instance, one researcher may try to keep value judgments completely separate from research, whereas another's value stance entirely permeates empirical analysis. Differentials like this one suggested that I might be able to identify the cultural logics of methodological practices if I could identify various ways in which such practices thread together the four forms of discourse. Exploring the relations of discourses to alternative practices, and of alternative practices to one

1

another, might also reveal something about the overall domain of sociohistorical inquiry. In turn, understanding this overall domain might improve our local practices and sharpen our communication across divergent methodologies. Pursuing these possibilities is the project of the present book.

Chapter 1 introduces the project by describing my approach, which shifts away from considering knowledge as a purely philosophical problem of epistemology toward a broadly Weberian method of "hermeneutic deconstruction" that I use to analyze forms of discourse and practices of inquiry. Readers more interested in the results of this analysis than its rationale may read the book in other ways than beginning with chapter 1.

Each chapter in Part I takes up one of the four *forms of discourse* that I argue collectively structure practices of inquiry. These chapters develop sequentially. However, each formative discourse can reasonably serve as a point of departure in actual inquiry, and, in this light, each chapter on a form of discourse is relatively self-contained, so that it is possible to read selectively. For each form of discourse, I show that inquiry today confronts both legacies of historical development and characteristic philosophical, theoretical, and rhetorical problems which researchers address in conventional (or sometimes innovative) ways. Chapter 2 traces how discourse on *values* frames research projects and, in turn, how inquiry claims to offer knowledge of value about the sociohistorical world. Whatever the claims for inquiry within any particular resolution of the value problem, the chapter shows that a diversity of viable yet mutually contradictory value bases of inquiry coexist. Chapter 3 makes the case that *narrative* discourse is equally contested, but in different ways. It considers two broad problems: first, the question of how structural characteristics of narrative discourse shape both inquiry and life more generally; and, second, the issue of how narrative can be used as a methodology for research. Methodologically, the chapter differentiates between narratives that are established "intrinsically" – in the meaningful actions of people *prior* to inquiry's narration, versus "extrinsic" narratives that obtain their coherence in ways that are decisively based on the *ex post facto* activities of inquiry itself. In turn, chapter 4 develops a "theory of theorization." In the strong sense of the term, discourses of *social theory* involve efforts to make sense of sociohistorical phenomena on one or another *general* basis. Thus defined, any theory depends on some strategy of concept formation. Here, just as there are diverse plausible approaches to value discourse and narrative, theoretical discourse can conceptualize sociohistorical phenomena in multiple viable ways that cut across one another.

Some readers will want to interject that none of these discourses is really autonomous from the others. This is certainly my view as well. Therefore, in *codas* following chapters 2, 3, and 4, I explore how value discourse, narrative, and social theory lay certain claims on the fourth form of discourse – *explanation and interpretation*. Divergent resolutions of the value problem yield manifold projects in which explanation or interpretation might operate. Furthermore, both narratives and theories can yield explanations and interpretations in their own terms. However, "partialling out" valuational, narrative, and social theoretical claims still leaves a "core" discourse of explanation and interpretation, which I consider in terms of its own problematics in chapter 5. For this discourse, precisely the concern of scientists to differentiate explanation from "softer" approaches such as interpretation suggests a broad and contested terrain. In the most general sense, its discourse is concerned with *accounting* for sociohistorical phenomena and *adjudicating* among competing accounts.

Overall, examining the four formative discourses demonstrates that any given one of them reaches limits beyond which its problematics become articulated with other forms of discourse – values in relation to explanation, theory as an axis of narrative, narrative as explanation, and so forth. My central thesis is that sociohistorical research cannot be carried out wholly within the unalloyed logic of a single, "pure" formative discourse. To the contrary, actual inquiries depend on *hybrid* practices that involve extra-logical mediations among *different* formative discourses employed *in relation to one another*. That is, any given inquiry draws together value discourse, narrative, social theory, and explanation or interpretation. Thus, it should be possible to identify alternative methodological practices of inquiry as discursive hybrids that articulate relationships *among* formative discourses.

Pursuing this thesis, the chapters of Part II examine how the four formative discourses become drawn together in eight methodological *practices of inquiry*, which I elaborate by examining diverse historically oriented research studies. Chapter 6 describes my rationale for the typology of methodological practices that I propose, and table 6.1 previews the eight practices of inquiry that are considered in depth in chapters 7 and 8 (summarized in tables 7.1 and 8.1). Although the whole analysis is greater than the sum of its parts, readers most interested in particular methodologies of research can focus selectively on one or another practice.

Among the eight methodological practices, chapter 7 explores four *generalizing practices* oriented toward research intended to apply across multiple cases (even if only a single case is the focus of a given inquiry).

These practices, derived from a theorization of historical-comparative sociology, are (1) universal history, (2) the application of theory, (3) analytic generalization, and (4) the development of contrasts through comparison. In turn, chapter 8 differentiates four *particularizing practices* oriented to the conventional task of histories, ethnographies, and other idiographic studies, namely, the comprehensive analysis of a single object of inquiry. They are: (5) situational history, (6) specific history, (7) configurational history, and (8) historicism. Taken together, the eight practices offer a set of benchmarks for understanding sociohistor-ical inquiry as a methodological domain. However, none of the eight is epistemologically "pure" in its logic. Instead, they are hybrids that cobble together the various forms of discourse in culturally meaningful ways.

Chapter 9 concludes that sociohistorical inquiry is neither a single, coherent, epistemologically founded scientific enterprise based on pure reason, nor a Babel of languages beyond translation. It is a complex of interpenetrating discourses, each with its own internal conflicts open to multiple resolutions, lacking any inherent external alignment, yet articu-lated with one another in alternative discursive constellations of prac-tice. The possible practices of research are shaped by historical legacies, yet open-ended and emergent. Any new practice remains, like other practices, a hybrid cultural logic of "impure reason" that confronts – well or poorly – both the enduring problematics within various formative discourses as well as the problem of bridging among multiple discourses in the conduct of research.

Precisely because inquiry operates in these circumstances, a surprising web of affinities and shared problematics can be found in the manifold practices of sociohistorical inquiry (these relationships are summarized in an admittedly byzantine diagram, figure 9.1, that probably should be viewed only when sitting down!). Heterogeneous methodologies of research are not autonomous; they are deeply connected, and some-times dependent upon one another. These connections are often denied by practitioners who want to assert the purity of their own methods, maintaining the boundaries that mark off some epistemological Other. But ultimate claims for the superiority of any given practice are suspect, because alternative and sometimes conflicting kinds of knowledge are culturally constructed under the discursive circumstances of impure reason shared by all practices. Therefore, no rhetorical claims of superi-ority can unilaterally seal off a given practice from critical considerations that lie beyond its supposedly pure domain. In particular, practices of science are predicated, like other sociohistorical research methodologies, on one or another cultural logic. By the opposite token, practices of inquiry that are dismissed in some quarters as "unscientific" or "anecdotal" have their own viable rationales which, if pursued rigorously, are capable of producing knowledge deserving of attention even by scientists. These conclusions imply neither that all culturally constructed knowledge is equally plausible, nor that any culturally constructed knowledge is necessarily untrue.

As for the present inquiry, it uses tools that I have previously favored in comparative-historical and field research, notably the analysis of substantive phenomena in relation to ideal types. Because some readers may mistake the systematic aspects of this approach as marking an enterprise with modernist or foundationalist pretensions, two points are worth emphasizing at the outset.

First, I do not claim to "totalize" or "represent" inquiry. Instead, I present ideal types as heuristics for the critique and formulation of inquiry's practices. However much these heuristics offer interpretive leverage for understanding inquiry, they neither represent nor subsume empirical diversity. There is always difference. Perhaps the most interesting practices of inquiry are neither fish nor fowl, neither type A or type B. Yet relatively patterned methodological practices of sociohistorical inquiry have become consolidated over the past two centuries or so. In these circumstances, typification helps to address questions of whether and how such practices act like fish or fowl, like A or B, and where and how they transcend the binaries. Even at that, no battery of conceptual tools is all-powerful. As the enterprise of writing the present book tells me, inquiry is a flux of lived practice that cannot be totally reduced to any rationalized systematization.

Second, readers will find that I address a number of issues of "reflexivity" as they arise throughout the text. Included, among other discussions, are a phenomenology of objectivity, discourse about discourse, a history of values, comparison of historicisms, and a theory of theorization. Although I claim no foundation for this study, there is this: unlike *logical* arguments affirming relativism, my account of inquiry's cultures is not in performative contradiction with the methodological practices used to produce it. Instead, there is a mirror reflecting in both directions between the concept formation and perspectives of this inquiry and the discourses and practices of sociohistorical inquiry that it describes. It is a text that I have sought to make an explication of itself.[1]

1   Introduction: the Third Path

Across the social sciences, history, and the humanities, approaches to research often seem disparate. On one front, sociologists Edgar Kiser and Michael Hechter seek to defend the project of general social theory in comparative and historical sociology. Arguing that idiographic approaches and recent trends toward induction play into charges of superficiality, Kiser and Hechter promote the search for causal mechanisms through the deductive use of general theory. From a different direction, in *The Return of Martin Guerre*, historian Natalie Zemon Davis has reexamined old accounts about a village in the south of France, where one day in 1556 there appeared a man who said he was the husband of a woman named Bertrande. Martin Guerre had disappeared years earlier, leaving behind his wife of nine years and a newborn child. The man recounted the reason for his disappearance – he had gone off to war – and the village people welcomed his return. Bertrande took him into her arms. But eventually the Martin Guerre who shared a bed with Bertrande lost favor, and came to be confronted in court with the return of the real Martin Guerre. Did Bertrande know from the beginning that she was accepting an impostor for her husband? Davis weaves a story of complex truths submerged in contending agendas of disguise. In the bargain, she reminds us that secrets and lies make social "reality" a many-layered thing.[1]

As these two examples suggest, it is possible to produce radically different kinds of sociohistorical knowledge. Kiser and Hechter promote inquiry into causal mechanisms, whereas a reading of Davis suggests that even detailed knowledge – much less any general explanation – is tentative, incomplete, and doomed to remain so. How are these and other practices of inquiry to be understood – in their own terms, and in relation to one another? What are the possibilities of dialogue among them? These questions deserve consideration within a broad domain – one that encompasses the social sciences, history, the humanities, and interdisciplinary enterprises such as historical sociology, feminist theory, cultural studies, critical theory, and the new historicism. That domain, which can be called *sociohistorical inquiry*, recently has been the object of increased interest in rethinking relationships among disciplines and interdisciplinary programs.[2]

In important ways, the issues are methodological. As Reinhard Bendix observed in 1981, "Once we accept that knowledge in the social sciences has been cumulative only to a very limited extent, we are more likely to take a stronger interest in what has previously been excluded: a fuller understanding – admittedly incomplete and partly intuitive – of the parameters of the search for knowledge and its objects of inquiry."[3] By questioning the potential of the social sciences for cumulative knowledge, Bendix implicitly linked them to history and the humanities. By distinguishing between knowledge and its objects, he drew into question any simple account of a representational correspondence between concepts and reality.

I take up Bendix's project of understanding inquiry here under circumstances in which the philosophical examination of claims to knowledge – epistemology – has been challenged by accounts of knowledge as a social construction subject to political and other extra-scientific influences. Yet social constructionists have not found it easy to move beyond general claims, to describe the specific cultural rationales that inform alternative constructions of knowledge. Nor have the social and historical critiques easily avoided circular problems of reductionism. When they focus on the conditions under which knowledge is produced rather than whether it is valid, such approaches fail to account for the significance of knowledge itself, and fall into the performative contradiction of delegitimating their own accounts as ones that may be reducible to external causes.

Contemporary controversies over knowledge derive in no small part from a vexing problem encountered by Immanuel Kant – that pure reason cannot contain inquiry concerning sociohistorical matters within its boundaries. As Kant understood, sociohistorical knowledge cannot be established entirely within the realm of pure reason, for human affairs conflate moral, intellectual, and empirical issues.[4] Given that pure reason at best offers only an incomplete basis for sociohistorical research, it is necessary to supplement Kant's own critique with a "critique of impure reason." As a contribution to the latter critique, the present study charts a "Third Path" that leads beyond objectivism and relativism to an understanding of inquiries in cultural terms – as structured practices with roots in shared discursive resources that facilitate communication about the sociohistorical world. This analysis takes as its point of departure the assumption that sociohistorical research is a craft activity carried out in professional worlds oriented to inquiry, akin to the art worlds that Howard S. Becker has shown are coordinated through the negotiation and use of "conventions" – working agreements about how things are to be done.[5]

The craft activities of research and their conventions might be investigated in many different ways. Others have studied the social, political, and economic contexts of everyday research practices. But there is another important aspect. Inquiry involves researchers, their audiences, and sometimes wider publics in the production and deployment of meanings. This feature implies that it should be possible to investigate the "cultural logics" that inform the conduct of research. Rather than approaching issues of methodology as matters of philosophical debate, a cultural analysis of this sort assumes that inquiry, like cultural logics elsewhere (for example, in religion), is a bit messy, resistant to thoroughgoing rationalization, and open to challenge from other cultural standpoints. On the basis of this assumption, it is possible to shift Max Weber's *verstehende* (or interpretive) method of cultural analysis from the investigation of meanings in the wider sociohistorical world toward the study of meanings in sociohistorical inquiry itself. To address the reflexive problem of circularity – conducting inquiry about inquiry – in the remainder of this chapter I review contemporary methodological conflicts and propose how to assay inquiry's prospects in light of them. In brief, that approach, which I call *hermeneutic deconstruction*, balances the critical power of deconstruction to unmask hidden meanings with the interpretive power of hermeneutics to identify coherent meanings in cultural constructions.

By investigating cultures of inquiry, I mean neither to exoticize inquiry as the domain of distinctive academic subcultures (microeconomics, ethnomusicology, Asian studies, and so forth), nor to essentialize Culture as a mysterious overarching spirit of Academe. Instead, I take inquiry to be cultural because it depends upon historically embedded and socially practiced activities of cultivating the soil from which knowledge is produced. Clearly, distinctive cultures of inquiry can be identified in diverse research programs, disciplines, interdisciplinary research agendas, and critical projects. But, in the interests of promoting a methodological debate about the inclusive domain of sociohistorical inquiry, I do not focus on local cultures of inquiry in their substantive specificities. Instead, I show how diverse methodological cultures are intimately connected by their alignments and oppositions to one another.

Overall, the Third Path transcends, on the one hand, foundationalism and objectivism, and, on the other hand, the more solipsistic and totalizing versions of skepticism and relativism. My approach can broadly be construed as "pragmatic," but it goes beyond a general affirmation of pragmatism to identify alternative pathways to knowledge and their potential grounds for communication with one another. This approach addresses workaday issues of research methodology, and simultaneously develops a sociology of sociohistorical knowledge – what Steve Fuller has called a "social epistemology" – that speaks to longstanding controversies concerning how inquiry is, and ought to be, constructed. Specifically, it is an essay in the project that Karl Mannheim once proposed – in the words of Dick Pels, "a sociological *reconstitution* of questions of truth, rationality, objectivity, and value" that shifts from foundationalist Epistemology to "small e" epistemology.[6]

From the foundations of knowledge to the cultures of inquiry

The conventional task of epistemology is to "found" inquiry on a single, logically consistent theory of knowledge. As the twenty-first century dawns, this project has become highly suspect. From one direction, in *Philosophy and the Mirror of Nature*, Richard Rorty has questioned the possibility of sustaining any general claims about knowledge. From an altogether different point of departure, Jacques Derrida uses deconstruction to seek out the unspokens and the unwrittens – silenced truths that haunt the texts marked by their absence.[7] There is serious contention about the ideas of Rorty and Derrida. But controversies over inquiry go well beyond philosophy and textual criticism. New voices have shifted the debates on a wide range of substantive topics – to name a few, the Holocaust, the colonization of the western hemisphere, the empowerment of women, and the political significance of popular culture. Doubts about general sociohistorical knowledge, deconstructive assertions about absent truths, and the new substantive debates converge in a situation that prevails for anyone who would practice inquiry. We all must suspect that, from someone else's point of view, our own efforts can be criticized as untenable. The methodologies that yield knowledge are manifold, and no one of them convincingly asserts its primacy. For sociohistorical inquiry, this is the modern/postmodern condition.[8]

Responses to this condition are several. Those scholars already committed to a discipline or research program, or to Reason as universal logic, may simply ignore external critique. Having invested whole careers in particular institutional arrangements and philosophical commitments, many scholars will continue their conventional disciplinary practices – art history, literary criticism, economics – as the crafts of intellectual guilds.

A second alternative is to join the ranks of methodological anarchists who assert that a single, objective, universal "Reason" must be displaced by multiple pathways to knowledge.[9] But this response begs questions about the character of these pathways and their merits. The methodologies of inquiry are not infinite in their variety, and no inquiry can do everything at once. Thus, anarchism still requires choice, and that choice may work out better if it is an informed one.

A third broad response is to establish a new practice of inquiry. On this front, certain recent exemplary studies address important puzzles – of how to reconcile theory with historicity, the material world with meaning, obdurate reality with the ephemeral social moment. Lynn Hunt's book *The Family Romance of the French Revolution*, for example, undertakes a critical use of Freudian theory to examine desires to rid the country of its royal "parents" that permeated the French political unconscious during the revolutionary period. On a different subject, Stephen Greenblatt's *Marvelous Possessions* describes how European "discoverers" found an imaginary new world by seeking to impose their visions from the old world onto the Americas.[10] These books artfully demonstrate that new approaches can create new knowledge by breaking the molds of old conventions.

The promise of the new exemplars, however, is not always reflected in broader currents of inquiry. Some new approaches resurrect old issues that are easier to resolve in rhetoric than in practice. Various "turns" – the historic turn in literary criticism, the cultural turn in history, the realist turn in historical sociology – help consolidate new practices of inquiry. But such moves do not necessarily resolve the enduring problems of the practices to which they are turning. For example, as I argue in chapter 8, the "new" historicism does not confront, much less resolve, the difficulties of the *old* historicism. What Pitirim Sorokin once called "fads and fashions" of inquiry often simply escape old problems only to arrive at new problems (at least new for their new proponents) that are equally intractable, and equally in need of critical thinking about how to conduct inquiry.

The repression of the old Methodenstreit

Inquiry reached this point, I think, because the classic late nineteenth-century conflict over methodology – the German *Methodenstreit* – has returned to haunt modern claims to resolve it. The *Methodenstreit* raised a series of linked questions – about the objectivity of science, the significance of values in inquiry, the relation of cultural science to natural science, and the prospects for generalization in the face of the uniqueness of history.

An intriguing stance toward these issues was promoted by Max Weber in the early years of the twentieth century. Working in the borderlands between history and the social sciences, examining the relationships between theory, methodology, values, and knowledge, Weber took up a position elsewhere than among the foundationalists or the relativists, the general scientists or the cultural historicists. Acknowledging the perspectival basis of sociohistorical knowledge, he sought to affirm inquiry as something other than science, which nevertheless amounts to more than opinion. Because Weber recognized that social conditions would affect the production of knowledge, he refused to be bound by philosophical analysis that treated inquiry as a strictly logical problem. But neither could he be satisfied by social relativists' indifference to the problem of epistemology.[11]

The methodological issues that Weber engaged are still disputed today. Indeed, we confront a new *Methodenstreit* for reasons that have much to do with how sociohistorical inquiry became institutionalized during the twentieth century. The problems of the old *Methodenstreit* were not resolved; they were shunted to the side by modernist totalizations of inquiry within autonomous domains of knowledge – science, aesthetics, and so on. Weber figured in these developments largely by the perverse appropriation that others made of his approach to values. Lifted from the context of Weber's methodology, the term "value freedom" was invoked to legitimate formalized "social science."[12] This dispensation met opposition from scholars such as the critical theorists of the Frankfurt School, C. Wright Mills, and Alvin Gouldner. But their reputation as mavericks underscores the modernist institutional interest in maintaining an aura of objectivity by policing an absolute distinction between facts and values. Economics, sociology, anthropology, and political science as social sciences, and history in its own special fashion, aspired to the objectivity presumed to protect the supposed "hard" sciences from any claims about social and historical contamination of knowledge. In an oddly parallel way, the humanistic disciplines became bastions intended to protect aesthetic and moral judgments from the taint of historical or sociological "reductionism." Values, to be worthy of the name, had to be freely chosen. Neither the creative act nor the moral choice could be reduced to any external determination. The various domains – natural science, social science, history, and the arts and humanities – could be autonomous only if values were partitioned off from "facts."

The program of isolating facts from values has by now become deeply problematic. This development affects all disciplines and methods, but it poses the greatest challenge for the legitimation of science. Here, positivism's philosophical prospectus once held out the hope of establishing a method for successively approximating true knowledge, subject to validation or disproof, that would not depend on metaphysical, ontological, or other assumptions, nor on mere opinions of investigators. But fulfillment of the positivist vision has proved elusive. By now, both on the basis of internal critique and because empirical evidence undermines claims for science as an autonomous enterprise, the modernist faith of positivism is widely (though not universally) discredited.[13]

The positivist project initiated by August Comte in the early nineteenth century underwent multiple incarnations – most notably, John Stuart Mill's inductive approach, Emile Durkheim's rules of sociological method, the logical positivism of the Vienna circle and Carl Hempel, logical empiricism, and the falsificationist strategy championed by Karl Popper. Positivists themselves identified a labyrinth of *internal* difficulties – for instance, the intractable problem of establishing a "law," the difficulty of separating the hypothesis of interest from untested assumptions, and the question of whether it is possible to establish a shared, theory-neutral observation language in which symbols "correspond" to empirical phenomena.[14]

Beyond these epistemological issues, early twentieth-century scholars like Max Weber and Karl Mannheim posed questions concerning how ideas and "knowledge" become socially distributed in the world. Specifically addressing the production of knowledge in professions, Weber analyzed institutional circumstances, and he asked how intellectual work is framed by ethical and value orientations, and how it is driven by processes such as rationalization (for example, in theology). For his part, Mannheim explored the cultural histories and meaningful ideological structures of mentalities such as conservative thought and the liberal-humanitarian idea of progress.[15]

In its modern American dispensation, especially at the hands of Robert Merton, the sociology of knowledge became increasingly concerned with distinguishing "scientific" from biased forms of knowledge. But social studies of science have had consequences that Merton did not intend. Thomas Kuhn's *The Structure of Scientific Revolutions* argued that the most dramatic scientific changes occur not through gradualistic testing of hypotheses, but in revolutionary shifts that sweep away paradigms previously protected through the practice of normal science. In the wake of Kuhn's pathbreaking book, diverse studies have pointed to historical circumstances, the political economy of knowledge interests, the social organization of inquiry, ideology, funding, competition, social networks, and communication processes as factors that undermine the autonomous integrity of science through external contamination of its practices.[16] Even the last defense of science – the demonstrable power of its theories – no longer necessarily legitimates its claims to generalized, objective knowledge. As Bruno Latour argues, there is no need to deny science's empirical demonstrations in order to show that science socially constructs discrete "nature–culture" complexes out of manifold latent possibilities.[17] Biological knowledge, for instance, connects selected aspects of natural phenomena with scientific techniques in ways that sometimes create organisms such as killer viruses and processes such as cloning; when deployed, such constructed novelties become elements in emergent biological systems. Biology does not simply study the world; it combines technology and nature to create phenomena that become new parts of its field of study.

The character of knowledge has also been reconstrued on other fronts over the past three decades, most notably in critical theory, feminist theory, subaltern studies, anthropology, history, and cultural studies.[18] Deconstruction is the iconic development, because it casts doubt on any rational apparatus for representing things, either within texts or beyond them. Jacques Derrida's analysis, with origins in the poststructuralist critique of structuralism, holds that any coherence in a text – whether of fiction, ideas, or events of the sociohistorical world – can be achieved only on the basis of linguistic feats that mask textual contradictions and ellipses. The practice of deconstruction erases any charitable "suspension of disbelief" about texts in order to investigate how they accomplish their sense of being *about* something, which no longer can be construed as "representation" of anything. The implications for inquiry are unnerving. "Deconstruction," philosopher Joseph Margolis writes, "demonstrates that, in any [our own] historical setting, it is always possible to construe any established schemata for analyzing and interpreting familiar phenomena as more restrictive, more distorting, more inadequate than another that can be generated, now, by submitting the one or ones in question to the process of supplementation." As anthropologist Clifford Geertz has remarked, the collapse of distinctions between categories of storytellers means that "the very right to write – to write ethnography – seems at risk."[19]

Small wonder that assertions about the relativism of enveloping yet unstable textuality meet resistance. To note an emblematic case, feminist theorists are justifiably critical of research that fails to come to terms with gender, and they have raised serious questions about whether methods of inquiry are gendered in how they produce knowledge. Still, the alternatives to the false objectivism of patriarchy can be disconcerting. One argument holds that people of one gender lack any basis to speak about those of another. But certain feminists criticize such strong relativism. Thus, Donna Haraway acknowledges, "The further I get in describing the radical social constructionist program and a particular version of postmodernism, coupled with the acid tools of critical discourse in the human sciences, the more nervous I get." And, while Sandra Harding recognizes that white feminists cannot presume to speak for feminists of color or women in general, she nevertheless warns against essentializing subject positions as sources of validity, and she remains committed to improving inquiry so that women can produce knowledge beyond mere opinion.[20] These feminist interests are shared by modernists and critical theorists who remain skeptical toward deconstruction because it seems to eclipse normative issues, and to encourage a culture of nihilism that denies the emancipatory potential of knowledge.[21] Facing the deconstructionist challenge, those who hope for rational discourse about the social questions refuse to admit their incarceration in the "prison house of language." They want to reach beyond the walls of the text to analyze our collective prospects.

From the end of purifying binaries to the Third Path

The significance of deconstruction will continue to be debated. But its critics seem right in one respect: the assertion of equality among the claims for all ideas is mistaken. Quite apart from the argument's performative contradiction, embracing it would require a pretense of naiveté that works no better in inquiry than it would in everyday life. The challenge posed by unconstrained relativism can be found in assertions that the Holocaust never happened.[22] But despite the pressing need to reason, as Jean-François Lyotard notes, the Enlightenment's ideals of progress through science, reason, and freedom have become subjects of critical doubt. For his part (and he is hardly alone), Lyotard favors postmodern "incredulity toward metanarratives."[23] In this climate, the status of Reason as a universal procedure can no longer be taken for granted.

The standoff over modernism and postmodernism, however, seems arbitrary. After all, the binary distinction between Reason and relativism is itself modernist, and it may distort our ability to understand the potential for knowledge. Inquiry is faced with a false choice – either formulate a new general account of knowledge that reasserts some solid way of connecting representations and their referents, or succumb to the bedlam of texts. But the rejection of foundationalism should bring with it neither a stalemate in inquiry nor a legitimation of mediocrity. Conversely, the anti-relativist nostalgia for procedurally guaranteed truth not only ignores the internal crisis of epistemology; it also tends to sidestep questions about the interests served by institutional arrangements through which scientific knowledge is produced, thereby masking relationships between power and inquiry.

A number of scholars have described the binary oppositions that frame the standoff. Hilary Putnam laments the opposition between Reason and relativism. For Richard Bernstein, the central problem concerns reconciling objectivism and relativism. Jeffrey Alexander writes of a disjuncture between science and relativism, and Randall Collins argues the claims of objectivism versus subjectivism.[24] These oppositions are formidable, but we need to reframe the problem in nonbinary terms if we are to avoid a dialectic of entrapment. Yet, paradoxically, any effort to transcend the oppositions on some *general* basis would simply replicate the totalizing and purifying impulses of modernity. Unfortunately, reactions against Reason, against theory, against representation sometimes fit this pattern: they become uncritically infused with the very modes of thought that they reject. It is too easy to reinvent modernist totalization through its destruction, by totalizing relativism via some critique of Reason or essentializing the world as a text.[25]

In these admittedly pragmatic calculations, the binary oppositions – between modern and postmodern sensibilities, between Reason and relativism, between science and its Other – seem overdrawn. We live in a world where, difficulties notwithstanding, inquiry is practiced and claims of knowledge are made. Each in its own way, either relativism or a monolithic Reason subverts critical inquiry – defined simply as the willingness to call into question any assumption, theory, or hypothesis.

Past the overdrawn binaries lies the Third Path to knowledge. This path is deeply connected both to modernist inquiry and to postmodern critique, but it moves beyond both. It marks the end of philosophy as an autonomous enterprise and the end of relativism as a self-contradictory totalizing claim. And it requires a new understanding of binary oppositions. Modernism, as Bruno Latour has observed, thrives on an odd contradiction: the assertion of sharp distinctions in principle, whereas, in practice, the powerful substantive demonstrations of modernist inquiry often depend on the construction of "hybrids" to connect the very things that the ideology of science must analytically distinguish – the vacuum and the machinery used to produce it, for example.[26] In the realm of sociohistorical inquiry, there is an analogue to Latour's account of hybrid relations between natural science and its objects – namely, the possibility of examining hybrid relationships across putatively "pure" regions and objects of inquiry.

One of the most imposing binaries is the one that worried C. P. Snow during the 1950s – the divide between "two cultures," the sciences and the humanities. This distinction continues to have its force – both in general (witness recent antipathy to historical and social studies of science) and in the intermediate realm of sociohistorical inquiry, where (shifting) boundaries continue to divide scientific and humanistic approaches. Yet the antipathies simultaneously mark and blur the boundaries with which they are concerned. By now there are widespread suspicions that art and science are intimately connected: science as art, rhetoric, and metanarrative, and art as something other than the free play of aesthetics, values, and ideas in an autonomous realm of creativity. Each culture has become historicized to the point where neither is autonomous from external influences. Yet efforts to erase the divide have not given rise to a scientific humanism or a humanistic science. And they have resulted not in one culture of inquiry, but many.[27]

Friedrich Nietzsche once suggested, "History must solve the problem of history, science must turn its sting against itself."[28] Reading Latour suggests that Nietzsche needs revision. Neither science nor history is up to the task of self-study, for they are hybrids, deeply interfigured with each other. Historians once claimed to proceed without theory, but they are now much more ambivalent about this point. Economists used to assert the neat boundaries of their discipline, but those boundaries seem less sharp today. Literary criticism, and especially deconstruction – are they not hybrid activities too?

The Third Path leads beyond modernist efforts to purify foundational logics of inquiry and postmodern critiques that simultaneously reject and recast modernist purifications. It uses a hybrid inquiry to identify the hybrid practices of inquiry. This route depends on understanding inquiry as the product of meaningful social *discourse*. As Seyla Benhabib delineates this shift, it can yield "an epistemology and politics which recognizes the lack of metanarratives and foundational guarantees but which nonetheless insists on formulating minimal criteria of validity for our discursive and political practices." Understanding inquiry as discourse makes it possible to explore the shared cultural worlds of rhetoric and reason, epistemology and ideology, knowledge and its purposes.[29]

Inquiry and its frames of reference

To investigate inquiry as discourse on the basis of some transcendent "view from nowhere" would make no sense. What approach, then, might be congruent with present doubts concerning secure foundations of knowledge? Almost paradoxically, there is a point of departure adequate to this situation. It entails acknowledging a circumstance of inquiry that can be identified via theories of subjectivity, namely, that research is undertaken by socially interacting individuals employing various "frames of reference" that orient meaningful activity.

The major strands of subjectivist inquiry – hermeneutics, phenomenology, symbolic interactionism, and *verstehende* sociology – together suggest a sociology of knowledge that describes both inquiry and meaningful conduct in general. As subjectivist approaches emphasize, socially shared knowledge is possible only because meaningful understandings emerge in the unfolding "here and now" of everyday experience – what the social phenomenologist Alfred Schutz called the "lifeworld."[30] In Schutz's account, social actors – politicians, nurses, peasants, children, carpenters, and others – make meanings about the world in relation to personal interests, knowledge, categories, and experiences that come to the fore in their individual streams of consciousness.

Lifeworldly circumstances shape both the subject matter of sociohistorical inquiry and its relationship to that subject matter. In the words of Anthony Giddens, sociohistorical research is engaged in a "double hermeneutic" – giving second-order interpretations to social phenomena, such as the Vietnam War, ethnic inequality, theatrical productions, and so on, that are themselves already matters of (often contested) meanings. Under this circumstance, sociohistorical inquiry imposes asymmetric power relationships of dominance and subordination that effectively replicate subaltern colonialism. That is, the double hermeneutic of inquiry places the meanings of its "subjects" in contexts alien to them. But this is not the end of the matter. Certain feminist epistemologists point out that inquiry's meaning-production occurs in the lifeworld, and that the observed subjects themselves gaze back at the observers.[31] The observed, and people in general, can make meaning about inquiries' projects of meaning-making. This circumstance reflects a general condition of "reflexivity" – that social actors make meanings about other meanings as part of everyday life. This condition has sometimes been regarded as an obstacle to rigorous inquiry, but, more recently, efforts to come to terms with reflexivity have been proposed as a basis for, as Loïc Wacquant puts it, transforming "the social organization of social science as an institution inscribed in both objective and mental mechanisms."[32]

The mental mechanisms that concern Wacquant can be sketched initially by describing the frames of reference available to inquiry. Research is meaningful lifeworldly action. It transpires under specific historical, social, and economic conditions, at particular times and

Table 1.1: *Types of meaning produced via alternative frames of reference*

	FRAME OF REFERENCE		
	Social actor's lifeworld orientation	Observer's lifeworld orientation	Observer's objective orientation
TYPE OF MEANING	Subjective meaning	Observer's subjective interpretation	Observer's interpretation of meaning in objective context

places, through lived social relationships, on the basis of more or less institutionalized conventions for producing and exchanging ideas and knowledge. Because inquiry takes place in the lifeworld, even if it produces specialized meanings, there is no reason to think that the frames of reference available to it are intrinsically different from those available to people in general.

Alfred Schutz analyzed such possibilities in his famous critique of Max Weber's *verstehende* sociology. According to Schutz, each person makes subjective meaning richly and more or less continuously in the flow of everyday experience and action – directed not only to the immediate present, but also to anticipated futures, to memories, and to dreams and fantasies. Each person is simultaneously oriented as both an *actor* and an *observer*, interpreting experience by reference to her own stock of knowledge. Meaningful cognition is a complexly orchestrated mélange of different mental acts in the course of unfolding life, but, analytically, three component frames of reference of these acts can be identified. Most obviously, there is (1) the *social actor's lifeworld orientation* as "author" or "agent" in the conduct of life through meaningful social action and interaction. Beyond this frame, Schutz differentiates two other orientations that individuals have available to adopt as *observers* of phenomena: (2) an *observer's lifeworld orientation* that seeks to apprehend original ("subjective") meanings held by other social actors in their own situations, and (3) an *observer's objective orientation* that apprehends social and other phenomena via some interpretational matrix available to the individual through a general stock of knowledge – for example, religious norms, historical memory about Winston Churchill, psychoanalytic interpretation, business procedures, political ideology, and on and on (see table 1.1).[33]

These alternative frames of reference are only schematic, and they are manifested in intricate ways, both in everyday life and in inquiry.

Distinguishing frames of reference does not resolve inquiry's ontological debates about any supposedly ultimate nature of the world, and it does not privilege one perspective over another – either one that depends on some, "objective" frame of reference, or "lifeworldly" approaches such as *verstehende* sociology and feminist-standpoint epistemology.[34] Instead, it describes a general condition – that multiple frames of reference coexist (1) on the basis of differences between observers' lifeworldly attempts to discern other people's subjective meanings versus observers' efforts to apply objective categories to analysis, and (2) because observers' objective analyses may draw on diverse interpretive schema. Given this general condition, unless and until some descriptive ontology becomes warranted as valid independent of theory, any inquiry must be assumed to have a perspectival status that draws on an observer's lifeworld orientation and/or one or more observers' objective orientations toward framing phenomena, and to make meaning on the basis of the orientations employed. In lifeworldly terms, without denying the potential power of scientific knowledge, we have no reason to assume that science was ever so detached and privileged as the modernist prospectus for it envisioned. On the other hand, even critical practices such as deconstruction do not spell the end of inquiry, for they also depend upon one or another frame of reference, subject to the reflexive gaze of other perspectives.

The hermeneutic deconstruction of inquiry

Once the perspectivity of all inquiry is acknowledged, we can ask how inquiry works when its approaches are culturally structured in alternative ways. This question can be pursued by using a strategy of "hermeneutic deconstruction" – a hermeneutic supplementation of deconstruction – to examine practices of research as cultural *bricolages* of discourse. Overall, this approach tempers the critical power of deconstruction to expose ellipses and contradictions of discourse with the reconstructive power of hermeneutics to tease out meanings in their cultural coherence.

As a way of analyzing inquiry, hermeneutic deconstruction takes inspiration from social epistemology, the sociology of knowledge, feminist theory, rhetoric, pragmatism, and critical theory. It might be thought of as a Foucauldian archeology of knowledge, reflexively directed toward inquiry. The predominant trope – discourse – is theorized by analogy with the work of Jean-François Lyotard. In terms of table 1.1, the central frame of reference is an observer's objective analysis of meaningful discourse, specifically, by way of Weberian ideal types –

sociohistorical models of patterned meaning complexes – used for purposes of cultural interpretation. The project takes inspiration from Karl Mannheim's investigation of ideological and utopian mentalities, but it differs from Mannheim (1) by drawing on strategies of discursive analysis that have emerged since he wrote; and (2) by focusing the sociology of knowledge reflexively toward understanding the possibilities of inquiry itself.[35]

This program of investigating inquiry as meaningful cultural activity has its general warrant in Hilary Putnam's pragmatist agenda of shifting from the search for a single encompassing Reason to recognizing different historically formed modalities of small-r reasoning. Given that my investigation cannot transcend its own account of knowledge without engaging in a performative contradiction, I cannot make any claim about its ultimate truth. But Ian Hacking cites the research-program strategy of Imre Lakatos as suggesting an alternative to the standard of truth as a criterion by which to judge inquiry, namely, whether it "opens up new things to think about."[36] In the terms suggested by Putnam and Hacking, the present study is a local project of reasoning that seeks to open up new ways of thinking about meaningful methodologies of sociohistorical inquiry.

A general philosophical strategy for studying inquiry in this way was elaborated by Richard McKeon in the 1950s. McKeon argued that different kinds of inquiry directed toward the same ultimate subject matter can be generated by alternative ways of combining multiple discourses.[37] How might this McKeonian insight be used to understand sociohistorical inquiry? The method of hermeneutic deconstruction draws on both the work of Jacques Derrida and the hermeneutic tradition, but it does not rigidly follow either one.

Deconstruction, totalization, and supplement

There is an interesting warrant for offering hermeneutics as a supplement to deconstruction. As Derrida made apparent in his 1967 essay, "Structure, sign, and play in the discourse of the human sciences," the study of discourses is crucial to the poststructuralist critique of structuralism. In this essay, Derrida described the "centered structure – although it represents coherence itself" as "contradictorily coherent." To illustrate the problem, he reviewed the famous mythic structures of "savage" and modern thought that Claude Lévi-Strauss had depicted in *The Savage Mind*. From what standpoint could Lévi-Strauss's discourse on these mythic structures proceed? Derrida insisted that the search for an epistemological foundation should be renounced in favor of a discourse that "must have the form of which it speaks": in Lévi-Strauss's case, discourse on myth "must itself be *mythomorphic*." This approach is necessary, Derrida suggested, as an acknowledgment that no attempt at "totalization" – encompassing everything within a coherent framework – can be assumed to have a privileged status.[38]

Indeed, any totalization gains coherence at the expense of the aspects that it omits, suppresses, or subordinates, and it is vitally dependent on these textual solutions. Therefore, a "supplement" may be developed to identify *absences* – those things not contained by the attempted totalization. There is always "play" between totalization and supplement, and, in turn, a tension between this textual play and history. Put differently, every coherent discourse is incomplete and subject to the exploration of its omissions, which are prefigured by the explicit or implicit principles that yield its coherence. A totalization of liberty versus tyranny, for example, might be deconstructed in relation to the absent construct of community. Similarly, any coherent inquiry based on elaborating the principle of social class *per se* tends either to exclude ethnicity and gender, or to place them in derivative positions. Elaborating such relationships is the task of deconstruction.

Yet is the identification of present (implied) absences the end of the matter? After Derrida, is all else supplementation? The answer, at least for Derrida, is that it is not. If, between two strands of a double-helixed terrain of inquiry, one strand "dreams of deciphering a truth or an origin which escapes play and the order of the sign," while the other one "affirms play," Derrida refuses the choice between the two, first because it is "trivial," and second "because we must first try to conceive of the common ground, and the *différance* of this irreducible difference."[39] A point not often acknowledged bears emphasis: although Derrida's deconstruction is sometimes presumed to render all totalizing frames of reference irrelevant, Derrida himself proposed a dialectic of totalization and supplement.

In the present study, deconstruction offers a vital strategy for moving beyond the surface claims of various methodologies, to see how each is constructed as a conventionalized totalization of inquiry, the supplementations of which are equally totalized alternative methodologies. Yet in light of Derrida's interest in a dialectic between totalization and supplement, this project of deconstruction itself ought to be supplemented as a way to avoid totalizing its analysis. For the study of inquiry, this supplementation can be pursued via a hermeneutic recovery of meanings.

Hermeneutics after poststructuralism

If the study of inquiry were pursued as a purely philosophical project, it would fall into a circular begging of the question – what is the epistemological foundation for studying the epistemological foundations of inquiry? But the hermeneutic method follows a different route. From origins in scholarship devoted to exegesis of biblical texts, practices of hermeneutics have found their way into diverse efforts to gain interpretive understanding of meanings, no longer confined to sacred texts, or even written ones.

This shift in interest, originating in the late nineteenth-century *Methodenstreit*, yielded multiple approaches to interpretive understanding. Most notably, Wilhelm Dilthey proposed a program of biographical history, and Max Weber emphasized interpretation of observed meanings. More recently, programmatic solutions have included Hans-Georg Gadamer's interpretive historicism, Charles Taylor's emphasis on meanings shared in common, Paul Ricoeur's temporally grounded emphasis on discourse-as-text and action-as-narrative, and Clifford Geertz's anthropological practice of "thick description." Along with the proliferation of methods, the objects of analysis have widened as well. Today, texts are to be found both in the utterances and interactions of people, and in the cultural products of social action – from sermons, talk at the dinner table, etiquette guidebooks, television commercials, and cityscapes, to social theories and studies of historical events. Yet these texts no longer have any stable relationship with authorship or meaning. The reasons for this are diverse. From one point of view, Jürgen Habermas takes issue with any effort to privilege an individual's or social group's self-interpretation to the exclusion of critical discourse. From another, the poststructuralist movement heralded by Derrida's deconstruction converges with phenomenological accounts of reading and writing. Both emphasize the historical and existential instabilities of meanings.[40] Synthesizing, a poststructuralist and postsubjectivist model of textual production and reception emphasizes a historicity of textual circulation in which neither the autonomy of the text as symbolic structure nor the meaning-making agency of any temporally stable "author" or "reader" can be theoretically privileged in advance.[41] With the collapse of the fixed subject and the fixed symbolic structure, phenomenology and poststructuralism converge in pointing toward manifold historically unfolding textual circuits of meaning operating in the lifeworld and media connected to it.

The present study directs interpretive understanding toward the circuits of meaning whereby sociohistorical research is carried out. This hermeneutic strategy builds upon contemporary work on rhetoric. Studies by scholars like Wayne Booth on fiction and Donald McCloskey on economic discourse have helped unmask the devices by which texts convince readers of their integrity, independently of the factual basis of their claims.[42] In its hermeneutic aspects, the present study supplements rhetorical analysis of the *products* of inquiry by explicitly considering how meanings shape the *conduct* of inquiry. The idea is not to assert the ultimate validity or invalidity of various methodologies, but to examine how they assemble meanings from diverse discourses into culturally coherent practices.

In turn, this hermeneutic program has a deconstructive dimension. Using the term "deconstruction" here may stretch some conventional understandings, because hermeneutics emphasizes identifying meaningful cultural logics, not their absences. But it would seem paradoxical to totalize deconstruction in a way that excludes the present practice. Deconstructive supplementation is play rather than structure, and texts can be subjected to its scrutiny in various aspects – ranging from grammar, punctuation, and word usage to basic concepts of philosophy.[43] The task here is not to describe an overarching meaningful structure of inquiry. Instead, deconstruction is used to identify multiple kinds of totalizing coherence and supplementary contradiction that coexist in unevenly connected alternative practices of inquiry. This analysis demonstrates why there is an *absence* of totalization among methodological practices.

Making meaningful discourse the object of hermeneutic deconstruction is an arbitrary decision (in that another choice could be made), but the reasoning behind the choice at least can be identified: it is directed toward clarifying the cultural rationales of inquiry (hence the hermeneutic emphasis) – an objective that can be judged by its results and not by *a priori* claims about any supposedly essential character of discourse. The strategy employed draws broadly on Michel Foucault's studies of knowledge and more explicitly on the perspective developed by Jean-François Lyotard in his book, *The Differend*.

The forms of discourse and practices of inquiry

Foucault's initial account of the human sciences, *The Order of Things*, published in 1966, argued that a certain "positivity" of knowledge in the "human sciences" is obscured by sterile debates over whether they can be "sciences." Convinced that the human sciences "are not sciences at all," Foucault sought "to determine the manner in which they are arranged in the *episteme* in which they have their roots; and to show, also, in what respect their configuration is radically different from that of the sciences in the strict sense." He traced the differences between human sciences and strict sciences to two dimensions of the human condition: (1) reflexivity of consciousness, "the transposition of external models within the dimension of the unconscious and consciousness, and the flowing back of critical reflection toward the very place from which those models come," and (2) historicity, a feature of social life that "surrounds the sciences of man with a frontier that limits them and also destroys, from the outset, their claim to validity within the element of universality."[44] Three years later, in *The Archaeology of Knowledge*, Foucault called *The Order of Things* "a very imperfect sketch." He recast his position by defining the "episteme" as a totality of relations among sciences understood as discursive regularities, and he proposed to search out "unities of discourse" that are identified not in any shared features or coherent logic but, rather, in "systems of dispersion."[45] In this account Foucault describes the general approach he employed in substantive studies such as *Madness and Civilization* and *Birth of the Clinic*. His strategy suggests a similar project for sociohistorical inquiry.

What Foucault called "systems of dispersion" can be identified in inquiry by mirroring Jean-François Lyotard's treatment of discourse in his book, *The Differend*. Lyotard contends that all discourses are composed by drawing from heterogeneous phrase regimens. For example, "What is a door?" and "Open the door!" belong to different phrase regimens – one interrogative, the other a command. Different phrase regimens, Lyotard shows, cannot be "linked" to one another in any "pertinent" way. But despite this heterogeneity of phrase regimens, phrases from different phrase regimens become drawn together in genres of discourse – orderings of phrases that themselves have some purpose, such as persuasion or entertainment. Any genre of discourse has something at stake, which Lyotard describes as based on "a single, universal principle, shall we say that of 'winning' or 'gaining.'" However, the stakes in any given genre of discourse are distinctive, and two different genres of discourse therefore may be marked by a "differend" – an ultimate incommensurability between them. The leverage or gain pursued within one genre may have nothing to do with that sought in another. The stakes of an ethical debate, for example, are not typically the same as those of a strategy discussion among politicians.[46]

Lyotard offers his model of phrase regimens and genres of discourse on a level of generality that transcends inquiry. It is not just a matter of philosophical, scientific, or critical discourse: there are discourses of politics, love, and work. The model thus has an affinity with recent efforts to analyze discourses in the world in general.[47]

My purpose here is similar, but I use Lyotard's model of genres of discourse and their constituent phrase regimens as an analogue to inquiry itself. Specifically, I explore sociohistorical inquiry as an arena contested by alternative *practices of inquiry* – relatively conventionalized methodological approaches to the production of sociohistorical knowledge (for example, universal history or, on a different front, analytic generalization). However, these practices cannot be assumed to be logically coherent enterprises; unless otherwise demonstrated, they must be provisionally regarded as logically impure hybrids.

How can these hybrids be described? Just as Lyotard's genres of discourse draw together heterogeneous phrase regimens, practices of inquiry submerge methodological issues not just in rhetoric, but in logical and analytic problems that are the prior subjects of contestation within distinctive zones – for example, social theory. These zones I call *forms of discourse* (or sometimes, "formative discourses"). I do not mean by "form" an entity having autonomous existence. Rather, it is a zone where particular discursive precepts and strategies help "form" practice. Issues relevant to any formative discourse are subject to contestation over alternative conventional resolutions. "Forms of discourse" are thus to be located somewhere between what Aristotle designated as *topoi*, or commonplaces available to all rhetoric – whether of science, law, or love – and what he identified as special topics – lines of argument relevant only to particular subjects. Formative discourses are domains where alternative commonplaces are contested in relation to specialized problems of methodology relevant to how inquiry is conducted.

For any form of discourse, hermeneutic deconstruction can seek to identify its distinctive problematics concerning how to construct coherences about things that in themselves lack any single coherence – namely, the actualities of sociohistorical phenomena. As with Lyotard's phrase regimens and genres of discourse, various forms of discourse in relation to practices of inquiry are like shoes and a coat that both clothe the person but work in different ways. They need not be equivalent in their structure or relations to inquiry. Pursuing this analogy, there is more than one kind of shoe or coat, and alternative *regimens* can order any formative discourse in different ways, thereby affecting how it gets drawn into one or another practice of inquiry.

Identifying formative discourses of inquiry is partly a theoretical task rather than solely an empirical one. As the phenomenology of reference frames (table 1.1) suggests, concepts are not simply representational; rather, they "bring things into view" from one or another perspective. The perspective here is oriented toward unmasking how multiple discourses structure inquiry's practices. In the absence of any assumption concerning the ultimate validity of categories, I do not claim *a priori* that the way I conceptualize formative discourses is somehow definitively "correct." Instead, the procedure is best judged by the interpretive leverage that it yields – namely, whether it offers a useful way of understanding sociohistorical inquiry.

My conceptualization of discursive forms is based on a survey of research exemplars and epistemological writings on social science, history, and humanistic inquiry. The results of this survey are embedded in the present study. In brief, I have found four distinctive forms of discourse that are widely shared across diverse methodologies, research agendas, and disciplines. All four can be conceptualized as constituent discursive zones, each necessary but no one of them sufficient to the consolidation of any practice of sociohistorical inquiry:

1. Discourse on *values* contests the goals and purposes held to legitimate inquiry, their implications for how inquiry is structured, and the relevance of knowledge produced. As chapter 2 shows, this discourse has a long history of mediating how inquiry is construed.
2. *Narrative* discourse constructs "stories" – in a nonpejorative sense – about events germane to inquiry. Chapter 3 investigates how alternative precepts shape the culturally universal activity of storytelling into a discursive aspect of inquiry.
3. Beginning concertedly in the nineteenth century, discourses of *social theory* are used to identify sociohistorical phenomena in relation to one or more conceptual frameworks. The alternative conceptual bases of theory construction are theorized in chapter 4.
4. Discourse of *explanation* (or, with greater humility, *interpretation*) is concerned with proper strategies for offering and adjudicating among accounts that attempt to make sense of sociohistorical phenomena. Chapter 5 explores explanation and interpretation as a distinctive zone of discourse.

All four of these formative discourses have been the subjects of considerable scholarship in their own right. Because the present study is centrally concerned with how methodological practices constitute *networks* of relations among precepts and strategies drawn from multiple discourses, the chapters on formative discourses focus on internal contestations about each discourse and their implications for precepts and strategies of inquiry. The codas to chapters 2, 3, and 4 – on values, narrative, and theory, respectively – examine these three discourses in relation to explanation and interpretation, in anticipation of investigating core issues concerning that discourse in chapter 5.

This approach can be foreshadowed by briefly considering one contested zone of discourse. In the realm of social theory, as Jeffrey Alexander describes it, the merits of answers to questions can be considered on the basis of theoretical logic, without reducing the enterprise to ideology, games of power, empirical questions, sociohistorical determinants of science, or some other deconstructing frame.[48] How does this depiction of theory align with my model of formative discourses? Certainly, social theory can be considered in the self-contained way that Alexander describes. In turn, a particular regimen of social theory could be used to order other forms of discourse within an overall practice of inquiry, as a way of centering the practice. But, as Lyotard suggests more generally, the converse possibility cannot be ruled out – that social theory might be invoked within the frame of some other formative discourse (for example, a narrative discourse about a political movement that draws on social theories relevant to offering a history of the movement's growth). Indeed, a wholly alternative approach – for instance, a thoroughgoing historicism – can consolidate a project of sociohistorical inquiry in which general social theory is not just reduced to a subordinate moment of supplementation. Rather, an attempt can be made to deny its validity altogether, at least in any terms understood by social theorists. In short, whatever the autonomous logic by which social theory is developed, practices through which inquiry proceeds can invoke theory in alternative ways, some central, some peripheral or implicit.

Formative discourses may be relatively autonomous, but they are not absolutely autonomous. Substantive inquiry about the sociohistorical world can be carried out wholly within a single form of discourse no more easily than a conversation could be conducted using only interrogatives. Whether the endeavor is ethnomusicology or macroeconomics, any practice of inquiry presupposes some stance about how to theorize, and, similarly, about the ways that values, narrative, and explanation or interpretation come into play. Formative discourses are not types of inquiry; they are constituent elements of it. Thus, the ability to carry out research depends on resolving various problematics within different forms of discourse (such as social theory), but the solution to a problematic within a given form of discourse is not isolated. Instead, any resolution to issues within one form of discourse becomes articulated with resolutions to problematics from *other* forms of discourse (e.g., theory with narrative). Compositions that align resolutions to problematics from multiple forms of discourse amount to practices of inquiry. To paraphrase Lyotard, a *practice of inquiry* links *regimens* from multiple *forms of discourse* in a way that establishes distinctive stakes for inquiry.[49]

Overall, hermeneutic deconstruction of sociohistorical inquiry (1) examines forms of discourse in order to show how problematics internal to each discourse become resolved in alternative regimens that have implications for the structuration of full-fledged practices of inquiry, and (2) identifies methodological practices of inquiry that draw together such regimens of formative discourses. To show that the methodological practices I describe are indeed relevant to how inquiry is actually practiced, chapters 7 and 8 consider exemplars of substantive research where the cultural meanings of inquiry are in play. As Foucault noted, issues of time and historicity pose critical problems for sociohistorical inquiry. Therefore, I draw those issues out by focusing on exemplars oriented in one way or another toward *historical* analysis. But because practices of inquiry as ideal types are generic abstractions, they potentially bear relevance to a wide range of scientific, ethnographic, interpretive, and other research across the humanities, cultural studies, history, the social sciences, and even the biological and physical sciences. At least that is what colleagues have suggested to me. Readers, I hope, will test that claim themselves.

To sum up, investigating the cultural constructions of "impure reason" in sociohistorical inquiry depends on recognizing that practices of inquiry are shaped by the formative discourses on which they draw. I therefore map four central forms of sociohistorical discourse as they have been staked out through debates within and about their zones. Because contending regimens from these formative discourses become appropriated in alternative practices of inquiry, I do not try to resolve epistemological disputes within formative discourses through logical analysis – a Sisyphusian task at best. Instead, in order to connect the diverse strands of these disputes to their implications for multiple practices of inquiry, I focus discussion on alternative ways that problematics have been conventionally resolved within each form of discourse.

This analysis opens the way for the subsequent task – exploring how regimens from the four formative discourses become articulated with one another in alternative practices of inquiry. To be sure, all concrete sociohistorical inquiries have their own distinctive characters. But by analyzing exemplars of concrete inquiry in relation to practices of inquiry conceptualized as ideal types, it becomes possible to clarify the cultural logics of research without getting so caught up in the inevitable empirical differences among practices as to fail to understand their commonalities.[50]

By looking to how inquiry's practices draw together multiple forms of discourse, hermeneutic deconstruction decenters and renders to inspection the seamless meaningful fabrics of research methodologies, so as to unravel the tangled web of debates and strategies that have accumulated during centuries of efforts to "rationalize" inquiry in various disciplines and philosophical arenas.[51] This amounts to an examination of what Derrida called the "contradictorily coherent" aspects of inquiry through "supplementation." It will show that alternative practices of inquiry are generated out of shared forms of discourse, yet link regimens from them in counterposed ways that produce different and sometimes conflicting kinds of knowledge, even when they are used to analyze the same phenomena. Any given practice of inquiry is a dialectical supplementation of other practices, positioned simultaneously as a negation of them and as an affirmation of an alternative method. But the *logical* coherence of any practice is belied by the way in which it draws multiple forms of discourse into a *bricolage*. Its coherence is cultural, not purely logical.

As I will show in the conclusion, taking the Third Path leads to evidence of how sociohistorical inquiry operates under conditions of "heterology" – the coexistence of alternative culturally conventionalized kinds of knowledge. It shows that the practices of sociohistorical inquiry are neither isolated provinces with distinctive autonomous logics nor the single province of a general epistemology. Instead, diverse practices of inquiry that might seem incompatible with one another – thoroughgoing historicism and theoretically driven analytic generalization, to take two extremes – are at once bound together and separated by their uneven, differential, and contradictory connections to shared formative discourses.

By understanding the heterological condition, we can become clearer about the potentials and limits of alternative methodologies of inquiry, their spheres of knowledge, and the possible bases of communication and gaps between them. Such clarifications have practical implications for research: they help address questions about whether differences in knowledge – even concerning "the same" phenomenon – are prefigured by the formative discourses and research practices through which inquiries are pursued. It is thereby possible to challenge the skeptic's conceit that we are trapped within multiple, equally illusory ways of knowing by emphasizing that any cultural practice has (contestable) criteria for producing and assessing knowledge, and that alternative practices are neither necessarily isolated from one another, nor equivalent in their cultivation of knowledge. It also becomes evident why epistemological differences are endemic. Even seemingly empirical disputes, and certainly disputes over method, have less to do with any ultimate validity of contending practices than with the values and purposes of inquiry. It is to discourse on those values and purposes that I now turn.

Part I

Formative discourses

2   Value discourse and the object of inquiry

The topics of sociohistorical inquiry are not pre-formed things in the world itself. Instead, inquiry draws aspects of the world into focus through concepts like "industrialization," "social movement," "coup d'état," and "citizenship." It also proceeds by "colligating" – grouping together – "historical individuals" like "European feudalism," "the Tai Ping rebellion," "the Holocaust," and "the US labor movement." At the outset, we are best served by assuming that these organizing rubrics are not only historically saturated but also mediated by a welter of meaningful interests that shape inquiry. Conflicting preferences for one kind of knowledge over another, and assessments of their relative worth – in a word, values – shape the conduct of inquiry. Because the goal of a presuppositionless foundation of knowledge has proved elusive, at least initially, all "facts" about the world must be considered value- (or theory-) laden. And even if efforts to realize "objectivity" and "rational discourse" prove successful, they too embody value commitments – scientific ones that may crowd out others, such as emancipation, authenticity, and representation. Because competing ways of assessing inquiry's objects, purposes, and findings coexist, undertaking any research depends on a preparatory enterprise of clarifying the meaningful stakes of inquiry. This chapter describes that enterprise by considering what I call "the problem of values" – how contending discourses on ultimate purposes, goals, and routes to their realization frame the significance of an inquiry and its object, and in turn give meaning to, about, and from the sociohistorical world.

The value problem has somewhat different expressions within the social sciences as opposed to history, ethnography, and cultural studies. Historians began during the nineteenth century to aspire to write history as an objective account of a period, a nation, a historical transformation. But at the end of the nineteenth century, with rising interest in the problem of subjectivity, the significance of historical events became relativized. In either case, whether history was taken to have an existence "out there" or in the eye of the beholder, historians faced the "problem of selection" – reappropriated in the latter part of the twentieth century as the "crisis of representation."[1] What, critics asked, is a workable relationship between events posited to have occurred *in* history and historians' characterizations *of* history? The social sciences face a parallel question: is there a single objective procedure for producing knowledge by applying universal standards of validity, or does the pluralism of value stances necessarily result in a mosaic of conflicting methodologies? On the surface, there is a difference between history's (and ethnography's and cultural studies') question about representation and the question in the social sciences about the potential for objective knowledge. However, the two questions share concerns about how values mediate the relation between the object as constituted through inquiry and the flux of the sociohistorical world.[2]

Attempts to establish a workable relation between values and inquiry frame central projects of the Enlightenment and its critical alternatives. Tracing them thus would be a major project of intellectual history. Here, I explore historically emergent stances toward the value problem but my purpose is not historical. Instead, I want to show how divergent approaches to the value problem frame inquiry by differentially construing objects of inquiry and research methodologies to study them. Specifically, I describe five exemplary proposals for resolving the value problem: (1) attempts to use inquiry to chart objective values in historical processes; (2) Max Weber's "value-neutral" resolution that balances a value-relativity of cultural significance with a commitment to science as a vocation; and the major alternatives to Weber's position – (3) more thoroughgoing value-relativity that treats any inquiry – scientific or other – as value-laden and therefore perspectival rather than objective; (4) attempts to establish science as an objective value with significance that overcomes cultural and value heterogeneity; and (5) the efforts of critical theorists like Habermas to reestablish objective values, but in ways that transcend either objective science or objective historical representation. My survey of these counterposed positions cannot claim to adjudicate among them, but identifying important alternative approaches to the value problem that have emerged does reveal an empirical condition under which contemporary inquiry proceeds: given the coexistence of alternatives, whatever our own preferences, we engage in inquiry in a climate of value heterogeneity. As the coda to this chapter shows, the consequence of this condition for the discourse of explanation and interpretation is that divergent projects of inquiry coexist prior to any internal questions about the logics or validity of their accounts. In chapters 7 and 8, I explore the significance of divergent value resolutions and projects of inquiry for how alternative practices of inquiry are formed.

Objective values as selection in historical representation

Walter Benjamin once observed, "A chronicler who recites events without distinguishing between major and minor ones acts in accordance with the following truth: nothing that has ever happened should be regarded as lost for history." The question remains: would Benjamin's faithful chronicler produce specifically historical knowledge? Probably not. It seems that if historians are to contribute distinctive knowledge, annals of events have to be ordered according to some principle. The alternative, as Immanuel Kant worried, amounts to nothing more than a "planless conglomeration of human actions." But what might serve as an ordering principle? This question in turn raises other questions. Does history have meaning? Shape? Pattern? Direction? Stages? Does it amount to the vacillation between opposing forces, ideal or material, now in ascendance, later in decline? Are stages punctured by revolutionary shifts? Historically, these questions in the philosophy of history were not simply academic. Thinkers like Augustine, Kant, Comte, Hegel, and Marx had central concerns about the relation of history to divine plans, moral principles, or human emancipation. Philosophical histories, in other words, trace theologians' and social philosophers' answers to the question of how empirical history is connected to some principle of objective valuation that displays the ultimate significance of historical events.[3]

Without cataloging all the proposed answers, it is possible to identify two broad strategies for positing an overall meaning to history. On the one hand, there have been efforts to identify a somehow simultaneously transcendent yet immanent process *of* history that gives meaningful shape to the flux of events. Alternatively, assertions about any ultimate meaning of history can be held in abeyance, and, instead, a matrix of values or metaphysical constructs external to the object of inquiry can provide a barometer used to measure the historical flux of the human condition.

Meaning in history

The first solution – meaning *of* history – takes many shapes, from the fulfillment of God's purpose in the account of Augustine to nineteenth-century formulations such as Leopold von Ranke's scientific tracing of the divine plan evidenced by events, August Comte's "positive" formulation of the stages of history, Hegel's dialectic of spirit, and Marx's dialectic of material forces. Each posits a total history as a thing-like teleological process that gives significance to particular events within its domain. The differences among these accounts are substantial, but they center on the specifics of teleological processes and how they are to be discerned. In each case, history has meaning because it is infused with objective value significance. The outlying example is Ranke, who, after all, famously sought to formulate a "scientific" history that would tell "what actually happened." But this is not Ranke's only side. He also held that scientific objectivity depended upon understanding history's ultimate meaning or significance, that is, the plan of God. Scientific history could simultaneously reveal what actually happened and unveil the mystery of God: "Every action of the past gives evidence of God, every moment preaches His name."[4]

Marx's solution differs from Ranke's by its secular, rather than religious, dispensation. The *Economic and Philosophic Manuscripts of 1844* revealed no divine plan; they instead described an ontology of humankind that has at its center the alienation of labor as the estrangement of people – from nature, from themselves, from the products of their labor, and from each other. But Marx did not use this ontology to read history based on a moral standard. Instead, alienation reflects the origins of Marx's analysis in Hegelian thought: it is embedded in the historical process. In *Capital*, class conflict – the engine of history – unfolds as a dialectical process founded in the material conditions of alienation that yields a teleology of becoming, toward the promise of a future redemption from alienation.[5]

Because not all reflections about history are speculative philosophies, Alex Callinicos has proposed to distinguish "philosophies" of history from "theories" of history, on the grounds that the latter are not concerned with questions about the ultimate meanings or "discernible lesson" of history.[6] Yet this distinction draws too neat a dividing line. "Theories" sometimes take on the trappings of "philosophies," and efforts to extract lessons from history can be derived as well from theoretical analysis as from speculation about some posited *Geist* or dialectic. What matters is how the value problem is resolved. When the meaning of history is located in an objective value process working itself out *in* history, values, theory, and history become blurred. Once an initial assumption about a specific telos is granted, inquiry obtains a particular kind of "objectivity," by claiming to do nothing more than look to that which is real, which gives history its shape and meaning. Valuation orders inquiry from the beginning and permeates its every moment, but the locus of that which is valued is posited to exist within sociohistorical processes themselves.

The possible formulations of meaningful teleology range widely, from the city of God to the conflicts of humankind as the engine of history, to social evolution. What they share is an extra-empirical totalizing schema that points to the core value-relevant processes embodied within history as an object of inquiry. History can be read as the play of God and Satan. Progress can become an *élan vital* that works itself out on many fronts. Processes of class struggle can encompass the state, culture, and household life. Totalizing accounts of this sort cannot easily be disproved in their own terms. So long as the valuation reflected in a teleological schema is presumed to reflect the most important dynamics of sociohistorical process, contradictory evidence at most would point to the need to refine the account of telos in relation to the real as a standard.

Ultimate meaning as moral barometer

The second broad way of connecting inquiry to objective values is more epistemological. Like the solution linked to immanent processes of history, it asserts objective values in order to constitute an object for investigation. But values are not presumed to have some telos working itself out in sociohistorical processes. Instead, the calculus of values is a facet of inquiry: particular concepts are valued for how they orient the pursuit of knowledge. As a case in point, in one kind of Christian theology, sociohistorical process is not assumed to derive from any divine predestination, yet inquiry is ordered by theological questions about the nature of God's will. A parallel shift in Marxism abandons the materialist dialectic as an embedded and necessary process in favor of using a dialectical framework to orient analysis. Alienation shifts from immanent dynamic to conceptual barometer (and class struggle becomes an analytic construct) used to chart the vicissitudes of movement toward a more humane social order. The comprehensive analytic framework can be justified by the "objective" value significance of the issues addressed – alienation and class struggle, for instance – without presuming any teleology of historical process.

The valuation of a framework for analyzing phenomena represents a departure from immanent teleologies, whatever their specifics, toward the problematic of knowledge launched by Immanuel Kant. However, as I will show, formulating an objective framework of valuation is problematic, and the shift toward observer valuation thus opens up problems of value pluralism that mark a neo-Kantian pass-age to relativism.

Kant's approach to the problem of a "universal history" was to treat conceptual benchmarks for interpreting history as value constructions. He recognized that "It is strange and apparently silly to wish to write a history in accordance with an Idea of how the course of the world must be if it is to lead to certain rational ends," but he could not accede to a view of history as a "planless conglomeration of human actions." Facing this dilemma, Kant argued that proper study might reveal history's "guiding thread" tied to a gradual movement toward enlightenment. Even though there is no way of confirming the existence of "a natural plan," if history were studied in light of the assumption that such a plan exists, it could offer a way of charting "how the human race finally achieves the condition in which all the seeds planted in it by Nature can fully develop and in which the destiny of the race can be fulfilled here on earth." Kant could thus propose to study history in light of "the question of what the various nations and governments have contributed to the goal of world citizenship, and what they have done to damage it."[7] By distinguishing between ultimate destiny and its uneven earthly fulfillment, he left room for a moral realm that makes sense only on the basis of assuming an element of freedom in human action. A "natural plan" might have no causal necessity, but moral discourse could exam-ine history in light of it.

Kant's philosophy is built on the delineation of a realm of universal reason, but reason operates in relation to concepts that are construc-tions: even with reason, what we know about the world is mediated by our concepts. Examining experience by use of reason helps us find out about the world, but, because of the mediation of concepts, there is no hope for knowledge of the world as such. Indeed, pure reason does not establish social and political valuations of history, a point that Kant implicitly acknowledged in his discussion of universal history.[8] As neo-Kantians later argued, a general inference follows from the hiatus between *a priori* reason and the valuations that guide production of sociohistorical knowledge: radically alternative ways of knowing may be constituted by their distinctive valuations and conceptual frameworks.

Overall, Kant himself replaced the attempt to trace the telos of values in history with an effort to study history in relation to values. For the communal exercise of reason that Kant sought, it is necessary to assume that the values animating such an inquiry into the significance of history are "objective" in the specifically social sense that they are nearly *univer-sally shared*. However, this assumption is not easily sustained from a neo-Kantian position, for there are likely to be gaps between phenomena and observers' conceptualizations of them. This problem of multiple perspectives has given rise to two broad alternative resolutions to the value problem. First, there is Max Weber's stand for truth in the midst of unending value conflicts. Second, the identification of alternative value spheres of knowledge has been used to sustain a different neo-Kantian position – a perspectivist relativism.[9]

Max Weber and the valuation of truth

In the neo-Kantian climate of the late nineteenth-century *Methodenstreit*, the question of whether and how to construe values "objectively" continued to be the hinge on which the status of inquiry turned. Max Weber came to stand at the center of the controversy at the beginning of the twentieth century, and today his position offers a reference point from which to chart alternative possibilities. Weber insisted upon both causal and meaningful standards for sociohistorical explanations. He also distinguished sociohistorical inquiry from the natural sciences on the basis of the former's interpretive interest in phenomena of "cultural significance." Today, we question the autonomy of natural sciences from cultural significance. But in any case, cultural significance is a matter of valuation, and consistent with Kant, Weber resisted the idea that values could be justified scientifically. In "Science as a vocation," he argued that, despite the power of science, it cannot answer questions of ultimate meaning: "'Scientific' pleading is meaningless in principle because the various value spheres of the world stand in irreconcilable conflict with each other."[10]

How is sociohistorical inquiry to be conducted under conditions of irreconcilable value conflict? Guy Oakes maintains that Weber resolved such questions by turning to his contemporary, the philosopher Heinrich Rickert, who held that the value basis for inquiry is no different in sociohistorical inquiry than in the natural sciences. For both pursuits, Rickert asserted, truth possesses "unconditional general value," or what I will call "objective" value, that is, value which does not depend on one's perspective. Without this primordial valuation, any attempt at science would be self-contradictory. Moreover, in Rickert's view, this claim could not be dismissed by way of argument, for such argument would make sense only if truth has value. Thus, assaults on science by critical theorists, deconstructionists, and others might be taken by Rickert to vindicate truth's value as something worth struggling over. But the gain seems small. Even a general embrace of truth promises only a potentially endless struggle over the value of specific methodologies and concepts as paths toward realization of truth. Rickert's victory is Pyrrhic.[11]

Weber did not subscribe to Rickert's theory of objective values.[12] Instead, he sought to maintain a delicate balance, recognizing the *relevance* of values in the formulation of questions for sociohistorical inquiry, yet maintaining inquiry itself under the flag of "value-neutrality."[13] In a Kantian vein, Weber held that conceptualizations do not exhaust reality; they bring aspects of it into focus. Acknowledging that "the problems of the social sciences are selected by the value relevance of the phenomena treated," he viewed sociohistorical inquiry as the practice of one or another *cultural* science, and he maintained that valuations of answers to empirical and scientific questions are distinct from the value of pursuing knowledge through inquiry. Why an economic market in certain commodities takes a specific form, and what laws or social processes might account for its developmental tendencies – inquiry into these questions says nothing about whether a market should exist, or what form it ought to take. Nor are any of these questions – either the empirical or the normative ones – necessarily of cultural significance. For Weber, value relevance is not an objective phenomenon; it is a situational one driven by the interests of a lesser or greater number of people, shifting according to their perspectives and over time: "The cultural problems which move men form themselves ever anew and in different colors, and the boundaries of that area in the infinite stream of concrete events which acquires meaning and significance for us, i.e., which becomes an 'historical individual' [e.g., the Renaissance, the Cold War], are constantly subject to change." In line with this formulation, Weber recognized his own inquiries as Eurocentric in their concerns about the circumstances of modernity, and he made no wider claims for them. These concerns (on which, after all, his entire life's work was based) were necessarily partial: "all knowledge of cultural reality," he wrote, "is always knowledge from *particular points of view*."[14]

For Weber, values are central to the consolidation of objects for investigation, but inquiry itself ought to value the stark intellectual pursuit of truth. Guy Oakes maintains that this position can be sustained only if objective inquiry is somehow sealed off from the conflict of irreconcilable values that Weber posits as a generic feature of social life. In this view, standards of truth would have to exist independently of value judgments concerning the significance of what is found to be true. Thus, highly contested valuations of freedom to choose abortion versus sanctity of life might raise empirical questions about abortion, but the empirical questions would be settled by evidence in relation to shared commitments to the value of truth. In turn, empirical knowledge about the developmental biology of the fetus would not confirm or reject any value commitment, though it might shed light on empirical issues relevant to particular value concerns. In similar ways, research on environmental policy, educational attainment, or other matters might yield valid knowledge that could speak to questions of value significance.

However, there is an obvious difficulty: political and cultural antagonists often do not agree on the value significance of research questions. For example, opponents of abortion may not care one way or another about research concerning the health or social implications of outlawing abortions, because their ultimate commitment to the right to life makes such research moot. Similarly, proponents of individual freedom may not care about the health implications of what they regard as victimless crimes, because the implications are irrelevant given the value of individual freedom. Possibilities like these serve notice that knowledge produced through inquiry may be relevant only to those individuals who accept the value significance of the inquiry, even though the proponents of particular values may proclaim relevance of the knowledge for a much wider audience, by asserting inquiry to be "objective" in its methods, and thus supposedly objectively relevant for everyone. By this slippery passage between truth and other values, science becomes the servant of politics. But, as Weber emphasized, "scientific truth is precisely what is *valid* for all who *seek* the truth." Even if truth is sustained epistemologically, its relevance is purely cultural, not based on any objective, universal value.[15]

Weber was much more the perspectivist than Rickert. This lends special importance to Oakes's claim that it would be inconsistent for Weber to seal off truth from the irreconcilable conflict of values. Unless truth is a sacrosanct value somehow protected within its realm from the play of other values, Oakes suggests that objectivity, hence, the possibility of science, is lost. However, there is another way of understanding Weber. For Oakes, Weber's strategy is "to take the heroic course of arguing that the irrationality of their [sociocultural sciences'] constitutive values is completely inconsequential for the theoretical rationality of the sociocultural sciences." The word "heroic" is well chosen here. Yes, Weber wanted to keep value significance of questions separate from judgments based in the intellectual valuation of truth. But did he advance a purely epistemological formulation in which, as Oakes puts it, "theoretical values have a special immunity"? To think that he did is at odds with Weber's own empirical depiction of potentially irreconcilable struggles over values (of love, justice, truth, and so on). It would be far more consistent for Weber to argue that the distinction between other values and the valuation of truth *ought* to be maintained *if* the interests of science are to be served. In this reading, the immunity of truth as a value could hardly be guaranteed: it would be approximated, if at all, only through effort. The separation between the realm of science and other realms is not established through logic, it is advocated as the condition for science as an activity ordered by an uncompromised *ethic* of value-neutrality.[16]

Various of Weber's statements support such an interpretation. In "'Objectivity' in social science," he proposed that judging the validity of values "is an act of faith," presumably one that would apply to truth, like other values. Similarly, in his essay on "The meaning of 'ethical neutrality,' " Weber admonished the advocates of an "ethical economics": "even if the moral law is perfectly unfulfillable, it is nonetheless 'imposed' as a duty."[17] Weber did not divorce science from values by some epistemological slight of hand. Instead, he offered a more lifeworldly analysis of how values figure in the actions of scientists or anyone else: ultimate commitment to a value is marked by a willingness to try to suppress other values that conflict with it. The scientist worthy of the name may be animated by other values, but she must set aside those values during the course of research, strive to serve truth, and be willing to be judged on that basis.

As Wolfgang Schluchter has observed, Weber used his famous lecture "Science as a vocation" to propose two reasons for pursuing truth independent of other influences. First, in the midst of conflicting values, it is the only way to make science "possible"; second, science is for Weber "desirable" because it can confront its audiences with "'inconvenient' facts" and "self-clarification" in relation to their value positions. The quest for truth places science in a special position as an instrument of rational discourse relevant to politics.[18] But in this value-neutral stance, Weber burdens inquiry with the claim that knowledge, even if it ever might approximate "truth" in some methodological sense, necessarily is animated by one or another culturally limited interest. Weber thus refuses the objectification of values as a basis of inquiry, but nevertheless consolidates a cultural science that is less than totally relativized.

The relativism of multiple value objectivities

From Weber's position, modern resolutions of the value-problem can be traced in three broad directions – toward an unrelenting value-relativism, toward positivism and other proclaimed formulations of objectivity, and toward critical theory as value affirmation. The first alternative to Weber – relativism of knowledge derived from the incommensurability of values – either (1) can be formulated on grounds that acknowledge the value differences of acting subjects and their cultures, or (2) it may take the form of "methodological relativism," tied to the value orientations of observers. The former version – "cultural relativism" – has multiple incarnations. Certain historians, for example, hold that any given sociohistorical object – a person, a religious group, a revolution, a nation – is absolutely unique, and meaningfully understood only in terms of its own distinctive values. In cultural analysis, a similar hermeneutic claim can be made about the absolute distinctiveness of an object (such as a painting or novel) as an interpretive locus. The same sort of formulation may be found in both "emic" and postmodern ethnography, which refuse to interpret a culturally defined group in the alien frame of anthropological concepts. These practices share the thesis that important unique qualities of sociohistorical phenomena would be missed if inquiry were based on categories derived from an observer's analytic interest. Pushed in this direction of cultural relativity, inquiry into a distinct sociohistorical object proceeds through the observer's engagement with the object's self-referential meaning, for example, in the hermeneutic circle by which part and whole are interpreted in relation to one another, as described by Gadamer.[19]

In contrast to cultural relativism, methodological (or epistemological or judgmental) relativism suggests that potentially incommensurate values shape not only questions (Weber's formulation) but also methodology. Guy Oakes rightly identifies this position with Georg Simmel's theory of aesthetics. Like Weber, Simmel understood conflicts between alternative values as potentially irreconcilable. However, Simmel could not affirm the pursuit of truth as a domain to be separated from other value controversies. Instead, the character of truth itself would be value-relative. Put differently, any given value complex might have its own standards of judgment that could be considered "objective" in the specific sense that they would be external to the phenomenon, and applied according to observers' clear decision rules (see table 1.1). However, if multiple values and their local objective standards coexisted, there would be no reason to expect that such standards could be aligned with one another. It would not be easy, for example, to reconcile two different "objective" judgments of a painting if one of the objective judgments were derived from the aesthetics of romanticism, the other from cubist ones. By analogy, even an "objective" study of a given war from the standpoint of Marxist theory might be incommensurate with an "objective" political history for reasons that have nothing to do with "facts" and everything to do with the purposes to which facts are put. In short, criteria for evaluating data may be bound up with values, such that there is no meeting ground of truth in general – no way to adjudicate truth disputes between inquiries based on heterologous problematics. Under this dispensation, any inquiry tied to distinctive aesthetics or value significations becomes beholden to those standards alone.[20]

This resolution of the value problem, at first inspection, leads in the direction of endless difference, signaling the eclipse of any solid basis for communication, much less knowledge. But as uncongenial as thoroughgoing value-relativity may seem, Simmel's formulation of it is worth inspecting. True, he emphasized the ever problematic character of knowledge, but he regarded ideas of "truth, value, objectivity, etc." as "products of a kind of relativism that signified no longer the dissolution of all uncertainties, but precisely their guarantee by means of a new conception of certainty."[21] For Simmel, answers to the question "what is truth?" are themselves driven by valuation, and they will differ, no doubt, between theologians and warriors, but also for alternative kinds of sociohistorical inquiry. Even assuming a topic of shared cultural significance (Weber's formulation), there may be an inability to resolve disputes because of a disagreement about alternative ways of evaluating data. We can anticipate this possibility, to take a very basic example, in the different valuations of *historical* versus *theoretical* accounts about objects as diverse as literary texts and social revolutions (see the codas to chapters 3 and 4).

In light of Simmel's theory of aesthetics, inquiry seems inevitably multiple in its disciplines. Sociohistorical phenomena are subject to a variety of kinds of knowledge, predicated both upon divergent *questions* of cultural significance and on alternative valuations of *methods* for assessing data during the search for knowledge (disciplines, in Foucault's double sense of the term). However, the difference between Weber and Simmel should not be overdrawn. Weber did not proclaim an absolute standard of truth, nor did Simmel accede to total relativity. Precisely because aesthetics of judgment can be made explicit, Simmel found it possible to identify coherent disciplines of inquiry, albeit ones that would be heterological with respect to one another. Any given discipline, with a communally shared significance/method complex, would facilitate sorting through disagreements about particular accounts concerning an object of inquiry. Simmel's relativity is thus *conditional*, in the sense that a socially coherent domain of inquiry might be carved out on the basis of agreed-upon issues of significance and methods of inquiry. A domain like this is not so far from a cultural science of the Weberian sort.

The difference from Weber depends on the issue of aesthetic judgments in inquiry. The strong version of value-relativism assumes a radical disjuncture between any two judgment complexes. However, the infusion of values into methods of data assessment also might yield a blurred relationship between two approaches. Some methods and standards of evidence may be specific to particular value stances, yet *a priori* or other shared standards of reason may still provide grounds for translation or adjudication among findings produced through divergent value-based perspectives. This would amount to an *incomplete* relativism. Between genres of pastoral photography and pastoral painting, for example, at least some aesthetic criteria of judgment (e.g., composition) might be shared, even though other criteria of interpretation (e.g., use of lenses) are relevant for only one medium, not the other. Similarly, historians' and social scientists' use of statistics may differ substantially, yet still share standards of measurement adequacy. Insofar as criteria of judgment are shared by inquiry across divergent value domains, there is a possibility of adjudicating certain issues among them.

Simmel's treatment of aesthetics and the value problem results in aesthetic perspectivism, not solipsism. Yet perhaps because it draws into question the possibility of even a value-neutral cultural science, there has been no rush to follow in Simmel's footsteps. To the contrary, sociologist Don Levine has described a "flight from ambiguity."[22] But toward what? Recent approaches to the value problem in effect revisit the possibilities considered so far, by developing one or another of them in relation to contemporary sensibilities about knowledge.

Values, objectivity, and science

Max Weber was enough of a value-relativist that he did not formulate an objective value basis for inquiry. Nevertheless, as I noted in chapter 1, his concept of value-neutrality became a touchstone for legitimating social science. Such an appropriation could be accomplished only through a creative and superficial reconstruction of "value-neutrality" as scientific "objectivity." But how this move works is affected by the problematic relation between causality and cultural significance, anticipated in the nineteenth-century *Methodenstreit* issue concerning whether to distinguish between natural and cultural sciences, and, if so, on what basis. This issue can be addressed either by formulating a difference between explanation and understanding (the position of Wilhelm Dilthey) or by emphasizing a distinction between individualizing science and generalizing science, as Weber did. Dilthey's approach divides sociohistorical inquiry from natural science by claiming that, because social life is structured by meanings, causal explanation is inadequate. Weber's distinction, on the other hand, acknowledges the possibility of generalizing about sociohistorical regularities that obtain either despite or by way of their incorporation into meaningful actions.[23] But Weber's distinctive resolution of the value problem raises the question of what the role of cultural significance might be in relation to a generalizing, "causal" social science. Efforts to answer this question circumscribe the dilemma of positivist science and the rise of "postpositivist" responses to it – ranging from realism, through conceptual constructionism, to conventionalism. These efforts, I argue, fall short of their objectivist ambitions and return us to culturally significant value-neutral inquiry in the Weberian mode.

The positivist dilemma

No research proceeds independently of individual and institutionalized value interests, but the positivist assumption is that such interests – whether in finding a cure for a disease or in creating a biodegradable plastic – do not affect the conceptualization of a virus or a polymer in its causally relevant aspects. The cultural significance of a phenomenon presumably counts for nothing in its conceptualization. This formulation suggests why promoters of a generalizing social scientific positivism sought to appropriate Weber's ethic of value-neutrality to their own ends: the problem of values could be restricted to identifying investigators' predispositions and value judgments in studying controversial issues such as abortion, revolutionary movements, and the like.[24] Weber's approach could be retooled as positivistic American social science if matters of cultural significance were somehow reduced to mere issues of "choice of problem," "context of discovery," and "bias of analysis."[25]

However, the only way to achieve the positivistic appropriation of value-neutrality is to separate problems of how social phenomena are conceptualized from issues of cultural significance. The question is, on what basis could this be accomplished? The difficulty of attaining a solution represents the repressed scandal of science. As Peter Halfpenny has shown, positivism is caught between two horns of a dilemma. On the one hand, the *logical* attempt to establish a correspondence between empirical phenomena and general concepts (such as "class" or "anomie") without making specific theoretical or metaphysical assumptions has produced dismal results. Increasingly, philosophers have had to acknowledge that observations of the world are theory-dependent, and that it is therefore difficult to subject theories to unambiguous empirical testing. On the other hand, in a tilt toward *empiricism*, measurements are not connected to general constructs, and the problem of theory-dependent measurement is thereby eliminated. But the cost is the collapse of science as a specifically theoretical enterprise.[26]

Halfpenny has suggested that the paths out of positivism's dilemma lead in two directions: (1) toward a *realism* that (from the positivist standpoint) depends on metaphysic ontological assumptions about the world, or (2) toward some version of *conventionalism* that depends on shared assumptions of investigators, and thus emphasizes the constructed character of knowledge. These alternatives are rightly considered *postpositivist* in that they do not claim any foundational basis for knowledge.[27] But the two paths are not really independent. Whatever the status of realism as a general ontological claim, as I will argue, realism gives way to cultural construction via convention when it faces the task of conceptualizing "reality."

Realism

The initial realist turn away from positivism can be marked by the emergent position of Karl Popper, who recognized the theory-ridden (and conventional) nature of observation, yet sought to posit the possibility of objective knowledge in a way that ducks the problems identified in social and historical studies of science. Affirming a metaphysically "critical" (rather than naive) realist belief in a world that exists independently of our knowledge about it, Popper envisioned an "evolutionary epistemology" open to self-correction partly on the basis of increases in objective knowledge. Roy Bhaskar has proposed a similar approach for sociohistorical inquiry. Bhaskar calls for a metaphysical presupposition about existence of a reality external to any observer that acknowledges both the sociohistorically constructed (and thus ephemeral) character of this posited reality, as well as the gap between reality and any conceptualization thereof. For Bhaskar, hermeneutics and historical and sociological critiques of science fail because they mistakenly target an admittedly bankrupt positivism. Realism, he tells us, can escape the hermeneutic critique if it can affirm that the knowledge yielded by hermeneutics (or any other inquiry) depends on real structures or mechanisms. Bhaskar recognizes that the social sciences face special challenges, in that the structures and mechanisms cannot exist except as historically contingent products of social activity, shaped in part by how actors conceive of their activities. These constraints lead him to identify the reality of societies with social "relations" that transpire "between people and each other, their activities, nature, and themselves." But a great puzzle remains: society "can only be known, not shown to exist." In Bhaskar's view, to investigate society is to study its effects – like Durkheim's social facts (e.g., language), themselves operative mediations of the social as reality.[28]

A realist philosophy of science like Bhaskar's is anathema for any positivist account of knowledge because it embraces metaphysical assumptions rather than trying to avoid them. The objects of inquiry – "properties and powers of real objects, structures, and processes" – are assumed to be real "even though," as Halfpenny notes, "these may be operationally inaccessible."[29] Thus, the central problem for Bhaskar's realism is how to conceptualize reality in a way that is aligned both with metaphysical assumptions about processes and mechanisms, and with the complexities entailed by the ongoing, reflexive activities whereby acting subjects emergently construct or reenact social reality. More simply put, when it comes time to move beyond metaphysical affirmation of reality and get on with research, realism must confront the problems of observation, description, and measurement, and in these circumstances it easily falls into an objectivism (in Bhaskar's case, a Marxist one) that faces difficulties conceptualizing the circumstances of multiple social realities.[30]

There is a fundamental problem with much discussion about realism: it has an abstract and unreal air about it. When we move from philosophical positions to trying to analyze the sociohistorical world, the "things" and "relations" that are awkwardly characterized as acts, norms, processes, and so forth all elude any straightforward realistic conceptualization.[31] The problem does not stem from granting realism as a metaphysical assumption. Instead, granting the assumption lacks any practical benefit: realists do not agree with each other about the reality (e.g., of "intelligence," "class conflict," "industrialization," "kinship") that supposedly is knowable. This problem, serious enough in the natural sciences, is compounded in sociohistorical inquiry by social actors' reflexive and multiple meaningful social constructions of reality, because controversies about the definitions and categorizations of situations permeate social life. The "realities" of economic class, race, and power are themselves socially contested, and in ways that suggest limits to attaining any conceptual closure. In short, accepting realism metaphysically cannot entail reducing the character of reality to any particular realist description (e.g., of "gender"). Thus, practically speaking, metaphysical realism is hard put to offer the social ontology that it would claim to warrant.[32]

At its extreme, the realist approach devolves to positing the terms of a scientific theory as real, using them to represent reality, and analyzing the relationships that obtain when phenomena are categorized under that system. In the absence of any scientific basis for privileging the particular realist metaphysic, inquiry is pushed in the direction of asserting the objective salience of its concepts in a way that reopens the problems faced by objectivist philosophies of history. Indeed, any theoretical approach that would totalize the object of its inquiry reaches this destination.[33] Under the flag of realism, as with the objectivist telos of history, the problems of value bias for specific investigators are rendered moot, for the overall valuation is established at the beginning – in the metaphysical realist scheme itself.

Pragmatic realism as conceptual constructionism

One way to try to advance the case for realism is to acknowledge the limited advantage gained by making metaphysical assumptions. Thus, historians Joyce Appleby, Lynn Hunt, and Margaret Jacob argue for a "practical realism."[34] They recognize the gap between assuming the existence of reality and any description of reality, and nevertheless search for formulations about the world that are "reasonably true." This stance avoids some difficulties of a strong realist position, but its implications ought to be noted. So long as controversies arise about the characterization of social things (even if the worldly referents of the characterizations are granted to be real, or at least real social constructions), the practical realism that Appleby, Hunt, and Jacob advocate seems best understood in relation to the constructionist circumstances of knowledge that can be derived from Kant: given multiple structural and cultural realities and the mediation of knowledge by concepts, no description of reality can be regarded as definitive. In these terms, practical realism must confront the role of values in constructions of knowledge, and the potential for objective concepts in the cultural sciences is therefore limited.

Weber once suggested, "Every concept that is not purely classificatory diverges from reality." He left open the possibility of formulating certain basic concepts in an "objective" fashion, for example, in the distinction between an "open" or a "closed" social relationship, or between production for market and an *oikos* (estate) economy. But he held that "the discursive nature of our knowledge" produces an interest in culturally enriched concepts and thus dictates the use of ideal types, which depart from description of reality by definition.[35] In this formulation, beyond basic distinctions, the cultural significance of inquiry makes conceptual constructions inevitable, and any sociohistorical ontology amounts to a one-sided accentuation that throws into relief certain aspects of a phenomenon. As a cultural construction, such an ontology is not any more "real" than alternative ones. For this reason, an advocate of realism, philosopher William Outhwaite, acknowledges that a metaphysical assumption of realism cannot help us choose among various contradictory ontologies, each purporting to describe the ultimate nature of social reality. "What it *does* provide, however," argues Outhwaite, "is a framework in which these alternative social ontologies can be rationally compared and discussed."[36]

Outhwaite's approach has consequences for the relation between values and concept formation that can be considered by taking the present inquiry as an example. In chapter 1, I sketched a provisional ontology of the individual's dual perspectives as actor and observer. In turn, this ontology identifies alternative observers' frames of reference for inquiry – *Verstehen* and objectivity – that support diverse, more specialized ontologies. But the problem of value significance, and thus the choice of what perspective to adopt, remains unresolved. Under these conditions, Outhwaite, like Weber, will allow the choice of a perspective – on the socially real, let us grant – to derive from the purposes at hand. Issues such as whether to study agency versus structure Outhwaite treats as "methodological questions about appropriate levels of abstraction, governed in each case by the pragmatics of the research process."[37] This stance seems perfectly workable for research, but it fails to achieve any objective basis for constructing objects of sociohistorical inquiry in relation to the world of social life. Realism is thus forced back into confronting issues of value-relativity already considered: either an ontology organizes the conceptualization of social reality on a metaphysical basis that replicates all the problems of establishing values objectively, or metaphysical realism gives way to conflicts over alternative cultural constructions of concepts, measurements, and observations.

Conventionalism

It is but a small step from the pragmatic realism advocated by both Outhwaite and Appleby, Hunt, and Jacob to the second major postpositivist approach to concept formation – conventionalism. The difference is that conventionalism makes no ultimate claims about reality. Instead, it resolves the dilemma of positivism by granting that there can be no basis for establishing a theory independent of metaphysical assumptions. Rather than trying to eliminate assumptions, the conventionalist strategy is to specify them as statements, neither true nor false, that identify the grounds on which inquiry proceeds. Conventionalism sidesteps logical problems of concept formation by looking instead to researchers' ongoing struggles over knowledge and the procedures for evaluating it. This understanding of inquiry began to crystallize even as logical positivism reached its internal crisis, and it gathered further support in the light of social and historical studies of science. Michael Polanyi, following

Nagel, recognized in the 1960s that science could not depend on a philosophical foundation; instead, he argued, it depends on the "self-coordination" and "mutual authority" of scientists who "keep watch over each other."[38] Building on such a move both affirms the significance of longstanding institutions of science such as peer review, and reflexively brings social and historical critiques of practice to the service of science.

In this vein, Sandra Harding calls for transcending the weak model of objectivism based on value-neutrality and the control of subjectivity by pursuing what she calls "strong objectivity." "The requirements for achieving strong objectivity," she argues, "permit one to abandon notions of perfect, mirror-like representations of the world, the self as a defended fortress, and the 'truly scientific' as disinterested with regard to morals and politics, yet still apply rational standards to sorting less from more partial and distorted belief." Harding does not cite Imre Lakatos, but Lakatos's formulations about "research programs" in effect sketch certain empirical conditions that may contribute to strong objectivity. His research-program model is an effort to describe what scientists actually do when they are successful. By backing off from strict "naive" experimental falsification and attending to the ways scientists develop a patterned "hard core" of ideas that generates further ideas and subsumes anomalies, Lakatos advocates a methodology for producing research findings "which can be evaluated in terms of progressive and degenerating problem shifts." Despite Lakatos's doubts about whether social science would ever sustain the conditions that he described, this model has been widely invoked as worthy of emulation in sociohistorical inquiry.[39]

The research-program approach accounts for science as knowledge that is socially and culturally constructed in conventionalized worlds of inquiry akin to the "art worlds" described by Howard S. Becker. However, it leaves open the possibility that divergent and contradictory research agendas will be undertaken in different research worlds. In sociohistorical inquiry in particular, as Paul Diesing observes, research communities proliferate "on the basis of some initial text, paradigm, method or concepts." Within communities there may be a conventionalized "objectivity" – some collective agreement about how to construe reality. Such conditioned objectivity may even constitute a domain of research in which open and replicable procedures of science applied to empirical material can be used to weed out arbitrary or invalid statements, thus yielding advances in knowledge. But this model falls short of Harding's call for strong objectivity because questions about embedded cultural values typically remain masked by the research-program narrative of legitimation. Agreement of like-minded researchers can establish concepts, theoretical formulations, and hypotheses by which to proceed with inquiry, but the resulting knowledge is ipso facto culturally circumscribed by the conventional construction of reality that produces it. Beyond a given community of convention seemingly lies the abyss. Any claim to objectivity is supported neither by ontology nor by a foundational philosophy of knowledge such as logical positivism. Instead, the choice among research programs is, in Simmel's sense, a matter of aesthetics. That is, there is no strategy in a conventionalist approach for constituting the object of inquiry on a basis that transcends the preferences of the community of researchers. Thus, the choice is philosophically "arbitrary," and open to the extra-scientific play of value interests and power.[40]

Promoters of the research-program approach who embrace strong objectivity might counter that science is its own corrective. The research program can establish rigorous criteria for assessing the adequacy of how an object of inquiry is conceptualized. Under this regimen, any research program will yield "findings," and such findings may lead to rejection of a given theory within the program's domain and its displacement by a more encompassing theory. The possibility of adjudicating theories on an empirical basis may be claimed as a protection against arbitrary value biases.

Such a claim, however, does not immunize the approach from the central problems of value-constituted discourse – which research program to undertake from among the multitude that might be undertaken, and through what conceptualization of the object of inquiry. Possible research programs are manifold – the study of sociobiology by use of theories about natural and cultural evolution of races, inquiry into inequality based on a theory of class exploitation, and so on. Under the research-program adjudication claim, each such program presumably would be open to theoretical advance. Yet this is not the end of the matter. As Outhwaite laments, research programs are likely to be incommensurate with one another.[41] This incommensurability in part is the consequence of different research questions. But divergent questions in turn are shaped through differential valuation. This does not necessarily invalidate the knowledge gained through research programs, and it does not preclude the possibility that carefully designed research might adjudicate the claims of incommensurate research programs, but it does mean that any research program – in its own terms – ends up where Weber ended up: claiming an arena of truth-seeking as science, but within a practice of inquiry that is formed on the basis of values. Like the pragmatic version of realism, the progressive search for truth via conventionalism, when put through the crucible of the value problem, becomes clarified as a relativized cultural science of the Weberian sort. Both conventionalism and pragmatic realism, as well as metaphysical realism, leave science failing to achieve its goal of objectivity. Realism and conventionalism are as saturated with values as transcendental objectivity, value-neutrality, and cultural relativity, and in one or another of the same ways. In *post*positivism, the accent falls on the "post."

Critique as a value

Despite differences, positivism and the postpositivist strategies of realism and conventionalism all value some version of scientific inquiry as the road to truth, legitimated as superior to other kinds of inquiry. By contrast, the point of departure for critical theory as an emancipatory project is the rejection of any privileged science. Max Horkheimer's 1937 essay "Traditional and critical theory" does not just call into question the value-neutrality of "traditional" scientific inquiry. It also asserts the potential for critical theory to transcend the division between theory and practice by recognizing theory-based knowledge as historically bounded, and produced via historically situated activity.[42] In this line of development, the attempt to consolidate a general theory of class struggle is displaced by analysis of historically concrete processes of class conflict. Yet a value problem persists for critical theory, and for strands of feminist and other inquiry that acknowledge the conditions of inquiry described by critical theorists, namely, whether and how to make objective claims for knowledge that is developed out of historically situated practice.

Science and the problem of relative values

As framed by Theodor Adorno, critical theory initiates its analysis with the assertion that science breeds ignorance:

Within positivism, it becomes a maxim of knowledge itself that one should not eat from the tree of knowledge. Curiosity is punished in the novelty of thought; utopia must be expelled from thought in every form it takes – including that of negation. Knowledge resigns itself to being a mere repetitive reconstruction.[43]

For critical theory, the ethic of value-neutrality has a feature that is not seriously considered in merely epistemological debates: it tends to legitimate science over other kinds of knowledge. A claim of value-neutrality makes sense, however, only if knowledge is indeed neutral in relation to various social interests. Yet there is reason to suspect that inquiry is dialectically incorporated into power arrangements that themselves are supposed to be objects of inquiry. Empirical claims about this possibility have been made by critical theorists ranging from Horkheimer and Adorno to Jürgen Habermas, by French social philosophers such as Michel Foucault and Jean-François Lyotard, and by feminists such as Sandra Harding and Patricia Hill Collins. In different ways, they all argue that "legitimate" sociohistorical knowledge contributes to the possibilities of social power that derive from treating people, social arrangements, and actions like nature – as objectified things. Equally important, the exercise of power may restrict the production and distribution of emancipatory kinds of knowledge.[44]

However, rejections of science's claim to value-neutrality (itself a weak claim compared to objectivity) shift the problem of values into the terrain of relativism again. This result is more palatable for some critics of science than others. Foucault did not seek foundational ground for his analysis of knowledge and power; to do so would have been a contradiction in terms. Similarly, Lyotard considers the relativity of discourses to be a condition that can be neither denied nor transcended, and some feminists would embrace rather than oppose the relativity of knowledge. But for critical theorists, feminists like Sandra Harding, and others who act on the basis of value commitments, this solution may not be a happy one, because it undermines the broader significance of knowledge gained from inquiry informed by any specific ultimate value. For this reason, Harding's promotion of strong objectivity acknowledges the relativities of knowledge, yet still claims room for the exercise of logic in the evaluation of arguments.

The stakes are high. If the affirmation of an ultimate value can be coupled with the creation of value-relevant knowledge, the project of inquiry can be shifted away from serving science's unevenly empowering production of knowledge, and toward serving values presumably more directly connected to broad social needs. Once inquiry is freed from a supposed neutrality that functions ideologically, knowledge can be pursued in relation to practice. "Praxis" becomes a way that people can act in concert with one another, for instance, in pursuit of an ultimate value in an actively engaged social movement committed to racial equality of opportunity. However, the potential of praxis to engage a wide following for an encompassing project hinges on the general acceptance of an ultimate value from diverse perspectives. Otherwise, the claims of knowledge hold only for those individuals who embrace the particular value that informs a given pursuit of knowledge. This problem leads critical theory back toward the attempt to establish values objectively, reentering the terrain previously explored in Christian, Kantian, Hegelian, and Marxian philosophies of history.

From Marx to negative dialectics

The efforts among critical theorists to ground a value position are diverse. Following Marx, a central strategy is to develop an ontological, rather than purely metaphysical, approach. As Seyla Benhabib has shown, Marx took over from Hegel the ontology of work. By designating his focus on work as the valuation of the ontologically real, Marx could develop a dialectical history of the totality. Yet in the formal analysis developed from it, Marx did not leave much room for the agency of either workers or capitalists, and his theory failed to anticipate historical developments – such as the *embourgoisement* of workers – that tended to negate it. Critical theorists thus confronted the central issue of how to shift from this totalization of history toward an alternative basis of counter-bourgeois theorizing.[45]

Even before the establishment of what came to be called the Frankfurt School, Georg Lukács sought to preserve the Marxian ontology of alienation, yet develop a position distanced from any dialectical teleology. Like Marx, Lukács proclaimed the standpoint of the proletariat as the key to understanding the historical development of capitalism. But instead of positing abstract categories to map the functional contradictions of a totalized system, Lukács used ideal types in the Weberian style to describe the dialectic in the historical process itself.[46] Lukács's solution harks back to Kant's use of value benchmarks to chart the progress of history toward certain presumed ends. But Lukács's ends are not the "natural plan" that Kant posited; they are the historically located interests of social collectivities.

Frankfurt School theorists Max Horkheimer and Theodor Adorno followed a different historicizing turn. In their formulations, the fact of historicity meant that there could be no general theory of society. The requirements of critical knowledge thus were dialectical, but only in a "negative" sense, since totalized outcomes resulting from developments bridging different social domains could not be anticipated. Adorno's negative dialectics envisioned the analysis of contradictions between (1) ideological constructs and (2) differentially and incompletely disjoined historical elements (such as elite versus popular culture) without imposing the teleological baggage of synthesis, either of dialectically opposed concepts or realities.[47]

Both the solution of Lukács and that of Horkheimer and Adorno leave knowledge, as Adorno put it, "conditioned." Truth is relative, but it can be revealed by a privileged relativized perspective that preserves history writ large as subject – either through the perspective of labor (Lukács's proletariat) or method (Adorno's negative dialectics). However, neither of these approaches resolves the value problem for critical theory. Even if Lukács did not anticipate the collapse of the historical mission of the working class as a revolutionary force, he understood that the standpoint of the proletariat could not validate its knowledge, because of the problem of false consciousness. For different reasons, Adorno's historicized negative dialectic of enlightenment also seems incapable of coming to terms with the value problem. As Benhabib suggests, "It is unclear . . . that these 'ciphers' of possible emancipation to which Adorno appeals can justify the normative standpoint of critical theory."[48] The negative dialectic failed to deliver praxis. The historicized critique of domination left unresolved Lenin's question, "What is to be done?" These difficulties do not necessarily stem from any inherent defect in the idea of forming inquiry around an explicit, value-driven agenda. They simply mean that Horkheimer and Adorno did not fully succeed in consolidating such a project.

Habermas and the objective value of communication

Given the value instability of historicized knowledge, the strategy advanced by Jürgen Habermas somehow does not seem surprising.[49] Like other critical theorists, he initially sought to historicize social theory, most notably in his 1962 book, *The Structural Transformation of the Public Sphere*, which traces the origins of a bourgeois public sphere and its increasing irrelevance in a late capitalist state where opinion and voting have become commodified through the triumph of advertising culture.[50] This historical trajectory was subsequently subsumed by Habermas within his theorizing about an evolutionary tendency toward a disjuncture between "system" and "lifeworld."

Concerned with theorizing structural transformations of social life as a whole without claiming a privileged class vantage point, Habermas has affirmed more than some of his predecessors that a critical theory must stake a claim to generality. This claim he has sought to advance on the basis of a universal value. If he could establish such a value, Habermas's project might order all knowledge in relation to human needs. He could thereby affirm a reinvigorated modernist ideal of progress as something other than the increase in purely technical and scientific control, of either things or people. Habermas's solution to the problem is complex, and it is tied to a close reading of social theory.

Essentially like Marx's, it is an ontological one. But in place of Marx's ontology of work and alienation, in *Knowledge and Human Interests* Habermas proposes an ontology of consciousness framed by three "knowledge-constitutive human interests":

Orientation toward technical control, toward mutual understanding in the conduct of life, and toward emancipation from seemingly "natural" constraint establish the specific viewpoints from which we can apprehend reality as such in any way whatsoever.[51]

Unlike Horkheimer and Adorno, Habermas does not directly challenge science – with its distinction between facts and values. Instead, he argues that science is only one form of knowledge. Habermas had already sketched this account by 1968, and he has elaborated it in *The Theory of Communicative Action*, published in 1981. Science depends on the lifeworld for its very possibility, Habermas maintains, but, perversely, scientific knowledge tends to establish an affinity at the institutional level with an emergent "system" that "colonizes" the lifeworld. Science is a form of knowledge connected to technical control, and technical control specifically subordinates human interests by treating the zone of human life – the lifeworld and its contents – as objects. The human interest in emancipation thus faces the task of establishing an emancipatory knowledge that is powerful enough to undo the system's colonization of the lifeworld. Yet such knowledge must not be arbitrary, and, therefore, it depends upon an objective value – one that holds for everyone, beyond social contentions.

What might this objective value be? In *The Theory of Communicative Action*, Habermas develops an idea already nascent in his earlier work: that social interaction that mirrors an ideal speech situation – where communication is rational and uncoerced – holds emancipatory potential. Habermas wants to ground this ideal ontologically, and his "reconstructive science" thus invokes theories of cognitive possibility, such as Piaget's research on children.[52] The work of Piaget may be criticized in substantive terms, of course, just as the ideal speech situation may be dismissed by critics as a utopian precept that denies cynical possibilities of motivated speech. But the central question here concerns the universal value itself. Habermas posits a collective interest in discourse that works toward mutually acknowledged truth. Without such a value, argumentation would not even be undertaken in the first place. That is, if discourse is more than an empty charade enacted in bad faith, it must presume such a value.

Habermas's cognitive interest in consensus on truth-seeking discourse has deeply Kantian sources, and it bears a striking similarity to that earlier neo-Kantian attempt by Heinrich Rickert to establish the objective value of truth as a basis for knowledge. Rickert's purposes in seeking to salvage historical inquiry from relativism were scientific, and thus different than those of Habermas. But the solution is effectively the same. In both cases, the search for truth is transcendentally established. As Rickert put it, "We can define the governing value, whose transindividual and unconditionally general validity is beyond doubt, with reference to its *content.* . ., namely, as the value of natural scientific truth or knowledge." Yet Rickert was more modest than Habermas, for he rejected as "pseudonaturalistic" any claim about "the gradual perfection of the intellect." Here, Rickert anticipated Habermas's turn toward an ontological description of human nature as a basis for reconstructive science, and he rejected it.[53]

Habermas and his critics

In *The Theory of Communicative Action* Habermas's proposal for communicative rationality brings discourse on the problem of values full circle, back to the hope for an objective basis for knowledge. Habermas offers humanity the hope of writing its own history, by affirming rational discourse as a value. The Enlightenment metanarrative of progress is not abandoned. Instead, inquiry is organized on the basis of communications about human interests in a way that exceeds science.

To date, Habermas is the last best hope of the Enlightenment. In the absence of value, history would lose its status as a totalized subject that possesses transcendent meaning. The struggle over valuation of inquiry is not simply an issue for science; it is crucial for any culture of inquiry in a modern dispensation. Habermas seeks to forestall the loss of meaning signaled in various postmodern accounts by moving beyond the materialist dialectic as meaning, beyond science as technical knowledge, toward self-conscious communication as the rehabilitation of the Enlightenment project. For him, the alternative to communication is irrationality. Indeed, even arguments for irrationality depend on rational discourse.[54] Habermas is willing to disagree, but he cannot countenance a refusal to engage in arguments.

Here, the post-Wittgensteinian debate among Habermas, Gadamer, and Lyotard poses a crucial puzzle. Wittgenstein's theory of language as a game, when applied to inquiry, defines for Habermas the problem of incommensurability and relativity. In the Wittgensteinian metaphor, each game has its boundaries, beyond which its moves and rules lack meaning. But the problem of translation between language games eluded Wittgenstein. Facing this issue in the 1960s, Habermas wanted to use Hans-Georg Gadamer's characterization of "porous," interpenetrating language games as a solution to the relativism that he found in Wittgenstein's position. Yet to adopt Gadamer's solution, Habermas had to reinterpret hermeneutics, for he found in Gadamer's approach a "prejudice in favor of the legitimacy of prejudices (or prejudgments) validated by tradition." Habermas regarded this prejudice as unacceptable because the hermeneutic commitment to self-understanding thus defined denies "the power of reflection." He acknowledged, "Certainly, reflection can no longer reach beyond itself to an absolute consciousness that it then claims to be," but insisted, "The right of reflection requires that the hermeneutic approach limit itself." In other words, interpretive traditions are inadequate in and of themselves. Specifically, any interpretive tradition is embedded within arrangements of labor and of domination. These arrangements are not merely symbolic, Habermas asserted, and they deserve investigation in terms that may eclipse "tradition."[55] Already in the 1960s Habermas both anticipated and denied a fully textual turn. He was attracted to Gadamer's vision that directed hermeneutics toward understanding socially embedded yet historically emergent meanings because it offered a model of communication oriented to mutual understanding. But in the final analysis, Habermas rejected hermeneutics because Gadamer could not be employed to support his own project of establishing a rational universal discourse that transcends meanings based purely on actors' and traditions' self-understandings.

Because Habermas seeks a historically engaged and reflective process of communication, postfoundationalist philosophers label him as a modernist who maintains the faith of a "metanarrative." For Richard Rorty, the attempt to create a transcendental standpoint is misguided. Gadamer regards the search for absolutes as "totally absurd." In his biography, Gadamer reasserts "the universality of hermeneutics" as a condition that precludes other kinds of absolutes and maintains that "Habermas has never gotten over an Idealistic understanding of the hermeneutic problem."[56] Lyotard is particularly emphatic: Habermas wishfully seeks a unity of experience that links the realms of knowledge. Lyotard regards this as "neither possible, nor even prudent." Instead he embraces a more anarchistic pragmatics. In this postmodern formulation, inquiry can be reckoned as a language game in which rules cannot be the basis for the suppression of ideas, and legitimation comes not through metanarrative, but piecemeal, in language-game "moves." These are "played in the pragmatics of knowledge" by leaping beyond what is conventionally settled knowledge. For Lyotard, "It is producing not the known, but the unknown."[57]

Disagreements notwithstanding, however, Habermas and his critics do not seem so far apart. Even though Habermas undertakes a quest for a new grand narrative of communication, like Richard Rorty, he disavows the project of epistemology. "The theory of communicative action that I have since put forward [after writing *On the Logic of the Social Sciences* in the 1960s]," Habermas insists, "is not a continuation of methodology by other means." Nor does Habermas reject out of hand the formulations of seemingly alien thinkers. Commenting after Foucault's death on the contradiction between Foucault's critique of power and the normative standards of truth that such a critique both depends upon and undermines, Habermas suggests that Foucault in the end resolved the contradiction by returning to "the philosophical discourse of modernity." In this account, Habermas affirms that historically instituted reason can be brought to bear on the critique of historically instituted reason. Moreover, Habermas asserts the salience of his own project "for the existing diversity of those who encounter one another – even when they fail to understand one another."[58] In these ways, Habermas seeks to engage his critics in a deeper conversation.

Despite his critics' apparent antipathies to the conversation, there are certain strands of convergence. Habermas the modernist and Lyotard the postmodernist share much of an outlook, perhaps rooted in their different but fruitful confrontations with Kant. Juxtaposed to each other, their ideas sweep away old issues and generate a new problematic. Both Habermas and Lyotard recognize that established institutional arrangements of technical knowledge production create power-based impediments to the production of nonconforming ideas. And both have a utopian bent. Habermas's ideal speech situation must be regarded as ironically utopian not only in societies ordered by despotism, but also in many bureaucratically institutionalized spheres of ostensibly democratic societies, including those where the production of scientific knowledge transpires on a large scale. Lyotard too is utopian in his own way: strong on showing the "terror" of modernist science, he posits the transcendence of the system by normatively liberated scientists and an information-accessing public as the basis of "a politics that would respect both the desire for justice and the desire for the unknown." Even if Lyotard does not project a value consensus, still, he advocates an ideal – nonauthoritarian communication – that Habermas shares. It is thus significant that Seyla Benhabib has been able to shade Habermas in a more Lyotardian direction, by offering an untotalized reformulation of Habermas's approach to communicative reason.[59]

In some ways, the overlap in these contentious but not completely incongruous positions is consolidated by the new pragmatism that has been advocated as an alternative, nonfoundationalist path to critical discourse. Benhabib thus distinguishes between "neo-pragmatic" recognition of a pluralism of research techniques versus a postmodern "'aesthetic' proliferation of styles" of writing history/fiction. And Cornell West wants to move beyond the narrow Euro-American bases of postmodern and critical theory, yet his communicative and cooperative project of creating knowledge sounds broadly postmodern and vaguely Habermasian.[60]

Such proposals for postfoundational production of knowledge may seem distant from workaday sociohistorical inquiry. But the implications are direct. Surveying the problem of values has shown that inquiry can be construed alternatively as a search for the ultimate significance in history, as an enterprise bounded by value significance, as either a positivist or a value-neutral version of science, or as a value-based project of creating emancipatory knowledge through critique. This range of possibilities underscores a general worldly circumstance of inquiry, namely, that actual sociohistorical inquiries are informed by *divergent* resolutions of the value problem. The empirical condition of value-relativity among multiple inquiries makes the very object of inquiry and its conceptualization matters of basic contention. Given this circumstance, it does not matter whether a particular inquiry claims to proceed under an objective resolution of the value problem. The diversity of value positions informing actual research means that neither a nonmetaphysical ("positive") science, nor any realist or conventionalist research program, nor Habermas's normative consensus about communicative reason empirically holds sway. Even for science and for Habermas, and certainly for conventionalists and pragmatists, inquiry proceeds today under conditions of value heterogeneity. Because neither realists, advocates of research programs, conventionalists, nor critical theorists have found a way to transcend the value constitution of their ontological and theoretical frames of reference, sociohistorical inquiry to date has fallen short of either positivist or humanistic objectivity. Yet this circumstance does not preclude efforts to evaluate evidence, theories, and arguments, and thus to refine knowledge – within some value-constituted frame of reference.

What are inquiry's prospects under these conditions? There are several possibilities. It may be that the heterogeneity of values yields potentially irreconcilable conflicts of interpretations between diverse frames of reference, as Habermas's critics suggest. Perhaps certain pathways of discourse transcend heterogeneity. Or maybe an emergent normative consensus on communication could establish an ever widening arena of rational discourse. These possibilities can be given proper consideration only at the conclusion of the present study. As a first step toward that end, in the coda to this chapter I raise the question of how conditions of value heterogeneity delimit alternative regimens within the formative discourse of explanation and interpretation, thereby giving rise to divergent projects of inquiry.

Coda 2   How values consolidate projects of explanation

When the problem of values is considered in its own terms, contentions arise about dramatically different ways of constituting sociohistorical inquiry. But one reason these contentions matter is that alternative value resolutions have implications for the formative discourse of *explanation*. There is no point here in proposing a narrow definition of explanation, when its character is at issue in sociohistorical inquiry. Precisely to explore that issue, I will exceed conventional scientific usage by treating approaches such as "interpretation" within the domain. Generally then, in research, explanatory discourse offers one or another *account* concerning an object of inquiry. This coda shows that, although value discourse does not subsume explanation, it does frame the stakes of the discourse in ways that consolidate alternative *explanatory projects* of inquiry.

In the first place, as I have already noted, the object of inquiry does not spring from raw empirical data: activities of selection and colligation (or drawing together) compile data that construct an object of inquiry according to a principle not inherent in the flux of the empirical world. Selection of such a principle is ultimately an issue of value preference. Either values would have to be *objective* in the specific sense that they would hold in general and for everyone, or a *relativity* of values would admit to differential selection and construction of the objects of inquiry according to local preferences – whether aesthetic, moral, or theoretical – that lack any generally compelling justification. If the value problem were resolved objectively, either science as a value or some other general preference would inform the consolidation of objects of inquiry. On the other hand, value-relativity would imply a diversity of constructed sociohistorical objects, even in reference to "the same" events in the world. In short, the consolidation of inquiry's subject matters depends on how the problem of values is resolved.

Second, quite apart from the value construction of objects of inquiry, we need to consider the relation of values to explanation, namely, the question of whether researchers can account for inquiry's objects in ways that hold independent of values. To think otherwise is to entertain the possibility that inquiry offers nothing more than perspectival knowledge, with no particular interpretation necessarily better than another.

The best-known attempt by proponents of science to avoid this threat is Hempel's "covering-law" model, which proposes that explanations are adequate when conclusions can be deduced logically from the combination of (1) a set of true initial conditions obtaining at a particular time and place, and (2) "universal hypotheses" about empirical regularities under a range of conditions. Thus, Hempel's classic example describes what happens when a car is left parked outdoors, its radiator filled with water, during a night when the temperature falls from above 32 to below 32 °F. That the radiator bursts as a consequence of these conditions can be deduced from a universal hypothesis concerning the relationships between water temperature, volume, and pressure. Despite the elegance of this example, however, the covering-law model has encountered serious questions about whether it can be sustained in general, much less in sociohistorical inquiry. In the face of critiques about the model's potential for tautology and its failure to encompass otherwise reasonable patterns of explanation, some philosophers now seek to warrant scientific knowledge under postfoundationalist conditions.[1] Failure to do so, the fear runs, means the end of rationality, since the alternative is to acknowledge the subversion of explanation by considerations that have no connection to logical criteria of truth.

On the route of the Third Path, however, a stark choice between rational science and relativism neither captures the epistemological possibilities nor describes actual practices of sociohistorical inquiry. A different way of construing the implications of values for explanation opens up if we consider the *social* activities of inquiry, and describe these activities in phenomenological terms. Here, Alfred Schutz's delineation of the "because" motive versus the "in-order-to" motive suggests a basic problem. These two motives describe alternative formulaic ways that people have available for offering accounts. Actors and observers can treat given events either as (1) "caused" by the past or (2) made meaningful by goals in relation to the future ("I became a bricklayer because of family expectations," or "in order to gain a living"). These alternative formulae yield wholly different kinds of accounts. But any attempt to justify one or the other approach depends on yet another account that must itself be justified ("She chose the 'because' motive formula 'because,' or 'in order to' . . ."), and so on. The question-begging can go on ad nauseam. However, the potentially endless regress is usually not allowed, and in any event it does not preclude the production of knowledge. As George Simmel suggested, "it is a characteristic of the human mind to be capable of erecting solid structures, while their foundations are still insecure."[2]

Phenomenologically, the worst threat to some universal standard of reason is the human condition: knowledge amounts to one or another kind of social construction. Whatever standards people invoke and negotiate for evaluating accounts produce a particular ordering regimen that shapes explanation as discourse. People who disagree can thereby focus on sorting things out, trying to gain leverage in ways that even their opponents will acknowledge as legitimate. But how do values condition alternative regimens of explanation?

Hempel's approach, like most models of science, depends on the value autonomy of inquiry: values may prefer or abhor an explanation, but such evaluations have no bearing on its logical or empirical adequacy. This value autonomy of a single logic might operate in two different ways, depending on how the first issue identified in this coda – value construction of inquiry's objects – is resolved. On the one hand, the phenomenon in its salient features could be construed as constituted *objectively* (that is, independently of values, theory, or "point of view"). In this case, with a single logic and an object of inquiry constituted objectively, two adequate accounts of the phenomenon could not coexist, and assessing an account would depend on a positivistic process of evaluating its adequacy.

Alternatively, following a "value-neutral" ethic of inquiry, divergent value purposes of inquiry might yield alternative objects of inquiry, even in relation to the "same" empirical material. But even if value preferences determined *what* was to be analyzed, under the uniform-logic-of-explanation thesis, value preferences would have no implications for the adequacy of the analysis itself. All explanations would remain subject to the same criteria of evaluation, and it would be possible to adjudicate the adequacy of alternative accounts *of the same object*, even if not of ultimate reality.

Overall, the boundaries of science in either its positivist or value-neutral mode are fixed by explanation independently of values. What about the alternative possibility – of acknowledging accounts to be *shaped* by values? Although Georg Simmel argued for an aesthetic relativism of disciplines (see chapter 2), the suggestion that procedures for the adequate analysis of a phenomenon can be shaped by nonlogical considerations amounts to a virtual heresy of science.[3] Even Sandra Harding, a sharp critic of science, seeks to strengthen objectivity, not do away with it.

A caricature would envision "political" standards of "correctness" defining what makes a good explanation: an account that conflicted with cherished values could not draw those values (which lie beyond empirical adjudication) into question, and so the research methods or findings would have to be rejected. On the face of it, such a stance subordinates inquiry to theology, moral philosophy, or political dictates – to dogma, "natural law," the corporate social interest, or "scientific values." So it is that religious fundamentalists find fault with Darwinist explanations of evolution, and that scientific Marxists publishing in the journal *Science and Society* used to rail at the proletariat for failing to fulfil its theorized role.[4] But these amount to clumsy value-based rejections of empirical findings. Taking them as exemplars makes it too easy to dismiss value-informed analysis in general, thus avoiding the hard questions. What if criteria of adjudication could be defined on the basis of values, yet within those constraints alternative accounts could be differentiated from one another in their empirical adequacy? This activity would not be untouched by values, yet neither could it be dismissed as simply unconstrained exercise of bias.

At first inspection, to mix value-based and logical adequacy seems to challenge prevailing justifications of science. Yet if we look at practices of inquiry rather than its supposed norms, criteria for adjudicating among accounts often are structured by value considerations. Consider the AIDS epidemic. In the United States, early research on social pathways of the disease – for example, on sharing of needles by drug users – received scant attention because its implications would require the State to shift its public moral stance by acknowledging the realities of drug use. In other words, during the early days of the epidemic, there was an allocation of research effort on the basis of the moral acceptability of the premises of an explanation. This kind of practice presumably does not affect the validity of research on needle sharing; instead, on a value basis, it limits in advance what knowledge will count as relevant. The subordination of science to political power is obvious. But what about accounting for the disease itself? Here, inquiry faces complex questions about retroviruses, their relationships to DNA sequences, the interplay between DNA and RNA, RNA effect on cell activity, and a host of other questions of biochemistry. These complexities may place any full account of the virus and the syndrome years, possibly decades, into the future. Yet coming to understand AIDS is an urgent matter. We may not expect a full explanation anytime soon, but we can hope on the basis of a pragmatic standard that incomplete knowledge will improve prevention and provide a cure for AIDS.[5] In this example, ultimate scientific criteria for adjudicating among accounts may be fixed, but social criteria for evaluating knowledge are pragmatic.

In turn, the example of AIDS brings us to another value consideration. The commitment to cure AIDS is itself a historically contingent construction. Whereas the allocation of substantial resources to AIDS research was once controversial among cultural conservatives – when AIDS was considered a gay disease – the commitment is now nearly universal. This emergently universal commitment raises the question of whether projects of inquiry more generally could be guided by widely shared (hence "objective") social values. Could objective values other than science shape the character of accounts that are produced through inquiry? The affirmation of this possibility can be found in Habermas's critical theory. For him, communication as a value inspires theorization of social processes intended to show how human emancipation is undermined by system "colonization" of the lifeworld; when multiple ways of analyzing an object of inquiry coexist, standards of adjudicating whether an account is any good become defined on the basis of increases in communicative potential. Without apology Habermas produces a highly sophisticated synthesis of social theories, yet engages in inquiry based on standards of knowledge that he believes to be transcendent to the technical reason embodied in any formal logic of explanation.[6]

Defenders of science might retort that the value constraints at work in the examples of AIDS and Habermas's social communication do not really touch the core logic of explanation. Partly to escape any determinant effects of values, some epistemologists have wanted to distinguish between the "context of discovery" of knowledge and its "context of justification." Under this dispensation, no matter how much the topics that AIDS researchers address may be shaped by values, their methods are subject to rules of procedure, and their findings to scrutiny and critique. The social and historical conditions under which researchers came to explore ideas would make no difference for how they – and, later, others – would evaluate those ideas. Even the Nazi scientist presumably would use the same procedures as the next scientist, and come to the same findings about a question.

However, because values can so deeply permeate the institutionalized production of knowledge, Sandra Harding calls into question the distinction between discovery and justification contexts, at least in any given cultural context. And even without looking to the extreme case of Nazi scientists, an examination of the relationship between values and criteria of justification suggests that she is right. To take an example well within the boundaries of institutionally legitimated inquiry, criteria of justification sometimes differ according to the disciplinary- or field-specific context in which objects of inquiry are investigated (e.g., in history, versus economics). But it is doubtful that the choice of field or discipline to study a phenomenon can be adjudicated on a purely logical basis, and, thus value considerations seem central to criteria of what is taken to be a "good" account. Under these conditions, two or more value-informed accounts of "the same" phenomena cannot necessarily be reconciled with each other in terms of their relative adequacy.[7] Even with political, social, and moral valuations to one side, the issue of value-preferential explanation persists in the choice of intellectual perspective.

Philosopher Richard Miller recently has sought to reckon with these circumstances by elaborating a pragmatic approach to explanation. Miller acknowledges that values may operate both outside and within fields and disciplines as the arbiters of explanation criteria. For any disciplinary- or field-specific line of inquiry, he suggests, a "standard causal pattern" – i.e., a "stopping rule" that is *"extra-scientific"* – will determine the sufficiency of explanation.[8] By this move, Miller hopes to preserve the realists' affirmation of coherent phenomena that are ultimately knowable, even in the face of multiple accounts about those phenomena. Yet recognition of diverse explanation criteria and stopping points seems to render philosophical realism moot. Once the pragmatics of inquiry are acknowledged, whatever the reality of social events and processes, alternative explanation patterns become generated out of divergent value interests. Whereas foundational science – for example, in Hempel's epistemology – is guided by the principle that there is a single valid explanation for a given occurrence, the pragmatic turn surrenders this principle to a *relativity* of explanations, even under the assumption of an *absolute* reality.

Miller draws the prospects of objective explanation further into doubt by acknowledging that the status of realism itself may vary, both among alternative fields of inquiry and within less coherent ones. In his view, for "(field specific) realism" to obtain, a field must have "a real foundation," in the sense that disputes must be about truth.[9] But Miller acknowledges that there are "fields without foundations." He points to literary criticism and music theory as examples. What is distinctive about these fields, Miller finds, is that multiple explanatory frameworks remain in play. A work of art may be interpreted not only by attempting to infer the intentions of the artist, but also by examining it in relation to some observer's objective frame of reference based on aesthetic criteria. To analyze a work of art requires choosing a frame of reference capable of yielding some truth, even if it is no more tied to ultimate truth than another. "But," Miller assures us, "a situation in which different explanatory frameworks are in the field, attributing contrary explanations to the phenomena, is no crisis. For accepting a theory, approach, or explanation only requires belief in its adequacy to cope with the phenomena."[10] But this position encourages strong contentions over inquiry, for in effect a criterion of adequacy can be based on a dictated ontological focus ("No explanation will be adequate unless it takes x into account"). Colonists will have one understanding of events, the colonized another. Feminists will examine issues from multiple standpoints without allowing the terms to be dictated by outsiders' criteria. Under such "positionalist" approaches, accounting for sociohistorical phenomena becomes an enterprise in which the results of inquiry are judged not by any single standard of empirical truth, but by their production of knowledge assessed by negotiated criteria which depend on the interests that give rise to inquiry in the first place.[11]

In Miller's view, fields with foundations are those in which rival hypotheses cannot both be taken as true. These fields with foundations are more "realist" than fields with multiple frames. Thus, economics would seem like a discipline based in realism because mainstream economists are in basic agreement about appropriate "standard causal patterns." Yet critics will argue that any agreement among economists has less to do with the obdurate reality of the discipline's foundations than with the degree to which economists have succeeded in excluding alternative ways of accounting for economic phenomena.[12] As a field, economics possesses a high degree of hegemony concerning the kinds of accounts that its more mainstream practitioners will entertain. But competing frameworks do exist, and thus any "foundation" of the field is a matter of extra-scientific commitments. Given that multiple frames of reference are available even for "the dismal science," the implication for sociohistorical inquiry in general is clear: any regimen of explanation is but one among multiple ways of accounting for a sociohistorical phenomenon. Hopefully accounts are at least adequate to their own principles. But the line that might divide values from science is blurred.

To sum up, when considering how values shape ways of accounting for sociohistorical phenomena, two dimensions often conflated with one another need to be disentangled: (1) whether or not the values that constitute *objects of inquiry* (a) have an *objective* basis – one that holds for people in general – or (b) are *relative* to a particular value- or theory-based frame of reference, and (2) whether explanation is subjected to *criteria for adjudication* among accounts that are (a) *independent* of values other than the scientific valuation of truth, or (b) *shaped* by political, ethical, or scholarly values, including preference for particular theoretical or disciplinary stopping rules. To simplify, the crosstabulation of dichotomies on these two dimensions defines four ideal-typical projects of explanation in inquiry, each ordered by a distinctive resolution of the

Table 2.1: *Projects of explanation according to value assumptions concerning the constructed object of inquiry and criteria for adjudication of alternative accounts concerning it*

| | | CRITERIA OF ADJUDICATION | |
		Universal	Value/theory-relative
BASIS OF **OBJECT OF** **INQUIRY**	**Value/theory-relative**	Value-neutral explanation	Interpretive explanation
	Objective	Objective explanation	Value-objective explanation

value problem: (1) value-neutral explanation, (2) objective explanation, (3) interpretive explanation, and (4) value-objective explanation (see table 2.1). Each value-configured approach structures inquiry in a distinctive way – as scientifically objective, or value constituted but scientifically guided by a single logic, and so forth.

In whatever way a given project is framed by values, it remains open to alternative specific procedures of inquiry. Thus, for instance, if all inquiry were ordered via narrative as a formative discourse, we would identify four value-based projects of narrative. These possibilities are exemplified in (1) value-neutral inquiry into historical problems of cultural significance by Weberian historical sociologists such as Reinhard Bendix; (2) projects of "scientific" universal history such as world-systems analysis; (3) the recent surge of interest in history as an interpretive enterprise of storytelling (for example, in the work of Simon Schama); and (4) value-objective narrative in critical-theory accounts of the public sphere. Similar alternatives could be sketched for theoretical discourse. But the general point is already clear: alternative ways of coming to terms with the value problem order inquiry in ways other than simple matters of "bias." Values centrally condition both what the object of analysis "is," as well as the criteria for adjudicating among alternative accounts of it.

This analysis elaborates a point Foucault has made, that ideological elements do not necessarily undermine knowledge claims of inquiry, and, by the opposite token, that increased rigor and clarity do not purge inquiry of ideology.[13] Given the alternative projects framed by the problem of values, there can be no extra-valuational basis for privileging a single approach to finding truth. Even proponents of scientific objectivity define explanation on the basis of a value preference that displaces other kinds of inquiry, and they do so despite evidence that alternative approaches yield socially meaningful knowledge grounded in empirical analysis. Contending interests based on values – including various dispensations of science as a value – give rise to divergent ways in which a discursive regimen of explanation can be structured. They thus infuse inquiry with moral, ethical, and other knowledge-preference considerations.

Yet the very circumstances of value diversity define a *general* social condition in which inquiry takes place. Despite the aspirations of scientists and critical theorists to construct objects of inquiry on an objective basis, the positivist goal of theory-free measurement remains elusive, and the claim of critical theory to objectivity depends upon drawing a general public to its enterprise. For the foreseeable future, multiple value-based projects of explanation are likely to continue to coexist. Within the boundaries of any given research program, agreed-upon criteria for judging the adequacy of alternative explanations undergird a value-neutral project. But because research programs are diverse, neutrality holds only within the program, not outside it. In the wider sphere of sociohistorical inquiry, multiple criteria remain in play, and field- or program-specific explanations thus amount to particular approaches to explanation within a wider palette of possibilities. An explanation taken to be value-neutral within a given research program may be construed as value-relative by researchers outside the program who are interested in similar questions. Here, we arrive at an interesting situation: under the lifeworldly conditions of inquiry that exist at this historical juncture, no account of a phenomenon – even an objective explanation – can be considered absolute; instead, it is only relative to the value position that legitimates its criteria. In short, there is little reason to expect some general "solution" to the value problem. This circumstance, however, is not the end of the matter but the beginning. Inquiry can become increasingly self-critical and reflexive by taking into consideration the conditions in which it operates. The task that remains is to examine inquiry's discourses and practices when multiple value constructions of them remain in play.

3   Narrative cultures and inquiry

Values are central to how inquiry is conducted, but their consideration often remains only implicit in actual research. Narrative is more obviously a formative discourse, but its status is tied to values, for narratives often engage the dilemmas of meaningful choice. The power of novels like Jane Austen's derives from how their protagonists confront conflicts between existential acts and moral implications that become apparent to protagonists and readers only as the plot unfolds. Inquiry's narratives share this capacity for moral drama with fiction, even though sociohistorical narratives are conventionally distinguished by their concern with telling "what actually happened."

In inquiry, narrative is conventionally defined as an account draped on the framework of an overall plot that connects events, actions, and subplots to one another; textually, the plot is developed through devices such as flashbacks and cuts between different scenes that establish some kind of narrative time. Even outside history, ethnographic narratives and qualitative sociological research still embody its principal features. And within history, the textual character of the form comes through even in a highly telescoped passage concerned with religions and nations:

The prospect of a Protestant succession so alarmed Philip II that he entered into a formal alliance with the league of French Catholics created by the Guise family: the Sainte Union . . . There seems to be no doubt that this alliance, the treaty of Joinville (signed on 31 December 1584), frightened England.[1]

This passage reflects broader realist and objectivist use of narrative in inquiry, centered on testing alternative constructions of plot by considering which of them most effectively organizes known facts and informed hunches into a coherent arrangement that avoids anomalies and contradictions.[2]

Even if the narratives of inquiry are about real events, however, critics of objectivism argue that they are not radically different from fictive narratives, either in their discursive structures or their mediations among author, story, and audience. Assuming adequate knowledge about a wide range of real occurrences relevant to the study of a finite set of events – say the assassination of John F. Kennedy – any narrator still must employ a set of "lenses" that will move closer to or further from occurrences on the basis of some logic of exposition that is not dictated by the events themselves. Both on the basis of plot structure and because of shifting perspectival lenses, even narratives about real events create constructed textual worlds. This overall problem – of a textual reality that takes the form of a story about the real – finds its obverse when deconstructionists and postmodernists posit the text as the real and treat the sociohistorical world as having the character of a text. Overall, narrative seems firmly entrenched in worldly conditions of storytelling.

Well before the postmodern turn, the gap between events and their narrative "representation" already raised a host of questions.[3] How do the characteristics of narrative affect its status in inquiry? Does sociohistorical narrative differ from fiction? What is the source of plot? Does the genre of a narrative shape understandings in ways that transcend events? Can narrative yield any sociohistorical knowledge beyond the "facts" that it incorporates, and, if so, what is the character of such knowledge? Prior to the issue of how narrative discourse should be employed, these questions give pause to wonder whether it has a place in inquiry at all.

Indeed, a number of historians have pursued other rubrics of inquiry. Practitioners of *Annales*-style structural history, Marxian social historians, historical sociologists, and, more recently, cultural historians inspired by Foucault and psychoanalytic theory have subordinated narrative in favor of puzzles, comparisons, and other expository devices. On a different front, anthropologists have come to distrust the classic ethnographies that were written within what is now seen as a hegemonic metanarrative of colonialism. And, among sociologists, the "mainstream" interest in the discipline's professional legitimation as a science continues to render narratives of naturalistic field research suspect.

Yet, despite these doubts, blanket dismissals are not persuasive. As a target of deconstruction, narrative probably fares no worse than scientific discourse. Moreover, even researchers who do not center their work in narrative cannot seem to avoid it. The most structuralist historian studying the decline of feudalism tells stories. The quantitative survey researcher sometimes sketches a plot when asking an individual to respond to a questionnaire. The laboratory social psychologist often narrates a definition of the situation to subjects participating in small-group research. More widely, scholarly articles and books routinely use narration to recount the process of research.[4] In short, criticizing narrative is easier than purging it from inquiry. Indeed, as exemplars considered in chapters 7 and 8 illustrate, how narrative works in relation to other discourses will vary, but it becomes infused into virtually all sociohistorical research.[5]

Overall, there are complex tensions between narrative as story and narrative as representation of social reality. A variety of approaches explore these tensions, but none of them can reduce narrative to its own claims. Formal and rhetorical approaches yield insights about the structure of narrative as text – what Hayden White calls "the content of the form." But this perspective is necessarily incomplete, for people tell stories. Both in daily life and in inquiry, a web of narration connects storytellers and audiences, giving substance to social meaning and historical experience as a constitutive practice of social life itself. If narrative were considered only in its formal structure, the often problematic lifeworldly relations between events, narrative, narrator, and audience would be lost to inspection. White's formalist thesis thus needs to be balanced by a counterthesis about "the form of the content." The only way to fully address the problem of how narrative operates in inquiry is to include consideration of its reflexive relation to the narrations of social actors.

To connect the historicized lifeworld and the textual structure as frames for understanding narrative, the present chapter addresses four interrelated topics: (1) the formal and conventional features of narrative as discourse, (2) narrative as cultural discourse that enables and shapes socially located reason, (3) theories of the meaningful exchange between narrator and audience, and (4) the unfolding play of social life as embodying features of narrative and plot. On the basis of these considerations, I then describe two alternative emphases that can order inquiry's discursive regimen of narrative – the *intrinsic* search for actual lifeworldly connections among events that existed prior to inquiry's narration of them, versus the *extrinsic* enterprise that draws on some objective scheme of interpretation to order the analytic construction of a narrative. Following the chapter, a coda anticipates the discussion of explanatory and interpretive discourse in chapter 5 by asking about the potential of narratives as explanations.

Genre as metanarrative

Exploring narrative as literary form is an activity of "objective" cultural analysis that brings into question narrative claims to objectivity. That is, in relation to the frames of reference described in table 1.1, formal textual criticism places any narrative within an objective analytic frame that is external to any subject's intentional actions of creating narrative.

Formal consideration thus elides the very feature most compelling to narrative discourse, namely, its idiosyncratically personal yet seemingly transparent ability to relate "what happened."

Nevertheless, even formal analysis cannot completely detach narrative genres from their historical contexts. Indeed, the narrow sense of the term "narrative" does not really capture the rich possibilities of the discourse. Fables, myths, legends, tales, epics, stories, allegories, journals, biographies, memoirs, and life histories are all narratives, and each bears a certain claim of truth. Thus, the means of ordering narrative are various. The problem is suggested by Claude Lévi-Strauss in *The Savage Mind*. In different social groups, Lévi-Strauss argued, reality may be apprehended through either of two ordering strategies – "synchronic" catalogue or "diachronic" historicity – the former as taxonomy, the latter as series. Either of these ordering schema offers a way of organizing social knowledge about events, but neither is dictated by some essential character of reality.[6]

Lévi-Strauss's deeper point is that various kinds of social representation are connected to qualitatively different patterns of social organization. Narrative, in the narrow modern sense, treats events that build upon one another, that is, "history." Myth, by contrast, consolidates an epigrammatic, self-contained plot that surfaces *outside history* ("once upon a time," but at no particular time). A story with a mythic structure – the parable of the prodigal son in the Bible's Luke 15, for instance – is self-referential, rather than consequential for some larger story. By comparison, narrative in the modern sense is better suited to representing events with linear historicity. But this difference between myth and historical narrative cannot simply be mapped onto societal development, with the former displaced by the latter. To the contrary, even within the modernist "historical" approach, narrative as a form of discourse does not necessarily represent events in objective, chronological time. Alternative strategies are available for narrating the temporal pace, structure, and connections among manifold chains of action and events – even for "the same" sociohistorical phenomena. Outside modernist history, forms such as myth (and epic, fable, and so on) are testaments to myriad other possibilities of narration.[7]

In an inclusive sense, then, a narrative tells a story. Literary theories suggest a range of basic plot genres – tragedy, comedy, and so forth. But even though these genres are cast in abstract and general terms, they are distinctly Western conventional constructions. There is no narrative in general, only historically specific and culturally embedded ways of telling stories (which, to be sure, can be subjected to theoretical analysis). Consider the emergence of modern Western historical narrative. Historically, it became particularly compelling with the rise of nation-states and the world economy. As Jean-François Lyotard has argued, the civilizational enterprise of modernity depends on narrative – specifically "metanarrative" – as a vehicle of legitimation. In Lyotard's narrative, with the advance of modernity, older narratives of traditional peoples – legends, stories, histories in the plural – are displaced by more encompassing value-based narratives that proclaim their own objectivity.[8] In turn, as either the triumph of Liberty or the march of Reason, these metanarratives legitimate inquiry through stories that tell why the production of knowledge is important. These metanarratives are already apparent in valuations of history via religion (see chapter 2). And, as Lyotard would expect, a similar relationship surfaces in science. There, the conventionalized narratives of research reports are legitimated by their connection to a metanarrative that speaks to the question, "why science?"

Because metanarratives are central to legitimating inquiry's projects, they have become the sites of conflict over the meanings of history and science, fueled both by counterhegemonic inquiry and by narratives that infuse the past and present with new meanings, based on alternative values. "Whose story?" becomes a matter of dispute. Examples of these shifts abound. The European colonizing expansion across North America is now widely seen as something other than "manifest destiny." And from multiple value directions, narratives are "making sense" of the Holocaust in new ways – from neofascist denial to deep condemnations of German society and culture.[9]

These varieties of historical revisionism raise a basic question: how do the valorizations of metanarratives come into play in ostensibly factual narratives of events and their significance? Hayden White has addressed this question by asking how historical narratives render events intelligible. In *Metahistory*, White characterizes the enterprise of writing history as a concatenation of two cultures – art and science. On the side of art, poetic acts of textual construction prefigure the works of historians independently of the actual subject matters of their studies. As White shows, in the works of Tocqueville, Ranke, Burckhardt, and others, formal affinities forge connections between ideology, mode of emplotment, and trope of argument. For instance, conservative history in the work of Ranke solves the problem of how to select events by the trope of *synecdoche* – by using a part (such as the State) to represent the history of the whole. This trope lends itself to an emplotment of *comedy*, in which the dramatic tensions arise out of the problematic relations between parts, and these eventually become resolved in a synthetic climax that affirms rectitude for the whole.

Historians today may think their methods more sophisticated than Ranke's, but White argues that the favored emplotment of contemporary historians – satire, with its associated trope of irony – has no more compelling validity than other narrative genres. Instead, he suggests, historians have become cynical about other emplotments, "since they can be deployed only in the belief in language's capacity to grasp the nature of things in figurative terms" – a view that now seems naive. White concludes that the conventional distinction between philosophical history and "history proper" is arbitrary, since proper history does not avoid the metahistorical conceptual constructs that are so obvious in philosophical history; instead it buries them in narratological and tropic devices that give history a credible quality.[10]

In other words, even with irony, narrative superimposes meanings. Like fiction, histories about real events face expository problems of how to structure a story's plot. Just as two novels may render the same general story as either tragedy or satire, so may inquiry. Just as the novelist may choose to take the viewpoint of one or another character or observer, so may the historian. Just as novels exercise poetic license in the characterization of events, so sociohistorical narrative arranges observations according to one or another rationale that lacks necessity. Overall, the implications are substantial. By choosing among alternative genres – tragedy, comedy, and so on – a narrator has the capacity to establish a textual coherence that does not depend on any singular coherence in events themselves. Once a particular transcendent coherence is given, a cascade of events can be fitted into that coherence (or appended to it through the use of "asides," or ignored). Conflicts between two narratives about the "same" events thus are not always easily resolved by "facts," because alternative coherent emplotments of narratives can emphasize different facts and give divergent meanings to the same facts.

That multiple possibilities of coherence are shared by historical narrative and fiction evidences more than simply a confrontation between alternative professional approaches to history. It suggests that professional history shares a terrain – uncomfortably – with wider practices. In the nineteenth century, historians sought to distance their efforts from fables, legends, and historical satires. Today, historians worry about blurred boundaries with historical fiction (such as *The Thorn Birds*), docudramas on subjects like World War II, and poeticized history (in the widely acclaimed writings of historian Simon Schama).[11]

Popular and fictionalized histories obviously threaten professional standards meant to protect disciplinary legitimacy. But what is the relation of professional standards to genres seemingly less tainted than fiction and legends – "annals" and "chronicles," for instance? Annals provide information but fail to offer plot: they log events that match a series of years, but without making apparent connections among events. As antecedents of modern historical narratives, chronicles are more complex. They open up the possibility of ordering events by topics, or they invent topics that make the ordering of events possible. But unlike full-fledged modern narratives, chronicles lack closure. Yet as White emphasizes, the plot choice among alternative beginnings and endings cannot be derived from events themselves. Life goes on. Thus, any effort to move beyond chronicles raises the classic historiographic problem of "periodization" – how to construe historical temporality. Indeed, it is the beginning and end that yield coherence. As Lyotard writes of narrative, "Wherever in diegetic time it stops, its term makes sense and retroactively organizes the recounted events."[12]

Modern historical narratives differ from annals and chronicles by giving meaningful shape and boundaries to a set of events. But what is the source of meaning? White identifies a source equivalent to the one that shapes Lyotard's metanarratives – namely, "moral principle." As White puts it, "The events that are actually recorded in the narrative appear to be real precisely insofar as they belong to an order of moral existence, just as they derive their meaning from their placement in this order."[13] In conflicts of historical interpretation, narratives lend credence to one view or another by way of some moral standard that resolves the meaning of events through a plot. Thus, modern historical narratives – of a labor movement, economic history, the Cold War – bear the weight of moral baggage that does not emerge from events themselves. How different are these narratives from myths? As Roland Barthes once observed, "The reader lives the myth as a story at once true and unreal."[14] Modern historical narratives are based on different conventions of genre, still capable of truth and still unreal. Moral principle effectively folds narrative into one or another metanarrative. Thus, the end of modernity would come only with the end of stories with endings. But the end of stories with endings could come only with the end of moral stakes for narratives. And this is a prospect that even supposed opponents of modernity find difficult to embrace.

Narratives as cultural communications

Although narratives are shaped by their genres, philosopher Paul Ricoeur argues in *Time and Narrative* that textual deconstructions do not drain narratives of their moral significance. Ricoeur refuses the end of modernity, the end of practical reason, and the end of history – which he sees as linked.[15] His refusal, based on a value stance that embraces narrative as a basis for agency, derives moral power from the potential of narratives as cultural communications that produce people's self-understandings. This account raises the question of how culturally specific genres of narrative work in various times and places. This question can be addressed by comparing annals to two types of narrative found outside the realm of inquiry – journalism and the *I Ching*, the Chinese Book of Changes.

As White has shown, annals match events to a series of years, but they lack the kinds of connectedness that *themes* give to chronicles and that morally coherent *plots* – with beginnings and endings – give to modern historical narratives. Annals seem like sets of disjointed entries. Thus, a portion of "The Welsh Annals" runs:

917   Queen Aethelflaed died.
918
919   King Clydog was killed.
920
921   The battle of Dinas Newydd.[16]

Some years lack any event that merited an entry; and if connections might be inferred among the reported events, they are not suggested. Annals like this do not offer even the protonarrative of chronicles – themselves unfulfilled by plot resolution. Yet it would be anachronistic to view annals as incomplete historical narratives. Their significance can more likely be found in their relations to the social groups in which they are constructed. In the absence of a story, why is anything recorded at all? In a minimalist way, annals construct historical time – but not history – out of endlessly passing duration. Although they lack any narrative of a morally infused subject (such as the fate of a nation), presumably a community existed for whom the entries marked widely known and important events. Annals, in this interpretation, may have been mnemonic devices for the production of collective memory (organized today through much more complex devices of narration, such as public and mediated ceremonies noting the anniversaries of symbolically important events).

A distinction between "stories" and "news" suggests a way to speculate about the social contexts of annals as written constructions of historical time.[17] In modern journalism, "stories" weave together events into coherent narratives ordered by plots. On the other hand, reports of "news" offer basic information about events, leaving readers to construct meanings on their own. In this light, the obviously disconnected quality of written annals may reflect their relationships to now inaccessible oral traditions about significant events. Whether public oral traditions served as "stories" or "news," descriptions of events by a figure like the "town crier" might leave people to weave meanings into their own stories that they pass along in more intimate episodes of "gossip." In other words, early written annals are probably surviving artifacts of once ongoing and much richer social intercourse – what Margaret Somers calls "ontological narratives," which she defines as "stories that social actors use to make sense of – indeed, to act in – their lives."[18] Somers's important point in invoking ontology is that some narratives not only make sense of the world; they constitute the world and our identities in relation to it. Ontological narratives may be simultaneously bound up with both moral principles and concrete orchestrations of ongoing social life.

The ontological powers of narrative can also be seen in cultural genres of narrative that structure other lived temporalities of social existence than the Western linear time that marks annals, chronicles, and modern historical narrative. Consider a classic work of Chinese philosophy, the *I Ching*, or Book of Changes. The *I Ching* does not describe "the past"; it identifies a matrix of alternative "present" situations that social actors may face. This matrix is defined by "upper" and "lower" trigrams – symbols consisting of three horizontal bars for which binary alternatives are defined by whether the bar is continuous or broken. Combinations of two three-bar trigrams yield a set of sixty-four six-bar hexagrams used to represent archetypal moments of biographical existence – situations such as "youthful folly," "splitting apart," and "abundance." Each hexagram also identifies possible changes leading to other situations, themselves defined by other hexagrams. Users of the *I Ching* either throw yarrow sticks or toss coins in order to identify their own hexagrammatic positions and lines of change toward other hexagrams. On this basis, they may consult the text for commentaries on their present circumstances and transitional possibilities.

To take one example, the hexagram *Ko*, revolution (molting), is composed of *Tui* as the upper trigram, standing for "The joyous, lake," and a lower trigram of *Li*, "The clinging, fire." For this hexagram, the "Judgment" reads: "Revolution. On your own day/ You are believed./ Supreme success,/ Furthering through perseverance./ Remorse disappears." The Book of Changes offers an "Image" of "Fire in the lake. . ./ Thus the superior man/ Sets the calendar in order/ And makes the seasons clear." As for numbers associated with specific lines of the hexagram, "Six in the second place [line] means:/ When one's own day comes, one may create revolution./ Starting brings good fortune. No blame."[19]

It might be argued that the *I Ching* is nothing more than an oracle or a device of divination, but this seems mistaken. As Richard Wilhelm, the German translator of the *I Ching*, pointed out, "fortune telling lacks moral significance," whereas, in the *I Ching*, "Each situation demands the action proper to it."[20] A person can reflect on an archetypal situation that might play out in a number of different ways, depending on how he or she acts. The *I Ching* offers accumulated wisdom organized in relation to a codification of these archetypal situations. The work is neither chronicle nor historical narrative: it is a typology of alternative situations and biographical possibilities, elaborated through trajectories toward other positions in the matrix. The *I Ching*'s effectiveness thus depends either on a world that is recursively patterned on archetypal events, or, at least, on the capacity of its users to identify aspects of unique events by archetypes of recurrence. I am not suggesting that the *I Ching* substitutes for narrative in a civilization with a nonlinear sense of time.[21] Rather, the *I Ching* offers a serviceable matrix that people can use to understand their own situations by reference to generic situations of social existence. But the understanding is classificatory and complexly cyclical, not "historical."

Narrative is not just text. As Somers holds, it is also embedded communication that connects an audience to meaningful situations and courses of action in the social world. Agreed-upon or "conventionalized" textual genres, plots, and scripts offer bases for communication among people who narratively enact life – in work, home life, politics, and elsewhere.

In this light, narratives – broadly understood as meaningful stories – will have diverse cultural conventions and significance. Whatever the relationships of annals to enacted cultures, the striking contrast between them, the *I Ching*, and modern historical narrative demonstrates that the latter is but one alternative among diverse conventionalized types of narrative communication. There is thus good reason to expect that changes in narrative produce innovative ways of making and communicating meaning. At the dawn of the twenty-first century, this possibility has yielded a new sense of inquiry's reflexivity. Advocates of social transformation are not abandoning narrative; they are coming to the view that modernity's narratives are exercises in cultural hegemony, either challenged or not, and they are searching for new approaches that hold some promise of empowerment to the dispossessed. As Renato Rosaldo has noted, the result is a clash of cultural epistemologies. Feminists who criticize the patriarchal character of conventional narratives are experimenting with ways of freeing individuals from cultural scripts inflected with heroic masculinity and romanticism. An alternative scenario offered by Jean Baudrillard depicts a postmodern world where mass-produced "simulacra" give the appearance of reality but overwhelm it with a hyper-reality. In this unreal world of real illusion, a narrative of one's own is displaced by mass distributions of scripts that lack an author or a subject. Whereas feminists seek to reestablish women as agents, Baudrillard offers agentless scripts. The distance between these positions suggests both that narrative is a central site of contestation over the possibilities of agency, and that inquiry needs to chart shifts in how narrative constructions are employed in everyday life.[22]

As a form of discourse that bears both moral concerns and lived agency (or lack thereof), how might narrative enter into inquiry at a time when the grand metanarratives have become suspect? Paul Ricoeur maintains that narrative can amount to more than mere elaboration of metanarrative. Like Habermas, Ricoeur wants to salvage the project of emancipation. He argues that, because narrative allows people to consider their own agency in relation to a world that is increasingly organized along systemic lines, it promotes socially located reason. This enterprise Ricoeur connects even with Foucault's discursive formations surrounding madness, economics, and other institutions that transcend narrative agency. For Ricoeur, Foucault brings into view the historicity of consciousness not as a transcendental Subject, but in multiple forms marked by periodical shifts in the possibilities of narrative discourse.[23] Foucault might have refused Ricoeur's formulation. But evidently the relation of narrative to both modernist and postmodernist projects remains open, and its significance is not completely constrained by textual forms or metanarratives.[24] At the dawn of the third millennium of the modern era, we are only beginning to understand narrative's manifold communicative potentialities for inquiry, ontological agency, and future constructions of social existence.

The social relationship between narrator and audience

Given the potential power of narrative, the question of how it works is paramount. Answers to this question have been formulated in perspectives ranging from psychoanalysis to rhetoric, speech-act theory, and phenomenology. These have their differences, but, by identifying narrative as a vehicle that transposes meaning between author and reader, they all suggest the incompleteness of arguments concerning poetic structure and textual form.

Theories of rhetoric shift attention away from the internal features of a text to the problem of how the reader is engaged by the author. Research on this question – from Wayne Booth's studies of the author's role in realistic fiction to Donald McCloskey's analyses of textual accomplishments in economic discourse – suggest that, independently of structural form, strategies of communication influence how readers assess the plausibility of content. Thus, extra-logical devices like "voice" and "point of view" are important for persuading the reader. Whatever the venue – whether the narrative is a conventional plot, a story of research, or a metanarrative of science – when rhetoric succeeds, it engages a reader by affirming stylistic conventions. An effective communicative voice meets the reader's standards for warranting the discourse.[25]

Like analyses of formal textual structures, rhetorical analysis is often taken to undermine the significance of truth claims in narratives, either historical or scientific. But rhetorical analysis transcends formalism by emphasizing the lifeworldly continuities between inquiry's narratives and other activities of communication. This underscores the double reflexivity of what Habermas calls communicative action. Narratives *are* kinds of social action, and they thus may be read as analogues of everyday actions (and conversely, in the strong poststructuralist thesis, actions in the lifeworld may be read as narrative texts). On the basis of this resonance, both lifeworldly and other narratives serve as representations *of* actions – not only about "the past," but about the recurrent ("recipes"), the imaginary ("fantasies"), and projected futures ("scenarios"). Narrative is used not only to describe action (e.g., the activities of work as an unfolding sequence), but also to construct meaningful models of action (procedures and practices of work), and to coordinate action (accounts about how to handle situations as work unfolds). The events and the narratives told during their unfolding in turn can be recalled (stories about work), imitated (dramatizations of work), and interpreted by others ("that's not such hard work," or "maybe I can get a job like that," or "we workers need to stick together").

When narrative is considered as a model of lifeworldly action, it becomes an explicit focus of social theoretical discourse (discussed in chapter 4). Remaining for the present within strictly narrative discourse, the key lifeworldly issue centers on the narrator's relation to readers. A linguistic approach to this issue – derived from Austin's theory of speech-acts – treats narrative as a speech-act broadly akin to verbal utterance, in a situation constructed as a relationship between a speaker and an audience.[26] The audience engages in what Erving Goffman (following Coleridge) calls a "suspension of disbelief" that ignores the obviously constructed features of narrative in order to "get into" the realm depicted within its frame. Most famously, Aristotle described this transformation via a model of catharsis, suggesting that readers give emotional energy to the dramatic tensions set up by narrative, thus becoming invested in the outcomes of situations constructed within the narrative. Readers adopt the tensions of the narrative as their own. This cathartic model is underspecified as to any cognitive process of investment, but it is at least a suggestive metaphor about narrative communication.

The cathartic model of narrative can be mapped in terms of Alfred Schutz's lifeworld phenomenology, particularly his theory of relevance. Describing an individual's stream of consciousness, Schutz defined as *topical relevances* issues that *might* come to the individual's mind (from the ultimate meaning of life to where to get something to eat). When someone actually thinks about a topical relevance, Schutz would describe the topic as having become "thematic." But an individual's focus on a thematic topic does not come to mind preinterpreted. Instead, any resolution in relation to a topical relevance is based upon two additional kinds of relevance: (1) *interpretational relevance*, that is, the elements of an individual's "stock of knowledge" available for assigning meaning in relation to a theme; and (2) *motivational relevance*, or the specific concerns, goals, and objectives that may affect what the individual "makes of" a particular thematic issue.[27] This account is suggestive about the complex relation between narrative and audience. In Schutz's terms, no narrative can be meaningful in its own right, for people will pay attention to it in relation to their own structures of relevance. People make meaning *out of* narrative, rather than apprehending "the" meaning *in* narrative. Thus, literary critic Harold Bloom regarded every critical reaction to a poem as necessarily founded in *mis*interpretation, reading as an activity of "creative misunderstanding."[28] Everyone who reads also "writes" – through the activity of reading.

By understanding narrative as social process, phenomenology blurs the analytic isolations of text, narrator, and audience. Rather than treating each as a separate entity that somehow "affects" the other, a phenomenological approach recognizes the textual mediations that connect writers and audiences in intersubjective relationships. When I read, I pay attention (more or less) to a stream of words on paper. To the extent that I as a reader "give myself over" to the writer's stream of words, I can explore the writer's own train of thought – filtered by my own ways of making meaning. But "giving oneself over" to reading amounts to "taking on" the writer's stream of words as though they were my own. Deep reading amounts to a communicative structure of sociation that makes an edited and revised version of the text a part of my own stock of knowledge. Thus, Wolfgang Iser proposed, in his

phenomenological theory of reception, to show how the text offers win-
dows by which the "implied reader" can "wander" through the world
made present by the text.[29] This narrative possibility is sustained in
inquiry by devices and conventions that are not so distant from the
strategies of realistic fiction. As Felix Gilbert observed, in *The History
of the Popes*, Leopold von Ranke "avoids summary statements and lets
the narrator disappear from the story so that the reader is directly confronted with facts and events. Ranke wants the reader to experience the
story as a participant."[30]

Both speech-act and phenomenological approaches emphasize the
connections between reading printed narratives and attending to spoken
narratives in everyday life. In the lifeworld as narratological world,
people search for conventional cues in order to frame experiences via
one or another "accent" on reality. People try to determine whether
someone is acting seriously or facetiously, pretending or mocking. We
engage the lifeworld as something of a text, while conversely we can
engage written narratives in ways that allow us to treat them as imaginary lifeworlds. Thus, the argument that literary texts are imaginary
might seem to suggest a fundamental divide from the lifeworld, but the
relationship is more complex: the lifeworld itself is partly constructed
both through imagination and by engagement with texts (ritual, news,
humor, and so on) that frame reality in divergent ways.

How readers make meaning out of any narrative is shaped by personal
stocks of knowledge and immediate situations. What someone makes
of a business proposition will depend upon the standing in which the
listener holds the narrator. A US politician and the surviving daughter
of a fatal causality will read a history of the Vietnam War in different
ways. Rather than passively "taking in" meanings already contained in
narratives, readers actively make new meanings out of narratives. There
are thus diverse receptions of narratives in the lifeworld. Once this is
acknowledged, it becomes possible to align phenomenological theories
of narrative with historical and Marxist theories of meaning – for
example, the work of Hans Robert Jauss and the "new historicist"
movement of literary criticism. Although opponents claim that "reader-
response" theories fall prey to an ahistorical "textualist fallacy," the
potential is quite the opposite: narratives, produced as acts in history,
can be charted in their reception, reading, and reinvocation in historical
narratives of memory, fantasy, and action by particular individuals and
communities.[31]

Overall, at some remove from inquiry, I have traced a wide arc of
narrative – as poetic structure, culture, agency, and communication.
First, plot coherence derives in part from the structural properties of

narratives, producing meanings not inherent in events themselves. Second, myriad possibilities of cultural expression yield alternative practices of narrative sense-making that reflexively shape social existence. In the production of meanings about the past, the present, and the future, life itself is in part constructed through narration. Third, rhetoric supplements narrational content by techniques of presentation such that the text is a superadded product of the authorial capacity to project a vision effectively. Focusing on the author in turn raises the question of the audience, and speech-act and phenomenological approaches again return narration to the lifeworld in its historicity. Taken together, these considerations undermine claims to establish narrative as "objective" description of "what happened," but they unveil narrative as a sense-making enterprise deeply connected to the existential circumstances of historically situated social life.

How, then, to tell a story? With the rise of skepticism in the late twentieth century, narration has become the subject of considerable contention. Readers now expect a more self-conscious narrator, one who does not try to hide "backstage" during the act of narration. Pushed in this direction, narration ultimately becomes a story of the narrator's activities (I scratch my ear and look over my notes. Perhaps what to say next will come to me after I go to get a cup of coffee and gaze out at the spring morning, pondering the crises reported in the newspaper. I should save this file before getting up. [control-S] I saved the file; I am getting up.) There is a tradeoff: playing with the forms of narrativity can shift away from other "subjects" to the narrator as subject. On the other hand, such experiments do show that any narrative is an odyssey in voice, emplotment, flashbacks, and other strategies.[32]

Plot in/of the lifeworld and the quest for intrinsic narrative

Given the range of possibilities, there can be no hope of consolidating a definitive narrative method for inquiry. My enterprise is different: I want to identify two alternative regimens of narration that follow from the distinction between an *observer's lifeworldly* versus an *observer's objective* frame of reference (identified in table 1.1). This distinction will differentiate between narrative oriented to the *intrinsic* meanings in play in events themselves versus narrative driven by *extrinsic* schemes of interpretation.[33] I describe the intrinsic possibility here; the following section considers extrinsic narrative (chapters 7 and 8 show how these possibilities of narration are connected to alternative ways of practicing inquiry).

If historical writing is assumed to describe immanent meanings embedded in events themselves, then the problem of narrative concerns how to ascertain and represent such meanings. One possibility is that the immanent meanings involve the working out of a transcendent meaningful telos *in* history, as expected by metanarratives of philosophical history. This view has fallen on hard times. To be sure, as White argued, the line between philosophical history and history proper is arbitrary. But, even so, Kant seems well grounded in thinking that philosophical history is an activity centered in the narrator's viewpoint.[34] If intrinsic narrative is to avoid metanarrative, the task of uncovering immanent meanings leads away from philosophical history, toward the hermeneutic discovery of how events become meaningful intrinsically – for social actors themselves. At the extreme, the intrinsic narrative is a story told in the first person, from one or another subjective viewpoint in the course of unfolding events. Of course, no observer can regain this viewpoint of an acting subject, but the observer engaged in inquiry can inquire into subjective meanings held by other social actors. To paraphrase Weber in a crude way, no one can be Caesar, but it is possible to try to understand the meaningful circumstances of action from Caesar's and other individuals' existential viewpoints. This orientation – in terms of table 1.1, an *observer's lifeworldly* frame of reference – directs analysis toward an *intrinsic sociohistorical object*, a web of lifeworldly connections among historically emergent actions, events, and meanings. Such an orientation differs from an *observer's objective* frame of reference – oriented toward issues such as the causes of capitalist development, the periodization of a nation-state's political history, the relation of resource mobilization to success of social movements, and so forth. Emplotment of an intrinsic sociohistorical object yields a narrative of events that are connected through the orientations of social actors toward objects of attention that they share – even when the actors are opposed to, or unaware of, each other.

The relationship of inquiry to an intrinsic sociohistorical object is variable. In ethnographic and participant-observer field research, the narrator interacts with individuals in a "we-relationship." At the other extreme, in historical research concerning long past events, the construction of an intrinsic narrative depends entirely on artifactual evidence and social memory. But the project is similar. In both cases, inquiry's emplotment becomes bound up with the identification of "plots" (not just in the conspiratorial sense) constructed in the course of actual life – through enactment, and by way of fantasy, anticipation, and memory of social actors.

In this theorization, sociohistorical objects subject to intrinsic emplotment include family politics, economic competition, social movements, wars, and other events that are rendered meaningful by social actors. In addition, cultural history may meet the criterion of mutual orientation insofar as the coherence of the culture that is traced is established by actors who either *serially* replicate (and are dialectically replicated by) cultural patterns, or engage in *sequential* modification of cultural meanings and practices.[35]

There is a nearly bottomless infinitude to intrinsic sociohistorical objects. The events are manifold, and, as Hayden White suggests, the connections among events that can be construed as plots exceed what any given narrative can characterize, even if a particular plot may accord better or worse with (always incomplete) information. Toward the end of the nineteenth century, Wilhelm Dilthey wanted to start from the biography as a unit for building up history, but he was overwhelmed by the task because any person's course of life has an oversupply of episodes that can be linked with intrinsic emplotments. These circumstances again underscore that narration cannot be reduced to faithful representation of "what really happened." We may thus expect diverse projects of intrinsic narrative. Foucault's archeology of disciplined practices is altogether different from Dilthey's interest in biography.[36] But the two share something. Both Dilthey and Foucault concerned themselves with unveiling the meanings of historicity marked by the orientations of acting subjects in particular sociohistorical arenas. The difference between the two – which spans a broad range of hermeneutic possibilities – depends upon Foucault's relative emphasis on "objective" stocks of knowledge versus Dilthey's concern with biography.[37]

For Dilthey and Foucault, and in general, narratives of intrinsic sociohistorical plots are directed to understanding the specific means by which the world is given a semblance of coherence by the existential meanings that social actors produce – before, during, and after events. Intrinsic narratives thus offer counterpoint to observers' objective frames of reference – theorizations of history, objective conceptual schemes, and metanarratives (themselves theoretically structured) – that define external criteria by which events obtain their analytic significance. The goal of intrinsic sociohistorical narrative – to emplot a play of events – depends on *Verstehen*, interpretive understanding.

Verstehen is concerned with people's subjectively meaningful actions that transpire in unfolding lifeworldly time, i.e., at actual moments of life.[38] Because subjective meaning is *temporally* constituted, any project of *verstehende* narrative at least implicitly embeds a textual representation of temporality. This connection between time and narrative has been widely noted. Among literary critics, Bakhtin showed how various genres of fiction are infused with alternative forms of temporality – everyday time, adventure time, and so forth. These possibilities, he argued, establish continuities between the novel and temporalities of actual life. Like Bakhtin, Paul Ricoeur resists identifying any essential character of temporality. Instead, he treats narrative as a problematic shared by fiction and historicity, and directs inquiry toward a hermeneutic analysis of its manifestations. In this vein, my own field research in utopian communal groups of the American counterculture shows that unfolding social time comes to be constructed in alternative ways. For example, "warring" apocalyptic social movements enact a *strategic time* of struggle against "forces of evil," whereas other apocalyptic groups construct their existences as "heavens-on-earth" in which time is construed to approximate a *timeless* tableau. These and other investigations suggest that social events are shaped through temporalities of meaningful social action and interaction, prior to inquiry's emplotment and narration of them.[39] Intrinsically meaningful social life does not simply take place *within* a homogeneous linear time; lived engagements of sociohistorical actors in meaningful social relationships give shape *to* time. There will be certain temporalities of action in a bureaucratically ordered realm, others in the interplay of pure sociability, altogether different ones in the performance of ritual, yet others in the conduct of war and revolution.

However, empirical temporalities do not amount to "eternal" structural features of different social arenas. To the contrary, the lived temporalities of meaningful actions intersect with one another in unfolding social life. As Erving Goffman has shown, we act *out* our actions, playing roles – well or poorly, shifting between frontstage performances and backstage rehearsals, framing scenes as we go.[40] This dramatic character of life is not limited to single episodes. Rather, lived temporal enactments in any one episode frequently become conditions of subsequent actions serially linked in temporally discontinuous, trans-episodic "plots" – social interactions with stakes – that are themselves the foci of social conflict, cooperation, ploys, and stratagems. People engaging in a political campaign, for example, do not just act in a self-contained here-and-now; at a given moment, they make coordinated plans for future activities, the success of which in turn is affected by events subsequent to the formulation of plans, which the campaigners may or may not learn about in time to take into account. In this instance, and in general, narrations are more than just observers' accounts of events after the fact. The regimen of intrinsic narrative depends for its very possibility on previously enacted events. As Wilhelm Dilthey made it his life's work to show, narrative is a basic constitutive rubric of interpretation in unfolding meaningful life.[41] People invoke narratives ("stories" we can call them, so long as we don't take this term to signify any judgments about truth status) in multiple ways. Narratives can be used by people to "construct" reality for other people by providing representations of events beyond their own personal knowledge. People also individually and jointly compose "scripts" and "scenarios" to make narrative sense of projects that they plan to undertake in the future. In addition, narratives can be used to "reconstruct" past events, and they can "deconstruct" competing narratives in advance, as events unfold, and after the fact.[42]

In all this, people act on the basis of knowledge – true or false – that they both construct and receive through narrations. They also sometimes seek to resurrect memories and reconstruct "what happened." Some stories prevail publicly. Others get maintained in private yet enduring ways. Some narratives promoted by one person or group are ignored or modified by others, according to their own circumstances of interpretation. Thus, part of the drama of life on the ground hinges on the unfolding constructions of past, present, and future history by its participants.

For example, during the August 1991 events in the then-USSR that led to the fall of Premier Mikhail Gorbachev (and ultimately to the collapse of Soviet communism), both the gamut of Soviet political actors as well as other nation-states needed to evaluate a number of possible plot lines (coup? revolution? thwarted rebellion?) that did not conflict with available evidence but yielded strikingly different interpretations of a situation that was in a high degree of flux. Initially, on the eve of the signing of a confederation treaty of union, certain of Gorbachev's aides announced a new "State Committee for the State of Emergency" to save the Soviet Union from ethnic disintegration and economic chaos. Gorbachev faced an "inability to perform his duties for health reasons," they reported, and was undergoing medical treatment while on vacation at the Black Sea. They hoped Gorbachev, "as soon as he feels better, will take up again his office." In response, Boris Yeltsin stood defiantly on a tank outside the Russian parliament building, denounced the ouster of Gorbachev, and rallied the masses to oppose what came to be understood as a coup. Facing widespread strikes and demonstrations, the coup leaders seem to have weakened in their purpose and lost control, and Gorbachev managed to return to Moscow, where he said of the coup leaders, "They lost." The Soviet news agency Tass returned to the Gorbachev side with a bulletin reporting that Gorbachev was "in full control of the country." But ultimately Gorbachev lost out to the man who had demanded his return, Boris Yeltsin.[43] Thus, in an interesting way, the validity of differing ambiguous narratives in progress ultimately depended on the power of Yeltsin and the inability of Gorbachev to orchestrate subsequent events that "fixed" the meanings of earlier events.[44] As this dramatic example from a world-transformative episode suggests, facts are never pristine; they are already enveloped within (often contradictory) layers of interpretation. No reconstruction, by participants or observers, before, during, or after the fact, gets the whole story. There is no whole story, only stories from various points of view.

Given the manifold narratives that go into an intrinsic object of inquiry, we must expect a fundamental tension between the object and any narrative emplotment of it. Outside inquiry, narratives are not often concerned with the niceties of epistemology or the philosophy of history, and criteria of truth remain highly ambiguous. Meaning is constructed through cultural use of available materials, and individuals, groups, entire nations often have vital interests in believing or rejecting particular versions of events. Moreover, intrinsic narratives on the ground sometimes become inserted into competing "intrinsic metanarratives," each with its own superadded moral significance. Thus, the surface "facts" – about the partitioning of an ethnic group, the accuracy of a newspaper report about a crime wave, or the emergence of a New World Order – cannot be the sole basis for considering their narratological importance, for individuals and groups can embrace meaningful definitions of situations that can themselves be consequential, whatever their "truth." Narration, both in lifeworldly conduct and in inquiry, is a narration of narration, the interpretation of preinterpretations. It is a journey into the hall of mirrors.

A series of parallels thus obtains between the narratives of social actors and the narratives of sociohistorical inquiry (and fiction, although it is not the issue here). In both cases, narration involves multiple plots (as meaningful efforts to sequence actions and events) and multiple emplotments (as meaningful descriptions of such sequences). Both the narratives of social actors and those of inquiry contain the reflexive possibility of becoming reincorporated into subsequent action. And, in both cases, narrative can become endlessly submerged in details, or fail to obtain dramatic closure for lack of critical information. Yet these commonalities underscore important differences. In everyday life, narratives may be subjected to various cultural conventions, but they are not the focus of efforts at institutional regulation, except in discrete arenas such as courtroom proceedings (testimony of witnesses) and religious organizations (confession, conversion stories). Ordinarily, people can let the pragmatic limits of interest establish the boundaries of their accounts, or they may keep secrets, dissemble, or embellish.

By contrast to lifeworldly narratives, narrative in inquiry is constructed through more institutionally conventionalized approaches to issues such as selection of events, adjudication of plot conflicts, and establishment of linkages among events. The classic narrative question – "what happened?" – depends on the establishment of some thematic boundary that sets the limits of the story – what Lawrence Stone has called a "pregnant principle." Certain narrative emplotments may not stand up under the weight of contrary evidence.[45] But, like lifeworldly narratives, alternative narratives in inquiry can yield divergent understandings of the same events. According to Jean-François Lyotard, such interpretive conflicts cannot be resolved, for "litigation" would assume a universal standpoint, whereas narrative, intrinsic or otherwise, necessarily involves the absence of such a standpoint – if for no other reason, because of its production at a specific historical time.[46]

Even without claiming a universal standpoint, however, intrinsic narrative may hope to seek out the lifeworldly connectedness of actions, including embedded actions of constructing and distributing stories. To be sure, the narrator has a viewpoint and telescopes events. But even if an intrinsic narrative cannot recount all events and meanings, it can aspire to offer one portrayal of events and meanings that does not contradict available information. In the limiting case, a fully intrinsic narrative might only seek to describe meanings of participants.[47] However, the hermeneutic description of actors' meanings does not exhaust the possibilities, even of intrinsic narrative. Indeed, it places a narrator in a position of performed naiveté in which nothing can be known except from the viewpoints of previous actors. Such a stance restricts the narrator to weaving together received stories. Yet, like any other restriction on the narrator's voice, this one can only be a convention, one that binds the narrator to particular viewpoints, or maintains the pretense that there is no narrator. Intrinsic narration spans a broader range of possibilities. It does not require an exclusively subjectivist account of social action or an idealist perspective on social phenomena more generally. To the contrary, intrinsic narratives widely address the play of scripts, cultural schema, economic interests, institutions of power, and other external circumstances that are not purely matters of subjective intention.

In representing intrinsically connected events, the narrator can be foregrounded or obscured but not erased. Whenever an intrinsic object is emplotted by someone other than one or another participant in events, this activity has its own, superadded concerns. The implications are spelled out in a deconstructive study of historical writing by Sande Cohen. As he shows, the sense that historians' narratives are "about" something depends on expository devices that transcend whatever empirically demonstrable connections may exist among events: at least some narrative connections are *extra*-intrinsic products of inquiry, not derivatives of causal or meaningful sequences in unfolding history.[48] Similarly, Lyotard notes that narrative discourse has a distinctive capacity to envelop diverse "phrase regimens" from other discourses.[49] An author can use substantial shifts – between scene-setting descriptions, ruminations of actors, and so forth – to lace a story with philosophical argument, history, poetry, and endless other matters. In inquiry, this makes it possible for intrinsic narrative to consider manifold issues relevant to plot development – the mental condition of a king, the food supply of a welfare class, weather conditions during a war campaign, and so on – even if individuals most directly involved in the intrinsic plot lacked awareness or interest in them. Narrative thereby becomes a vehicle for wide-ranging discussions that transpire "outside" the narrative time of plot development, yet become embedded within its frame by a narrator whose knowledge and interests exceed those of the narration's subjects.

Intrinsic narrative in inquiry sometimes is held to differ decisively from lifeworldly narratives because its narrator typically knows what is unknown to the actors at a particular juncture, namely, outcomes of certain events. Inquiry's narrator is able to give shape to the intrinsic plot through techniques of foreshadowing that are unavailable to the actors. However, this sense of closure is illusory, for the perspective from which foreshadowing occurs is not fixed. It depends on how a historical subject is constructed after the fact. Inquiry's questions, periodizations, and analyses may attain a history of their own, established within one or another discursive community – for example, historians debating whether the events in seventeenth-century England constituted a "revolution." These points suggest that any narration other than a contemporary account of an open-ended, unresolved plot is a retrospective superadded construction, even when its standard of coherence is established intrinsically, by attention to the mutual orientations of social actors toward a set of events.

Overall, inquiry's narratives differ from everyday narrative in their institutional circumstances and conventions of construction. However, these differences do not transport inquiry's narrators beyond the lifeworld. Whoever writes intrinsic narrative, at whatever time, proceeds on the basis of necessarily fragmentary information, from a limited perspective, by use of lesser or greater amounts of elaboration according to the richness of sources. Yet paradoxically, the pieced-together fragments that are the building blocks of narrative can give the reader a rich sense of experiencing events. In part this trick of narrative works because readers absorb stories in empathic relationships to everyday and imagined experiences. Pithy evocations of a "seedy jungle town" or a "refusal of the judge to rush to a decision concerning a person of political stature" can allow the reader to grasp a situation and "come to rest" at a subsequent point in the story. Even when an intrinsic narrative is carefully constructed by use of historically surviving artifacts, its evocation of a lifeworld must be something of a Potemkin village: the thickly described world gains its verisimilitude by the installation of images along the route of the text. Meaning is opened up through illusion.[50]

Extrinsic objects of inquiry and the passages from narrative

Narrative, as I have considered it so far, has a distinctive potential for catharsis because it can engage readers to take on a story and make it relevant within their own experience. It thus bears a strong capacity to make the unfamiliar meaningful. This capacity is readily apparent in intrinsic narrative, my neologism for what in a simpler age was the conventional fare of historians' inquiries about real events "in" history. Yet many historians regard constructing this kind of narrative as a tedious, potentially fraudulent task, one that merges with fiction by giving more drama to events after the fact than they possessed in their unfolding. Indeed, much history – the gradual improvement of agriculture, for example – may lack drama altogether.

However, the intrinsic approach does not exhaust the possibilities. Not only can narrative subsume other forms of discourse within its frame, the opposite is also true: narrative itself may be subordinated to other forms of discourse. As we have already seen, discourse on values plays a significant role in constituting an object of inquiry. It is also evident that intrinsic narrative can be juxtaposed with arguments about evidence, claims about the significance of events, and so on. But there is more. If the subordination of narrative is pushed to an extreme, we may imagine inquiry in which occasional snippets of narrative are ordered by some other discourse than narrative *per se*.

The potential importance of extra-narratological discourses suggests that there is an alternative to intrinsic narrative. Much historical writing does not locate the coherence of its objects in the mutual orientations toward events by individuals and groups in history. Instead, the narrator's own analytic interests predominate, and those interests shift the focus toward *extrinsic narrative*, that is, narrative about an object of inquiry for which the "pregnant principle" holding the plot together is a product of inquiry rather than intrinsically connected events.[51]

For self-consciously extrinsic narrative (and against Sande Cohen's deconstruction), the use of transcendent staging devices to constitute the object of inquiry does not necessarily signal a failure to "represent" reality. Instead, optimally, the transcendent devices of linkage reflect some coherent rationale of inquiry that exceeds any attempt to describe an intrinsic plot. Thus, the question of why modern capitalism emerged first in Europe not only depends upon a viewpoint unavailable to historical actors during the time when the emergence was under way; recent controversies about the validity of the question itself suggest that it does not necessarily even concern any intrinsically connected set of events. The sprawling array of developments relevant to the emergence of modern capitalism does not rule out narrative, but any such narrative will be an extrinsic one. The plot is – or ought to be – a narrator's self-conscious model, theory, argument, or set of juxtapositions.[52]

Inquiry can construct an extrinsic object in a variety of ways – all of them quite different from intrinsic narrative. What extrinsic narratives share is the relocation of narrative's axis beyond the *verstehende* concern with a course of events meaningful to actors themselves. One prominent approach – what might be called general history – locates diverse developments with a "larger" course of history in objective time. By this device, historians fit particular developments ("the Korean conflict") within a more encompassing story ("the Cold War"). As extrinsic narrative becomes concerned with ever more encompassing patterns, it increasingly approximates the approach of Fernand Braudel, the famous *Annales*-school historian. Braudel wanted to displace narratives about *l'histoire événementielle* by giving primacy to broader ecological and structural forces. In *The Mediterranean*, his conventional political narrative about Philip II came after a more encompassing structural and ecological history (of *la longue durée*). This version of *Annales* history did not so much change the character of political narrative as it elaborated a geographical and institutional history as the context of plot.[53]

Braudel's approach marks an important reconfiguration of narrative in relation to conventional political history, but it does not represent the French historical tradition in all its diverse practices. Some studies by later *Annales* historians, like Le Roy Ladurie's account of the Pyrenees village of Montaillou during the fourteenth century, retain ecological features but narrate the lives of peasants and shepherds – people typically ignored by historians interested in the march of History. Other *Annalistes*, as well as anthropological historians like Robert Darnton, have displaced the intrinsic object as the basis on which they would select facts (e.g., about *mentalités* or novels) to be explored through narrative.[54] The diverse topics range from climate, demography, technology, and trade routes, to the relations between land, village, town, and city, and on to printing and pornography. Overall, French historians have reconstructed historical inquiry itself. The "pregnant principle" is no longer "what happened" in the sense of any intrinsic plot; instead, the principle may have diverse sources, from a functional theme (e.g., privacy or discipline) to an ordering based on theorized dynamics such as the circulation of capital.

It is worth asking whether these *Annales* writings transcend narrative altogether, or simply expand its horizon. How this question is resolved in effect defines a boundary between narrative and other forms of discourse. But the boundary is not a divide between the micro analysis of everyday life as narrative and the macro analysis of structural history, for, as the range of *Annales* studies suggests, even the most everyday events can be constituted as objects of extrinsic analysis. One boundary between narrative and other discourse could be drawn from Lawrence Stone's assertion that narrative engages in "answering the *what* and the *how* questions in chronological fashion." This definition might seem to hold both for intrinsic narratives concerning mutually oriented social actors and for extrinsic narrative where plots exceed any intrinsic meaningful coherence. If so, by widening the time frame, as Braudel did, even ecological, demographic, and structural considerations can be incorporated within an extrinsic narrative.[55] Leopold von Ranke's program for writing the history of human society is shifted to an even grander scale. The logic of narrative potentially encompasses the broadest and longest swaths of events; plots range from the moment-to-moment unfoldings of a group of friends to the epochal transformations of whole civilizational orders and ecological transformations of societal environments.

An alternative argument, by Paul Ricoeur, insists that, when inquiry loses touch with human action, it exceeds the discourse of narration. In this view, physical events in the past may be subjected to a sort of geological "history" as "retrodiction" – talking about what is past – but this is not narrative because it is severed from the human intentionalities that figure plots.[56] Ricoeur argues for a divide between narrative, concerned with meaningful human experience, and other kinds of descriptions, of brute material causality. In this formulation, purely physical events of temperature, wind, and precipitation have no history; they can be described as a series of interconnected contingencies, but unless they are linked to human endeavors they lack the social meanings that are the hallmark of narrative. Narration – by the human affairs it describes – transforms an earthquake, for instance, from geologic "event" to "disaster." This boundary work does not preclude extrinsic narrative; rather, it suggests that even extrinsic narrative is concerned with phenomena that bear the marks of human agency.

For all the resilience of narrative, I suspect its borderlands lie near the line that Ricoeur draws. As this chapter has shown, narrative is a formative discourse infused with both superadded moral principle and lifeworldly capacities to mediate meanings. Whether narrative takes an intrinsic or extrinsic orientation, its salience derives precisely from these properties. The very possibility of telling a story depends upon the narrator's capacity to shift between one voice and another, and to consider diverse issues – from psychoanalysis to geology to economics. Yet narrative does not encompass everything. Although narrative is a sponge that can absorb discourses on subjects like demography and biology, doing so presumes that those subjects exist in their own right, in forms that are not preeminently narratological. Ricoeur wants to fold various other discourses of inquiry into narrative, but this move seems foreshadowed by his own goal of constituting narrative as an inclusive project of inquiry. The following coda considers the viability of this project by addressing the question of whether narrative can subsume the discourse of explanation.

Narratives often shift to other discourses – the author's assessment of
alternative plots, discussion of economic practices in a given country,
an inquiry into theories about charismatic bandits. Because such shifts
seem nearly pervasive, it is worth asking whether narrative discourse in
itself is capable of constituting a comprehensive basis of inquiry. One
way of addressing this question is by asking whether narrative can subsume the formative discourse of explanation and interpretation.

Answers to this question are mixed. Poetic and rhetorical critiques,
as well as Lyotard's claims about the incommensurability of multiple
narrative viewpoints, imply that the potential contribution of narrative
to inquiry is quite limited. A more sympathetic view holds that a well-
wrought narrative itself is an explanation, and thus subject to universal
criteria of adjudication.[1] To render a narration of *how* the Vietnam War
began is to offer an account of *why* the war occurred. A different narrative would amount to an alternative explanation. However, this argument requires that empirical regularities often discussed in other terms
either be dismissed entirely or presented through narrative. How can
narrative contend with conflicting causal claims, for example, that the
Vietnam War resulted from neo-imperialist power imperatives of the
United States as a core country in the world economy during the Cold
War era? Or that the war was the consequence of an ideology of anti-
communism that led the US government to mistake nationalist revolutions as threats to its national security?

Let us consider the potential of narrative for strong explanation in its
own terms. Paul Ricoeur argues that narrative's dramatic power stems
from its capacity to display the meaningful world of social actors pursuing their intentions, and he thereby emphasizes agency over causality as
the medium for recounting events. If we follow Ricoeur in taking agency
as narrative's defining trait, to succeed in offering a strong explanatory
account without resorting to other discourses, narrative would have to
locate all salient externalities within an analysis concerned with the
intentional orientations of social actors. Whatever the "outer" events of

the world, they would become relevant only insofar as they were relevant to actors themselves. As it turns out, this characterization of narrative as explanation has been vigorously championed by Frederick Olafson, in his 1979 book *The Dialectic of Action.*

Debates over narrative now connect social theory and politics to historicity in ways that spill well beyond the discourse of narrative *per se*, and into the broader practices of inquiry that I describe in chapters 7 and 8. Indeed, Stone's claim in 1979 that the return to narrative signaled a much broader shift of inquiry was nothing less than prescient. Yet in these recent reconsolidations, the status of narrative depends very much on the potential for adjudicating among alternative narrative explanations. Because Olafson develops a thorough case for narrative explanation, concentrating on his argument offers an efficient way to consider the viability of "strong narrative."[2]

Olafson proposes that the phenomenology of actors' intentions is central to historical inquiry. From this starting point he must directly address the challenge of subsuming "causal" analysis within narrative. How does he try to do this? Consistent with his phenomenological bearings, Olafson argues that what makes a narrative hang together is its thematic concern with actors' agency. History is not just an assemblage of events rendered meaningful by the historian's interest; it is not an account of an extrinsic sociohistorical object. Rather, narrative in the strong sense concerns what I have called an "intrinsic object" – one that was rendered meaningful in the past by the ways individuals acted in relation to the world as they saw it. In Olafson's view, the historian shares the circumstances of social actors in history more generally; even if they have diverse interests, each is endowed with "intentional access to past events and a capability for logically cumulative description of subsequent events in the light of such past events."[3] Narrators' knowledge, like that of other individuals, is constrained by their own historicity. Whatever pretensions historians may harbor, they cannot hope to explain the past in any veridical way that corresponds to "facts." Like anyone else, they must make sense of what they can come up with and, if they are honest, adopt a certain humility by accepting the tenuous character of their claims.

However, in Olafson's strong version, no sociohistorical account can lie outside narrative. How, then, does narrative handle non-narrative moments, such as the shift from plot to analysis?[4] What is going on when a narrator describes the social composition of the town where a protagonist was born, or investigates the state of the economy at a critical juncture? Indeed, what about phenomena that lack agency, but nevertheless affect the course of history – personality attributes, climate, locust plagues? Olafson proceeds by distinguishing the social from the nonsocial. Social analyses, he argues, are telescoped reductions from narratives, marked by the potential to be written as fullblown narratives.[5] On this view, even if action sequences are routinized by conventions or institutional practices (for example, in con games, and other relatively coherent action sequences), it should be possible to specify "plot" patterns of action. True to the project of intrinsic narrative, the capacity to elaborate a description or analysis by way of a narrative discourse would offer a test of its specifically social character.[6]

Nonsocial phenomena create more intractable problems for Olafson. Almost heroically, he argues for their assimilation into narrative by maintaining that factors such as disease, climate, and spatial logistics are salient only if they are conditions under which concrete human action transpires. Insofar as agents themselves take conditions into consideration – for example, by trying to intercept someone by taking a shortcut, or using the physiological effects of liquor to loosen up the sensibilities of a potential customer – material conditions and properties become incorporated within narrative by the agents' intentional social actions.

Yet the question remains: are there not still some remaining regularities of the nonsocial world (and perhaps, of the social realm as well) that affect what happens without being incorporated by conscious action? Olafson tries to dismiss this possibility by trivializing it. "Non-historical regularities of natural science" may exist, he acknowledges. "But this ever-present natural or cosmic background is of comparatively little relevance to the work of the historian." Because the historian deals with issues that are "actional in character," "there is no realistic prospect of our being able to extend the chain of derivation and establish a linkage between historical regularities and nonhistorical laws of unrestricted universality."[7] In other words, although Olafson is ready to admit to nonhistorical regularities, he will not accede to their significance outside intentional social action that can be described through narrative.

Olafson frames his phenomenological analysis by defining narrative as the representation of an intrinsically coherent set of events that were meaningful to social actors. Yet this approach has its problems. A phenomenological account can as easily be tilted in the opposite direction, toward recognizing that the narrator in inquiry may come upon knowledge unknown to historical actors who are the subjects of narration but nonetheless relevant to explaining historical events in which they were involved. Thus, Olafson forces narrative into a matrix more narrow than a comprehensive phenomenology would suggest. Moreover, by acknowledging the salience of both social and nonsocial regularities that may find their ways into telescoped narratives, Olafson undermines his own position. If demographic forces have their significance for social actors, understanding them has long depended on the search for regularities by use of non-narrative procedures. Narrative discourse seems to require non-narrative inquiry, even if such inquiry is treated as grist for storytelling by incorporating its knowledge within narrative accounts. Olafson thus probably would have to give some ground under pressure. But I suspect that he would reaffirm his basic thesis, that narrative is the approach to accounting for phenomena specifically appropriate to sociohistorical inquiry.

How, then, is Olafson's approach related to the other kinds of knowledge that he recognizes only in the breach? This issue can be addressed by considering narrative in relation to Karl-Otto Apel's 1979 "transcendental-pragmatic" study of explanation and understanding. Apel argues (against Olafson's position) that all efforts to reduce explanation to the understanding of social action typical of narrative (or conversely, to subsume narrative within causal explanation) are futile, because they mistakenly assume that the two approaches compete for the right to fulfill the same purpose. Apel holds instead that to explain a given person's action in causal terms scrutinizes that action under a type of technical reason that asks something like, "under what conditions of variation external to action itself can the given action be predicted to occur?" But the historical past is not open to experimental variation of conditions, and despite all the efforts to use causality for accounts of purposive activity, Apel holds, causality is not equipped with a logic that can deal with "internal" matters of an acting subject's practical interests. The effort to understand action is oriented toward a different sort of question than causal explanation, with a different purpose:

> The positive accomplishment of this form of knowledge does not lie in the "explanation" of why, under specific conditions, a specific action – i.e., an event at a specific time – *had* to occur (or in the case of a how-possible explanation, *could* occur). Rather, it makes a specific action that actually did occur at a specific time intelligible from the inside, as it were, as an action suggesting itself to and binding on the knowing subject (under appropriate suppositions with regard to will and belief).[8]

For Apel, the conflict between understanding and explanation dissolves once the divergent interests are recognized. The two approaches do not answer the same question in different ways; they address alternative questions, even in reference to the "same" phenomenon. Unlike Olafson, Apel does consider it possible for the human sciences to draw on causal explanation. But he does not think that causality can subsume agency. Instead, he holds that the distinctive concerns of interpretive understanding are left untouched by the admission of causal regularities.

By rejecting any proposal for scientific analysis of meaning, Apel in effect locates intrinsic narrative in a domain where universal standards of adjudication do not obtain, and assigns extrinsic narrative to the regions of value-neutral and objective explanation (see table 2.1).[9]

Olafson and Apel work to legitimate narrative in different ways, Olafson by subsuming explanation within narrative, Apel by establishing critical theory and hermeneutics as projects of interpretive understanding that cannot be eroded by any "subsumption-theoretic" (covering-law) model of explanation. But neither narrative nor the understanding – explanation complex is exhausted by these alternative possibilities. A third approach posits a working relation between narrative and scientific explanation.

Georg Henrik von Wright explored this possibility in a 1971 study that sought to incorporate narrative within a more comprehensive logic of explanation. His approach distinguishes meaningful action from other processes by explaining action as a *logical* relation, rather than a causal one.[10] To develop possibilities of meaningful explanation, von Wright identified a series of "internal" needs and wants (e.g., psychological "drives") and "external" circumstances that might affect action. In addition, he considered the possibility of explaining action in generalizable terms, by using teleological models and rational-actor theories. Von Wright acknowledged the importance of intrinsic narrative concerned with the history of contestedly meaningful events, but he sketched a stronger capacity of the narrator to go beyond interpretive understanding of meaningful action, by shifting into extrinsic narrative where emplotment amounts to the narrator's explanation of how diverse events are causally connected in their developmental significance.

Von Wright's scientistic approach would satisfy neither Olafson nor Apel, but it does point again to that widely acknowledged characteristic of narrative, namely, its capacity to shift to other discourses to explore arguments *outside* the rhetoric of emplotment. Hard as Olafson struggled, he could not completely eliminate this possibility. Apel did not even try, instead finessing the question by invoking a criterion of value relevance that distinguishes interpretive understanding as a wholly different enterprise than scientific explanation. In either approach, questions remain about how sociohistorical inquiry operates in ways that do not depend on narrative as an ordering discourse.

The discourse that looms largest as an alternative to narrative as the ordering discourse for inquiry is social theory. Indeed, one view suggests that any narrative is inherently theoretical.[11] This point already surfaces in the dependence of extrinsic narratives on frames of reference external to events themselves. But issues of meaning are subject to theorizing as well. I therefore turn now to social theory – first as a relatively autonomous domain of discourse and then, in a coda, in relation to the formative discourse of explanation and interpretation. Together with the explorations of values and narrative, these considerations bring us to the issue, addressed in chapter 5, of whether explanation has properties of a formative discourse in its own right. Overall, evidence mounts through the consideration of inquiry's discourses that any one of them – say, narrative – is neither partitioned off from other discourses nor randomly associated with them. Instead, different patterned relationships among the four formative discourses undergird alternative ways of practicing inquiry. These alternative practices of inquiry are the subject of chapters 6, 7, and 8.

4 The conceptual possibilities of social theoretical discourse

Rejecting social theory is easier said than done. Deconstruction, for instance, purports to show how elisions shape theoretical systems of analysis by their vital absences. Yet deconstruction itself is deeply theoretical. On a different front, Margaret Somers's archeology of the concept of "citizenship" shows that theoretical concepts are cultural products, heavily freighted with ideological baggage that often becomes invisible in "naturalized" academic discourse. As Somers emphasizes, historicity means that there can be no ultimate foundations for social theory. Given both the ubiquity and historicity of social theoretical discourse, its role in sociohistorical inquiry calls for clarification.

As Martin Jay has artfully suggested, opponents can only submerge their theoretical acts, not purge them. This does not mean that theory must be embraced, only that it ought to be engaged. Peoples subjected to domination rightly wonder whether they ought to learn the category systems of their oppressors or displace them. But Henry Louis Gates argues that black literary critics are better served by selectively reconstructing theory within a black vernacular idiom rather than abandoning it. Gates will neither dismiss theory nor fetishize it. This approach strikes me as reasonable for theory more generally. In this chapter, I consider social and cultural theories rather than literary ones. And as important as the development of vernacular idioms is, I concentrate on the other side of the dialectic – understanding theories in their basic conceptual and methodological construction, how they work, and to what effect. My analytic strategy is to identify major conceptual approaches to theory as discourse so that – in chapters 7 and 8 – implications of those concepts and their vernacular usages can be discerned in the practices of inquiry in which they are embedded.[1]

Not surprisingly, there is considerable disagreement as to the nature of theories and their relation to empirical phenomena. Positivist proponents of linking theory to science seek to unearth general propositions that are subject to empirical disproof. Postpositivists want to maintain positivist rigor but they acknowledge that there is no theory-free language for description of "empirical" objects. Some Marxists, rational-choice theorists, and others purport to develop comprehensive general theories. Sociologists in the Weberian tradition use ideal types – theoretically specified models of sociohistorical phenomena – for comparative analysis, while cultural critics seek to develop one or another theory of the text that will inform their interpretive projects. In a different way, Habermas's version of critical theory identifies multiple domains of theorizing, each with different implications for emancipatory projects.

Theory is not sealed off from narrative. As I noted in chapter 3, meta-narratives can be structured theoretically. More complexly, theories infuse narratives with conceptual representations, however implicit. But prior to their inflection of narrative, theories have their own internal properties that offer decisive counterpoint to narrative discourse. As I construe them, social theories transcend disciplinary boundaries, even the social sciences over and against history and the humanities. Whatever their specifics of approach and subject, social theories – including critical and interpretive ones – share a discursive project: a social theory purports to account for fundamental phenomena on the basis of a mutually coordinated set of concepts. Specific sociohistorical objects – from a literary text to the industrial revolution – may be "theorized," as contemporary usage has it, but such accounts depend on prior theoretical frameworks for analyzing, interpreting, explaining, and otherwise making sense of the world.

Theoretical discourse defined in this way cannot be reduced to the conventional positivist image of universal "covering laws." True, for any specific case, a proposition derived from a social theory – about demographic pressures, or gender and class conflict – may seem lawlike. But, as the coda following chapter 2 concluded, competing resolutions of the value problem yield divergent projects of inquiry. Given value heterogeneity, the overall domain of theoretical discourse encompasses much more than covering laws. In the most general sense, theory challenges idiographic approaches concerned with the uniqueness of specific events. Because social theories involve efforts to conceptualize sociohistorical phenomena in comprehensive, internally consistent ways, despite their diversity, their discourse is based on a shared premise. Insofar as unique sociohistorical phenomena can be subsumed (analyzed, interpreted, explained, etc.) by reference to a conceptual framework or theory taken to hold across objects of inquiry, investigation of unique circumstances by other means (such as narrative) is only supplementary. Social theory claims analytic priority for the general over the specific.

Understood as general analytic frameworks, social theories can be assessed not only empirically, but also in terms of their "theoretical logics" – how they work as theories *per se*.[2] In these terms, there is a task that precedes either examining the internal coherence of any given theory or adjudicating disputes between theories: effective theorizing depends on understanding how theorization "works." What possibilities of conceptualization are generated from its properties as a form of discourse?

To begin with the obvious, competing ways of constructing social theories coexist. Any given social theory – a materialist one or a textual approach, for example – must either "crowd out" alternatives such as functionalism or market analysis, or provide a "multidimensional" way of combining heterogeneous theoretical concepts. Either way, any social theory builds upon certain ways of conceptualizing phenomena and excludes others. Yet the excluded others are not inherently irrelevant. They simply carve up the attributes of empirical phenomena in alternative conceptualizations. Under these conditions, understanding theory as a discursive domain calls for a "theory of theory" that identifies alternative conceptual vocabularies, their internal "grammars" (or ways of theorizing), and the kinds of theories that can be formulated by drawing concepts together in distinctive ways.

To initiate the project of mapping theoretical discourse I identify two broad approaches to concept formation that are mirror images of each other – using concepts to describe case-like patterns, and using concepts to describe analytic aspects of phenomena in terms of variables. Although these two mirrored approaches can be found across the entire range of social theory – from literary criticism to demography, sociohistorical inquiry faces a distinctive challenge in theorizing meaning, and the issues are thus crystallized in a particularly revealing way in theories that conceptualize social action. I therefore consider the case versus variable approaches by way of an iconic divide between two key modern sociological theorists of social action – Max Weber, who used "ideal types," and Talcott Parsons, who asserted the primacy of variable "analytic elements" over ideal types. Charting this divide raises a question as to the limits of either approach as a basis for mapping social theoretical discourse. The source of these limits can be clarified by considering the ambivalent relations of both Weber and Parsons to yet another modern sociological theorist, Georg Simmel.

Exploring Weber, Parsons, and Simmel is a catalytic process by which I precipitate out the theorization of four broad approaches to social theoretical discourse: a *hermeneutic approach*, an *interchange approach*, a *dialectical/functional approach*, and a *formal/structural approach*. As I show at the end of the chapter, identifying these approaches helps to pinpoint internal debates and relationships among (and multidimensional syntheses beyond) contemporary social theories such as network, rational-choice, normative, feminist, and systems approaches. It would be impossible in the present chapter to consider theories in depth, but surveying contemporary theoretical practice illustrates the interpretive utility of the metatheoretical map of social theoretical discourse that I propose.

My own relativist, culturally constructionist standpoint in this analysis acknowledges the multiple frames of reference both of inquiry and of social actors in general (see table 1.1). This standpoint finds common cause with postmodern, feminist, and other critical concerns about "totalizing theories" that subsume subjects and their agency. A parallel point is that there are less formal approaches which infuse interpretation and explanation with theory. To explore issues related to totalization and the potential for less formalistic theorizing, in the coda following this chapter I consider problems of agency and historicity, and their implications for explanation and interpretation. This analysis suggests that there are nontotalizing ways to theorize. Ironically, although totalization might seem implied by the typology that I map from binary oppositions, I do not claim that the present analysis is either objective, exhaustive, or definitive of social theory's "essence." The point is altogether different: to offer one potentially useful way of thinking about alternative conceptual logics of social theory.

Case-pattern and analytic-element models

As Charles Ragin and David Zaret have shown, the possibilities of analyzing sociohistorical objects depend upon a fundamental relationship between "cases" and "variables." Cases (social movements, picaresque novels, conversations, and so on) have attributes that can be specified by a series of variables (e.g., narratological point of view, degree of solidarity, turn-taking). Given this relationship, a data matrix can list cases in rows and variables in columns. At the intersection of each row and column is a value for a case measured in terms of a variable attribute. Two basic methodological strategies derive from this relationship. In one, cases are compared to one another in their patterns of similarity and difference along variable dimensions. In the other, relationships among two or more variables are analyzed on the basis of their values for a set of cases.[3]

The case–variable relationship is well developed in methodological terms, but its importance for the construction of social theories is less widely understood. To get at the difference between *case-pattern* versus *analytic-element* theoretical concepts that parallels the case–variable distinction in methodology is a first step toward identifying fundamental alternatives for conceptualizing social, cultural, and historical phenomena. In turn, as I will show, there are different ways of construing case patterns and analytic elements, and these give rise to heterologous approaches to social theory. To chart these developments, we can begin by examining the divergence between Max Weber and Talcott Parsons.

Critics have sometimes paraphrased Parsons's famous first lines of his 1937 book, *The Structure of Social Action* by asking, "Who now reads Parsons?" Nevertheless, Parsons produced arguably the highest of high modern social theories, he retains importance for neofunctionalist theories, and his differences with Weber have implications far beyond his own approach. In *The Structure of Social Action*, Parsons wanted to consolidate a general theoretical schema for conceptualizing voluntary social action, in part by drawing on Weber. But Weber posed a serious obstacle, for his approach to social action was not geared to the formulation of a general social theory. Instead, Weber defined an array of ideal types – what I am calling more generally "case patterns" – comparable to empirical cases. These types Weber then employed in the sociological analysis of historical change. Parsons praised Weber's substantive achievements, but he went to great lengths to reject ideal-type analysis in favor of a "more parsimonious" approach to concept formation – what he called "analytical realism." Parsons wanted to study the world with concepts that would "adequately 'grasp' aspects of the objective external world."[4]

The epistemological struggle by Parsons against Weber marks a key divergence in theory construction. Essentially, Parsons sought to displace (1) a broadly qualitative and historical-comparative case-oriented approach that attends to emergent *patterns* of action and interaction, in favor of (2) a more abstract analytic approach focused on describing *variable elements* of action and interaction. This divergence has its origins in mirror-image procedures of concept formation. But, as I will show, it has a substantial consequence. Parsons's shift orients theory toward specifying relations among abstracted, atemporal analytic elements in a way that fails to accommodate the historicity of social action, and substitutes for it the historicity of a posited totality. Yet the two approaches are connected to one another. An array of analytic elements can describe a case-like pattern, and patterns are constellations of analytic elements. Because of this relationship, the binary opposition between case-pattern and analytic-element analysis can be transcended in a way that identifies alternative approaches to social theory in more general terms.

Exploring the divergence between Parsons and Weber suggests how this can be done. Weber constructed his concepts in a way that would counter antitheoretical historicism, evolutionary or stage-theory metan-arratives of history, and deterministic social theorizing. He did so by defining ideal-type models that could be used as standard benchmarks for comparative and historical analysis of meaningful social action complexes. Weber did not question the possibility that propositions about relations between variable analytic elements might be specified and tested; he simply argued that value interests tend to place "historical individuals" (that is, sociohistorical objects, or cases) at the center of inquiry. Weber's ideal-typical comparisons in his studies of the world religions – in China and India, for example – thus identify distinctive civilizational complexes in their meaningful structurations.

Parsons's differences with Weber should not be inflated, for he aligned his voluntary action schema with Weber's principle of *Verstehen* as a postulate requiring reference to "real subjective processes." Parsons's main problem concerned ideal-type analysis. He complained that Weber failed to identify a general set of analytic elements that would define the conceptual relations *among* ideal types. Such a move, in Parsons's view, would advance the scientific goal of parsimony.[5]

The logic of Parsons's claim is straightforward: a large number of case combinations can be specified from a small number of analytic-element concepts by systematically varying the values of the elements. As Parsons recognized, ideal-type analysis and his own "analytical realism" are mirror images of each other. In table 4.1, for example, three binary analytic variables specify eight case-pattern combinations. A single matrix arrays hypothetical analytic-element variable distinctions in the columns (diffuse versus specific social relationships, for example), and a value for each case listed in the rows is measured for each variable. Ideal types (e.g., "legal-rational bureaucracy") are case patterns that identify theoretically coherent constellations of elements. Thus, ideal type VIII is defined by values of "1" on variables A, B, and C. Comparisons from row to row gives rise to an analysis of diverse empirical case patterns (such as actual organizations) in relation to ideal types as theoretically defined case patterns. Alternatively, inquiry oriented toward the columns permits the study, for sets of cases, of variable relationships between analytic-element dimensions. For example, analysis could focus on the relationship between "diffuse versus specific social relationships" (variable A) and "office management based on training in a specialized field" (variable C). Overall, ideal types and cases on the one hand and analytic variables on the other are connected by measurements that relate each to the other.[6]

As Parsons recognized, theory development could move in either the

Table 4.1: *Hypothetical case patterns and ideal types specified as unique combinations of values on three binary analytic-element concepts*

		BINARY ANALYTIC CONCEPTS		
		A	B	C
	I*	0	0	0
	II	1	0	0
CASE	III	0	1	0
PATTERNS	IV	0	0	1
AND	V	0	1	1
IDEAL TYPES	VI	1	0	1
	VII	1	1	0
	VIII*	1	1	1

*Signifies ideal type.

case-pattern or analytic-element direction. After all, Weber had defined complex ideal types ("status group" and "market," for example) by building from analytic-element concepts about characteristics of action, social relationships, and the like.[7] But Weber did not formalize a theory that integrated a systematic matrix of analytic elements and ideal-typical case patterns such as the one in table 4.1.[8] For his part, Parsons did not deny that formalization of Weberian-style ideal types could yield general theory.[9] Instead, he argued that a fundamental limitation of ideal-type analysis favored using analytic elements to theorize. Any ideal type, Parsons argued, consists of a constellation of elements *fixed* in relation to one another, whereas in empirical phenomena the different elements may *vary* independently of one another. Thus, "rational capitalism" as an ideal type involves rational calculation of profits, universalistic rather than particularistic social relationships among participants, and so forth, whereas empirical capitalism, when described in relation to the same analytic distinctions, may differ from the model (e.g., the difference between ideal type I and case pattern III in table 4.1). This hiatus between fixed ideal types and empirical cases, Parsons argued, creates a source of bias in inquiry.

Thus, Weber's focus on *rational* capitalism singled out a particular aspect of the considerably more complex empirical phenomenon of modern capitalism. As Parsons observed, it misses the interaction between *rational* and *adventurer* capitalism that was important to capitalist development. This is a point well taken, but, unfortunately for Parsons's argument, it demonstrates the strategic importance of Weber's methodology. By conceptually distinguishing adventurer and rational capitalism in order to analyze their interrelations, Parsons employed ideal-type analysis while purporting to show its difficulties! He thus implicitly acknowledged that, although empirical phenomena often involve complexities beyond the range of any single ideal type, these complexities can sometimes be disentangled by using theoretically coherent, internally consistent models.[10]

Jeffrey Alexander once called Parsons's epistemology "his most fundamental theoretical contribution."[11] It does not necessarily stand or fall with Parsons's particular social theory. However, Parsons's epistemological vision – framing strategies of concept formation as a choice between use of ideal types and his own preferred analytic-element strategy – blocked adequate understanding of social theory. In order to show how this occurred, I take up two questions in the following sections. First I ask about the consequences of the preference for analytic theory that Parsons promoted. Second, I pursue the question of whether the discursive space of social theory is adequately described by the binary opposition between ideal-typical case patterns and analytic elements.

Meaning, historicity, and general theory

It is my contention that Parsons's dismissal of Weber's ideal-type approach in favor of analytical realism finessed any conceptualization of meaningful social action. During the 1950s and 1960s, this move by Parsons helped consolidate an alignment among functionalist, systems, and positivistic approaches to social theorizing. In this alignment, Parsons's original 1937 goal of formulating a voluntary action schema was relegated to a theoretical cul-de-sac, separated from the very considerations of meaning, temporality, and historicity that presumably would be central to theorizing social action and interaction. Despite the surge of interest in historical sociology beginning in the 1960s, this disjuncture between formal social theory and the problem of historicity has yet to be effectively transcended.

In part, the tradeoffs between Weber's and Parsons's approaches are matters of strategic choice in research. Is it more efficient to study the social world by using ideal-type concepts that can be constructed as close analogues of empirical phenomena? Or is more leverage offered by studying the variation of analytic elements? Parsons argued for the parsimony of analytic elements. But research sometimes favors substantive parsimony over theoretical parsimony. Ideal-type concepts tend to be less "distant" than analytic elements from the empirical sociohistorical world. This is so because sociohistorical phenomena are often structured in ways that ideal types can closely approximate, either (1) in strongly contrasting formations, for instance, feudalism versus capitalism, or (2) in closely related and easily transited patterns, such as variants of feudalism that hinge on the character of fief or rent. Similar strong contrasts and closely related patterns can be found in research on individual social actors. Thus, Weber's famous study of the Protestant ethic opposed work-asceticism versus a motive structure that regards work only as a means to a livelihood, and it also identified nuanced differences within work-asceticism by reference to specific variations in Protestant theology.[12]

In short, it is empirically possible that cases would either cluster together in related patterns or sort into radically alternative patterns, rather than varying continuously. Another way of putting this is that analytic-element values may be correlated with one another in distinctive ways for different subsets of cases. To display these possibilities, let us examine again the hypothetical example of table 4.1, where ideal types and case patterns are defined as combinatories of analytic-element values. It is possible to diagram transitional paths between case patterns in terms of analytic-element values. In figure 4.1, strongly opposed ideal types and case patterns are those which have the greatest "distances" from one another, e.g., 000 versus 111 (or 001 versus 110, and so forth). The transition between closely related case patterns, on the other hand, requires a change in the value of only one analytic element, and, in the figure, the transition between such case patterns is indicated by a line. This hypothetical example approximates Weber's practice of concept formation. Many of his ideal types – such as rational versus traditional action, or modern versus patrimonial bureaucracy – contrast strong patterns on multiple fronts (000 versus 111). But Weber also calibrated concepts to their substantive problems, sometimes specifying subtypes (001, 010, 100), for example, of charisma, in order to typify closely related alternative patterns of social organization and the pathways of transition between them.

For Weber, ideal types have to be "fictions" because they are abstract. However, he argued, "To compensate for this disadvantage, sociological analysis can offer a greater precision of concepts. This precision is attained by striving for the highest possible degree of adequacy on the level of meaning." According to this principle, a meaningfully adequate ideal type defines a pattern of meaningful elements that fit in relation to one another in a culturally noncontradictory way. (For example, "stable, rule-bound distribution of authority" is a feature of modern legal-rational bureaucracy as an ideal type.) Paradoxically, even though ideal types are "fictions," they are hypothetical cases, and thus they are more richly comparable than analytic elements to empirically observable social phenomena, ranging from a patrimonial family or political party

Figure 4.1: *Hypothetical case-pattern models based on combinations of values on binary analytic-element concepts indicated in table 4.1, with transitional possibilities to each of the three most similar case-pattern models specified by connecting lines (after Kauffman 1995). Additional binary analytic-element variables could be depicted graphically only in a greater than three-dimensional space.*

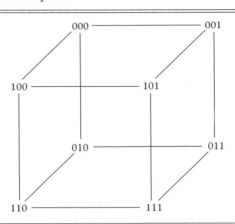

organization to a capitalist economy. Because ideal types characterize social reality in case-like patterned terms, Guenther Roth prefers to call them "sociohistorical models." Like other concepts, the furthest they can be carried on a purely theoretical basis is to clarification of their logical coherence, their meaning adequacy, and their posited properties, including dynamic and developmental tendencies. But in substantive research, as case-pattern analogues to lifeworldly situations, they provide an efficient means for comparatively analyzing social processes at work in events themselves.[13]

Even Parsons did not reject ideal-type concept formation; he sought to subsume it in a comprehensive approach that positioned analytic elements at the center of theoretical discourse.[14] Despite its deep connection to Weber's case-oriented interpretive sociology, however, Parsons's solution reinforced the tendency of modern social theory in the post-World War II era to become oriented to the formulation of abstracted relationships among analytic-element variables – what Andrew Abbott has called "general linear reality."[15]

Perversely, not withstanding Parsons's founding commitment to a theory of voluntaristic action, his embrace of analytical realism disjoined theory from consideration of meaning and the historicity of contingent action. This eclipse of meaning and historicity becomes starkly apparent in the theoretical moves that Parsons made after writing *Structure*. In the 1950s he elaborated analytical realism in a functionalist direction, theorizing an abstracted analytical "interchange model" of a social system that requires for its continuance the fulfillment of four interconnected functions – Adaptation, Goal attainment, Integration, and Latency (or pattern maintenance) – the so-called AGIL functions. By turning his analysis from voluntary action to the social system, Parsons shifted theory beyond the bounds of *Verstehen*: the analytic significance of action became reduced to its systemically functional or dysfunctional consequences.[16] In terms of table 1.1, Parsons displaced an "observer's lifeworldly" frame of reference that would theorize people's subjectively meaningful actions with an "objective observer's" framework based on systems functionalism.

Parsons's shift had these consequences because ideal types are more suited than analytic elements to conceptualizing subjective meaning, social action, and interaction. Why would ideal types have this property? The answer has to do with conceptual relationships among abstractions, meaningful action, and temporality. Abstractions – symbols, ideas, motives, norms, and values – like the abstractions of Parsons's analytical elements, lack agentic qualities of duration or spontaneity; they are in effect "atemporal." In one version or another, such atemporal elements may be available in an individual's stock of knowledge as "cultural structures" – what William Sewell calls "schemas."[17] However, in contrast to the atemporality of cultural structures, social action is inherently temporal. People act in the here-and-now on the basis of meanings that come into play in our individual temporally unfolding streams of consciousness. Thus, for instance, rational action gains its specific meaningful qualities through a temporal orientation to the anticipated *future* completion of a goal, whereas traditional action invokes a remembered (and thereby reconstructed) *past* as the guide for conduct. In complex ways, temporal constructions of subjectively meaningful action become dialectically connected to social constructions of temporality. Thus, a modern "bureaucracy" is coordinated via objectivized temporality of the clock and calendar, whereas a "community" is marked by the creation of collective consciousness through shared events in the here-and-now.[18]

Because meaning-in-action is marked by one or another specific temporal quality of sociocognitive process, the capacity to specify a distinctive structure of subjective and social temporalities is a decisive test of whether a theoretical construct adequately conceptualizes meaning. Ideal types are uniquely suited to the task of reflecting subjectively meaningful action and social interaction because they are case-pattern analogues, and these analogues can describe a hypothetical meaningful situation of an individual or complex of individuals acting in the course of temporally articulated life – e.g., undertaking traditional action versus working in a bureaucracy. By contrast, Parsons's analytic-element approach (and more generally, any analysis of interrelations among variables) disaggregates analytic elements and studies their relationships "outside" any temporally unfolding situation, hence losing conceptualization of meaning.[19] This loss occurs because the capacity of analytic elements to signify meanings depends on arraying them in combinatory patterns. In Weber's theorizations concerning the Protestant ethic, for instance, the analytic element of "ascetic self-denial" operates in one temporally meaningful way if it is oriented to an "other-worldly" concern with life after death, and becomes part of a wholly different meaning complex when associated with an "inner-worldly" concern about conduct in daily life. In other words, conceptualization of meaningful action depends on specifying existential connections *between* meaning elements, because different temporal patterns of meaningful action and social organization (and their sometime institutionalizations) derive from alternative socially constructed relationships among atemporal symbols, ideas, and motives.

By displacing ideal types with generalized functions and "pattern variables" such as universalism versus particularism, Parsons shifted to a set of independently varying analytic elements, no one of which can reflect subjective and social temporal structures that are the hallmarks of meaningful social action and interaction. This move allowed Parsons to align the *functions* of actions with the atemporal Durkheimian collective cultural domain of norms, myths, symbols, and system goals. But as a consequence, what presumably would be the focus of his original voluntary action schema – lived subjectively meaningful action in unfolding time – drops out of the theory. Thus, for example, neither pole of Parsons's binary pattern variable, universalism versus particularism, describes a temporally structured existential moment of action.[20]

For any inquiry concerned with the historicities of meaningful actions, constructing an isolated general theory is a flawed enterprise. The consequences of this enterprise are a matter of historical record. When a general theory eclipses interpretive categories of social action, its propositions take forms at odds with Parsons's voluntary action schema – namely, "pure functionalism" (i.e., devoid of comparative case/ideal-type analysis) and positivism aimed at identifying lawlike relationships between analytic variables by scientific testing of hypotheses. By these moves, a continuum of analytic variables – describing everything from materially causal processes to analytic aspects of meaningful action, and on to teleological processes – can be integrated into a general theoretical model. As Parsons sometimes seems to have intended, the whole range of variables can thereby be connected with quantitative social scientific practice. Yet because general theory and analytic-element quantification sacrifice the conceptualization of meaning, inquiry in their terms is cut off from *verstehende* analysis.[21]

Parsons was originally interested in theorizing voluntary action and, for this reason, his ambivalent turn toward analytic-element theorizing brings its contrast with case-pattern theorizing into particularly strong focus. However, general analytic theorizing is hardly Parsons's province alone: it is a trademark of much contemporary social theory, to be found in diverse approaches embodying varying degrees of formalization – for example, Jonathan Turner's theory of social interaction, Margaret Archer's theory of culture and agency, the structuralist theory of Peter Blau, the rational-choice theory advanced by James Coleman, and the revision of structure/agency theory advanced by William Sewell, Jr. In these instances of general theory and more widely, the central task is to frame a set of relationships among analytic elements that offer a framework for analysis of diverse empirical phenomena.[22] Yet this commonality hardly implies that all theorists who use analytic elements to specify general relationships are "like Parsons." Thus we come to the second issue that I identified at the beginning of this chapter – whether social theory is adequately described by the binary opposition between ideal-typical case patterns and analytic-element variables. Given the range of phenomena that can be measured by use of analytic variables – from demographic rates and structural aspects of organizations to cognitive dimensions and consequences of action – the contrast of analytic-element with case-pattern concept formation can be regarded only as an initial step in mapping social theory. How, then, can the description of discursive space be deepened?

Analytical realism and the terrain of theoretical discourse

For all Parsons's claims about the potential of universal lawlike propositions, he did not go far in that direction. More often, he used analytical-element concepts to describe empirical "systems." But despite the strong contrast that Parsons drew between ideal types and analytic elements, "system" was a generic and flexible metaphor. Parsons defined systems concepts in heterogeneous ways. Exploring the alternative kinds of relationships he posited among analytic elements and the alternative case-pattern (for him, systems) concepts they entail serves as a first pass at delineating a wider set of approaches to theorization.

Ideal type as "system" of meaning elements

Sometimes Parsons used system language to describe systems of meaning that amount to bootleg ideal types – the personality system and the action system, for example. Richard Münch has shown how Parsons used analytic elements to develop a theory of socialization. In Weberian terms, the result is a model that focuses on the instrumental and emotional aspects of meaningful actions, the significance of the particular ethos toward which socialization is oriented, and so forth.[23] In a similar way, systems language can describe role relationships in social groups interacting in unfolding event time, as Parsons and his followers have done. In these theorizations, a pattern of analytic meaning elements delineates an ideal type. The word "system" simply amounts to a modernist trope of Parsons's era.

But de facto ideal types and parallel descriptions of empirical meaningful situations do not exhaust Parsons's system metaphor. There are two additional ways in which he conceptualized systemic relations among analytic elements: (1) as functional and dialectical relations, and (2) as inputs and outputs, including exchange. The first move is the better known of the two, because it was central to Parsons's famous AGIL schema.

The functional or dialectical system

By developing his famous societal functions – Adaptation, Goal attainment, Integration, and Latency (or pattern maintenance) – in relation to social systems, Parsons invoked a general logic of functional and dialectical analysis. This logic proposes a solution to an enduring theoretical challenge – how to conceptualize relations among unintended yet interconnected consequences of actions and events that occur at disparate times and places. As chapter 3 showed, unless some theoretical or historiographic synthesis links phenomena "extrinsically," narrative can proceed only "intrinsically." In a parallel way, unless empirically disparate phenomena (transportation infrastructure and political legitimation, for example) are linked via some general framework, social theory cannot offer a general analysis of social processes. If a system is specified in functional or dialectical terms, it offers a possible solution – a meaning-transcendent concept that nevertheless serves as a case-pattern counterpart to actual cases. The functional or dialectical juxtaposition of autonomous interacting elements permits the analysis of far-flung events in relation to the system as a totality. The analytic "level" of the system conceptualization is open: it can be located in societies, social institutions, and system sectors, or more concretely in world economies, states, organizational fields (e.g., the health care industry), organizations (corporations, government agencies, families), and so forth. Each such system can be analyzed in relation to its subsystems, other systems, and more encompassing systems within which they are all enmeshed.

If the system language is functional, it suggests feedback and adjustment processes that align events with a telos of system balance or evolution in objective time. On the other hand, dialectical discourse moves in the direction of analyzing contradictions between objective systemic tendencies. In this approach, each element is essential to the system in its state at a given point in objective time. Therefore, social responses to contradictions that pose problems for one element of the system may forestall system transformation, but the responses themselves (even radical ones, such as revolutionary transformations) may generate new contradictions elsewhere in the system. Whether the language is functional, dialectical, or a combination of the two, the discourse develops an observer's objective frame of reference. In terms of values, such a framework could be based on the modest claim of its relevance to social questions at hand, but the tendency in both functionalist and dialectical theories has been to assert the general relevance of the analytic categories for use in what, broadly construed, can be called objective explanation (see table 2.1).

Functional and dialectical systems theories yield models of societal integration and contradictions, and, by their incorporation of evolutionary or revolutionary dynamics, they can theorize secular (i.e., long-term) change, such as proletarianization or the emergence of value contradictions in societal cultures. But such theories face difficulties in addressing what has come to be called the micro–macro problem.[24] In their core logics, functionalist and dialectical theoretical discourses obtain coherence by way of the system as a construct, without any necessary conceptualization of the concrete processes that connect action with functions or contradictions of large-scale sociohistorical processes. Thus, actual social relations tend to "drop out" of systems analyses. The result is remarkably similar for otherwise diverse approaches that theorize a systemic "totality." On the one hand, Parsons's social-systems theory tends to emphasize order, consensus, equilibrium, evolution, and teleology. By contrast, in Marxian dialectical analysis, the totality undergoes a dynamic of revolutionary ruptures rather than system evolution. What either approach has difficulty theorizing is the system's relationship to the relativity of means and ends of diverse social actors and the contingent historicity of their interplay.

The system of exchange

Beyond "systems" ideal types and functionalist/dialectical theorizing, the systems metaphor was used by Parsons in a third way. Following a basic idea of utilitarian theory, in the 1950s he began to identify certain systems as based on relationships of exchange (or "interchange," to follow Parsons's neologism) that depend on "generalized media."[25] In this theorization, money is the medium of exchange for goods, services, labor, and other transactions in the economic subsystem; power is the medium for the political subsystem; and so on. If interchanges are theorized in abstract terms, this approach maintains the functionalist discourse. Yet an interchange system model can shift the specification of relationships among elements from an *analytic* to a *concrete* basis, where exchanges take place between empirical entities such as individual actors, groups, and social movements. As economists have found, models that describe empirical "systems" of exchange lack any overall telos other than the developmental outcomes of emergent relationships among the parties involved. Conceptualizations of concrete interchange systems that depend on generalized media thus exemplify a third mode of case-pattern theorizing – treating "social systems" as established in their coherence by relatively stable, institutionally reproduced meaningful exchanges among social actors and groups, using currencies such as economic, political, social, and cultural capital.

Here the systems language of Parsons again intersects with Weber, who used notions of exchange to define various ideal types of meaningful interaction patterns, for example, models of patrimonial social organization, and hierocratic domination in religious organizations – the latter based on the supplicant's exchange of submission to authority for dispensation of grace. The main difference is that Weber's ideal types – keyed to empirical sociohistorical formations – sometimes "mix" what Parsons regarded as analytically distinct subsystems of interchange. Thus, for Weber, patrimonialism as an action complex may align diverse kinds of exchange – of power, money, allegiance, knowledge, and so forth – but strictly speaking these are neither "contained" within some discretely bounded patrimonial "system" nor differentiated into separate subsystems; instead, they form a relatively identifiable pattern of interaction that arises in relation to a distinctive set of wider lifeworldly conditions (e.g., the unfolding interests of social actors in relation to families, wealth, political power) that cannot necessarily be fully characterized solely within an interchange system model.

In more formalized approaches to markets, relationships among actors and groups are theorized by reference to an institutionally bounded pattern based on a single medium of exchange. This conceptualization, widely applied to economic markets, also has been used to study other market interchanges, for example, in the analysis of cultural capital as the basis of class-based status orders by Pierre Bourdieu and others. The attraction of an interchange model is obvious: when exchange is relatively institutionalized, conceptualizing it offers a basis for linking meaningful social actions with the "systemic" properties of a particular sphere of interaction. The drawbacks are equally obvious: to the degree that exchange is socially constructed by participants without the benefit of any tangible "currency" like money or votes (for example, in exchanges based in social or cultural capital), there is no assurance that any socially fixed medium of exchange exists. In using a systems concept to model extra-organizational processes of exchange, it is thus important to differentiate instances in which the media of exchange are rationalized, externalized cultural objects from relatively unrationalized "systems" like patrimonialism and metaphoric economies of cultural capital.[26]

Concrete interchange analysis differs strikingly from functional/dialectical systems theorizing in one important feature: the media of exchange are diverse, but they all ground systems discourse in the problem of subjectively meaningful action. That is, insofar as systems have as their elements concrete social entities capable of tangible exchange, their conceptualizations directly reflect the existence of individuals (or through imputation of collective action, groups) who undertake actions in unfolding time by orienting to exchange as a meaningful activity. It is social actors who construct and act in terms of "systems." Developmental trajectories are to be discerned, if at all, in cumulative consequences of social actions and their institutionalizations – in organizations, in markets, in political systems where traffic involves lifeworldly transactions like the exchange of allegiance for patronage benefits.[27]

Connecting analytic elements and case patterns

Parsons depicted conceptual space through a strong contrast between ideal types and analytic elements, and he conflated alternative regimens of theoretical discourse under a broad "systems" rubric. He was thus able to put forward a *particular* consolidation of systems theory as objective and analytically real. But, because Parsons was bounded by his own distinctive formulation, he prematurely closed off an overall understanding of the *general* conditions of social theoretical discourse. However, he was not so far wrong as to make such an understanding inaccessible. To the contrary, Parsons brought nearly all the aspects of theoretical discourse to light. As he saw, analytic elements and ideal types are reciprocal kinds of concepts. Moreover, he theorized relationships among analytic elements by using several kinds of "systems" concepts. When the postulate of *Verstehen* is recouped through ideal types and exchange models, general theory is no longer isolated as a realm unto itself. Instead, the analytic-element axis of social theory is drawn into working relations with the case-pattern axis and, thus, with the analysis of concrete meanings, temporalities, and historicities. This range of possibilities brings us tantalizingly close to consolidating an overall "map" of theoretical discourse.

The ellipsis: Simmel and social forms

When the full range of Parsons's theoretical discourse is considered, two anomalies become apparent. They have to do with the styles of analytic theorizing that he employed, and the relations that he developed between analytic-element and case-pattern concepts. The examination of these anomalies is a first step toward specifying a typology that describes broad alternative approaches to theory. In turn, by exploring Parsons's ambivalent and unresolved relationship to Georg Simmel as a social theorist, the anomalies can be used to consolidate the theorization of theory.

The first anomaly concerns a gap between the alternative kinds of analytic-element relationships that Parsons identified and his own theoretical practices. Ironically, Parsons identified alternative routes to concept formation that are more general than his own systems theory, but these possibilities have remained obscured by the importance that his systems theorizing gained in modern social theory. The initial impulse in *Structure* was to emphasize the deconstruction of ideal types into freely varying analytically abstracted meaning elements. But this approach opened the way toward others. One route, anticipated in *Structure*, would join the voluntary action schema with theorizations of causal relationships among analytic elements describing biologically and environmentally deterministic processes. In practice, Parsons did not pursue this positivistic direction with any vigor. Instead, he opted for systems models. Yet he had no single idea of how a system is to be conceptually specified. As I have shown, apart from rehabilitating ideal types by translating them into patterned "system" constellations of analytic meaning elements, Parsons employed two alternative approaches to systems theorizing – functional/dialectical and concrete exchange/interchange models.

Overall, four different kinds of relationships among analytic elements can be discerned in Parsons's work: (1) relations among analytic meaning elements, (2) causal relations, (3) functional and dialectical relations, and (4) exchange and interchange transactions based on general media. These four alternatives may be theorized as "dialects" of social theoretical discourse by describing them in terms of two fundamental dimensions.

The first dimension distinguishes theoretical relationships among analytic elements as describing phenomena in either *meaningful* or *non-meaningful* terms. Here, I am defining "meaning" in Weber's narrow sense as *subjective* orientation toward action by a social actor. Concepts not concerned with subjective meaning do not necessarily exclude the consideration of meaning from sociological analysis, but they tend to focus on shared objective meanings, their circumstances of production, and consequences, rather than subjective meanings *per se*.[28]

The second dimension differentiates between conceptualizations of phenomena that emphasize their *structural* versus *systemic* aspects. "Structural" conceptualizations describe phenomena in terms of a single, relatively bounded pattern of mutually determined or articulated elements, such as a given person, episode, or organization. "Systemic" concepts, on the other hand, designate interactive relationships among multiple, differentially located, relatively autonomous entities (e.g., social actors, organizations, texts, social classes, subsystems) that are theorized as operating in relation to one another within broader bounded contexts, such as communities, organizational fields, markets, discursive universes, or social totalities.[29]

A crosstabulation of the two dichotomies – meaningful versus non-meaningful, and structural versus systemic – specifies four alternative relationships among analytic elements (see table 4.2). As the table shows, the various moves of Parsons locate possibilities of theoretical discourse more general than his specific formulations.

However, mapping these relationships brings a second, more significant anomaly to light. There is a gap between Parsons's theorization of relations among analytic elements and his parallel theorization of case patterns. As Parsons understood, a set of analytic-element relations should translate into a case-pattern concept. Thus, a pattern of analytic elements that characterizes a structure of meaningful actions or social relations describes an ideal type. By the same logic, functional and dia-

Table 4.2: *Types of analytic-element relations according to subjective meaning adequacy and basis of concept formation*

		BASIS OF CONCEPT FORMATION	
		Structural	Systemic
BASIS IN MEANING ADEQUACY	Present	meaning elements	exchange/interchange
	Absent	causal/conditional	functional/dialectical

lectical analytic-element relations translate into a telic systems model that conceptualizes a totality. Third, what Parsons termed interchange relationships translate into patterns of exchange – what might be called in certain institutionalized circumstances, "markets," if the term is not construed too narrowly, or "networks," if the exchanges build up patterns of social relationships.

Yet there is a striking absence: Parsons identified no case-pattern concept that corresponds to the specifically "causal" relationship among analytic elements identified in table 4.2. Although Parsons recognized the possibility of theorizing nonmeaningful causal analytical relations between external phenomena (heredity, environment) and social action, he consistently rejected theoretical discourse that was, in his view, not based in his voluntary action schema. Perhaps for this reason, Parsons failed to incorporate within his approach any case-pattern counterpart to analytic elements theorized as causal relations. Thus the question of the missing term: what alternative concepts of social theory might employ analytic-element relationships to describe nonmeaningful causal patterns? Here, Parsons's avoidance of Georg Simmel becomes salient.

In *Structure*, Parsons treated analytical realism as the obvious alternative to ideal types. Interestingly, however, when he later looked back on his earlier claims for convergence among earlier social theorists toward a voluntaristic theory of action, Parsons recognized that Simmel's approach did not fit his thesis. Indeed, Parsons drafted a portion of a chapter for *Structure* that discussed Simmel at some length, but excised this portion of the text, in part because he admitted, "Simmel's program did not fit my convergence thesis."[30] In the published version of *Structure*, Parsons mentioned Simmel only in passing.[31]

Why did Parsons find Simmel's program incompatible with his convergence thesis? There are several reasons. In the first place, Simmel's methodological relativism of values (see chapter 2) played into a kind of historicism that Parsons sought to displace with his move to general theory. If Parsons wanted to deal with meaning on Simmel's terms, he would have had to accede to a theoretical relativism predicated on the relativity of historical meanings.[32] Second, as Parsons observed, Simmel wanted to establish only one analytic science for the entire sociohistorical field, and this approach was at odds with Parsons's attempt to offer an intellectual foundation for disciplinary boundaries based on the delineation of societal subsystems. Third, even though Simmel wanted only one analytic social science, he, like Weber, resisted the idea that a general theory of society could be established. Fourth, as is widely noted, Simmel's substantive essays – on mental life in the metropolis, sociability, secrecy, and so on – display a genius that cannot easily be reduced to his theoretical sociology, and, on the face of it, seems at odds with Parsons's systems approach.[33]

The fifth and most central difficulty Parsons shared with Weber. It concerns Simmel's concepts that describe "forms" of interaction and sociation. Characterizing forms as concepts has proved a stumbling block for Simmelian social theory. It would be mistaken to draw a rough parallel between them and Weber's ideal types. In contrast to Weber, both methodologically and substantively, Simmel strongly distinguished "forms of interaction" from their "contents," namely, "everything that is present in individuals (the immediately concrete loci of all historical reality) – drive, interest, purpose, inclination, psychic state, movement." As Donald Levine has pointed out, Simmel thus divorced his basic theoretical constructs – forms – from the very characteristic that Weber held central to social theoretical concepts – their adequacy for describing subjectively meaningful action and interaction. Simmel's forms identify patterns of sociation held to operate *across* meaningful situations.[34] Simmel thus departed from Weber's construction of ideal types as meaningfully adequate models to be used in *verstehende* analysis. But he did not move in a direction that interested Parsons. Whereas Parsons wanted to translate ideal types into analytic elements and their relationships, Simmel regarded forms as descriptions of concretely occurring processes. In Simmel's view, forms such as sociability are not ideal types that "approximate" reality; they are sociations that actually occur, even if not often in their "pure" forms. Patterns of sociation and interaction have an "objective reality." In a way that parallels other structuralist concepts – e.g., Marxian conceptualizations of modes of production – Simmel held, "These forms do not *make* for sociation; they *are* sociation."[35]

Simmel's theorization differs from that of either Weber or Parsons. For his part, Weber referred readers of *Economy and Society* to Simmel on the concept of "understanding," but he faulted Simmel's *Sociology* and *Philosophy of Money* for conflating objective and subjective meaning.[36] Parsons was similarly concerned about the character of Simmel's constructs. In the extensive fragment on Simmel that Parsons originally planned to include in *Structure*, he puzzled over whether Simmel's forms are abstractions equivalent to his own analytic elements. Parsons reasoned that "in spite of the abstraction involved it is a mode of abstraction which directly cuts across the line of analysis into elements of action which has been our main concern." Unable to integrate Simmel's forms within his own approach in *Structure*, Parsons characterized them as offering only "what may tentatively be called a 'descriptive aspect,'" and he asserted that Simmel's program must be regarded as "very severely limited in its capability of development into systematic scientific theory."[37]

The objections of Weber and Parsons seem less concerned with assessing Simmel's approach than with protecting their own conceptual strategies. Simmel refused to conceptualize meaning and he drew a line between social theory as the investigation of forms versus other inquiry that examined the interaction of form with content – hence with meaning. This distinction between form and meaningful content positions research into the existential contingency of meanings in unfolding social life as a complement to "structural" (or formal) sociological analysis. On this basis, Simmel's approach has been invoked as a precursor by researchers who emphasize contingency and social construction – for example, symbolic interactionists and Erving Goffman.[38] Simmel's concepts bear a structural character that is shorn of meaningful content, as was his intention, but it is not because he excluded the problem of meaning from inquiry. Rather, he sought a different division of intellectual labor, in which the social regularities subject to general concepts are distinguished from historically variable meaningful contents.

Where, then, is Simmel's form as a construct located in relation to the approaches to concept formation that I have been mapping? This question can be addressed by considering Simmel's relation to analytic-element and case-pattern concepts. Here, the significance of Parsons's vacillation over Simmel becomes apparent: Simmel's forms are not equivalent to analytic elements at all; rather, as Simmel made clear, they are analogues to concrete situations, thus, case-pattern concepts – like Weber's ideal types but different, as Parsons observed at one point.[39] In terms of the two dimensions in table 4.2, Simmel clearly constructed his forms as structuralist concepts of social situations, rather than using a systems approach. But, whereas Weber defined structures by way of concepts that incorporated subjective meaning elements, Simmel specifically asserted an "objective" deterministic character of structures (i.e., "forms") divorced from meanings.

Because case patterns in general are defined via analytic-element concepts, the question thereby arises: what is the relation of forms as case patterns to analytic elements? In Simmel's vision, inquiry into the forms of sociation would proceed in two integrated ways. First, sociology would investigate forms using the analytic-element language of structural determination – "in regard to laws entirely inhering in the objective nature of the elements." For Simmel, "these laws must be sharply distinguished from any spatio-temporal realization; they are valid whether the historical actualities enforce them once or a thousand times." Their investigation, for Simmel, amounted to the search for "timeless uniformities," for example, into the structural circumstances of interaction in sociability or secrecy as social forms.[40]

Second, Simmel held, "the forms of sociation may be examined, with equal validity, in regard to their occurrence at specific times, and in regard to their historical development in specific groups." In this vein, he regarded the particular embedding of forms in concrete sociation and their concatenations with one another as subject to variable analysis. The rationale of this variable analysis is visible in Simmel's demonstration that the variable number of parties to interaction – a dyad, triad, and so on – structures the possibilities of interaction in ways that are prior to any meaningful content. Here, forms are structures, and variations in analytic-element characteristics (number of parties to interaction) define different forms.[41] In addition, a given theoretical form can coincide with another, as for example in the triad as a form engaged in the pure sociability of "the party." In Simmel's approach overall, then, social theory can conceptualize transcendent "structural" relationships among analytic elements operative in concrete processes of sociation that are variable in both their circumstances and their interplay with other forms.

Parsons established his theoretical program largely by reconstructing Weber's theory in systems terms. He avoided an alternative possibility by an act of silence. Having considered Simmel's structural approach in some detail, Parsons chose not to discuss it publicly. But today, despite Parsons's ellipsis, the possibilities of theoretical discourse adumbrated by Simmel's work cannot be dismissed. Quite apart from the revival of interest in Simmel himself, understanding his formal sociology helps resolve a puzzle about the terrain of social theorizing. Simmel's approach offers counterpoint to Parsons and Weber by "cutting across" their approaches, as Parsons had it, but not simply in a descriptive way, as Parsons wanted to think.

Table 4.3: *Four approaches to theoretical discourse with associated types of case-pattern concepts, according to subjective meaning adequacy and basis of concept formation, with type of analytic-element relation used to specify case-pattern concept listed in brackets*

		BASIS OF CONCEPT FORMATION	
		Structural	Systemic
BASIS IN SUBJECTIVE MEANING ADEQUACY	Present	*Hermeneutic approach* IDEAL TYPE [meaning elements]	*Interchange approach* "MARKET" SYSTEM [exchange/ interchange]
	Absent	*Formal/ structural approach* FORM [causal/ conditonal]	*Dialectical/ functional approach* FUNCTIONAL/ DIALECTICAL SYSTEM [functional/ dialectical]

Approaches to concept formation and the possibilities of social theory

Locating Simmel helps clarify the alternative approaches that can be used to construct social theoretical concepts. Specifically, Simmel's approach shows how causal and relational analytic variables are tied to a particular kind of case-pattern analysis – of social forms, or "structures." As table 4.3 shows, this move completes the typology of theoretical discourse. Using the same dimensions as table 4.2 – (1) basis of concept formation in "structural" versus "system" concepts, and (2) presence versus absence of subjective meaning as a component of concept formation – table 4.3 describes paired relationships between each of four types of analytic-element concepts and four case-pattern concepts.

Meaning elements specify ideal types; conditional and causal specifications identify forms; and so forth. These relationships between analytic-element concepts and case-pattern concepts delineate four alternative approaches to theoretical discourse. Like dialects in ordinary language, these theoretical regimens are not inherently isolated from one another; in the case of theory, this means that actual theories are not necessarily purely of one type or another. But insofar as these four types of theoretical discourse are meaningfully coherent, like dialects, they are subject to examination in their own terms.

1. A *hermeneutic approach* draws on "meaning elements" – binary oppositions, continua, and tropes of meaning – using configurations of these elements to specify "ideal types," that is, interpretive models intended to describe distinctive complexes of subjectively meaningful social action and interaction (including organized action), and their developmental and historical tendencies (Weber is the classic exemplar).

2. An *interchange approach* theorizes a concrete "market" or "network" system of meaningful social interaction that can be described by use of concepts of exchange, interchange, and their media of transmission (exemplars include semiotic theorists, network theorists, microeconomists, market institutionalists, and some symbolic interactionists).[42]

3. A *dialectical and/or functional approach* posits "objective" (i.e., action transcendent) consequences of actions as well as organized and non-organized social processes, all of which interact with one another to create a systemic dynamic that tends toward equilibrium and evolution, or dysfunction, contradiction, and transformation (Marx, Parsons, and functionalist approaches to world-systems analysis are exemplars).

4. A *formal/structural approach* theorizes transhistorical patterns of sociation, or forms, that operate in the same way in heterogeneous social arenas despite differences in subjectively meaningful content; the patterns are conditioned by causal externalities and structural features of social interaction (exemplars range from Simmel and formalist symbolic interactionism to structuralists and quantitative empiricists, depending on whether the case-pattern or analytic-element side of concept formation is emphasized).

These four approaches differ in how core concepts of theoretical discourse are constructed – as meaningful action complexes, as networks or markets of interaction, as totalized systems, and as forms or structures. In any of these approaches, the relations of social theory to other discourses, and to fully developed practices of inquiry, remain open questions. Concepts mediate between the flux of the empirical world and the constitution of objects of inquiry in manifold ways, even in the most antitheoretical studies. They may be invoked in a passing gesture during a historical or ethnological narrative; they may be deconstructed in a critical reading of a previous argument; they can be rigorously linked to other concepts in formal social theories; or they may constitute an entire enterprise of moral philosophy.

Indeed, given the coexistence of multiple observers' frames of reference (see table 1.1), any given sociohistorical phenomenon can be brought within the orb of inquiry via more than one approach to theorization. Social interaction can be conceptualized either in ways that dissociate meaning from content or combine them, and it can be the focus of both structural and systemic concepts. Similarly, norms and rules could be invoked in both a hermeneutic and an interchange approach; gender has been conceptualized in both formal ways that posit structural properties and hermeneutic ways that explore its social construction; class conflict might be construed in market, meaningful, formal, or dialectical terms; and as Weber noted, power can be identified as a phenomenon of both meaningful organizational and market relationships. These examples easily could be multiplied, opening out into a historical encyclopedia of social theory beyond the scope of this study. In the present context, two points clarify the prospects of social theoretical discourse today. First, the four approaches to social theory are not frozen in their development. Second, they are not isolated from one another.

The four approaches and developments of theory

As historical, conceptual, and substantive developments of social theory attest, theoretical concepts approximating each of the four approaches can be employed in a variety of ways. Sketching some of those developments demonstrates that the typology helps to delineate parallels, differences, and relationships among a wide array of social theories.[43] The exemplars approximating a given approach to concept formation often differ dramatically from one another, and they are sometimes controversial in ways that I will not take up here. But both the differences and the controversies attest to the breadth of theoretical developments that share any given approach.

To begin with, the *hermeneutic approach* is well known by its development in German social thought, centered in Max Weber's consolidation of *verstehende Soziologie*. Yet the lines of its development have moved far beyond any national or disciplinary boundary. Scholars like Alfred Schutz, George Herbert Mead, Hans-Georg Gadamer, and Charles

Taylor have explored epistemological issues of hermeneutics. W. I. Thomas, Herbert Blumer, and Peter Berger and Thomas Luckmann developed the approach within empirical sociology; Norbert Elias elaborated a historical sociology of social life in relation to "the civilizing process," and Clifford Geertz championed an interpretive anthropology. Recently, Dorothy Smith (influenced in part by Schutz's phenomenology) has taken the actor's personal knowledge as central to development of a feminist standpoint sociology, and William Sewell, Jr., has emphasized both the significance of events in relation to historical processes and meaning in relation to structures. In literary criticism, historicized speech-act theories, phenomenologies of reception, and discourse analysis follow a parallel hermeneutic track. Among feminists, Nancy Chodorow has explored the meaningful construction of motherhood in ways that take on theories of Freud (who himself developed interpretive models based on analytic-element relations among id, ego, and superego). In a different way, Lynn Hunt has drawn on Freud to study the "family romance" of the French Revolution. Feminist theorist Carole Pateman also engages in a broadly hermeneutic theorization by using an ideal-type methodology to explore "the sexual contract." Finally, though it may seem odd at first glance because of their intellectual origins in the French structuralist tradition, both Michel Foucault and Jacques Derrida have been centrally concerned with the problem of meaning. Derrida, after all, wants to deconstruct texts precisely to get at meanings that are occluded in structuralist reductions of them. And, in a different way, Foucault investigated the epistemic shifts in historically specific webs of meaning that occupy social categories such as "madness."

The *interchange approach* is strongly connected to hermeneutic theories because of their common focus on meaning. Conceptualizing either the interchanges of social interaction or exchanges and their media (money, power, and so on) depends on recognizing that meanings are in play for individuals who engage in exchange, as in any other kind of social interaction. However, the conceptual focus on interaction and exchange can lead toward theoretical possibilities that diverge from the hermeneutic approach, narrowly construed. Microeconomic theory finds its locus here, as do macroeconomic approaches that model markets, even though both theories tend to bracket the question of meaning bound up in the value preferences of economic actors. Spanning different routes of development and multiple dispensations, the interchange approach now includes two broad alternatives. On the one hand, emphasis on the social *relationships* of exchange moves in the directions of game theories of the sort proposed by rational-choice theorists and network theories such as those developed by Harrison White, Ronald Burt, Roger Gould, and Mustafa Emirbayer and Jeff Goodwin – the latter all undergirded by Georg Simmel's pathbreaking essay on "the web of group-affiliations." On the other hand, conceptualizations of economic, human, cultural, or social "capital" draw on the same basic conceptual motifs, but emphasize the *medium* of exchange in ways that yield more explicit models of interchange systems. Weber's theory of economic classes and their connections to market interests finds its locus here, as does the exchange theory pioneered by George Homans in the 1950s and elaborated by Richard Emerson. In a different way, exchange systems undergird the social structures that emerge from: gift-giving theorized by Marcel Mauss and Claude Lévi-Strauss, credential systems in the work of Randall Collins, class–status systems in the work of Pierre Bourdieu, and even a "political economy of signs" in the work of Jean Baudrillard. Equally interesting is the relative scarcity of feminist theory employing a theoretical approach centered on utilitarian issues; Rubin's study of "The traffic in women" offers a feminist critique of patriarchal gift-giving, but Randall Collins seems practically alone so far in using cultural-capital theory to analyze gender stratification.[44]

The theoretical transition from the hermeneutic and the interchange approaches to the *functional and dialectical approach* is marked by a shift from interest in meaningful actions toward theorizing their connections with extra-meaningful "objective" systemic conditions. As with all typological passages, the boundaries are fluid. Consider, for example, the dual possibilities of world-systems theorizing. On the one hand, if market relationships within a world economy are emphasized (as they sometimes are in dependency theory), the world system can be understood as a network. On the other hand, when the theory is elaborated in functionalist and dialectical directions, it posits that the system as a totality structures relationships among its parts. In the latter emphasis, world-systems theory becomes aligned with other theories that construe systems as having their own dynamics that cannot be reduced to interactions among component subsystems. These would include Marx's dialectical theory of capitalist class conflict set in motion by systemic contradictions that emerge from the quest for profit, Parsons's AGIL systems theory, and the less formalistic systems theorizing by Parsons's student, Niklas Luhmann, who investigates systems and their environments without assuming that all systems are integrated in an ordered social totality. None of these approaches denies meaningful action, but they do assert that action is on the one hand constrained and oriented by its systemic context, and on the other hand salient for its functional or dialectical consequences in ways that cannot be reduced to the meanings of social actors themselves. Thus, a systemic reality is posited that can be studied in its own terms.

Historically, the claim to a social reality over and above meaningful action has its origins, of course, in the claims of Emile Durkheim about "social facts." Although Simmel – the sociologist in whose work I initially identified the *formal/structural approach* – is not typically seen as a compatriot of Durkheim in social theory, their affinities come to the surface once we draw the connection between forms as case-pattern concepts and causal/conditional variables as analytic elements. Much more the positivist than Simmel, Durkheim centered his work on the problem of identifying society as something different than a purely economic phenomenon, which exists over and above the actions and intentions of individuals. He pursued this agenda in part by identifying structural forms like the division of labor that he could describe by use of analytic elements. Together, Durkheim and Simmel's strategies define a shared intellectual space that encompasses diverse possibilities of structural and formal analysis, developed during the twentieth century in relation to a wide range of topics. On the one hand, symbolic (and cultural) structuralism can be traced in linguistics, literature, and anthropology, in the works of Ferdinand de Saussure, the Russian formalist Roman Jakobson, Roland Barthes, Claude Lévi-Strauss, and Mary Douglas. On the other hand, societal structuralism and the identification of social forms find their micro development in certain approaches to symbolic interaction, and in Erving Goffman and Harold Garfinkle. Development of societal structuralism in macro directions includes the work of Peter Blau on structural features of social organization, structuralist theories of stratification and power such as the class analysis of Ralf Dahrendorf and the analysis of sexual stratification by Janet Chafetz, theories of social formations such as the models advanced by Barry Hindess and Paul Hirst, social structural models based on a positivistic version of rational-action theory in the work of James Coleman, Jeffrey Alexander's semiotic model of public ritual, and ecological models of organizational fields advanced by scholars like Michael Hannan, Paul DiMaggio, and Walter W. Powell. The specifics of these theories differ substantially from one another, but, as with other approaches, the very diversity of substantive phenomena to which the various theories attend suggests that the formal/structural approach is a robust basis for social theorizing, marked by a shared concern with identifying structured social patterns and processes that may operate in relation to meaning, but with mechanisms that can be identified independently of meaning.

The logical and dialogical connections of theoretical approaches

As distinctive as the four alternative approaches to social theoretical discourse are, it would be mistaken to think of them as autonomous of one another. In the first place, they share a deep structure that derives from their parallel development of case-pattern concepts by way of analytic-element concepts. More importantly, these theoretical approaches are not inherently isolated from one another. Although the concepts generated by these approaches cut into substantive inquiry from different angles, they are nevertheless often used together in more complex theoretical arguments. We already have seen the potential of world-systems theory to develop in both interchange and functional/dialectical directions. Similar sorts of theoretical "bridges" connect other approaches. For example, Durkheim's theory of ritual as the basis for the maintenance of symbolic and group boundaries can be regarded conceptually as a structural model describing a particular form of interaction. But once identified, this form of interaction can be analyzed for its functional or dysfunctional consequences for the social group – a strategy rightly called "structural functionalism." In other directions, Bourdieu has mounted a critique of formal structuralism based on analysis of emergent meanings in action (a hermeneutic move), and he has linked both action and structures to the socially constructed systems of exchange mediated by cultural and social capital (an interchange approach). Similar relationships among approaches arise on other fronts. The vocabulary of rational-choice theory may be used to develop ideal-typical models of meaning and exchange, or it may be taken in a more positivistic direction of building structural models. Jeffrey Alexander's structuralist model of public ritual naturally leads to questions of meaning; interchange-system markets can be theorized as operating within constraints that are structurally defined by their institutional contexts; and Baudrillard's approach to the political economy of signs neatly links markets and linguistic structures.

Beyond these conceptual bridges, certain multidimensional theories combine concepts from different approaches, as Jonathan Turner has done in a general theory of social interaction. Other synthetic strategies link different kinds of analytic elements and case-pattern concepts with each other. Anthony Giddens, for instance, has theorized "structuration" as an interplay between actions, structures, and systems, and, in a different way, Habermas has analyzed relationships between the system and the lifeworld, maintaining the two alternative approaches to theoretical discourse in their distinctive logics yet incorporating them within a comprehensive analysis.[45] In short, concepts, as the building blocks of social theory, can be drawn into theoretical discourses that transcend any single approach. These possibilities affirm the shared discursive terrain even of social theories that organize conceptualization in fundamentally alternative ways.

Although the modernist hope for a "general theory of society" now seems like a chimera, social theory continues to provide touchstones of conceptualization for inquiry – more or less integrated assemblages of constructs employed in the fabrication of knowledge. But, ironically, a recent claim for the continuing vitality of theory has been made through self-conscious narrative. In *Visions of the Sociological Tradition*, Donald Levine identifies the self-reflective narratives that theorists have used to describe the historical emergence of theory. He tells a story of stories, locating the widely acknowledged crisis of social theory in the failure of previous narratives – positivist, pluralist, synthetic, humanistic, and contextual – to account for social theory as an enterprise. In their place, he proposes a "dialogical" narrative, "one that connects different parts of the community while respecting what appear to be irreducible differences."[46] The present typological mapping of theoretical discourse, like Levine's historically grounded analysis, suggests that social theory has not found some philosopher's stone to integrate theoretical knowledge. Yet it also shows that integration does not depend solely on dialogue, for concepts can connected to one another by understanding their relations in theoretical logic.

It would be convenient, of course, if on purely logical grounds one or another theoretical approach could be identified as superior, others untenable. However, the situation is different. Even if alternative approaches use shared tools of concept formation – analytic elements and case patterns – they often "cut across" one another, analytically dividing up empirical phenomena in ways that move social theory in divergent directions. The value choice between directions of theoretical development is arbitrary in the following sense: any approach to theory occupies terrain that could be differently occupied by viable alternative kinds of concept formation. Even though they conceptualize objects of inquiry in fundamentally different ways, there is no *logical* primacy to ideal type over form, or system over ideal type, or exchange network over dialectical system. Each approach, we may hope and expect, is capable of giving rise to some knowledge unavailable to others. (Whether *empirical* inquiry can adjudicate among theoretical approaches is a question that can be addressed only by considering possibilities of translation between alternative practices of inquiry, an issue taken up in chapter 9.) Applying the present analysis reflexively, my survey of theoretical discourse cannot claim greater comprehensiveness of its typologies than the approaches that it describes; other arrays of analytic distinctions might display different affinities and disjunctures. As Levine shows, theoretical discourse is an enterprise in which earlier approaches are always susceptible to subsumption by later approaches. Indeed, neither the present typology nor any other conceptual construction is exempt from the theoretical discourse of deconstructionist supplementation. Social theory is a discursive field shared and fought over by deployment of emergent formulations that draw on previous conceptualizations and develop ever new ones.

It is also the case that theory has its limits. The present typology cannot account for either the significance of social theories or their lacunae, which may transcend their theoretical logics. Exemplary works of theory – from Weber, Simmel, and Parsons to Jürgen Habermas and Dorothy Smith – show us that theoretical discourse ought not be and is not an isolated enterprise: it obtains its significance in sociohistorical inquiry more broadly conceived. Max Weber's analysis of the Protestant ethic is dependent on its construction of ideal types, but Weber's thesis engages us not primarily because it uses ideal types, but for what his argument suggests about the emergence of modern capitalism. Similarly, Simmel's formal concepts make his theoretical investigations possible, but it is the content of his essays on the dyad, secrecy, and the stranger that is so captivating. The early versus the late Marx may be read for their formal versus dialectical arguments, but what really count are the thesis of alienation and the crisis of capitalism.

Because great theories are important for their substantive implications, the word "theory" has long been used to describe aspects of inquiry that exceed the boundaries of the discourse as I have delineated them here.[47] Often, theory is taken to mean "explanation" or "interpretation," and the term thus finds its way into inquiry by routes that are distant from social theory *per se*. For instance, historical sociologists will sometimes use the term "secular theory" to refer to an account of social change that is historically specific (as in "a secular theory of industrialization"). In this sense, much historical work constitutes its object of analysis by "extrinsic" narrative that in effect theorizes temporally unfolding developmental processes. These narratives bring into focus objects of inquiry ranging from social movement cultures, state formations, family patterns, and the like, to grander processes such as rationalization, modernization, proletarianization, and the rise of postmodernity. These analyses are historically saturated, and they cannot be reduced to formal theory, but they (like other historical approaches) are deeply structured by theoretical concepts.

On a different front, deconstructionists, as well as certain feminist theorists, develop theory in discursive and epistemological ways in order to describe the conditions in which the "representation" of phenomena through theoretical concepts yields both silences and tendentious caricatures. A related thesis, initiated by Horkheimer and Adorno but now connected to diverse strands of critical theory, is that general theory cannot capture the historical dialectic by which domination develops within a historically emergent capitalist social formation. In various ways, these historical and critical projects draw on the motifs of theoretical discourse described here, but they also demonstrate that social theory cannot be contained within its boundaries as a form of discourse. Theory seeps out into wider practices of historical and critical inquiry. We need to understand how this happens. A first step, taken in the following coda, is to consider the relation of theory to the fourth formative discourse considered in the present inquiry – explanation and interpretation.

Coda 4   The uses of theory in explanatory and interpretive accounts

Often only implicit, sometimes hidden within narrative, shaped by value considerations, theory is generated out of the conceptual languages by which inquiry brings sociohistorical objects into focus. But the grander aim of offering explanations by way of social theory – once a central goal of social science – has become controversial in recent years, for sometimes contradictory reasons. Those who assert the importance of human agency (if not the soul) refuse the determinism that they believe theoretical explanation entails; on the other hand, poststructuralist critiques deny the freely acting subject and they draw into question efforts to represent the world conceptually. Yet neither blind acceptance nor unrelenting rejection of theory seems very plausible.

This coda considers how different theoretical languages engage discourses of explanation and interpretation. Chapter 5 then builds on the codas to chapters 2, 3, and 4 by examining explanatory and interpretive discourse in ways not subsumed by values, narrative, and theory. As an ensemble, these investigations begin to suggest how ordering regimens within each of the four formative discourses – on values, narrative, theory, and explanation and interpretation – become aligned with one another in alternative methodological practices by which inquiry gets carried out (described in chapters 7 and 8).

Conventionally, epistemologists have sought a single valid account of explanation, but as the coda to chapter 2 shows, divergent values produce alternative ways of construing projects of explanation and interpretation. Similarly, the theoretical enterprise gives rise to alternative regimens of accounting for phenomena. Therefore, it does not seem appropriate to restrict explanation to any narrowly scientific definition. From a neo-Kantian perspective, more than one theoretical language can represent phenomena "objectively" – that is, on the basis of alternative observers' objective frames of reference (see table 1.1). This neo-Kantian circumstance raises the question of whether any particular conceptual representation of phenomena can be adjudicated as better or worse than another on empirical grounds. This question is not only important for scientific explanation; it is also a central concern of critics engaged in cultural interpretation, who debate whether some interpretations are better than others. Possibilities of adjudication can be addressed only in chapter 9, once actual practices of inquiry have been described. That issue aside for the moment, considering the role of theory in explanation and interpretation raises two connected issues – the possibility of voluntary action (the old problem of "free will," now the problem of "agency"), and the significance of temporally contingent historicity – each of which would undermine theoretical generalization. The following discussion of these issues reaches two conclusions. First, alternative uses of theoretical concepts crystallize different issues of agency and historicity. Second, any theoretical account is inherently incomplete, leaving core properties of the formative discourse of explanation to be understood in other terms.

Voluntary action and analytic-variable accounts

Among the most determined advocates of strong theoretical explanation have been Edgar Kiser and Michael Hechter. They invoke Hume's suggestion of a basic scientific working hypothesis under which inquiry ought to proceed – the assumption that observed events can be explained by causal uniformities. "In essence," Kiser and Hechter argue, "causal explanation works by subsuming events under causal laws, and causal laws, in turn, derive from general theories."[1] A good theoretical explanation, they emphasize, goes beyond mere identification of empirical regularities; it specifies causal *mechanisms* that account for them.

Kiser and Hechter's approach is workable within its own domain, but it tends to reduce theory to deductive theory, so it must be amended here to acknowledge the multiple approaches to theoretical discourse identified in chapter 4: in the broadest sense, theoretical explanation and interpretation are accounts that work by subsuming events under conceptual relationships and models, and these, in turn, derive from general theories that specify some mechanism by which the relationships obtain or the models operate. In this definition, interpretation versus explanation as theoretical accounts are not assumed to differ inherently in their conceptual structure. Rather, as table 2.1 shows, interpretation is simply explanation that occurs under conditions in which multiple criteria of adjudicating among accounts remain in contention with one another; under this condition, different theories may produce knowledge about a given phenomenon, each in relation to its own standards of evaluation. In other words, interpretation is a special case of explanation, and it faces parallel problems of adjudication.

For both explanatory and interpretive theories, a *ceteris paribus* assumption warrants claims: social theories do not specify exact outcomes; they offer accounts of the forces, processes, and meaningful relations held to operate across a range of instances, "other things being equal."[2] How, then, do considerations about voluntary action affect the character of theoretical accounts? As chapter 4 showed, any single analytic element on its own is inadequate for conceptualizing subjectively meaningful action. Universalism versus particularism, for example, does not specify a meaningful action. Yet a brief survey of the four types of theoretical concepts will show that, with the exception of the most material kinds of causation, all interpretive and explanatory accounts at least implicitly assume the operation of voluntaristic action that can be specified by way of "theory narratives."[3]

Causal-deterministic, meaning, and exchange relations

The most substantial challenge to the premise of a voluntary component to action is raised by "causal/deterministic" theories that describe relationships between social structural-element concepts independent of subjective or social meanings. Thus, Peter Blau and Joseph Schwartz theorize that certain social structural features – the size and heterogeneity of ethnic groups, for example – have consequences for relationships among the groups, such as patterns of intermarriage. On a different topic, historical geographer Len Hochberg theorizes that the spatial pattern of social settlement is a consequence of geographic features and technologies of transportation and communication, and that within a specified historical period this pattern affects the occurrence of social revolutions.[4] Such theories use structural-element concepts that do not reference meaning, and, in terms of table 4.2, they amount to causal/ conditional theories.

Yet it is important to clarify the character of these accounts. They cannot be translated into the Humean inference of deterministic causality at work when one billiard ball hits another. Instead, the theorized relationships are only deemed *likely* to occur. The accounts are probabilistic. But why do causal sociohistorical explanations tend to be probabilistic? This trait is not solely a consequence of complex empirical situations in which diverse unrelated forces impinge on the theorized process – a circumstance to be found in natural sciences as well, and one that could be handled under a *ceteris paribus* clause. It also obtains, I submit, because virtually all causal social theoretical explanations are contingent on actions that have a "voluntary" component.[5]

The contribution of voluntary action to the *probabilistic* character of sociohistorical "causality" is evidenced by the problems that confront any attempt to formulate an absolutely *deterministic* causality. For instance, weather conditions make it very difficult for anyone to grow corn in northern Finland, but they do not stop the determined person from trying, and perhaps succeeding. A social norm may make it prudent for people who value their reputations to act in certain ways, but it does not "force" people to act prudently. A given technology may enable a state to create weapons of mass destruction, but the existence of the technology does not mean that the state will do so. In general, other than materially causal processes (e.g., biological heredity when not socially manipulated through "genetic engineering"; neural processes when not influenced by drugs), social causality depends on social action, and, with any degree of voluntaristic "slippage" stemming from the operation of agency, causal theories describe only tendencies, not outcomes. Given social action, relationships between "predisposing" sociohistorical circumstances and outcomes can in principle be formulated as narratives, as Olafson has argued. Causal theories amount to shorthands for "theory narratives" in which the main plot is always approximately the same.[6] However, absent direct causal force, the general pattern is not determinative for the actors upon whose conduct the hypothesized causal relationship depends.

If, instead of causal theories, we consider interpretive and explanatory accounts that use meaning elements and exchange and network concepts as the analytic variables, Olafson's project of translating any theoretical account into narrative is enhanced. Accounts using meaning and exchange elements as theoretical constructs do not describe processes "outside" social action; they theorize about patterns of meaningful conduct subject to narration. The classic exemplar is the elective affinity that Weber theorized between Protestant inner-worldly asceticism and the spirit of capitalism. Unless we resort to idealism, which Weber rejected, this affinity depends on how people meaningfully regarded their actions. The same point holds for clearly "public" meanings, and for those based on exchange or interchange. A shift in the exercise of criminal punishment, for instance, does not occur outside meaningful social interactions, but through them. Similarly, networks depend on social action for their establishment and maintenance, as do economic relationships and productions of cultural capital.

Functional and dialectical relationships

Theoretical accounts using causal, meaningful, and exchange analytic elements can in principle be translated into theory narratives. The more vexing question concerns functional and dialectical relationships. It is for this analysis, after all, that Talcott Parsons labored so hard in *The Structure of Social Action* to establish a "voluntary action schema." He had little difficulty incorporating either external and hereditary *causes* or *meanings* into his schema. They became, on the one hand, the *conditions* and, on the other hand, the *content* of social actions. The challenge was to offer a voluntaristic theorization of how action becomes aligned with the fulfillment of societal *functions*. How, for instance, do individuals with their own personal agendas become caught up in ritualistic societal dramas that consolidate the moral boundaries of an established social order? Critics often have accused Parsons of theorizing a teleological system, but it is precisely the antivoluntaristic features of teleological thinking that he had to avoid if he was to sustain a voluntaristic theory. Parsons's solution to the functionalist puzzle invoked social norms, but he rejected idealism and refused to accede to what he regarded as Durkheim's "group mind" account of normative conformity. Instead, Parsons posited "effort" as a necessary component of action. "This is a name," he wrote, "for the relating factor between the normative and the conditional elements of action. It is necessitated by the fact that norms do not realize themselves automatically but only through action, so far as they are realized at all." Exactly what effort is and how it mediates conditions and norms are issues that remain rather mysterious in Parsons's formulation. But either, following Parsons, these are issues to be pursued through a voluntaristic theory that addresses the problem of meaning, or an alternative mechanism must be specified.[7]

Overall, except for the limiting case of purely material causation through direct effects, analytic-variable accounts of sociohistorical phenomena depend at least implicitly on intervening processes of meaningful agency open to specification as theory narratives, as Olafson argued. In turn, the voluntary component of any socially mediated process implies that outcomes could be otherwise. Thus, probabilistic "slippage" cannot be handled solely through a *ceteris paribus* clause acknowledging the operation of other external factors.

However, one point bears emphasis. Acknowledging meaningful social action as the medium of most social processes does not deny the potential of theoretical explanation and interpretation. Insofar as outcomes do not differ from a theory's expectations, the empirical plausibility of the theory is enhanced. Empirical inquiry disconfirms some but not all theorized relationships, and this suggests that some theoretical accounts are more compelling than others.[8] The question is, why? Assuming the potential for agency in social action, why are there differences in analytic power?

Jack Goldstone has addressed this question by pointing out that, in sociohistorical inquiry, theoretical explanations may not necessarily depend on deterministic predictions about the actions of *each* individual; instead, they may simply specify a probability that under specified circumstances a *sufficient* number of people will act in such a way as to precipitate a given outcome. In other words, there may be social ecological relationships between individual actions and aggregate processes. For example, under certain economic conditions, a given set of individuals may be theorized to have a .20 probability of engaging in revolutionary activity. Any single individual's actions are unpredictable, and specific events may be open to more precise analysis. But if the .20 probability obtains, significant numbers of people will participate in revolutionary activity, and this degree of involvement will pose a political threat to the established order. As this hypothetical example suggests, theory can be probabilistic, acknowledge agency, and still develop explanations of what Goldstone calls "robust processes."[9]

In sum, there is little reason to expect social theoretical accounts to describe deterministic processes, but theories offer a precise way of exploring the degree to which social action and its products are structurally or situationally influenced, institutionalized, meaningfully ordered, rationally oriented, routinized, or otherwise predictably patterned. The power of such theories depends on the degree to which action occurs according to script in ways that generate individual, social, or ecological consequences. Theoretical accounts are thus typically shorthand descriptions of relationships that are complex and probabilistic in character – in part due to the role of meaningful social action. Given this dependence of theoretical accounts on social action, they can be most richly specified through the formulation of "theory narratives" that display their assumptions and arguments concerning the relationships of theorized mechanisms to meaning and agency.

Time, historicity, and theoretical accounts

In turn, the potential of theory narratives as accounts is tied to issues of temporality and historicity that are central properties of all narratives. Time, both phenomenology and deconstruction show us, is socially constructed. Social practices construct socially meaningful temporalities not only by the clock and calendar, but in other ways as well – in the constructions of popular historical periodizations, in the differential experiences, hopes, and memories of successive generations, in tradition and nostalgia, in apocalyptic anticipation, and in the here-and-now.[10] Indeed, even for objective time, there is good reason to expect variability in the temporal unfolding of social processes, such that accounting for such processes theoretically is a distinctive challenge.

Historicity and theory

William Sewell, Jr., describes three ways that temporality can be conceptualized in inquiry: (1) *experimental time*, in which moments and sequences of historical time are "frozen" – conceptually abstracted from their concrete locations within webs of connected events and treated as equivalent to one another; (2) *teleological time*, where events of a historical present are ordered in relation to a transcendent process defined by anticipated future events; and (3) *eventful time*, which "takes into account the transformation of structures by events."[11] In terms of Sewell's typology, how do different types of theoretical interpretations and explanations come to terms with temporality and historicity? There is an overall pattern: *analytic-variable* accounts are usually located outside eventful time, whereas *case-pattern* concepts are invoked to construct various kinds of eventful-time accounts.

Especially when theoretical accounts treat sociohistorical phenomena within *experimental* time, they tend to be formulated in *causal* terms – as explanations, not interpretations. For instance, a strong advocate of deductive theoretical explanation, Edgar Kiser, has investigated the conditions under which tax collection in early modern state fiscal systems was organized by a state bureaucracy or, alternatively, by the contracting out of tax collection to independent tax farmers. His explanation – derived from a rational-choice theory – depends on general hypotheses about the conditions under which one or the other form of tax collection will prove most effective at maximizing revenues and cultivating the tax base itself. By the structure of Kiser's hypotheses, an equivalent set of cause-effect relationships should operate across all cases, despite differences in meaningful, historical, and spatial conditions. Kiser's study thus is situated within what Sewell calls experimental time.

Critics will point out that such theoretical explanation carves each case away from a wider array of causal mechanisms (the political economy of state interests in patrimonial relations, for example), much less the unique circumstances and finite interests and rationales of actors within concrete situations. Such points, however, simply suggest that a model is incomplete; they would not necessarily dispute an explanation that accounts for a large proportion of the variation across cases. But with respect to temporality, there is a more fundamental issue: theoretical accounts situated wholly in experimental time are atemporal and ahistorical unless time is included as a theorized variable (for example, in relation to phased periods in the emergence of the modern world economy). They also tend to assume cases to be independent of one another, rather than acknowledging the potential influences of earlier history on subsequent events. Moreover, whatever else causal models may explain, they do not address questions about how causal conditions arise or the consequences of outcomes in relation to other concrete historical developments.

Kiser recognizes these limits of experimental time, and he incorporates a different, historically developmental argument to suggest that in some cases the long-term decline of tax farming was due precisely to its refinement over an extended period of historical time: states shifted to administrative tax collection both to capitalize on the efficiencies first achieved in tax farming and to counter the threat of emergently powerful tax-farming organizations.[12] This extension of Kiser's argument does not contradict his general hypotheses. Rather, it demonstrates that general theory can increase its explanatory power if it is not constrained by the limits of experimental time.

Theorizing in *teleological* time is a different matter. Essentially it involves an argument that a future state of affairs required certain occurrences, as preparation, so to speak. In its fullest version, teleological time in effect transforms explanatory social theory into an overarching interpretive "theory of universal history" that characterizes the march of events as the playing out of a world-historical process. But teleological time also may be aligned more directly with strong theoretical explanation through *functional* and *dialectical* formulations. In these versions, processes and events are deemed significant for their consequences that are salient to the operation of a functional or dialectical system. Thus, as a systemic functional imperative, solidarity among system participants "requires" social identification of deviance. Development of capitalist trade "paves the way for" an industrial economy. Class conflict is "necessary" to the realization of the next stage of history.

Functionalist and dialectical accounts are currently in disfavor because, in the absence of an identifiable mechanism, theorizing a telos seems like positing a transcendent value operating as some sort of spirit-force *in* the sociohistorical world.[13] But there is an alternative possibility. Value as telos can be abandoned in favor of Kant's approach of using a construct as an analytic *benchmark* by which to measure historical change (see chapter 2). In this solution, a functionalist/dialectical benchmark is used to chart historically unfolding processes such as class conflict, the expansion of the world economy, decolonization, or globalization. Thus formulated, theoretical accounts in teleological time offer a basis for analyzing the conjunctural systemic consequences of far-flung events, by inverting the causal strategy of explanation found in experimental time: instead of looking at the results of causes, teleological accounts theorize about the necessary conditions for a given outcome and then search for the functionally equivalent combinations of circumstances that yield or fail to produce these conditions. For instance, if the development of modern capitalism requires predictable trade arrangements, there are multiple ways in which the predictability "requirement" may be fulfilled that would be sufficient for general economic development to occur. This analysis yields the important insight of "functional equivalence," namely, that *different* processes and events can lead to the *same* result. Revolutions, for instance, may emerge from more than one set of prior conditions. In such formulations, it may not matter when, how, or even why a developmental shift occurs. What counts is whether any given event, process, or conjunctural "moment" of the "system" has consequences for equilibrium, system breakdown, or the advancement to a new systemic condition. Used in conjunctural analysis, teleological time offers the possibility of theorizing long-term historical transformations that are complex and subject to alternative combinations of developmental conditions, each of which may be fulfilled in functionally equivalent ways.

Yet theoretical accounts in teleological time suffer an inverse defect: they do not typically address issues concerning the developmental sequences of events. Even if alternative combinations of circumstances can lead to revolution (and, similarly, even if capitalism can develop through alternative fulfillments of system conditions), the "path-dependent" ways in which processes unfold presumably affect the specific character of revolution (or capitalism). Insofar as teleological explanation fails to explore why *particular* developmental sequences occurred, it ignores a central question of sociohistorical inquiry.

This brings us to theoretical accounts in *eventful* time. Here, causal and dialectical/functional theories specifying interactions among *analytic-variable* relationships in experimental and teleological time give way to accounts using *case-pattern* theories better suited to the interpretive analysis of concrete situations. In turn, each type of case-pattern concept identified in table 4.3 – forms, systems concepts, and meaningful and market/network ideal types – has a distinctive potentiality.

To begin with, it is possible to model functional and dialectical processes in eventful time, thus describing a temporally unfolding *system*.

But systems theorists seldom offer eventful-time narratives. Instead, functional and dialectical analytic elements typically become assimilated into atemporal narratives of "eternal" system functioning or they find their ways into evolutionary or revolutionary historical metanarratives.

Event-time accounts can also chart the trajectories of structural *forms*, described independently of social meanings. Here, causality is transferred from a context of experimental time to an eventful, interactional, and contingent determinism. A particularly ambitious example of this is Claude Lévi-Strauss's structuralist projection of two practices of cross-cousin marriage – matrilineal and patrilineal.[14] Over time, Lévi-Strauss theorizes, strict adherence to one practice or the other creates a far-flung versus dense pattern of social solidarity among families. His model is an elegant one, but it is also the exception. Structural theories usually run into problems with explaining change. They are thus vulnerable to the sort of ridicule that E. P. Thompson heaped onto Louis Althusser's structural Marxism as a mechanistic clockwork devoid of history. As both Bourdieu and Sewell have pointed out, structural-form accounts of change ignore the play of actions and events that make a difference in whether and how structures shift.[15]

In order to conceptualize action, theoretical accounts in eventful time tend to incorporate *meaning, exchange,* and *interchange* elements. Here, analytic-element concepts are used to theorize ideal types and their developmental tendencies, and to characterize cases and their transformations. To take a famous example, Weber theorized that charisma is existentially unstable, and he therefore addressed the crucial issue of what directions "routinization" might take – toward office charisma, or the institutionalization of charismatic acclamation, or some other outcome. "Routinization of charisma" is a generic narrative plot of an ideal-typical situation that may be further specified with subtypes, and by comparison with concrete historical narratives of charismatic movements in eventful time.[16]

Weber's approach is widely, though not always explicitly, employed. Implicit use can be seen in a recent article by William Brustein that asks why the Italian fascist party gained electoral support. At the core of Brustein's explanation are assumptions drawn from rational-choice theory. But rather than applying a general model of rationality across a wide range of cases in experimental time, Brustein uses the theory to hypothesize about the differing circumstances of diversely situated voters living within a particular society, Italy, during a relatively brief period of historical time, 1919 to 1921. Brustein theorizes an array of ideal-typical voters who have class interests tied to their positions in formations of agrarian production. He then uses the ideal types of meaningful voter situations to predict changes in voting over eventful time across Italian regions, based on differences in the regions' predominant modes of agrarian production.[17] Because Brustein has chosen to investigate what may be called a "crucial moment" in the growth of the Italian fascist movement, his theoretical explanation establishes an important link in the more complex sequence of events of which it is a part.

Overall, theoretical accounts in eventful time emphasize the historicity of social processes. The theoretical motifs are variable: they can be structurally causal, systemically functional, or meaningful. What they share is the identification of case patterns and their event-time developmental trajectories.

In recent years, various formal methodologies have been proposed to evaluate event-time accounts of unfolding events and processes. These range from event-history analysis to Andrew Abbott's event-sequence analysis and Larry Griffin's narrative/causal event-structure analysis.[18] These formal methodologies are promising, yet they also have limitations tied to the issue of probability, and these underscore the inherent difficulties of trying to construct adequate sociohistorical interpretations and explanations based on theory alone. In principle, a theoretical account of a sequence and its outcome could be linked with past and subsequent sequences, yielding a causal chain that theorizes processes across historical time. Some research actually approximates this goal.[19] However, theoretical accounts in eventful time depend on agency; thus, like causal explanations, they are necessarily probabilistic. The consequences are disconcerting. If a given case-pattern sequence has a certain probability of a given outcome, the addition of each sequence in a chain reduces predictive power (e.g., if the separate probability of A resulting in B and B resulting in C is each .6, the probability for the two-sequence model would be .36). Even with relatively high-probability condition–outcome sequences, as models become more elaborate, the potential of explanation becomes weaker.[20] Thus, social theory will have its limits as a basis of predictive explanation not only in experimental and teleological time, but also within the time of unfolding events. These difficulties are not fatal – in part because sequence–outcomes could be theorized for long time spans or major historical developments that remain predictable despite the probabilistic character of the events and processes that comprise them. Still, the difficulties show that theory has limits, a point that even its strongest proponents acknowledge.[21]

Theory, historicity, and narrative

In this brief survey I have suggested that theoretical concepts used in explanatory and interpretive accounts display alternative kinds of historicity. As chapter 3 shows, historicities are also conveyed through different styles of narrative discourse. It thus should be possible to spell out affinities between the approaches to theoretical concept formation described in chapter 4 and the approaches to narrative described in chapter 3.

The theory/narrative binary, it turns out, is blurred by deeply theoretical substructures of narrative. First, when theoretical conceptualization employs ideal types, historicity is saturated with meanings represented through "intrinsic" sociohistorical narratives – narratives that are reflexively meaningful for their participants. Second, exchange and network ideal types mark a shift from intrinsic to extrinsic narrative, that is, to the delineation of an analytic model in which the social interactions of individuals have consequences for a plot – the story of a network, a market, an interaction order, or similar phenomenon – that encompasses but also begins to transcend them.[22] Third, in the Simmelian approach to structural forms, historicity and theoretical analysis become different enterprises entirely; the structured form is in a sense eternal; historicity is deviation from the form; it lies outside the theory, to be investigated by interpretive narratives of what may be called "historicism" that attend to the unique meaningful qualities of sociohistorical objects and the particular circumstances that give rise to historical shifts. Finally, in the functional/dialectical approach, historicity is theorized as the convergent unintended consequences of disparate actions, events, and processes; this theorization yields an objective history of the totality, sometimes tending toward a "universal history." These affinities suggest that representing historicity through narrative implicitly amounts to one or another theorization of historicity, and, conversely, that social theories have distinctive enterprises of narrative embedded within them.[23] As chapters 7 and 8 will show, these affinities among alternative discursive regimens begin to specify the conventionalized articulations of discourses connected to one another in alternative "generalizing" and "individualizing" practices of inquiry.

Yet despite the deep connections of theory to historicities, there is a final issue. It derives not from any given approach to concept formation but from the character of theory. As Stanley Lieberson has observed, even powerful theories do not explain everything. Partly this is so, Hume recognized long ago, because theories are applied in a world where complex processes interact with one another in ways that are not reducible to the theorization of any single process. As Hume put it, even strong general causal explanations can be expected to remain "imperfect." Thus, Lieberson suggests, theorists should not even try to explain some events: strange things can happen as the result of a series of disconnected and bizarre occurrences. Accounts of *particular* sociohistorical phenomena may not be reducible to a coherent *general* theoretical formulation, whether couched in case-pattern or analytic-variable terms.

Philosopher Richard Miller describes this problem for strong deductive theoretical explanation in a way that would seem to hold for theoretical accounts more generally. He argues that undue emphasis on deductive theory in sociohistorical inquiry unnecessarily undermines the potential of explanation, for deductive theories are likely to be most robust when causal factors are relatively easy to identify, observe, and measure. Yet these conditions, he suggests, are the very ones where the gain from explanation is limited: theoretical explanation thereby evidences a "bias toward the superficial" that can be corrected only by efforts to achieve greater "causal depth." Miller asserts that a cause must be considered shallow if its effect would have happened anyway, without the specific cause (e.g., by some other process), or if the isolated "cause" is merely an intermediate factor in a larger but dimly understood process.[24] We should be reluctant to adopt Miller's critique in the abstract, for the power of theory is empirically variable, and it is certainly possible for theories to produce powerful, counterintuitive accounts. Nevertheless, many of the sociohistorical phenomena that are objects of cultural significance, ranging from the social distribution of individual intelligence to the causes of the decline of the Roman Empire, are complex, only dimly understood, and resistant to parsimonious theorization. Given sociohistorical complexity, strong theoretical explanations are often shallow, and typically incomplete. And in certain resolutions of the value problem, the goal is nuanced interpretation drawing on multiple perspectives, rather than any strong version of theoretical explanation. The potential of theory for use in constructing explanatory and interpretive accounts should not be underestimated, but the challenge of achieving analytic depth raises the question of whether a residual core discourse of explanation and interpretation can be identified beyond the claims of values, narrative, and social theory.

5 The core of explanation and interpretation as formative discourse

In the former Soviet Union, why did the *putsch* in 1991 to restore hard-line communist power fail? Did the plotters miscalculate? Were they unwilling to use force? Had the communist state apparatus reached a point of no return? Did the responses of capitalist states give courage to opponents?[1] These questions raise a more general one: what is an adequate account? This question, like the others, lacks a definitive answer. Because of differing resolutions of the value problem, controversy promises to persist over whether "strong" explanation ought to be the preferred form of an account or whether all accounts are interpretive (see table 2.1). Nor, for those who embrace explanation, is there any consensual answer to the question of how a good explanation can be distinguished from a bad one. Given the intractable character of such controversies, sociohistorical researchers often regard philosophical discussions as irrelevant. In particular, naturalistic logical empiricists resist philosophers' attempts to prescribe standards of explanation.[2] A good explanation, they argue, ought not be thrown out on grounds that philosophers are not able to account for it.

No matter how arcane the philosophers' debates, there is a practical side to the matter. Empirical questions get asked, and accounts will address such questions, with or without the benefit of philosophy. But any survey of actual research will evidence profound divergences in approaches to explanation and interpretation. After the linguistic turn, some historians have renounced explanation; others have embraced narrative for its potential to help construct a meaningful politics. In anthropology, ethnographers with local knowledge as native participants have inverted the colonial moment of discovery and challenged the rationale of crosscultural analysis. In sociology, movements toward cultural, case, and historical inquiry gather momentum from critiques of causal variable analysis.[3] These developments show that the question of how to order the discursive domain that encompasses explanation and its pluralistic counterpart, interpretation, is hardly an idle one: it is an

Archimedean point by which inquiry can be shifted in one direction or another.

The crosspressures come from diverse corners. The codas to chapters 2, 3, and 4 show that discourse on values, narrative, and social theory all make claims concerning how to account for sociohistorical phenomena. Yet important considerations remain outside the boundaries of those discourses. Values frame alternative projects by delineating what is to be the object of inquiry, and what criteria are to be applied in adjudication of accounts concerning them (see table 2.1). However, even for a given resolution of the value problem, alternative procedures of accounting coexist, e.g., via narrative or theoretical discourse. In turn, narrative raises a different problem: with an artful story, the reader may become drawn into the seeming inevitability of a "naturalized" account, but explicit consideration of the account's viability breaks the spell of narrative through a rhetorical shift to other forms of discourse.[4] In a different way, social theoretical accounts, whatever their specifics, almost always leave what statisticians call residual unexplained variance.

In short, other forms of discourse are complexly interfigured with explanatory and interpretive accounts as enterprises beyond them. Thus, before turning (in chapters 6 through 8) to the combinatories of discourse that comprise distinctive practices of inquiry, it is important to consider the formative discourse of explanation and interpretation in its own terms. In the present chapter, I argue that, at its core, such discourse investigates how the play of contingencies yields specific outcomes in concrete events. In this view, the difference between interpretation and explanation does not derive from logic. Rather, the two projects operate under different conditions. Under a regimen of interpretation, multiple criteria for adjudicating among accounts coexist, leaving the validity of any single account open to external challenge, even when it is sustained internally (see table 2.1). By contrast, the regimen of explanation is based on the claim that there is only one appropriate set of criteria for evaluating the adequacy of alternative accounts about a given phenomenon. Despite these different contexts, however, as I am construing them, both explanation and interpretation share a core enterprise that tends to blur the line between them: they both draw on the most diverse evidence to make sense of phenomena, without any necessary commitment to narrative emplotment or social theory. In both regimens, the core discourse involves argumentation that analytically marshals evidence for and against alternative accounts. The discourse moves across time, space, and texts (and sometimes analogous cases invoked for comparative purposes), and it is especially open to idiographic consideration of complex interactions among processes, events, and meanings. The present chapter considers the character of such argumentation in relation to traditions of inquiry, explanatory-factor approaches, and issues of probability and contingency.

Traditions of inquiry

Core aspects of how explanation and interpretation characteristically operate are especially visible in what may be called "traditions of inquiry." Such traditions form around substantive debates such as why capitalism emerged in Europe, why the Holocaust occurred, or how culture affects individuals' performances on IQ tests. In debates like these, both *differing approaches* and *contending substantive accounts* come into confrontation, and those who privilege different discourses – intrinsic narrative versus Marxist theory, for example – need not accept claims internal to each other's methodologies at their face value. Thus, at their most compelling, accounts produced through explanatory and interpretive discourse are interpolative. They constitute, in Derrida's terms, *supplements* used to span the *differends* among diverse points of view.

An example of such interpolative discourse can be found in "the traditional blood sport of English historians" – debating the causes of the English Civil War.[5] As W. H. Dray has demonstrated, four conflicting interpretations of the Civil War differ in their discourses, strategies, and assumptions. In the Whig interpretation, Dray recounts, the war is framed in relation to the growth of a constitutionally legitimate opposition to royal absolutism, part of a centuries-long extension of English civil liberties. The second, Marxist, approach colligates the events in the wake of the Long Parliament of 1640 – including the Civil War – as a revolution, which then is explained on the basis of the ascendancy of the bourgeois class. Third, Lawrence Stone offers a comprehensive account of the interplay of factors including Henry VIII's disposal of monastic lands expropriated from the Church, the "relative deprivation" of a rising gentry class, and various triggering events. Finally, Dray points to revisionist explanations, such as that of Conrad Russell, which treat the Civil War as the result of what might be called historical accidents – miscalculations by a ruler and the conjuncture between the Irish Rebellion and events in England, for example. If Dray were writing now, he likely would include a fifth account, Jack Goldstone's identification of shifting historical dynamics driven by steady demographic change, episodes of state fiscal crisis, blocked elite intergenerational mobility, and the political mobilization of nonelite classes.

Both Goldstone's assessment of previous arguments as well as the controversy that his own book generated among reviewers are only the latest episodes of a debate with its own long, heated history. But what are the stakes of the debate? As Dray shows, the controversy is driven by competing conceptions about what approach ought to *count* as explanation or interpretation: Whig interpretations take narrative as their form; the Marxist reading derives from a general social theory; Stone combines covering laws with nontheorized conditions and events; and the revisionists move in the direction of purely contingent explanation. For his part, Goldstone constructs a quantitative "*political stress indicator*," *psi*. In turn, and characteristic of down-to-earth historians who resist the use of analytic (as opposed to empirically descriptive) quantitative variables, Lawrence Stone rejects *psi* as a "pseudo-scientific methodology."[6] These disagreements are centered on what is to be deemed a proper regimen of explanatory and interpretive discourse *per se*. In addition, the controversies derive in part from different value interests. The Marxist account has its moral vision of history, quite at odds with the Whiggish metanarrative.

Given these diversities, what common stakes make the "blood sport" into a sport? A distinctive form of interpretive and explanatory discourse interpolates in at least two ways, *rhetorical* and *logical*. First, rhetoric. For the controversy over the English Civil War, even if one approach emphasizes narrative while another works from theory, an overall terrain of explanatory and interpretive discourse has been carved out. Any account – no matter what its basis – must either hold its own within the general debate or lose ground. This debate does not admit to special pleadings for the value-based project of explanation or that of interpretation (delineated in table 2.1), for the superiority of narrative, or for the virtues of theory – either in general or in their specifics. Assuming relative agreement about *what* is to be analyzed, any inquiry's account must be defended within an arena in which rival accounts compete.[7] In this confrontation, detailed narratives or theoretical discussions do not necessarily matter, for within an overall tradition of inquiry, interpretive and explanatory discourse can often cut to the salient debatable points that advance or undermine particular arguments. In a sense the process of rhetoric works like that of a courtroom trial. Witnesses may offer their narratives and experts may assert causal theoretical linkages, but these are not dominant motifs that organize the overall discourse. They are discrete texts meant to advance or refute particular points within a process of debate which adjudicates among the weaker and the stronger of arguments. The courtroom analogy could easily be carried too far: rules of evidence lack any constitutional basis in the court of inquiry, and no judge sits ready to rule from the bench that the defense's

objection is sustained: the prosecution is intimidating historical witnesses. Yet, as in court, diverse strands of argumentation may be
invoked in inquiry to advance one account or refute an opposing one,
and with varying degrees of success.

In turn, the play of rhetoric raises questions about logic. Contemporary efforts to reconstruct the rationale of explanation trace largely from
dissatisfaction with the positivist model of scientific explanation,
specifically, Carl Hempel's covering-law approach and probabilistic
revisions (which amended it to admit less rigorous "explanation
sketches"). The positivist approach remains confounded by unresolved
problems of logic even for the general project of science, and the problems only intensify for sociohistorical inquiry, where the covering-law
model is overwhelmed purely on grounds of the complexity of sociohistorical phenomena *in situ*. Further, scholars such as Karl-Otto Apel dis-
count the covering-law model both because it fails to account
adequately for agency and because it yields only technical explanation
that ignores hermeneutic issues of interpretive understanding.

Because the covering-law model is based in formal scientific logic, it
is not well equipped to yield explanations in any but the most controlled
experimental situations or the simplest of nonexperimental ones. This
problem becomes especially apparent in efforts to account for situated
complexity. Consider Mark Traugott's study of the Revolution of 1848
in France. Trafficking in the most detailed history of events, Traugott
explores the central sociological question of how political mobilization
affected the reversal of the 1848 revolution's prospects between the
heady insurgent days of February and the failed Paris insurrection four
months later. Traugott's careful examination of details is framed in
relation to an overarching rhetoric and an expository framework that
together invoke a central concern with social scientific explanation
through the testing of hypotheses. This strategy helps Traugott sort
through alternative accounts concerning two "armies of the poor" –
the Mobile Guard that became coopted into defending the forces of
moderation, and the Parisian National Workshops, a paramilitary
organization of workers that contributed disproportionately to the insurrection. Overall, Traugott makes the case that short-term, emergent
organizational processes of cadre solidarity-building and social control
explain the alternative political mobilizations of the two "armies."

In its rhetoric, *Armies of the Poor* might be taken as the paragon of
scientific explanation used in historical investigation. Yet if we look at
the substance of the analysis, two points become clear. First, the hypotheses that Traugott evaluates as explanations are often *historical* explanatory hypotheses, not social theoretical lawlike propositions. Thus,

although one hypothesis that is dismissed – social class differences between the Mobile Guard and the National Workshops – derives from a Marxian social theory of revolutionary mobilization, another untenable hypothesis – age cohort differences between the two forces – invokes a conceptualization of generational interests that amounts a "rule of experience" rather than a well-developed social theory. As the latter example suggests more generally, a historical hypothesis need not necessarily have any particular law-like status. What matters is that it offer a potentially plausible account of a historical outcome, whatever its basis.

Second, the way that Traugott evaluates his own organizational-control alternative to class and age-cohort explanations is to delve into ever more detailed analyses that overwhelm the covering-law model of explanation. Traugott considers a series of contingent events that unfold in complex relation to one another over finite periods of time – months, days, sometimes hours. To be sure, he often formulates more specific hypotheses – poor morale in the Mobile Guard officer corps, the good timing of an effort to purge the corps – as possible explanations of particular events tied to the larger hypothesis-driven plot. Yet doing so reveals just how precarious any lawlike sociohistorical proposition can be, for the explanations hinge on contingencies like the strength of officer authority and the potential for extra-group fraternization that can be accounted for by reference to organizational dynamics, yet are not reducible to deterministic causal relationships. Given the multiple influences at work in rebellions and revolutions, Traugott judiciously concludes, "In the attempt to explain collective action, where the adoption of a group unit of analysis helps to reveal the mechanisms that may – or may not – translate dispositional influences into behavior, organizational properties will often prove decisive."[8]

Traugott explicitly considers a wide array of complexly connected issues by moving back and forth between hypotheses and detailed narratives of events. It would be difficult if not impossible to subsume his nuanced analysis within the logical structure of Hempel's "covering-law" and "explanation-sketch" approach. But on which side does the difficulty lie – with Traugott or Hempel? Because carefully argued sociohistorical inquiries typically do not fit Hempel's epistemology, philosophers now rightly question whether positivistic criteria of explanation should count for historians, or whether reasonable approaches might take a different form.[9] Thus, philosopher Richard Miller rejects the Hempelian approach and proposes instead to define as a cause "anything that helps to bring about something."[10] Examining this less positivistic approach can serve as a point of departure for delineating the interpolative process that lies at the core of interpretive and explanatory discourse.

Because Miller's definition of causes is so broad, the list of causes of a particular phenomenon might be long indeed. He therefore favors the elaboration of specific standards for particular fields of inquiry based either on logic or on pragmatic considerations such as parsimony. If a fire occurs, Miller suggests that we do not normally need to list oxygen as a cause even if it is a necessary condition for the fire to occur. "It is a cause that doesn't need to be named." Instead of trying to describe a single logic of accounting for phenomena, Miller argues that different kinds of inquiry will have their own approaches. Any given arena of inquiry may be based on a "negotiated order" in which certain arguments require no further explication (e.g., the wind caused the leaves to blow about), while other arguments will be in need of detailed justification. Each specific arena of inquiry depends on what Miller calls a "standard causal pattern" – a conventional set of precepts about what constitutes an adequate account within that arena. These precepts establish the "stopping rules" that define further analysis as either unnecessary or beyond the purview of the particular arena.[11]

Explanatory-factor frameworks

Because other discourses – on values, narrative, and social theory – help shape patterns of explanation and interpretation, they imply certain stopping rules for particular ways of accounting for sociohistorical phenomena. There will be different accounts, for example, in interpretive intrinsic narrative versus value-neutral theoretical explanation. But we need to ask whether there is also a range of interpolative patterns and stopping rules for explanation and interpretation *qua* discourse. The covering-law model tends to be discounted in sociohistorical inquiry, because of the complex, context-sensitive, culturally embedded character of sociohistorical phenomena. But in its place, some logics focus on diverse influences in relation to actual outcomes, in ways that roughly align with Miller's idea of multiple causation. These approaches I will call "explanatory-factor frameworks." The particulars differ, but the best such frameworks avoid either identifying a purely atemporal array of necessary and sufficient causal variables or engaging in a sequential narration that locates a series of events in relation to linear time. Instead, the task of explanatory-factor approaches is to identify the relationships among (1) what are variously called background factors, underlying causes, or preconditions, and (2) immediate causes or triggering events. These frameworks offer clear analytic alternatives to either causal, covering-law, or narrative approaches, but their analyses do not emphasize lawlike regularities; they explore interactive relationships among social processes and the "efforts" embodied in the agency of social actions. Here, the problem of "colligation" – how phenomena are analytically grouped together – becomes especially salient.

One study that uses the explanatory-factor approach is Lawrence Stone's account of the English Civil War, based on an analytic framework of preconditions, precipitants, and triggers. The first set of factors – the *preconditions* – (like oxygen for a fire) are held to be necessary if the outcome is to occur at all, but hardly sufficient. *Precipitants* begin to increase the likelihood of an outcome. *Triggers* are the decisive events and actions that bring resolution one way or another. They are not necessary: other factors might have brought about the same outcome, or there might have been a different outcome, but, given the preconditions and precipitants, they are sufficient causes.

An important ambiguity about colligation of phenomena in explanatory-factor approaches is apparent in Stone's threefold classification. As Dray observes, Stone's distinctions between types of causes may conflate (1) the degree of objective *temporal* distance between causes, with (2) *theoretical* differences between structural/processual causes and the history of events. For Dray, such distinctions lead to misguided philosophical debates about the significance of different types of causes.[12] Thus, there is the longstanding question about the relative importance of social forces versus "great" historical persons. This distinction between structure and action is only analytic, but explanatory-factor approaches tend to reify it in a way that ignores the empirical embeddedness of both structure and action in unfolding historical time. The problem goes back to the question of how an object of inquiry is constructed in the first place. As I argued in chapter 2, absent some such construction, the object of inquiry remains adrift in that vast undifferentiated sea of events noted by both Ranke and Simmel. But as a methodological strategy for ordering this flux (or more precisely, the artifacts and traces of it that survive and become known), the delineation of a "factor" colligates various phenomena together under a claim that they share empirically or analytically connected features (e.g., the English Long Parliament, the putting-out system, the French Revolution, lower-middle-class resentment, the anti-Vietnam War movement).

There can be little doubt of the need for colligation; without it, inquiry would lose its bearings in the sea of events, all unequivocally unique, none of greater significance than another. But Dray raises a thorny problem. Consolidating a structural or processual "factor" in explanation can easily mask the contingent significance of social actions for factors, thereby transforming histories of events into the play of temporally amorphous forces of history. Dray's critique of Lawrence Stone's schema illustrates this problem. In the debates over the English Civil War, many historians, including Stone, note the enduring fiscal difficulties of the crown. It is also widely accepted that the wars against the Scots in the late 1630s depleted the royal coffers. Both of these "factors," Dray agrees, were "necessary conditions for the collapse of the English government at the end of the thirties." Yet, he asks, would either of these circumstances have been fatal had Charles I not proved so inept at managing the affairs of his throne?[13] Simply posing the question shows how the actions of individuals in what Stone calls "triggering" events are themselves implicated in the colligation of earlier preconditions and precipitants by analysts who have the benefit of analytic hindsight. As William Sewell, Jr., has argued, events make a difference, even in "structural" history.[14] Had Charles I managed fiscal affairs more prudently (much less undertaken policies that resolved the crisis of revenues), certain colligations of events would dissolve as "long-term" factors. Factor theorists might retort that the king would have been swimming against the tides of history, but this argument hypostatizes tides into forces that are disconnected from individual and collective action. This position seems untenable. Whatever the tides of history, they are human tides, not simply deterministic processes.

As Geoffrey Hawthorn has noted, "a structure, we might say, is not an unchangeable state of affairs, but one that just happens not to have changed much."[15] Particularly when other conditions are fluid, the force of institutions and the playing out of processes can take on new qualities, subside quickly, or move along entirely novel channels. The structures may be formidable, but they are often unstable, and they sometimes shift on the basis of seemingly minor and highly contingent events. For this reason, Hawthorn encourages the consideration of "counterfactuals" – what might have been – as the basis for developing explanations. Such counterfactuals must be "plausible," he insists; they cannot simply "rewind" history or imagine radically different conditions than those which obtained. Perhaps, for example, if China had developed strong market capitalism in the sixteenth century, the French Revolution would not have happened in the eighteenth century. But we have no way of verifying this claim and, moreover, it bears little plausible relevance to the French Revolution. On the other hand, if in the seventeenth century, the drive of the French monarchy toward more effective absolutist power had either failed or, alternatively, succeeded in surmounting barriers to effective taxation, the French Revolution probably would never have happened in anything like the way that it did. As these examples suggest, structural formations themselves are contingent. This implies that, when an explanatory-factor model colligates preconditions, precipitants, and other factors, it can avoid reifying them only by acknowledging social actors' agency (or lack thereof) in constructing the concrete circumstances for which the colligated factor is argued to have analytic salience. The analysis of counterfactual possibilities of structures, processes, and actions can serve as a brake on reification.

To emphasize the agentic connection to phenomena colligated as "structures" and "factors" is not to advocate a "great-person" model of explanation; to the contrary, it simply points to a mutual reflexivity of events and actions that are conventionally differentiated into temporally sequenced "factors" and "triggering events." Attempts to account for phenomena in unfolding time offer an important opportunity to overcome the often sterile (because largely atemporal) debate about the relation between "agency" and "structure." But reified factors threaten to replicate this debate within a temporalized venue. Even if colligation into factors is a necessary heuristic of inquiry, inquiry must take into consideration actions carried out by individuals and groups with multiple agendas in a world of socially constructed and unevenly apprehended realities. How might explanation actually do this? The key to any solution must entail close attention to the contingent relationship between depictions of colligated factors and depictions of events that play out through social actions. But how to take contingency seriously?

Probabilities

One solution would treat contingencies as matters of "chance." Indeed, we have already seen in coda 4 that social theoretical explanations are almost always probabilistic rather than deterministic. Yet how is chance to be understood? Any sophisticated consideration of probability will deny that chance *per se* has causal significance as some sort of universalistic force. As Paul Humphreys argues, "That sort of modern Platonism must be resisted." Instead, in Humphreys's view, "chance" outcomes depend on probabilistic propensities for events to occur, but the propensities themselves lack causal force.[16]

Let us reexamine a standard example in debates about explanation: "Consider a man who, on a whim, takes an afternoon's motorcycle ride. Descending a hill, a fly strikes him in the eye, causing him to lose control. He skids on a patch of loose gravel, is thrown from the machine, and is killed."[17] Here, deterministic arguments about the flight patterns of flies notwithstanding, accounting for the outcome depends in part on acknowledging the "chance" collision of the fly and the motorcyclist, yet the causal force of the account has nothing to do with the chance of their proximity: it concerns what happened, *given* the chance proximity. Humphreys uses the example of the chance collision of the fly and the motorcyclist to argue against deterministic causal explanation and in favor of a clarified account of probabilistic explanation.[18] In this account, whatever the more or less settled regularities of our material and social world, outcomes partly depend on contingencies that cannot be predicted on the basis of regularities and, thus, are matters of "chance." Probabilities are not predictive for any particular event – the fly's position in relation to the motorcyclist – but the chance conditions still have consequences that may be important.

Considering social action pushes the example beyond probabilities and consequences, into the domain of meaning. Suppose that the motorcyclist is a smoker who has run out of cigarettes, and takes the ill-fated trip in order to buy a pack. Richard Miller adopts the famous historiographic position of E. H. Carr in arguing that the fact of running out of cigarettes is not a useful explanation, even though it was "necessary" in that the accident wouldn't have taken place without it. But Miller's adjudication of the grounds of explanation has nothing to do with whether the man's cigarette smoking helped "bring about" the accident; it is a pragmatic stopping rule based on the valuation of a particular kind of knowledge: knowing that the victim was a smoker doesn't help to reduce accidents.[19] My view is somewhat different. Certainly "going to buy cigarettes" adds nothing to a *general* explanation of accidents, but not all knowledge consists of generalized explanations, and, in the actual case, the genesis of the motorcycle trip is a necessary component of the account. The example is trivial, but it has implications for similar nontrivial inquiry. Even in the natural world, events depend on interacting concrete conditions. This matter of circumstance becomes all the more important in sociohistorical inquiry because conditions are not simply products of regularities and "chance" juxtapositions. There are additional components. Specifically, individual and collective social actors – pursuing potentially disparate agendas that may contingently intersect – meaningfully construct and apprehend the conditions of contingency themselves.

In the coda to chapter 4, I argued that the probabilistic character of social theoretical explanations derives in part from the "effort" upon which agency depends. Effort, I noted, remains analytically mysterious: the term does not ontologically establish the character of action; it suggests that how hard people try to secure intentions mediates social phenomena. In these terms, variations in effort and their consequences are often critical to contingencies that influence the play of one or another scientific "law."[20] Surely the law of gravity was in effect when two Catholic councilors of the Bohemian regency were thrown from a tower window in the royal palace on May 23, 1618. But for the purposes of sociohistorical inquiry, the contingent (and meaningful) act by which they were shoved out the window, not the always operative gravity, will be taken as the causally significant factor in the fall of the clerics.[21] In one respect, this sketch approximates Carl Hempel's "covering-law" model that makes explicit room for the role of generalization: the actual events in Bohemia are partly explained by a covering law and initial empirical conditions. But the example adds substance to Richard Miller's point that theoretical explanation on the basis of general laws is "biased toward the superficial."[22] In sociohistorical inquiry, even if interpretive and explanatory accounts assume a more or less settled, regularly operating natural world, the contingencies, not the regularities, are often the matter of primary interest. These contingencies may have their basis in social streams of action that intersect through what is colloquially called chance. But social chance (such as running into someone within an established social circle of acquaintances) is not the equivalent of probability, in part because of effortful social actions.

Contingencies

The substance of interpretive and explanatory accounts is open: no particular class of phenomena, events, factors, or contingencies can be ruled in or out in advance. Instead, any phenomenon of interest may be subject not only to regularities but also to happenstance, potentially of the most bizarre and unpredictable sort. Given the rhetorical character of explanatory and interpretive discourse as interpolation among disparate discourses and the substantive claims they produce, the discourse cannot be based solely on a single general social theory or typology of factors. To name only a few, phenomena as diverse as weather, disease, forms of organization, subterfuge, accidents, ambitions, class solidarity, and biological drives may inform analysis. Despite the colorful palette of possibilities, however, some rules of thumb concerning contingency have proven useful in formulating and assessing accounts.

Conjuncture

In the first place, effective analysis depends upon resolving complex questions concerning conjuncture – the simultaneous occurrence and mutual influence of originally disparate actions, events, and processes. Conjuncture may yield outcomes different from the separate effects of the same factors, each operating independently. Explanatory-factor approaches therefore attend especially to the *interaction* among phenomena described by analytically distinct factors. In a formalized analysis, such interactions may be modeled by Qualitative Comparative Analysis (QCA) – Charles Ragin's methodology developed from Boolean algebra tied to set theory. To take explaining social revolution as an example, among societies enduring seemingly unending economic hardship, revolution may be theorized to occur in some circumstances, but not others. On the other hand, in the *absence* of economic hardship, entirely different factors may be regarded as important. When the QCA approach is successful, it identifies alternative configurations of factors and their developmental tendencies. It thus offers one way to develop case-pattern theoretical generalization (considered in coda 4). Because this sort of case-pattern approach is intended to identify factors that operate in more than one case, it offers a methodology for certain generalizing practices of comparative analysis discussed in chapter 7, without resorting to the search for a single explanatory model of the sort that Arthur Stinchcombe and Charles Tilly have criticized.[23]

However, formal models of conjuncturally interacting factors have their limitations, which need to be understood if they are to be used effectively, and these limitations may require supplementation with other methods. Analyzing interactions among factors depends on effectively resolving problems of colligation and measurement. On the one hand, the more fine-grained the distinctions used to create factor categories, the more difficult it is to identify configurational patterns shared among cases. On the other hand, the broader the factor categories, the more that cases with *divergent* outcomes will have analytically *shared* features. For instance, "state fiscal strain" may lump together diversely consequential conditions, whereas "inefficient revenue collection" may isolate certain cases from others that share consequential fiscal crises. Moreover, factor-analytic realism does not necessarily establish neat analytic breakpoints. Many phenomena involve the simultaneous operation of analytically distinct processes – both intergenerational conflict over resources as well as class mobility, for instance. But, in the analysis of "conjunctural" phenomena, it is not always evident where one aspect stops, or whether that aspect shades off into another. How well can the effects of education be distinguished from those of family habitus, and indeed, are they perhaps conflated in their consequences for individuals' status attainment? Or how are we to know where the strategic calculations of a social-movement organization are to be distinguished from its capacity to recruit new members? These, of course, are longstanding issues of measurement and classification, but they become especially salient in explanatory and interpretive accounts that seek to address the conjunctural interactions of putatively separate factors.

It is partly because of these measurement difficulties that Arthur Stinchcombe proposes the analytic strategy of searching for "deep analogies" between aspects of multiple cases, rather than seeking a merely formalistic exactitude of measurement or exact parallels of process across whole cases. He wants inquiry to examine chains of a sequence by using analogical concepts that theorize particular links within the sequence, rather than explaining the overall process by reference to a single theory. And he argues that the concepts appropriate to this style of explanation will have a connection to people's individual and shared motives of action, even when these actions are shaped by structural circumstances.[24] This strategy pushes explanatory and interpretive discourse away from conjunctural factor approaches and toward a more nuanced, contingent, and *verstehende* analysis. But doing so raises a further question – whether contingencies in eventful time limit the viability of case-pattern generalizations based on factorial conjuncture alone.

Historical time

Thus, the second general issue of contingency concerns temporality, ranging from the epoch in which an event transpires to its momentary unfolding. The historical times of "eras," "epochs," and "periods" offer shorthand for describing causally unique factors that may be called "situational" in that they are not always operative. At a given time (and place), particular situational constraints and possibilities obtain. Processes of war, for instance, are affected by the technologies available in various eras. Boolean analyses like QCA do not force attention to this issue by their formal structure, but they can address this issue by defining period or era (or their attributes) as factor variables.

Beyond contextual period, historical time also is marked by unfolding and reflexively altered situations. Eventful time flows in one direction in this world, and subsequent events cannot be taken as direct causes of prior events (whether they may be teleological or functional "causes" is a separate question). Here, the limitation of formal factorial combinatory approaches such as Boolean algebra is that they do not directly model contingent or "path-dependent" sequences whereby events at one point in time may affect future channels of development. Thus, for instance, the early modern naval power of the Spanish and Portuguese was consequential for the character of the capitalist colonization of South America. To take a different example, the wide market share of

IBM-platform personal computers had consequences for the success of Microsoft disk operating systems, despite the early technical superiority of less widely distributed Apple personal computers and software. To analyze the significance of such path-dependent sequences in QCA or similar methodologies requires special analytic efforts. One approach would be to specify certain factors as "preconditions" and others as "triggers," thus permitting combinatorial analysis of which preconditions tend to produce which contingent outcomes, with or without one or another trigger. Alternatively, a specific sequence – such as "development of trade networks *before* colonial settlement" – could be defined as a factor itself, and studied in relation to the presence or absence of other factors. However, unless there are good theoretical reasons that inform these strategies, they can end up searching for needles in haystacks. The gains will be relatively limited if outcomes are driven by happenstance contingencies that lack any systematic character open to formal specification, yet still can be identified through detailed study of contingent developments.

Effort

In turn, the problem of temporality implies a third aspect of contingency. As I have already pointed out, we are far from agreeing on an ontology that construes any ultimate nature of "effort." Nonetheless, effort, defined as variation in the strength of intentionality, may be posited as one basis for the slippages between circumstances deemed to affect actions, actions themselves, and their consequences. As I argued in the coda to chapter 4, the effortful character of social action undermines attempts to explain sociohistorical phenomena deterministically. In this light, the problem of Charles I and his (lack of) effort to put England's fiscal house in order is emblematic of a wider phenomenon of contingency. Individual and collective actions can transform the context and significance of subsequent actions, as well as the salience of colligated factors and lawlike regularities. For this reason, the play of "effortful" action is important in relation to time. Outcomes of events depend on their sequence, as in the case of a military command group that initiates an action on the basis of false intelligence *before* finding out that its informant is a traitor. Specific sequence patterns are not always simply matters of chance or the configurational interaction of factors and events; they also can depend on effortful actions that construct the unfolding play of temporality. It is for this reason that unfolding events cannot easily be divided into stages or analytic factors by an objectification of temporality or the colligation of factors. Epoch and moment, conjuncture and sequence – the "outer" temporal horizons of events – are shaped through the interplay of meaningful social actions that have their "inner" social temporalities – the rhythms of daily life, the play of strategic action, the temporally rationalized operations of bureaucratic organizations, the episodic temporalities of courts of law, and so forth. The salience of effortful action underscores once again the limitations of general-theory or analytic-factor accounts, in part because effort is so dimly understood on any general theoretical basis. The analytic implications are clear. To the degree that effortful actions are consequential, interpretive and explanatory discourse must go beyond accounts of the operation of chance, theorized processes, hypostatized factors, or sequences. They must sort through evidence relating to complex temporal relations among contingencies.[25]

Pushed in this direction, inquiry often turns to narrative, the ultimate vehicle for elaborating contingencies. Yet when inquiry works to puzzle through the meaningful actions that narrative characterizes, it is caught up in what Geoffrey Hawthorn calls "disputable judgments of the similarly disputable judgments of the agents themselves."[26] As we have seen, even the "same" events are open to multiple emplotments. Any narrative must step outside itself and face off against competing accounts if it is to legitimate its claim. In doing so, it turns to the formative discourse of explanation and interpretation – the interpolative discussion and evaluation of evidence produced through alternative accounts of how the play of contingencies yields specific outcomes in concrete events.

Inquiry is torn between two poles that derive from alternative resolutions of the problem of values. On the one hand, an optimistic modernist vision seeks to establish certifiable explanation that will stand independently of value commitments. By contrast, modern and postmodern doubts transform the achievements of knowledge into value-infused, constructed interpretations that lack any analytically compelling justification over and against alternative interpretations. Each in its own way, narrative and theory as relatively autonomous discourses can be found on both sides of this divide. But neither transcends the binary division between objectivism versus relativism. By contrast, coming to terms with interpretation and explanation as an impure domain of formative discourse already inflected with values, narrative, and theory holds greater potential for surveying a Third Path.

The prospectus for assessing heterologous explanatory and interpretive accounts is more modest than the modernist claims once made for foundational knowledge, for it does not seem that the gap between sociohistorical occurrences and our multiple ways of accounting for those occurrences can ever be definitively closed. Yet against pessimistic postmodernism, explanatory and interpretive discourse supplements narrative and social theory by weighing arguments, from whatever quarters, on whatever grounds, so that the weaker arguments can be dismissed, stronger ones set against each other. Even if no account would ever be complete or adequate, efforts at formulating and assessing accounts ground whatever sense we make of our world.

Part II

Practices of inquiry

6   Discursive hybrids of practice: an
introductory schema

In recent years, the gap between objectivism and relativism has been remapped onto a divide between modern and postmodern sensibilities. Among strong postmodernists, the collapse of objectivity and science is taken as beyond serious debate, and inquiry is judged by humanistic and pragmatic standards of aesthetics, poetics, morals, and interpretive insight, rather than by objective standards of truth. But postmodernists can end up asserting a rejection of modernist inquiry that is paradoxically essentialist. Against this tendency, modernists recognize relativity, but work to salvage reason in the face of it. These tensions are not easily negotiated. However, the controversy shows how problematic both modernist and postmodernist positions can be, and this is a potentially fruitful result. Once the supposedly sharp lines between historical and fictional narratives, between science and interpretation, between text and world are drawn into question, it is possible to ask whether humanistic, historical, and social scientific inquiry – modern or postmodern – are really so distant from one another. Perhaps, instead, the inquiries conventionally allocated to history or science, modern or postmodern, depend upon an interconnected set of practices that transcend present-day disciplinary and interdisciplinary boundaries of the humanities, history, and the social sciences.

To anticipate such a possibility, the present chapter introduces a schema for examining how culturally meaningful practices of inquiry (such as "historicism" or "analytic generalization") become consolidated through mutual articulations among value discourse, narrative, social theory, and explanation and interpretation as formative discourses. In turn, chapters 7 and 8 use this schema to describe eight alternative yet interdependent methodological practices of inquiry that all draw on the four formative discourses. Because I believe that coming to terms with temporality is important both for cultural studies and for the social and other sciences (to say nothing of history!), I describe the eight practices by way of exemplars that involve one or another kind of historical investigation. But the cultural logics of practice should equally

169

bear relevance to both humanistic and scientific inquiry into relationships investigated "outside" historical time.

Overall, identifying a typology of methodological practices by way of their formative discourses serves dual purposes. First, as a chapter in social epistemology, it offers an alternative to foundationalism by developing a hermeneutic sociology of sociohistorical knowledge that brings to light various kinds of "impure reason" at work in sociohistorical inquiry. Second, in methodological terms, the typology clarifies various ideal-typical practices for conducting research, by laying bare alternative cultural logics connecting pure reason with inquiry via one or another hybrid of value discourse, narrative, social theory, and explanatory/interpretive discourse.

The typology that I develop is purposely systematic, for two reasons. First, I want to demonstrate that, even in modernist terms, sociohistorical inquiry as an enterprise cannot be reduced to the privileging of any *particular* discourse or practice. This is so because diverse practices of inquiry are hybrids of meaningful research actions that draw differentially on multiple discourses shared with other practices. Second, I want to show that the diversity of hybrid knowledge-producing practices notwithstanding, there is an overarching coherence to the ensemble, and that this coherence is undamaged – indeed, it is enhanced – by the critique of modernist purity.

The discursive articulations of practice

The coherent diversity of inquiry that I will describe derives not from the purity of any single approach to inquiry, but from the dependence of diverse practices of inquiry on shared forms of discourse that were the subject of hermeneutic deconstruction in Part I above. I do not assert some interdisciplinary working relation between fields as presently constituted. Nor do I make a preemptive claim for any single theory, method, set of ontological assumptions, or research agenda, whether modern or postmodern. It will not do, for example, to take the seemingly plausible approach that all inquiry is at least implicitly theoretical, and that therefore the first task is one of theoretical clarification: better to say, with Steven Seidman, that social theory must come to terms with narrative and moral purpose.[1] Just as untenable as the preemptive claim for theory is the notion that, because we are embedded in history, all inquiry must therefore take a narratological point of departure. For history itself can be interpreted as both a theoretical and an ideological value construction.[2] Equally, claims about textuality contribute to understanding of social action, including the mediation of inquiry by its forms of discourse. But strategies of textual criticism themselves employ practices of inquiry. In short, the hermeneutic deconstruction of inquiry's discourses draws into question any royal road to inquiry. However, it does not disclaim inquiry as meaningful social activity.

The point we have reached is different. Beyond the specifics, consideration of the four formative discourses yields two findings central to understanding inquiry. First, no domain of discourse is ordered by a single internally consistent logic. Each form of discourse encompasses multiple ways of resolving its issues. There are alternative viable regimens that can order the value problem, and there is more than one way to theorize, narrate, and interpret or explain.

Second, no matter how each form of discourse might be ordered internally, no discourse is more than a relatively autonomous register. In inquiry, the four registers are intermingled. Discourse on values affects other discourses – most notably through the construction of inquiry's objects, by legitimating a project of inquiry, and by defining the relevance of knowledge gained through inquiry. As for narrative, internally it is distinctive precisely in its capacity to incorporate other discourses within stories. On the other hand, externally, the enterprise of narrative depends on a resolution of the value problem, and relations to theory and explanation and interpretation. For theory, in turn, hermeneutic deconstruction reveals an integrated logical structure of conceptual alternatives. Within the general possibilities of its discourse, divergent ways of constructing theories coexist. However, theory is no more autonomous than narrative. Its development depends on the values that inform it, and, in turn, one or another conceptual vocabulary – of structural variables, ideal types, systems functions, or exchange transactions – constrains both the kinds of interpretive or explanatory accounts that can be formulated and how narrative can be employed. Finally, the discursive domain of explanation and interpretation encompasses distinctive problematics of supplementary interpolation, yet the discourse is precarious: wholly alternative approaches hinge on its articulation in relation to values, narrative, and theory.

In sum, there is complexity in both the individual discourses of sociohistorical inquiry and the interactions among them. This double complexity suggests that conducting research will involve engaging multiple forms of discourse and that the possible points of departure are diverse. The American philosopher Richard McKeon and a series of French thinkers have anticipated these points. Beginning in the 1950s McKeon sought to account for the diversity of generalized methods of inquiry. Various methods are not totally distinct, he observed, "for within the framework of each method the others are assigned a subordinate place which is sometimes important and sometimes trivial." Then, in the 1960s, in *The Archaeology of Knowledge*, Michel Foucault argued that relations among discourses are neither internal nor external to an overall discursive formation. That is, they are not purely matters of logical relations or rhetorical structure, or of form imposed from some external source. Foucault therefore proposed to identify any given empirical discursive formation by defining "the system of formation of the different strategies that are deployed in it." Michel de Certeau later considered a similar issue on a more specific basis: noting a disjuncture between two different discourses – "narration" and "logical discourse" – he described a hybrid intermediate form, "historical discourse," which, he suggested, mixes the problems of "temporal sequence" and "truth." The most systematic effort to address such issues was undertaken by Jean-François Lyotard in *The Differend*. There, he identified various "genres of discourse" both in inquiry and in life more generally – e.g., the scientific genre, dialectical discourse, economic discourse – constituted through distinctive ways of articulating different kinds of "phrase regimens" in relation to one another.[3]

Both McKeon and the French theorists have shown that multiple approaches become intertwined in inquiry. Following their leads, I have argued that sociohistorical inquiry is permeated with (1) distinctive regimens that order issues *within* specific formative discourses, and (2) alternative articulations *among* various forms of discourse. On the first point, I have shown that each of the four forms of discourse – on values, narrative, theory, and explanation and interpretation – is riven with internal disputes (e.g., the status of narrative, the proper basis of theoretical concept formation, and so on). In relation to the second point, it has become evident that the resolution of a problem internal to one form of discourse may have implications for other discourses. Thus, the emphasis on intrinsic versus extrinsic narrative is not independent from the construction of theoretical concepts. Similarly, a particular value resolution will articulate with a distinctive way of engaging in explanation or interpretation. In these terms, it is my thesis that "practices of inquiry" constitute specific relationships between the various formative discourses, either by articulation or insertion or some combination of the two.

It remains to show how actual practices of inquiry combine formative discourses on values, narrative, social theory, and explanation or interpretation. As any survey of inquiry's practices would show, the possibilities are manifold and historically emergent. Complexity overwhelms any attempt to contain inquiry within a categorization of its practices. But, as Weber argued more generally, in these circumstances ideal types can be used as analytic benchmarks by which to map how complex empirical practices approximate various meaningfully coherent practices of inquiry.

In the remainder of the present chapter I develop an introductory schema for typifying inquiry by taking up the issue of pandisciplinarity. For this issue, the old *Methodenstreit* evidenced a reasonable and relevant thesis, namely that different analytic purposes are served by *particularizing* versus *generalizing* orientations to inquiry. I resurrect this distinction here, in combination with the four previously identified forms of sociohistorical discourse, to offer an initial sketch of a typological framework that identifies eight ideal-typical practices of inquiry – four generalizing practices and four particularizing ones. Drawing on this framework, chapter 7 describes four generalizing practices of inquiry, each as an ensemble of relations among discourses on values, narrative, social theory, and explanation and interpretation. In turn, chapter 8 describes four particularizing practices of inquiry in the same terms.

The pandisciplinarity of inquiry

In the past three decades, the enduring puzzle of the nineteenth-century *Methodenstreit* has been pursued with particular force by historians and sociologists seeking to define an enterprise shared by the two disciplines. During its early phases, the discussion was framed largely through discussions of exemplary studies by scholars like Fernand Braudel, Reinhard Bendix, Barrington Moore, Charles Tilly, and Immanuel Wallerstein, and through inductive descriptions of various institutionally established approaches such as the *Annales* school, world-system theory, and neo-Weberian historical sociology. As Peter Burke put it, these activities helped to define emergent working relations between sociology and history by "working outwards from monographs." The schools and their exemplars inspired a generation of scholars trained in the 1960s and '70s who tackled topics ranging from the history of climates, labor history, economic history, and colonialism to women's history, mentalities, culture, Reason, and the body. These developments have helped consolidate substantive research agendas of historical inquiry and they have demonstrated the relevance of social theory to historical analysis.[4] But, as Andrew Abbott has shown, for all the important new work, no widely shared interdisciplinary enterprise has emerged. Instead, practitioners operate under a mélange of competing labels such as "comparative history," "historical sociology," "social science history," the "new social history," "world-systems analysis," "cultural history," and "the new historicism" – even though these labels do not necessarily identify either coherent practices or distinctive, self-contained agendas of inquiry.[5]

The unevenly interdisciplinary character of sociohistorical inquiry remains a matter of contention, I submit, because the problem largely has been approached inductively and through description of its practices as they have developed institutionally. Granted that purely philosophical consideration of inquiry might end up lacking relevance to actual practices, most efforts to understand the methodological circumstances of sociohistorical inquiry have erred in a different direction, and they have failed to yield an effective vocabulary for considering the diverse methodologies of inquiry. As a counterpoint here, I differentiate practices of inquiry on a more systematic basis. But, instead of turning to philosophy, I employ the Weberian approach of identifying meaningfully adequate ideal types – practices of inquiry that have coherence as cultural ensembles. By this approach, it should be possible to interpretively analyze the social practices of inquiry, while avoiding either empty formalism or empiricist induction. This strategy does not pretend to adjudicate between competing methodological claims. But it does not submerge them either.

How to construe the domain of sociohistorical inquiry has long been a puzzle. Some scholars, such as Christopher Lloyd, have recently sought to encompass the whole of inquiry within a *single* approach, but there are surprisingly few accounts of sociohistorical inquiry as an ensemble of alternative manifestations. One account, Peter Burke's, advances the idea that the realm is defined by a *continuum* between history and social theory. Burke fleshes out social theoretical concepts (sex and gender, class, mobility, and the like) in a way that can help bring historical inquiry to more self-conscious use of theory; however, he does not describe the meeting points on the continuum between history and theory except by example. Another account, by A. A. Van den Braembussche, specifies five strategies by drawing the line of its continuum between John Stuart Mill's method of agreement and his method of difference. The discussion is informative, but, as with Burke, the distinctions among the strategies along the continuum seem undertheorized.[6] Perhaps one-dimensional continua are conceptually inadequate for theorizing methodologies of sociohistorical inquiry. In any event, the two most elaborated efforts to describe sociohistorical research practices – those of Theda Skocpol and Margaret Somers, and of Charles Tilly – displace the idea of a continuum by specifying alternative *types* of interdisciplinary inquiry.

Skocpol and Somers used an inductive approach that initially identified three alternative logics of "comparative history" – one that involves the "parallel demonstration of theory" in different contexts, a second approach in which a single phenomenon (such as democratization) is studied through the "contrast of contexts" in different cases, and a third strategy, "macro-causal analysis," concerned with testing hypotheses through comparative analysis. Skocpol later slightly altered the labels for the three types to acknowledge the possibility of single-case analysis. At the same time she differentiated historical sociology from the detailed histories that historical sociologists often synthesize: "Historians, of course, also draw upon concepts and theoretical ideas, but they often do so implicitly rather than explicitly, and they may orient their research to describing a time and place rather than to a conceptual or explanatory problem."[7] Overall, Skocpol and Somers's discussion suggests that there are three core practices of interdisciplinary inquiry, and that focusing on a single case is not the sole province of historians: it can also proceed via a logic that is explicitly theoretical, and, in principle, comparative.

Charles Tilly has taken a different tack. Rather than consolidating practices inductively, he theorized a typology that differentiates alternative kinds of propositions studied through inquiry. And rather than including single-case analyses as special examples of more general logics of inquiry, he made the number of cases the second axis of a two-dimensional typology describing four alternative kinds of propositional analysis. On the first axis, propositions about a given phenomenon (e.g., class struggle) might range in application from one to multiple *forms* of the phenomenon (worker resistance, social movement, electoral politics). On the second axis, for any given form, propositions about a phenomenon could be directed to anywhere from one to all *instances* of that form. Four kinds of propositions can thereby be delineated: (1) "individualizing" propositions concerned with only one instance of one form, that is, a unique case; (2) "encompassing" comparison, dealing with multiple forms of a single overall instance (such as the world economy); (3) "universalizing" analysis intended to cover all instances of a single form of a phenomenon (such as a general model of all developmental economic growth); and (4) "variation-finding" analysis that seeks to uncover the patterns of a phenomenon for all cases, whatever their alternative forms. Although Tilly includes single-case and single-form poles in this typology, he rightly emphasizes that comparison is central to evaluating each kind of proposition. Even the propositional analysis of a single case of a single form (he cites the example of Reinhard Bendix's interest in British workers' political enfranchisement) employs comparisons that deepen the understanding of the phenomenon.[8]

Both Skocpol and Somers's and Tilly's typologies are important efforts to clarify the alternative methods of inquiry. Especially given the connections they establish between logical approaches and actual studies, they have a certain face validity to them. However, two points suggest the need to push further. First, Skocpol and Somers identify three logics of inquiry whereas Tilly's typology includes four approaches. The status of the two typologies would become clearer if the source of this difference could be understood. Are they wholly divergent ways of slicing through empirical variation, or are they similar enough that their differences can be accounted for in some more direct way?

Second, although both typologies make room for inquiry into individual cases, each emphasizes generalizing and comparative analysis. In Skocpol and Somers's approach, except for the uncharted activities of historians, the analysis of an individual case is a special instance of one of the three multiple-case research strategies. For his part, Tilly identifies only one type of proposition analysis directed to an individual case, and such analysis construes the case as a single instance of a single form rather than a unique phenomenon.

Are the possibilities of analyzing a single phenomenon adequately identified by reducing them to special instances of comparative inquiry? The question becomes especially relevant with the rise of postmodern thinking, for three reasons. First, once naive realism is supplanted by recognitions about the social construction of any object of inquiry, the question of what constitutes a case as an instance of a more general phenomenon becomes problematic, and it is important to ask whether inquiry on a single phenomenon can proceed without assuming a scientific logic of inference. Second, with the textual turn, poststructuralist and hermeneutic investigations of meaning have become more important to inquiry outside the conventional boundaries of the humanities, yet the renewed focus on meaning in history and the social sciences does not always depend upon the scientific logic of comparison (whether meaning itself is established through oppositions is a different question). Third, comparison often is based on abstract concepts (ranging from the concept of democracy to census categories) that are socially constructed either by historical actors or through the process of inquiry; in either case, concept construction and its relation to representations of cases become problematized through the textual turn.[9] These considerations do not deny that even the analysis of particularities involves comparison, nor do they exclude the possibility that analysis of a single phenomenon can be based on a practice of generalizing inquiry, but they do suggest that comparison may not always be a central activity in the analysis of singular phenomena, and, thus, that generalizing practices do not exhaust culturally coherent types of sociohistorical inquiry.

Indeed, there is a longstanding alternative to treating analysis of an individual phenomenon as a special case of generalizing analysis. In the interdisciplinary engagement of history and the social sciences, this alternative has been identified most often on the basis of positing a disjuncture between the sociological study of history and the historian's use of social science.[10] Such a disjuncture is anticipated by Skocpol's remark about historians, cited above. It derives from historical sociology's interest in theorization relevant to *generalizing* (typically in relation to multiple cases), compared to historians' typically more thoroughgoing *particularizing* orientation toward comprehensive analysis of a single phenomenon. Invoking this distinction raises the question of whether approaches to "particularizing inquiry" indeed parallel those that Skocpol and Somers found for the "generalizing" approaches of historical sociology. The best way to give full consideration to this question is to begin by assuming that distinctive alternative practices of inquiry can be identified in *both* generalizing and particularizing orientations. Two caveats. First, generalizing and particularizing orientations are terms of convenience and convention that cannot be reduced to disciplinary methods: a given historian (or a literary critic) may engage in a generalizing practice of inquiry, while some sociologists (anthropologists, economists, literary critics, etc.) effectively use the theoretical resources of sociology (anthropology, economics, literary criticism, etc.) to pursue particularizing inquiries. Second, any "particularizing" study of a single phenomenon – even those conventionally regarded as resolutely opposed to abstraction and generalization – must be understood as dependent on generalizing discourses – implicitly or explicitly, sometimes strongly, sometimes weakly. Conversely, all "generalizing" inquiry, even formal theory, runs up against issues of historicity and uniqueness. These caveats imply that the diversity of inquiry cannot be characterized by a single set of interdisciplinary practices that bridge two disciplines such as sociology and history. Instead the disciplinary boundaries themselves are erased by the recognition that sociohistorical inquiry as a terrain encompasses *all* theoretico-empirical inquiry into cultural and sociohistorical phenomena. The meeting ground of history, the social sciences, and the humanities is not interdisciplinary; it is pandisciplinary, even if any given practice is typically oriented either toward the particularizing analysis of a single phenomenon or toward generalizing in relation to one or more cases.

How might it be possible to acknowledge the distinction between generalizing and particularizing orientations, yet explore the shared terrain of sociohistorical inquiry? First, let us hypothesize that each of the four formative discourses I have discussed – on values, narrative, social

Table 6.1: *Practices of inquiry, specified in terms of dominant discourse that orders the four forms of discourse in the practice, and in terms of orientation of the practice toward inquiry*

Orientation toward inquiry	Dominant discourse that orders four forms of discourse			
	VALUES	NARRATIVE	SOCIAL THEORY	EXPLANATION/ INTERPRETATION
GENERALIZING	Universal history	Theory application	Analytic generalization	Contrast-oriented comparison
PARTICULARIZING	Situational history	Specific history	Configurational history	Historicism

theory, and explanation and interpretation – is capable of consolidating a meaningfully coherent practice of inquiry by serving as a *dominant discourse* that orders relations among all four discourses through internal subsumption and external articulation of them. In other words, I am proposing that, for example, if narrative discourse predominates, it will order the articulation among all four discourses in one distinctive practice of inquiry, whereas the predominance of theoretical discourse will order an articulation of discourses in an alternative practice. Under this assumption, it should be possible to identify four ideal-typical practices of inquiry.[11] (Whether and how cultural logics invoke such articulated discourses remains an empirical issue, to be taken up in the following two chapters.) Second, hypothesizing that generalizing versus particularizing orientations make a difference in how inquiry works, each dominant discourse – such as narrative – should order the four discourses in one distinctive practice in a generalizing orientation, and a different one in a particularizing orientation. Given four alternative ordering discourses and two orientations of inquiry, it thus should be possible to identify eight meaningfully coherent practices of inquiry. Table 6.1 anticipates this possibility by displaying the typological framework that is defined on one axis by the generalizing versus particularizing orientation toward inquiry and on the other axis by variation in which of the four forms operates as the dominant ordering discourse. For each combination of ordering discourse and particularizing versus generalizing orientation, the typology names each of the eight theorized ideal-typical practices of inquiry.

In order to establish that the typology delineates meaningfully coherent methodological practices at work in inquiry, in chapters 7 and 8,

I examine actual research studies that approximate each ideal-typical practice – identified as a distinctive articulation of the four forms of discourse, ordered by one of them. My central concern is to evoke an understanding of the practices themselves. However, the studies discussed as exemplars are not without their own historical contexts, nor are they disconnected from substantive controversies. These contexts and controversies underscore the reflexivity of inquiry's practices.

Necessarily, given my overall agenda, I do not discuss an exhaustive set of exemplars, and the exemplars that I do discuss cannot begin to capture the range of inquiries that employ any given practice. Topics of research are diverse in any event, and the pandisciplinarity of inquiry identifies commonalities in an enormous array of scholarship, ranging across literary and cultural studies in the conventional humanities, divergent approaches to the study of history ("social history," "cultural history," "oral history," etc.), and the conventional social sciences – divided by disciplines (economics, geography, etc.) but united both by shared substantive interests (markets, colonization, culture, etc.) and by shared practices across disciplines, from ethnography to statistical analysis. Given the diversity of research that falls within the general domain of sociohistorical inquiry, the exemplars considered in the following two chapters can only be illustrative. Hopefully their range will show that the distinctions conventionally used to mark off disciplinary boundaries and interdisciplinary enterprises are transcended by methodologies that are shared across boundaries. The eight practices are culturally coherent methodologies employed in the pandisciplinary realm of the humanities, history, and the social sciences.

7   Generalizing practices of inquiry

The principal inspirations for generalizing practices of sociohistorical inquiry include Alexis de Tocqueville's comparative studies, the comparative logic of John Stuart Mill, Marxist efforts toward a "scientific" history, Max Weber's comparative historical sociology, and the *Annales* school's program of structural and social history. These and other sources were brought into historical sociology as it became consolidated in the 1970s.[1] Taking stock at the end of the decade, Theda Skocpol and Margaret Somers argued forcefully against searching for a *single* methodological solution to establishing better interdisciplinary relations between history and the social sciences.[2] Instead they used substantive exemplars to sketch three broad strategies – the application of a general theory to explain history, the application of concepts to interpret history meaningfully, and the analysis of causal regularities. Their account raises two questions about whether generalizing practices of inquiry can be adequately described by the typology that I introduced in the previous chapter. First, is each of Skocpol and Somers's three alternative strategies a coherent practice of inquiry that can be described as a distinctive articulation among the four forms of discourse – on values, narrative, social theory, and explanation and interpretation? Second, is it possible to identify a fourth coherent generalizing practice, as we would expect if each of the four formative discourses is capable of structuring a distinctive practice of inquiry by defining a meaningful pattern of ordered relationships among all four formative discourses? Table 7.1 suggests an affirmative answer to both questions by presenting an overview that characterizes each of four generalizing practices of inquiry as an ordered combinatory articulation of the four discourses.

The present chapter gives flesh to this skeletal summary. The discussion follows the order of practices displayed in table 7.1. First, I show that "universal history" is a meaningfully coherent practice that can be distinguished from the first of Skocpol and Somers's approaches, "applying a general theory," which is discussed second. The remaining two practices are ones initially identified by Skocpol and Somers. Taken

Table 7.1: *Four generalizing practices of inquiry, described by how formative discourses contribute to each practice, with the discourse ordering each practice capitalized*

Generalizing practice of inquiry	Role of discourse			
	VALUES	NARRATIVE	SOCIAL THEORY	EXPLANATION/ INTERPRETATION
UNIVERSAL HISTORY	METATHEORY OF HISTORY	Subsumes cases under sociological theory	Derives theory from universal metatheory	Defines need for theory revision
THEORY APPLICATION	Knowledge by case theorizations	APPLIES THEORY TO EXPLAIN CASES	Subsumes case variation via theory	Incorporated in narrative via theory
ANALYTIC GENERALIZATION	Knowledge by "bounded generalizations"	Basis of analytic comparisons	TESTS HYPOTHESES BY COMPARISON	Controls or accounts for extraneous variation
CONTRAST-ORIENTED COMPARISON	Knowledge by "rules of experience"	Basis for developing contrasts	Establishes foci of narratives	ACCOUNTS FOR UNIQUE ASPECTS OF PROCESS

as a set, the four practices are widely employed in the social sciences (including occasional studies in the humanities that use social science methodologies), and they are central to the natural sciences.[3] Here, I focus on exemplary studies within the domain of historical sociology, since this is where interdisciplinary generalizing practices have been most self-consciously developed.

Totalizing theory as universal history

If each formative discourse is capable of ordering relations among the four discourses to yield a coherent practice of inquiry, four alternative generalizing practices of inquiry can be described, even though Skocpol and Somers identified only three. This discrepancy can be resolved if it can be shown that Skocpol and Somers's single category, "applying a general model to history," actually includes two meaningful practices that can be distinguished from each other as distinctive combinatory articulations among formative discourses. Briefly reviewing Skocpol and Somers's characterization of the application of theory suggests how this can be done. On the one hand, they discussed "middle-range" theories with distinct scope conditions, like the ones discussed in the section following this one. As I will show, this practice uses narrative to demonstrate the utility of social theories *in situ*. But there is a feature of "theory application" worth noting here: the practice operates by maintaining a strong distinction between theory and the object of its empirical analyses; theory is not a *comprehensive* representation of sociohistorical phenomena – it is a discrete model, a conceptual framework that will either demonstrate its power by its capacity to order an effective narrative or reveal its limits by its failure to do so. In this, the application of theory differs from an earlier established and enduring practice of inquiry that Skocpol and Somers discussed but did not explicitly identify, namely, providing a "theory of history."[4]

Such a theory, based on a realist metaphysic, can be formulated as either (1) an exhaustive, systematically integrated conceptual framework for the analysis of all sociohistorical phenomena, or (2) a temporally dynamic, systemically bounded "grand theory." From either of these starting points, the history of a totality becomes framed as the description of a holistic social system moving through objective time. History is different than the march of events or the play of autonomous social forces. Events and processes occur within encompassing systemic conditions, often marked by conjuncture and periodization. The overarching theory gives shape, significance, and developmental direction to specific events and processes and, more importantly, to central social patterns and transformations of History writ large.

In its historical emergence as a practice, "universal history" derives from wider and historically earlier interests in what is sometimes called "philosophical history." Usage for the two terms is not strongly fixed, but philosophical history is the more general one, with a rich heritage in theological and moral efforts to make sense of history, from those of the ancient Hindus and Jews through Kant. These earlier formulations can produce holistic accounts of the human condition, but they do not necessarily deploy the totalizing theory characteristic of universal history as I am defining it. For example, as I noted in chapter 2, Kant proposed to write what he called a universal history *as if* there were a guiding hand, by adopting a value stance in favor of enlightenment and citizenship, and tracing history in those terms. This philosophical – or better, moral – investigation is best understood as an antecedent hybrid practice that anticipates both universal history and the individualizing practice of "situational history," concerned with current historical conditions, their sources, and culturally significant alternative paths of development (described in chapter 8). During the eighteenth and nineteenth centuries, understandings of philosophical history underwent transformations in their metaphysical bases. Mainly, these changes substituted analytic categories for moral ones and inserted theorized systemic processes for mere historical stages or cycles of the sort theorized during the eighteenth-century German Enlightenment. The nineteenth-century developments – the idealist dialectic of world Spirit theorized by Hegel, and especially Marx's materialist inversion of Hegel – transformed philosophical history by proposing one or another totalizing and dynamic social theory. It was no longer just a matter of theological telos or a value-based framework for the arrangement of events. Instead, with the rise of empirical social theorizing, practitioners of universal history undertook the project of theorizing events and processes in relation to the historical totality as a closed system that could be represented conceptually.[5]

Totalizing theories are mostly greeted with suspicion today. Modern historians do not bestow favor upon them; most social theorists have moved toward theorizing more delimited processes rather than society as a whole; and recent poststructuralist philosophies have called into question anthropological, literary, and social theoretical procedures for positing structural totalities. The collapse of totalitarian regimes operating under pseudo-Marxist ideologies probably also contributed to the intellectual migration away from totalizing theories.

However, despite the understandable misgivings about such theories, we live in one world, increasingly interconnected. Thus, the question of whether or not world society is emerging on the basis of one or a series of interconnected dynamics – the economic and social dynamics of capitalism, for example – is best not prematurely closed off by fiat. Moreover, for all the current disdain toward universal history as a variant of philosophical history, Hayden White has argued that more conventional historical narratives themselves are infused with extra-empirical elements. In these terms, and in deconstructive critique as well, *all* history (and for that matter, inquiry in general) is "philosophical," and universal history cannot be singled out for criticism on that basis alone.[6]

Recent versions of universal history have been based both on systematic social theories and on dynamic theories of history; what they share is the ordering of inquiry through one or another value constitution of theory. One instance of the systemic approach is the evolutionary social-systems theory proposed by Talcott Parsons. The alternative possibility, of theorizing the dynamic processes that constitute history, is exemplified in the "strong" version of Immanuel Wallerstein's world-system analysis.[7] If these projects employ a practice of inquiry different from any of the ones identified by Skocpol and Somers, they should share a distinctive pattern in which one formative discourse meaningfully orders the articulation of all four formative discourses with one another. What might this pattern be? That is, which discourse is dominant, and how does it produce a distinctive pattern of relationships among formative discourses that defines a meaningfully coherent methodological practice?

I submit that value discourse is the axial discourse, and that it orders relations among discourses in a way that can be differentiated from "the application of social theory to cases," discussed below. Totalizing theories such as Parsons's and Wallerstein's entail an interest in accounting for particular cases. However, as we will see, the application of theory employs middle-range theories, and the practice is ordered by the use of narrative to explore theoretical versus contingent accounts. The project of universal history resolves the historian's problem of selection in an alternative combination of formative discourses: either it elides any differentiation between theory and "empirical" object by adopting the older philosophical solution of an analytic matrix based on value commitments, or it posits a realist ontology as a delineation of inquiry's object. Either way, the frame of reference becomes valued in a way that places it beyond empirical adjudication. Thus established the frame of reference can be used to produce an integrated account of the entire sweep of human history. Absent this characteristic value-theoretic totalization of inquiry's object, universal history gives way to some other practice of inquiry, for example, theory application or analytic generalization, or – among particularizing practices of inquiry – situational or configurational history.

Sometimes, as in totalizing versions of Marxism and world-system theory, the politics of universal history are explicit – in the case of Marx, the achievement of communism; for Wallerstein, the establishment of a "socialist world-government."[8] But not all universal history is based on explicit value commitment: the practice can be approximated by any theoretical system that represents its object through a comprehensive metaphysical ontology taken as the frame of reference for conceptualizing social reality as such. Such a metaphysic need not necessarily describe a dynamic theory of history, but theoretical totalization makes it in principle capable of doing so. Thus, even when the scope of a totalizing theory is initially limited to individuals and interpersonal relations (as with Freudian psychoanalytic theory, microeconomic theory, and sociological versions of rational-choice theory), it can be used to identify systemic historical dynamics. And even without the infusion of explicit value commitments, the "naturalized" realist metaphysic acquires an ideological valence when it is translated into a dynamic and totalized theory of history. It is on this basis that Freud's effort at universal history can so easily be read for its moral argument, and that the liberal ideology of progress is so identifiable in Parsons's evolutionary extension of his systems theory.[9]

Whether value commitments are explicit or embedded in ontological claims of realism, and whether theory is formal or historically dynamic, universal histories share distinctive features. The practice easily generates a research program that specifies further ways to elaborate and refine the theory, and the domain that it can claim to encompass is thereby open to expansion. Because any totalized framework purportedly brings to light axial processes obscured by empirical complexity, proponents typically advocate their preferred framework as the scientific basis of sociohistorical inquiry. But of course there are widely divergent metatheoretical frameworks, and even a single framework might be constituted in alternative ways (e.g., through different sets of rational-choice assumptions). Under these conditions, theoretical debates often take the form of contentions as to which metatheoretical framework offers the superior totalization.[10] But the most effective totalized theoretical frameworks can be used to account for all conceivable sociohistorical outcomes (God's intervention or forbearance, revolution or its absence, economic recession or growth, mania or depression, the rationality of altruism). Therefore any viable framework tends to become consolidated as a self-contained domain of discourse based on a theory that has a nondisprovable quality. Such domains easily become institutionalized as relatively impermeable "schools" of thought (or disciplines, if they become hegemonic) with their own problematics, their own journals, their own conferences and symposia.[11]

A fully developed universal history specifies an empirical phenomenon as a totality by way of its metatheoretical system. This tack results in a problem of how to generalize about multiple cases: because the object of study is a totality, all phenomena within the object are interconnected, and there is only one case – the system. Under these conditions, conventional scientific methods of sampling and case comparison lack salience. One way around this difficulty is to treat each object as a holistic system, while recognizing the existence of multiple systems as cases that can be compared (e.g., multiple isolated "world" systems at various historical junctures). This tack effectively moves away from universal history, and toward some other generalizing practice. But this does not resolve the difficulty in the practice of universal history *per se*. For large-scale theorized totalities such as *the* world system, scientific comparison of phenomena is thus problematic. To legitimate the practice, proponents point to sciences, such as astronomy, that posit a single totality yet still manage to analyze discrete phenomena within the totality. However well this solution works in astronomy, for universal history it is complicated by complex mutual influences of phenomena in unfolding historical time. Movements toward the modern state in Europe were not autonomous: what happened in one society had consequences for others. Similarly, the economic structurations of peripheral colonies are theorized to connect with core nation-states and the world economy as a whole. Coming to terms with these sorts of relationships can lead to two alternative specifications of the practice. On the one hand, the practice of universal history can be construed as the production not of scientific explanation but of a value-relevant interpretive analysis of the totality via the theoretical matrix. On the other hand, under a realist metaphysic, the proclaimed ontological basis of the theory's concepts yields distinctive analytic procedures for dialectical analysis of the totality. Absent some such solution, the claims to universal history to produce general knowledge are weakened, and generalizing inquiry is pushed toward less totalizing practices, sometimes using less totalized formulations of the same theoretical ideas.[12]

As an example of universal history, let us consider an empirical study that Skocpol described – Neil Smelser's structural-functionalist account of industrialization in the nineteenth-century English cotton industry.

In the 1950s, Smelser adapted Talcott Parsons's evolutionary systems framework to analyze structural differentiation within the cotton industry and among working-class families. His methodology was to locate both the cotton industry and the working-class family as sets of interlinked functional subsystems defined in terms of Parsons's four-function system AGIL model – Adaptation, Goal attainment, Integration, and Latency (or pattern maintenance). Smelser then charted the industry historically through seven steps of structural differentiation. He identified the importance of the spinning jenny, for example, by noting that its basic principles were invented some decades before any efforts were made to "specify" the invention (step 5) in ways that would make it the object of serious industrial innovation by entrepreneurs (step 6). Smelser affirmed the superiority of his functionalist analysis of system differentiation in two different social subsystems – industry and family – by comparing his account with others (including that of Marx), and by asserting the model's relevance to analyzing other changes during the industrial revolution – in religion, politics, and education.[13]

Characteristically for universal history, value discourse pervades and orders Smelser's account, not by looking for moral lessons of history, as Kant wanted to do, but in a much more subtle way – by inserting the realist ontology's metatheoretical categories in a way that frames topical analysis. Contingent explanation and interpretation are avoided because they would acknowledge an idiographic failure of the account; all *relevant* events are subsumed by the totalizing social theory. Strictly speaking, the theory is neither "tested" nor "applied" to a manifold history; it is employed as an orienting device to bring to the surface the relevant aspects of significant events. Universal history, in Smelser's study, offers an overarching framework for the selection of information and organization of a theoretical narrative about the sociohistorical world.

Under such a regimen, disjunctures between empirical data and social theory have a peculiar status. As Stanley Aronowitz has observed about studies undertaken through strongly theorized versions of world-system analysis, substantive findings that contradict the theory fail as critique insofar as they leave untouched the metatheoretical assumptions from which the theoretical argument is derived. This issue can be illustrated by considering a critical discussion of Smelser's study, Craig Calhoun's *The Question of Class Struggle*. Published in 1982, Calhoun's book argues that Smelser misrepresented the complex relationships of families to industrialization in England, and that this misrepresentation is theoretically based in the effort to subsume the phenomenon of industrial change within Smelser's totalizing theory. As Calhoun puts it, Smelser's "universal interpolation of 'family structure and values' as a key variable in every explanatory chain seems to be empirically quite arbitrary, following only from his general theory."[14] The differing accounts by Smelser and Calhoun can be argued on empirical grounds. But what about the theoretical stakes? From the perspective of Parsons's functionalist systems theory, Calhoun's critique could be construed as suggesting that Smelser failed to translate the general theoretical framework into a comprehensive substantive theory, or that he got the subsumption of empirical data into the (incomplete) theoretical frame wrong. Under these interpretations of the critique, the theory itself would remain unaffected by the substantive critique.

Any resilient universal history is based on a framework sufficiently flexible to accommodate substantive arguments that take one or another direction without violating the theory. Thus, for proponents who wish to sustain a totalizing theory, anomalies between historical "facts" and theory give rise to efforts to rejig these relationships by one of two strategies: either the data must be reinterpreted to show that the theoretical structure actually accounts for them "in the last instance," or the substantive analysis must be "retheorized" to account for the anomaly without contradicting the core postulates of the metatheoretical schema. For their parts, researchers who seek to test the theory *per se* either must evaluate universal history on the level of its theoretical logic or they must try to devise empirical analyses that test not just substantive expectations, but the adequacy of key metatheoretical assumptions. These challenges can be deemed successful when proponents find it increasingly difficult to sustain the theory, or when a critical mass of researchers recasts the basic problematic. In this regard, historically oriented Marxism (including some of Marx's own analyses), Niklas Luhmann's shift away from Parsons's totalized conceptualization of systems and recent refinements in studies of world economies show that it is possible to maintain value commitments and theoretical interests while rejecting the totalizing theory derived from a metatheoretical framework. But to do so is to move from universal history to some other practice of inquiry.[15]

The application of social theory to cases

The first approach that Skocpol and Somers described, the "parallel demonstration of theory," was later called by Skocpol "applying a general model to history" in order to encompass generalization in relation to a single case. In this approach, how a theoretical model is constructed is an open question; what matters is how it is employed in analysis.

Overall, the practice entails assessing the utility of a model according to what Skocpol and Somers described as "its ability to convincingly order the evidence" in one or more cases.[16] Inquiry thus uses narrative to analyze one or more cases as thoroughly as possible within a domain structured by explicit theoretical interests.

To explore an example of this practice, Skocpol and Somers chose *Agrarian Revolution*, Jeffrey Paige's 1975 comparative study of agrarian social change in less developed countries. Paige did not invoke an integrated and exhaustive formal theory of social change. Instead he proposed a substantive typological theory about social movements that emerge in contexts of agrarian social structures. His typology specifies four forms of agricultural production, each with distinctive developmental tendencies toward class submission or conflict. On one axis, it distinguishes *cultivators* according to whether their livelihood depends upon use of *land* or on earning *wages*; on the other axis, it differentiates *noncultivators* according to whether they derive income primarily from *land* or from *capital*. Each of the four possible combinations of livelihood for cultivators versus noncultivators specifies an ideal type of agricultural organization, which, Paige argued, favors a particular kind of cultivators' social movement. For example, the combination of landed noncultivators with subsistence peasants who derive their livelihood from the land defines the structure of a "commercial hacienda" that "pays its labor force in land rights and supports an economically backward upper class dependent on land as its only source of income." Under this structural condition, the noncultivating landed class proves unyielding in efforts to protect its privileged position, which strongly depends on the absence of markets in labor and land. The cultivating peasant class in this circumstance is "particularly incompetent" at organizing on the basis of collective solidarity. Social movements therefore are theorized to take the form of sporadic revolts such as land invasions. Using the same theoretical logic, Paige suggested different social-movement propensities for the other three types of agrarian organization – smallholding, plantation, and sharecropping/migratory labor agrarian structures.[17]

How are formative discourses ordered in Paige's inquiry? To begin with, is it value discourse that orders Paige's practice, as in the practice of universal history? I think not. Whereas universal history uses value discourse to establish a realist ontology, the value concerns that animate Paige's research form the backdrop rather than the ordering axis of analysis. To be sure, they are strongly present. Paige undertook his research in the shadow of the Vietnam War, which happened to be the very time when hopes for a scientifically legitimated historical sociology were waxing strong. Paige affirmed in a preface that he had "tried to report as objectively as possible the behavior of both the agricultural upper and lower classes," adding, "Nevertheless, it is important to note at the outset that this book grows out of the fundamental questions raised by United States' involvement in revolutionary movements in the underdeveloped world in general and Vietnam in particular . . . Most Americans will find that we have chosen strange allies indeed." Thus hinting at strong value commitments, Paige nevertheless worked under the regime of social science predominant when he wrote *Agrarian Revolution*. He maintained a strong distinction between "fact" and "value," such that diverse audiences could read his analysis as "objective." In the main body of the book, his prose has an even-handed, descriptive quality.[18] By working to maintain the fact–value distinction, Paige gave readers pause to reconsider political policies by presenting an analysis undertaken as a scientific enterprise. This value resolution, though frequent, is not inherent to the application of theory as a practice. More generally, the value of the practice lies in producing knowledge by viewing phenomena through a particular theoretical lens.

In any case, value discourse is not the central ordering discourse in the application of social theory to cases. Although value discourse defines Paige's topical commitment and its relevance to his audience, the axial enterprise of his inquiry is to focus the application of his theoretical model in case narratives. This narratological enterprise distinctively shapes the articulations among the four formative discourses. In relation to narrative, social theory figures in a way that falls outside the conventional social scientific interest in "testing" hypotheses derived from theory (described below within the practice of analytic generalization).

As with deductive uses of general theory, Paige's strategy is to derive empirical expectations from theory. But true to Skocpol and Somers's characterization, the stakes of Paige's theory concern "its ability to convincingly order the evidence." In these terms, his typological and developmental model supplies the central issues of plot analysis for his discussions of Peru, Angola, and Vietnam. Paige addressed the narrative question of "what happened" by exploring the adequacy of his theoretical predictions about the trajectories of social movements under alternative structures of agrarian organization. In contrast to more conventional histories, what might be called his "theory narrative" takes social theory for its framework. This narratological framework orders "parallel" efforts at demonstrating the theory's power. For instance, addressing the case of Peru, Paige described relevant export agricultural sectors in terms of his typology and narrated the histories of social-movement struggles by region and crop. With this strategy of exposition, his ordering discourse of narrative could keep to the theoretical theme, yet still acknowledge diversity of events. For example, he could argue "not only that strikes tend to occur in sugar valleys and land invasions in cotton areas but also that the number of strikes and invasions is roughly proportional to the amount of cotton or sugar produced in each province."[19]

The discourse of explanation and interpretation in *Agrarian Revolution* depends on its articulation to the overall practice centered on theory-oriented narration. Paige's typology defines case-pattern concepts that predict certain developmental trajectories in unfolding time. If this theory narrative is valid, it should account for the general features of narrated events within its domain of concern. The discursive role of explanation and interpretation therefore very much depends on defining the domain boundary of theory. This boundary establishes limits beyond which *non*theoretical explanations and interpretations can be invoked without drawing the theoretical account into question. On the other hand, the real power of the model is demonstrated by its capacity to account for contingencies *within* the domain boundary. That is, if a theory shows how contingent factors set general domain processes in motion in a particular case, the persuasiveness of the theory is enhanced. But if theoretical expectations within the domain boundary are forced into contention with unique events that undercut those expectations, the theory must be revised by induction; otherwise it loses force in favor of some alternative account, either idiographic or derived from another theory.

Paige advanced a robust, parsimonious theory that is largely effective in subsuming the discourse of contingent explanation and interpretation. The power of his approach derives from the capacity of his theoretical framework to encompass a wide range of events without ignoring or "explaining away" issues that do not fit his theory. For example, to come to terms with a seeming anomaly about highland Peru, Paige drew on his theory to analyze contingencies that produced the anomaly. In most of the region, he found that hacienda *campesinos* sided with their landlords against land-invasion movements initiated in indigenous communities. Around Cuzco, however, *campesinos* participated in the revolutionary uprisings *against* landlords. Why? In brief, Paige saved his theory from this seeming anomaly by showing that the spread of the coffee economy changed the economic balance of the Cuzco haciendas by reducing *campesinos'* forced-labor obligations to landlords and increasing their interests in acquiring their own land.[20] A less resilient theory, similarly challenged, presumably would give way to non-theoretical explanations and interpretations.

Agrarian Revolution is a strong exemplar of the practice of inquiry that applies theory to cases. However, it is important to note two variants of the practice. First, in Paige's study, theory is applied to several cases, and within each case to ever more specific places and events. But the coherence of the practice does not depend on the number of cases. Other scholars, such as Jack Goldstone, initially examine a single case (for Goldstone, the English Revolution) and later bring other cases within the sphere of the theoretical narrative.[21] Insofar as a convincing account is provided for each additional case, the theory can be regarded as increasingly persuasive.

Second, Paige's parallel accounts of cases show how social theory can structure narrative discourse. But in the occasional inquiry, logical and empirical critiques of previous studies are sufficient to organize the application of a theory to cases without extensive use of theoretically structured narrative. Here again, Jack Goldstone's consideration of England in *Revolution and Rebellion in the Early Modern World* illustrates the variation in practice. Because the longstanding debate about causes of the English Civil War is well rehearsed, Goldstone's critiques of other scholars' explanations offered a sufficient platform for developing his revisionist account based on demography, social mobility, state fiscal crisis, and political mobilization. Explication of one social theoretical account in relation to alternative ones could substitute for narrative, partly because alternative narrative plots had previously been articulated in terms of their theoretical implications, and partly because Goldstone invoked time-series data upon which he could drape a theory narrative. The conventional narrative on which the wider debate is based was a largely absent presence, yet this absence apparently was not a matter of concern for contemporary critics.[22]

More typically in the application of theory to cases, the explanatory and interpretive relevance of social theories has not been so well defined through previous inquiry, and narrative is the contested terrain of a theory narrative and contingent explanation and interpretation. Either way, the basic pattern of inquiry is similar: the narrative problem of selection is solved in favor of the social theory under consideration. That is, detailed examinations of cases serve as *in situ* applications of the theory. Under these conditions, application of theory does more than simply demonstrate that a theory offers one interpretive account of a particular case. The adequacy of knowledge is adjudicated by attending as exhaustively as possible to alternative theoretical and idiographic explanations and interpretations in relation to historical evidence, and, on this basis, inquiry explores the potential of a theory to structure a viable narrative of how a theorized process plays out historically.

Analytic generalization

In analytic generalization, the formative discourses of inquiry are ordered by the discourse of social theory, and the central concern is with empirically testing generalized hypotheses derived from theories and inductive insights. Historically, the practice has multiple origins: (1) the development of the comparative method – in its logic by John Stuart Mill in the 1840s and in its practice by analysts such as Alexis de Tocqueville, Karl Marx, Max Weber, and Marc Bloch; (2) the development during the twentieth century of inferential (as opposed to descriptive) statistics as a social scientific practice; and (3) the formulation of a method of "analytic induction" by sociologists interested in "grounded theory." In any of these dispensations, as Weber put it, research "seeks to formulate type concepts and generalized uniformities of empirical process."[23] This interest has been pursued by diverse research strategies, both of case comparison and of statistical analysis. What these strategies share is an interest in producing, refining, and evaluating theoretical formulations intended as adequate accounts of the processes at work in empirical phenomena.

Analytic generalization typically depends on the study of multiple cases, but not always. Indeed, its project is readily apparent in the distinctive way that Craig Calhoun approached "the question of class struggle" in a single case, the English industrial revolution. Calhoun began his inquiry not from a historian's starting point, but from an interest in "a rethinking of our theories of community, class, and collective action, of revolution and popular protest." From this point of departure, he used a critique of previous historical interpretations, most centrally E. P. Thompson's *The Making of the English Working Class*, to draw into question both structuralist and culturalist versions of Marxist class theory. In their place, Calhoun proposed a theoretical account of populist radicalism and political mobilization during the early phases of industrialization. This account emphasizes the importance of artisans and small producers, and of communally shared traditions.[24] Calhoun's study orders inquiry in a distinctive way that reflects a practice of analytic generalization in its overall features.

In this practice, theories identify alternative contingent lines of causation held to account for divergent empirical outcomes within a given domain. In turn, the thread of narrative is structured to offer the basis for theoretical adjudication. Simply put, evidence from case-comparative or variable-analytic research is used to elaborate and test hypotheses. The discursive emphasis on theoretical generalization orders the practice in its relation to values. The impartial evaluation of hypotheses central to analytic generalization depends on Weber's ideal of science as a vocation. There is an ethical obligation to separate the process of investigation from the value interests that shape the formulation of questions. Inquiry is thereby oriented to the development of generalizations that will carry weight for individuals who hold divergent values or theoretical positions.

Within inquiry framed by value-based questions, hypotheses are specified and studies designed to test them in various ways. The coherent character of analytic generalization does not derive from any single research design; it is shaped by a distinctive articulation of discourses ordered by social theory. How, then, does theory operate? As chapter 4 showed, it can be specified either in terms of analytic-element variable or element-pattern concepts. Tied to these possibilities, analytic generalization potentially encompasses the testing of hypotheses both through variable analysis and by strategies of case comparison. The sources of hypotheses are equally open. Skocpol emphasizes the inductive side of theory construction, in which hypotheses come from sources that include theories, analogical reasoning about case differences, and striking historical patterns. As Ragin puts it, induction "proceeds from the ground up, simplifying complexity in a methodical, stepwise manner." For Skocpol, "The crucial point is that no effort is made to analyze historical facts according to a preconceived general model." The strategy is to begin with an empirical puzzle, for which the task is to delineate one or more social theoretical accounts and evaluate their adequacy by comparing expectations with actual phenomena.[25]

This inductive approach has been criticized by proponents of research programs derived from formal theories, notably, Edgar Kiser and Michael Hechter. For them, Skocpol's emphasis on empirical adequacy overly emphasizes "contingency" and "context dependency." Kiser and Hechter argue that only a general theory can account for causal mechanisms, and that those mechanisms give rise to the patterned phenomena that may be revealed by inductive approaches.[26]

Despite the sharpness of this disagreement, so long as neither side seeks to propose a realist metaphysic as totalizing framework, the two sides are seeking to dominate the practice of analytic generalization, rather than advocating alternative practices of inquiry. This is evident because neither approach exceeds the boundaries of the practice. When analytic generalization is understood as a combination of discourses centered on theoretical discourse, its distinctive feature is its emphasis on developing theoretical formulations as a basis for testing hypotheses. Neither of the other generalizing practices that I have described so far – the application of a theory or universal history – is centrally concerned with this project. And this project is one that Kiser and Hechter share with Skocpol; they simply disagree about how to generate theory and what its character should be. Clearly, there are multiple ways of constituting theories including multidimensional approaches that combine different theories. Thus, *how* theory is constituted is a matter of internal struggle within the discourse of social theory, with important implications for the project of general theory tied to a research program, versus other projects, including inductive approaches that seek to develop theory by identifying general patterns in empirical phenomena.

The question is not whether there is a role for either general theory or inductive, historical, and "grounded" theories in analytic generalization, but whether any particular type of theory should be privileged as a basis of empirical explanation and interpretation. The answer seems obvious. Given the multiple kinds of social theory and the value-neutrality required for any fair test of theory, analytic generalization as a practice cannot presume to privilege one approach to constructing theory over another. The degree of formalization of theories is variable, and their value is judged on the basis of their analytic power in accounting for empirical phenomena, not on the basis of whether hypotheses are formulated inductively or deductively.

Whatever the source of its hypotheses, analytic generalization takes as its central task the development of a theory that accounts for a heterogeneous array of phenomena. Explanations and interpretations of contingencies and variations across cases therefore figure prominently. Consider Theda Skocpol's well-known historical-comparative study, *States and Social Revolutions*, which formulated a multicausal inductive explanation of social revolutions in France, Russia, and China that accounts for them as consequences of equivalent conjunctures of foreign and domestic crises. On the international front, Skocpol argued that old-regime states "suddenly had to confront more economically developed military competitors," and their state organizations were inadequate to respond to these challenges. Domestically, the regimes were saddled with agrarian structures that fostered peasant rebellions, and they faced revolutionary vanguards that worked to seize power during the uncertain conditions. Skocpol hypothesized that a conjuncture of external threat and internal upheaval would be present in regimes where social revolution occurred, and she argued that such a conjuncture was absent in other regimes such as Japan and England. Finally, for countries that underwent social revolutions, Skocpol sought to explain differences in the character of those revolutions on the basis of varying structural conditions.[27]

By the manner in which it proceeds, *States and Social Revolutions* reflects the key methodological assumption of social theory as a formative discourse – that theoretical accounts are more parsimonious than particularistic ones. First, it subsumes the theoretically relevant variation (presence or absence of social revolution) within the explanatory model; then it seeks to account for variations in outcomes by an explanatory analysis of social revolution, pursued on both a comparative and an idiographic basis. In contrast to Paige's application of social theory, Skocpol does not develop extended theoretical narratives of cases; instead, her analyses of cases are decomposed into their aspects relevant to a series of theoretical propositions being subjected to evaluation. Yet it is also clear that Skocpol's account is not narrowly derived from any single social theory, as Kiser and Hechter would prefer; rather, it is a multidimensional theorization of a historical social process marked by a characteristic set of conditions, sequences of events, and ranges of outcomes.

Overall, analytic generalization requires an explicit logic of analysis to structure comparisons that will yield knowledge about patterns of relations among cases and variables. Different sorts of studies can be designed to develop theories through inductive analysis and to test theories – whether derived formally or inductively. But whether the process is inductive or deductive, John Stuart Mill's logic of scientific method is central to the evaluation of hypotheses. This logic is not limited to a particular style or subject of inquiry. Its rules of inference find their ways into both comparative case inquiries and statistical analyses of variable relationships. In addition, analyses can be directed toward diverse phenomena, from structural societal change to face-to-face interaction processes.[28] In other words, against arguments for context-dependent epistemologies, those who follow Mill's methods assume that core rules of logic can be used to produce reasoned generalizations about the empirical world.

Mill asserted two complementary methods relevant to non-experimental research – the "method of agreement" and the "indirect method of difference" (indirect because it retools an experimental logic for use under nonexperimental conditions). The method of agreement is designed to isolate crucial similarities shared by a set of diverse cases. Its logic is most compelling when the selection of cases approximates random sampling: the very diversity of cases on other dimensions enhances the argument that similarities are patterned by whatever shared dynamic is identified. For instance, if patron–client relationships occur in the most diverse social settings, but, wherever they occur, there are substantial resource inequalities, the method of agreement will produce the inference that resource inequality is somehow connected to the occurrence of patron–client relationships.

In the indirect method of difference, on the other hand, the logic of control-group experiments is extended to nonexperimental inquiry by searching for contingent co-related variations. It is as though two different findings derived from the method of agreement were placed side by side. Thus, if a study of postcolonial nation-states finds that a propensity toward a particular type of state formation occurs *only* in former plantation slavery colonies, whereas diverse *non*plantation former colonies lack such a propensity, plantation slavery colonization may be identified, in Mill's words, as "the effect, or the cause, or an indispensable part of the cause." As with the method of agreement, the indirect method of difference is relevant not only to historical and comparative research, but also to statistical techniques.[29]

The procedures appropriate to analytic generalization can be quite rigorous, but, as with any research method, they are subject to methodological development and critique. One development, Charles Ragin's set-theory Boolean algebra extension of Mill's logic – Qualitative Comparative Analysis (or QCA) – marks an important advance over these possibilities, by analytically providing for the possibility that *different* sets of conditions or conjunctures of causes may yield the *same* outcome.[30] One issue of critique concerns size of the sample in a study. Even if Mill's methods are accepted for large numbers of cases, Stanley Lieberson has argued that for small numbers of cases they involve assumptions that are difficult to sustain.[31]

A separate critical issue has to do with concept formation and measurement – how to "operationalize" theoretical concepts such as "inequality" or "social revolution" in relation to the nuances of empirical diversity. Characterizing a diverse set of cases according to general standards is a risky business: concepts like "mode of production," "absolutist state," "rebellion," and "solidarity" may refer in different cases to theoretically heterogeneous phenomena. In the words of Arthur Stinchcombe, "Social theory without attention to details is wind." Stinchcombe argues that the crucial task of concept formation involves "deepening analogies" among various phenomena under study.[32] In Stinchcombe's view, the search for broad causal equivalences between cases as such is too crude, and we are most likely to find parallel patterns if we look to the details of how things happen at specific situational junctures. This task is not easily accomplished in the practice of analytic generalization simply by using a formal method. Thus, considering Kiser and Hechter's call for more attention to discovering causal processes and mechanisms raises a fundamental issue: the simple fact that an analytical generalization is parsimonious as an abstract formulation does not mean that a diverse set of specific Stinchcombeian analogies would not fit the evidence of various empirical cases as well, if not better.[33]

Any sensible application of Mill's method, Qualitative Comparative Analysis, or statistic inference will acknowledge that no research is an isolated enterprise. Especially when analytic generalization is employed in macro-historical comparison, it typically depends upon basic research, which itself may be controversial. Under these circumstances, either analytic generalization must operate on a level more general than any disputes among the specialists that it cites or, where one account is favored over another, the consequences of the alternative argument ought to be considered. But such disputes often rest on different narrative descriptions of events, a circumstance that obtains even when narrative descriptions are translated into quantitative classifications and measurements. Ironically, although analytic generalization depends upon clarification of narratives to help sort through the comparative puzzles that entangle theoretical discourse, it is designed to subsume particularity within theoretical explanation or interpretation of patterns. Analytic generalization thus brings the generalizing practice of inquiry closest to the ideal of modern social science: the structured dialogue between empirical phenomena and alternative theoretical ways of interpreting or explaining these phenomena.

Contrast-oriented comparison

The generalizing practices considered to this point encompass three different relationships to social theory: it may be assessed, applied, or used to subsume empirical phenomena within a universal history. But many researchers hold theory in any strong incarnation suspect; they invoke historicity, culture, and contingency as circumstances that draw into question any "overly theorized" view of the social world.[34] On a different front, as the coda to chapter 2 showed, any resolution of the value problem affects how the discourse of explanation and interpretation can be construed. In these terms, the practice of universal history is a value-informed approach that refuses explanation as either a value-neutral or positivistic exercise.

An alternative practice – contrast-oriented comparison – also opens up value-informed possibilities of inquiry, but in ways that differ dramatically from universal history. Instead of introducing a value-based totalizing theory, contrast-oriented comparison subordinates theory to explanatory and interpretive discourses. The practice of contrast-oriented comparison can be traced to strongly cultural and historical interests in understanding differences, already notable in Tocqueville's contrasting comparisons of the United States and France. In the twentieth century, scholars such as Max Weber and Marc Bloch similarly sought to arrive at limited and nuanced theoretical and historical generalizations by exploring contrasting particularities – Weber through his comparisons of the Protestant ethic in multiple sects, Bloch by analyzing variations in feudalism.[35]

It has been my thesis throughout that no inquiry can completely purge itself of theoretical discourse. Even the strongest skeptics draw on theory, at least in implicit ways – not only in history and the social sciences, but also in humanistic inquiry such as art history and literary criticism. However, contrast-oriented comparison evidences the possibility of deemphasizing theory while maintaining a generalizing orientation toward inquiry. Instead of developing theory in any detailed or systematic way, a researcher can make a value judgment about the cultural significance of a theoretical issue such as state formation, class mobilization, or the routinization of charisma, and use this issue as an orienting theme for theoretical conceptualization. Research then explores the theme in relation to particular objects of inquiry via narrative, which traces the concrete circumstances that give play to particular structural outcomes, cultural constellations, or other developments.[36] In this process, the contrast-oriented approach emphasizes the unique effects of situational genesis and context. Indeed, it is the discourse of explanation and interpretation that orders contrast-oriented comparison as a practice of contingent and idiographic analysis focused on social phenomena that are deemed broadly comparable in theoretical terms.

The rationale for contrast-oriented comparison is well captured by Reinhard Bendix's book, *Kings or People*, a sweeping analysis of royal authority and its transformation in the modern era. As a value commitment, Bendix undertook his study to create knowledge about past struggles of nation-building, the better to understand both the diversity of modern nation-states and the struggles of nation-building that continue in the contemporary world. To serve this value interest in an analytic way, he theorized a number of thematic issues – for example, the relation of kingship to religion, the interplay between central royal authority and local power, the secular historical trend toward the erosion of royal authority, the role of particular societies' educated elites in formulating alternative models of authority (in part by imitating developments elsewhere), and the unique national contexts that shaped how kingship became transformed into distinctive modern states legitimated by popular rule. These themes Bendix proceeded to explore through a series of historical narratives and typological summaries that identified parallels and divergences in the character of kingship and its articulation in premodern societies ranging from European kingdoms to Japan. In turn, he delineated mutually influenced national episodes of emerging popular rule – from the devolution of royal authority in England during the sixteenth and seventeenth centuries, to the problems of democratic legitimacy and nation-building facing new states in the wake of decolonization during the latter half of the twentieth century.

The watchwords of Bendix's study are "diversity" and "divergence" – of kingship structures in relation to aristocracies, of transformations toward modernity, and of modern state political structures legitimated through popular mandates. In part the bases of diversity and the spoilers for causal models are cultural. Ideas travel, and they are borrowed. Not only do cultural processes of diffusion contaminate any effort to isolate causally autonomous cases – France without England, Japan independent of the West; they also inject meanings into societal development that undermine any tidy structural determinism. Taking these considerations into account, Bendix did not deny the possibility of causal explanation, but he did suggest that, "without a knowledge of contexts, causal inference may pretend to a level of generality to which it is not entitled." Bendix thus embraced an alternative to other practices of generalizing inquiry. "In order to preserve a sense of historical particularity while comparing different countries," he wrote, "I ask the same or at least similar questions of very different contexts and thus allow for divergent answers."[37]

Proponents of scientific inquiry sometimes criticize contrast-oriented studies on the grounds that they miss opportunities for causal analysis.[38] Yet this view privileges an abstracted version of causal analysis and ignores the potential of alternatives. Contrast-oriented comparison at its best pursues Stinchcombe's goal of identifying deep analogies among instances. Rather than try to subsume a case as a whole within a general model, the practice analyzes cases through detailed investigations that are predicated on acknowledging diversity. Yet in diversity similar processes subject to theorization may be at work. The "deep" in Stinchcombe's deep analogies is thus tied to the depth of analysis where analogies emerge. They are relevant at specific junctures where analysis of particular sociohistorical situations can be connected to parallel instances and general arguments about social processes. The analogies on which contrast-oriented comparison depends for its coherence thus yield a different kind of general knowledge than abstracted causal explanation. By looking to both the deep analogies and the alternative ways that thematically similar social processes play out, contrast-oriented comparison approximates what Stephen Turner has called explanation by "translation" that looks to the parallels among the games, rules, and conditions operating for people acting in different social contexts.[39]

There are often good reasons for pushing comparative interpretation and explanation to the foreground by use of analogies and translations. Most importantly, a given topic may not lend itself to the overall theoretical generalization that is the goal of causal theoretical models. Indeed, treating case outcomes as equivalent "things" (e.g., social revolutions) is dicey at best, and, even charitably granting equivalence, heterogeneous processes may have similar consequences. For reasons tied to the general problem of equivalence, scholars with humanistic interests in the study of culture may resist a strong agenda of theoretical explanation, yet still employ comparative analysis to explore a thematic issue in diverse situations. Jaroslav Pelikan, for example, investigated how the symbol of Jesus has been invoked in diverse times and places. He was not interested in advancing a theory, and he claimed no definitive history, but his interpretive account enriches our understandings about the complex circumstantial meanings that a symbol can take. In a parallel way, Barrington Moore has examined privacy in ancient China and Greece, and other societies.[40] It would be mistaken to conclude that these studies fail to yield knowledge simply because they are not directed toward theoretical generalization across cases. To the contrary, comparison has the potential to yield analogical "rules of experience" that may be of import in research ranging from the assessment of psychiatric therapy interventions to comparative studies of fictions.[41] In such inquiries, what is contingently meaningful may be of greater interest than what is explicable across cases in general theoretical terms. Because the contrast of cases is ordered by the discourse of explanation and interpretation, it is positioned to bring to light the interplay of dynamics *in situ*. As a practice, it focuses on the play of context, contingency, voluntaristic "slippage," and "effort" that seem important to how social things happen but often residual to theoretical generalizations about cases.

More directly, methodological considerations also argue for the significance of the contrast-oriented approach. These can be framed in relation to John Stuart Mill's logic of inquiry, already discussed in relation to the practice of analytic generalization. Consider Bendix's study of European state formations, which emphasizes patterns of common genesis and mutual influence among cases. In such circumstances, "cases" involving parallel phenomena are not independent of one another, and common genesis and mutual influence contaminate scientific hypothesis testing, thereby forcing inquiry in an alternative direction. Specifically, if a researcher employs Mill's "method of agreement" – identifying uniquely shared causal features with shared outcomes across otherwise diverse cases – inquiry is required to assume causal independence of cases. This assumption is necessary because the method cannot differentiate between independent cause–effect relationships in diverse cases versus genetic or mutual influences that produce interdependent outcomes in the set of cases. Suppose, for example, that a study of sixty satanism panics in the United States showed that they emerged and developed in quite similar ways. The parallel event structures might seem to suggest a causal theoretical explanation, but alternative explanations cannot easily be excluded, because the satanism scares may not have been independent of one another; they equally could have occurred through sequential local adoptions of widely available scenarios, such that diffusion and imitation produced parallel developmental patterns.

The other of Mill's basic procedures, the method of difference, entails a second limit of analytic generalization that also underscores the importance of contrast-oriented comparison. In Mill's indirect method of difference, the task is to search for a "crucial difference" that can account for alternative outcomes among two sets of cases that lack any other consistent difference.[42] As Charles Ragin has noted, the immediate problem facing this method is that *equivalent* outcomes may be the products of *different* prior conditions. What is the status of these differences in prior conditions? Logically, they can be the subjects of efforts at explanation through theoretical generalization. But cases may differ on the basis of unique conditions and circumstances unsusceptible to theorization. The best tack for theoretical explanation under these circumstances is to shift to multiple iterations of Mill's method of agreement, to see whether particular combinations of circumstances (A, B, and C) consistently give rise to the same outcome, O – even though there is more than one pattern (A, B, and C, but also D and E) that will produce the outcome. Ragin's comparative methodology using Boolean algebra promotes evaluation of such possibilities by seeking to identify alternative patterns of contingent, conjunctural, "plural," and multiple processes that have similar consequences. However, Ragin's approach may reveal that there are certain "contradictory" combinations of circumstances (A, B, and C) for which a particular outcome, O, occurs sometimes but not always. Thus, the identification of decisive theoretical patterns can be an elusive enterprise. This implies, as Ragin recognizes, that general causal-factor patterns do not explain everything; when they don't, they can help focus the puzzles to be addressed, but detailed historical comparison of alternative unique outcomes is an important enterprise in its own right.[43]

Generalizing inquiry in each of the first three practices described in the present chapter – ordered by narrative, values, and theoretical discourse – seems to come up against inherent limits in its capacity to deal with complexity in sociohistorical phenomena. In its approach to complexity, contrast-oriented comparison offers an important alternative to other generalizing practices. The interest in "how . . . unique features affect the working-out of putatively general social processes" establishes a theoretical theme.[44] In these terms, either the study of contrasts through comparison can order inquiry as the contingent explanation of alternative outcomes through the use of deep analogies, or, alternatively, the interest in understanding culture and the pragmatic goal of identifying "rules of experience" offer rationales for contrast-oriented comparison that may yield other than scientific rewards. Under either dispensation, in contrast-oriented comparison, generalizing inquiry comes closest to its inverse – the comprehensive analysis of particularity.

8   Particularizing practices of inquiry

The specialists most concerned with particularity, historians, have long been resistant to the incursion of formalized methods into their provinces. Training in many departments remains largely a matter of historiography and apprenticeship. The institutional stakes of such training tend to promote ever more detailed analysis of particular times, places, and events. Historians thus sometimes reject comparison because it sacrifices detailed knowledge for greater breadth of analysis, and their impulse is to suspect theory of sacrificing empirical reality for systematic conceptual coherence. Yet there have been important countertendencies. Although Marc Bloch considered history more a craft than a science, he devoted considerable attention to detailing the techniques of that craft, and he regarded comparison as a central craft technique.

Moreover, historians do not have a monopoly on their craft. Recently, any neatly bounded autonomy of history has been eroded, first, by deconstructive criticism, second, as a consequence of intense efforts to thematize the relationships between history and other disciplines, third, because social science researchers have increasingly engaged in comprehensive single-case analyses, and, fourth, because a number of historians themselves have shifted practices to incorporate both the so-called linguistic turn and more theoretically informed analytic practices. However the boundaries of history may be construed, they are not historically immutable. In the wake of recent developments, we now have a rare opportunity to achieve a more systematic understanding of historians' diverse practices and their relationships to the wider domain of sociohistorical inquiry. This effort can be efficiently pursued by addressing the puzzle that single-case analysis raises for the two most successful efforts to account for methodological practices of sociohistorical inquiry – by Theda Skocpol and Margaret Somers, and by Charles Tilly.

As I pointed out in chapter 6, Charles Tilly has held, and rightly so, that comparison is central to the analysis of all propositions in inquiry. His typology includes the possibility of investigating a single instance (or case), but any given instance is *of* a thematically defined phenomenon (such as class struggle). By this delineation of inquiry's objects through thematization, Tilly in effect opts for a program of generalizing inquiry, even in the analysis of individual cases. This program, important in its own terms, nevertheless leaves theorization of particularizing inquiry (and possible roles of comparison within it) underdeveloped.

Theda Skocpol proceeded in a slightly different way. Following up on her and Somers's work on generalizing practices, Skocpol, like Tilly, sought to bridge sociology and history by treating single-case analysis as a special kind of historical sociology. But she also recognized that historical sociologists often draw on strictly historical studies as secondary sources. This acknowledgment, like Tilly's typology, leaves unanswered questions about how comprehensive analyses of singular phenomena are structured, and how these particularizing practices of inquiry should be understood in relation to the generalizing ones that I have already described. To address these questions here, I follow an approach that parallels chapter 7. Hypothesizing that social theory finds its way at least implicitly into even the most antitheoretical particularizing inquiry, I describe four ideal-typical particularizing practices of inquiry, each centered in the organizing logic of one formative discourse that orders a combinatory articulation among all four forms of discourse (see table 8.1). Three of the practices – situational history, specific developmental history, and configurational history – are derived from methodological practices of Max Weber, as identified by Guenther Roth.[1] The fourth practice is historicism, against which Weber reacted in his own work.

Situational history

In principle, values inform all inquiry. Typically, however, inquiry aspires to objectivity, and attempts are made to suppress other value considerations. But practices from Marx and Engels's *Communist Manifesto* to contemporary critical theory and feminist and subaltern studies attest to a different possibility. Inquiry is sometimes inspired by political and moral interests in producing knowledge that will prove useful or meaningful in a particular situation, and research is oriented toward serving those interests by making sense of the situation for people who share value concerns. Situational history, as Guenther Roth described it in Max Weber's work, raises the questions of "where we stand and are likely to go."[2] Value concerns order inquiries into these questions in varying ways. But whoever "we" are, and be the subject political,

Table 8.1: *Four particularizing practices of inquiry, described by how formative discourses contribute to each practice, with the discourse ordering each practice capitalized*

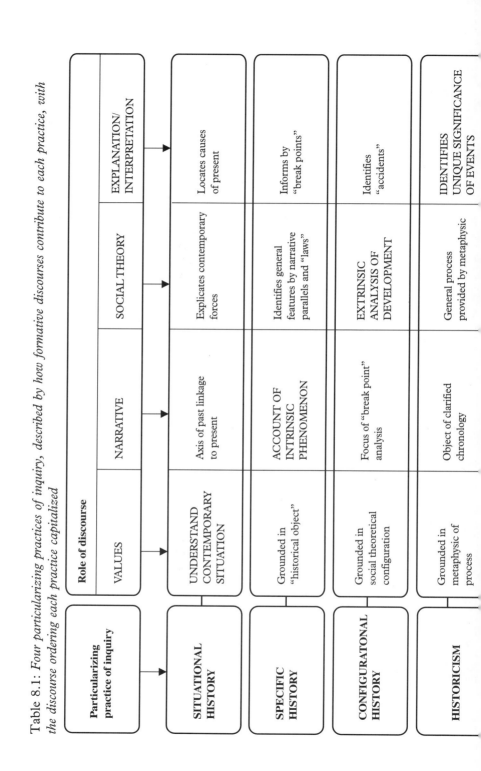

Particularizing practice of inquiry	Role of discourse			
	VALUES	NARRATIVE	SOCIAL THEORY	EXPLANATION/ INTERPRETATION
SITUATIONAL HISTORY	UNDERSTAND CONTEMPORARY SITUATION	Axis of past linkage to present	Explicates contemporary forces	Locates causes of present
SPECIFIC HISTORY	Grounded in "historical object"	ACCOUNT OF INTRINSIC PHENOMENON	Identifies general features by narrative parallels and "laws"	Informs by "break points"
CONFIGURATIONAL HISTORY	Grounded in social theoretical configuration	Focus of "break point" analysis	EXTRINSIC ANALYSIS OF DEVELOPMENT	Identifies "accidents"
HISTORICISM	Grounded in metaphysic of process	Object of clarified chronology	General process provided by metaphysic	IDENTIFIES UNIQUE SIGNIFICANCE OF EVENTS

economic, cultural, or religious, be it narrowly partisan or broadly civic, situational inquiry is marked by the predominance of value-based concerns.

A striking exemplar is Lenin's pamphlet, *What Is to Be Done?*, published in 1902, at a particular juncture in the development of the revolutionary movement in Russia. Lenin had returned from banishment in Siberia in 1900, and he devoted his energies to uniting diverse political tendencies into a movement opposing tsarist autocracy, organized under a Marxist ideology. As Lenin and his associates succeeded in their efforts, they moved away from factional participation in social-democratic politics. In his pamphlet, Lenin railed against what he regarded as sources of disorganization – the trade-union movement, "economism," "opportunism," and "spontaneity," and he called for a centralized organization with theoreticians at the core of a narrow, disciplined vanguard party that would orchestrate mass political education and revolutionary struggle. At the conclusion of his argument, Lenin described three periods of the Russian social-democratic movement – origins from 1884 to 1894, popularization from 1894 to 1898, and a third period, of disarray, beginning in 1898. His answer to the question of his pamphlet, "what is to be done?" – "Liquidate the third period."[3] *What Is to Be Done?* was a tract, written to advance a particular agenda at particular political moment. But there was much more than rhetoric: the tract depended for its persuasiveness on theoretical arguments about social movements, organizations, and class consciousness. Its narrative offered a situational retrospective and prospectus that drew on analyses of past and projected outcomes to argue for the strategic benefits of a course of action oriented toward political success.

Lenin must be regarded as an extreme example: in other situational histories, values order inquiry without the rhetoric of polemics. More generally, there is a sort of ad hoc stopping rule at work in the value standard of practical relevance, and value discourse can be eclectic in how it brings other discourses to bear in practice.[4] We thus may expect situational histories to differ in the uses of social theories and contingent explanatory and interpretive discourse to address value concerns. What they share is a value discourse that establishes a detailed analytic criterion of relevance by which other discourses come into play in the consideration of an object of inquiry.

A contemporary scholarly example is Carole Pateman's *The Sexual Contract*. Pateman acknowledges a feminist value inspiration for her critique of the modernist narrative that describes how contract societies have replaced status societies. She would displace this narrative by arguing that the supposedly modern social contract both denies and depends upon a "sexual contract." Pateman uses ideal-typical concepts of contractual arrangements – e.g., of wife, slave, and wage slave – to construct detailed yet theoretically focused narratives about the contractual bases of historically located social relationships. She is engaged in scholarship, not factional struggle. Yet her effort to displace the modernist narrative of social contract also serves to displace the public worldview shaped by contract theory, specifically as it informs feminist politics:

> To retrieve the story of the sexual contract does not, in itself, provide a political programme or offer any short cuts in the hard task of deciding what, in any given circumstances, are the best courses of action and policies for feminists to follow, or when and how feminists should form alliances with other political movements. Once the story has been told, however, a new perspective is available from which to assess political possibilities and to judge whether this path or that will aid or hinder (or bòth) the creation of a free society and the creation of sexual difference as diverse expressions of freedom.[5]

The Sexual Contract differs from *What Is to Be Done?* in its theoretical agenda: it pushes to the limit the single theoretical construct of contract. Nevertheless, Lenin's and Pateman's works share a central ordering of inquiry by value concerns, and, despite the differences in the stopping rules determined by the ad hoc value concerns, these value concerns similarly shape the overall practice of inquiry. In both cases, theories are salient as resources for resolving value-based problematics about social phenomena; explanation and interpretation tie theoretical discourse to the analysis of past, present, and potential futures, and narratives represent events relevant to the contested trajectories of a situated social movement.

For both Pateman and Lenin, value concerns focus analysis on a historical present – for Lenin, the revolutionary movement in Russia at the dawn of the twentieth century; for Pateman, feminist politics toward the end of the same century. Yet situational value interests need not necessarily focus analysis only on the present. It is equally possible for present interests to project analysis back onto earlier historical moments. As philosophers of history have emphasized, we do not study the past from a universal standpoint, but from positions themselves located in history and situation. When this perspectivity is embraced rather than repressed, inquiry even about times long past can gain special value. As Hayden White has suggested, narrative lends moral significance to events. Thus, narratives that legitimate national identities (or challenge them) are best understood as efforts of political agency *in* history. But even discounting the more obviously ideological national histories, value-based arguments over past history are often important as discourses with subtexts about contemporary politics and moral purposes.[6]

It would be very difficult today to study the histories of slavery in the United States, the Civil War, or black Americans independently of contemporary debates about inequality and affirmative action. Even topically focused studies such as Fogel and Engerman's study of the economics of slavery, *Time on the Cross*, often are explicit about the implications of their work for current history. Similarly, the 500-year anniversary of Columbus's first voyage to the western hemisphere occasioned a vigorous debate over celebrations of the event, along with a flood of revisionist and multicultural histories. At the crux of such controversies over events long past are moral questions about the political and cultural legitimacy of today's societies spawned by Europeans' conquest of the "new world."[7]

Like universal history, situational history gives primacy to value-based interests, and in this it resonates with Kant's idea that a transcendent value can shape inquiry. But, unlike universal history, situational history does not offer a dynamic theory of history. Instead, whether keyed to the distant past, the recent past, or the present, situational history is grounded in pragmatic and moral demands for knowledge meant to inform understandings of contemporary issues. These interests set the boundaries of relevance for narrative discourse about the past, potential present interventions, and a projected future, draped around a plot animated by value concerns. The task is less to evaluate alternative plots in relation to evidence than to provide an interpretation of situation that reveals to readers their opportunities to make history.

Both social theory and explanatory and interpretive discourse are crucial to situational history because they display the terrain of action as the interplay of constraints, dynamics, and possibilities. The task is to account for the unique course of events, processes, and institutional developments that are of situational value concern. But the explanatory and interpretive accounts themselves are not value-free: they are saturated by concerns about their implications for one course of action over another. Has a particular coalition entrenched itself in a political party apparatus that opponents seek to capture? Is a new religious movement gaining converts from institutionally legitimized religions? Have two nation-states changed in their political opportunities for alliance? These questions differ from others more in their import for particular audiences than in their substance: answers potentially can be used to empower individuals, groups, even societies – by puzzling out the situational context, the motives and intentions of actors in the situation, and the social processes, conjunctures, and contingencies that shape future possibilities.

In addressing questions of value concern, social theory and unique explanatory and interpretive accounts compete in explicating the circumstances to be understood historically and into the projected future. But the import of either theoretical or contingent accounts has to do with their heuristic capacity to inform situational analyses and prescriptions for action. For instance, it is conceivable that two accounts of patriarchy might be roughly equivalent in their plausibility, but that one of them offered a striking general challenge to conventional strategies of feminist politics, while the other was politically silent or failed to offer any widely relevant "rules of experience." Groups involved in political struggles may view questions of ultimate explanation or theoretical validity as beyond timely adjudication. Indeed, because situational analysis has a compelling concern with understanding ongoing events on the basis of particular values, any explanatory or interpretive account, theoretical or otherwise, need not be comprehensive. On a pragmatic basis, accounts with important political implications will prove more worthy of attention. Their value will depend on their potential for yielding not only truth, but also meaningful understanding and empowerment. Therefore, social theories constructed as case-pattern models that parallel empirical cases may be favored over analytic-variable theorizing, because they offer analogues especially meaningful to actors confronting concrete situations. Accounts are useful only insofar as they offer salient bases of intervention. Value concerns thus drive narrative to separate the wheat of usable knowledge about a situation from the chaff of information about other factors, even causally robust ones.

Specific history

Historians are not typically concerned with the present situation; periodization draws the curtain to a close much earlier. Nor do they usually orient analysis on the basis of explicit value concerns. And although writing about the grand march of world history is a venerable tradition, few historians attempt it. Instead, inquiry typically is directed to understanding what Max Weber called an "historical individual," which can be defined as a relatively self-contained set of events, sequences, patterns, or outcomes, rendered coherent by invocation of them as meaningful (e.g., "the Cold War"). The degree to which a historical individual as an object of inquiry is constituted "intrinsically" – that is, on the basis of an observer's lifeworldly orientation to historical social actors' convergent invocation of events – or "extrinsically," through inquiry's own objective frame of reference, is both a philosophical issue (discussed in chapter 3) and an empirical question of how inquiry is carried out. In relation to alternative ways of construing a historical individual, the practice of "specific history" is aligned with the "intrinsic" object, whereas "extrinsic" objects are the theoretically constructed themes of "configurational history," discussed below. That is, the practice of specific history is based on the *verstehende* project of identifying intrinsic sociohistorical objects meaningful to historically located individuals who participated in events subject to analysis through emplotment.

Any specific history is framed by an act of colligation that throws into relief a sociohistorical object such as feudalism, the Renaissance, or, more concretely, the Portuguese colonial enterprise, the Tai Ping rebellion, or the Dreyfus affair. But even if there is an intrinsic basis for a sociohistorical object, colligation is a value-based act. That is, because the plots of unfolding life are manifold and overlapping, any object of inquiry, even an intrinsic one, is framed by a criterion of relevance that delimits a particular specific history rather than other ones that could be colligated – even in relation to roughly the "same" set of events or "different" events involving some of the same actors. Acts of colligation that yield topics of specific history thus vary widely in their breadth of focus. Carlo Ginzburg's study of a single sixteenth-century person, Victoria Bonnell's analysis of early twentieth-century Russian radicalism, E. P. Thompson's account of poachers in eighteenth-century English forests, Rebecca Scott's treatment of slave emancipation in Cuba – these studies all deal with "intrinsic" sociohistorical objects.[8] That is, each concerns actual episodes that were meaningful to historical actors before they became meaningful as objects of inquiry.

The boundaries of specific history can be located by examining circumstances beyond which it becomes difficult to argue for the existence of an intrinsic object. Along the line of transition to an extrinsic object, the object of inquiry increasingly is colligated independently of its coherence for historical actors: some objective analytic distinction is used to assert the connectedness of phenomena independently of an intrinsic plot. Two themes of inquiry – cultural and structural – evidence the transition. A structural history such as Georges Duby's *Annales*-school investigation of medieval European rural economy identifies a relatively stable pattern that changes only slowly over centuries. Here the object of inquiry engulfs a multitude of intrinsic plots in an enduring world recognizable to its participants. The analysis describes, as it were, structure without event history, generic plots without developmental action, repetition as meaning. Other structural histories move beyond even constructions of generic intrinsic objects: they point to the "drift" of structures in ways held to lie beyond the consciousness of individuals, or they identify structural shifts over long periods of time that transcend the scales of intrinsic plots. In either case, inquiry moves beyond the ordering by narrative discourse that is characteristic of specific history.[9]

Cultural history spans a similar divide. For questions of culture, determining whether the object is intrinsic or extrinsic amounts to asking whether individuals and groups draw upon, rework, and transmit cultural meanings, techniques, tools, and the like in ways that can be reconstructed through narrative plot linkages. Intrinsic cultural history is a variant of specific history that concentrates on the socially mediated historical lineages of cultural replication, innovation, and diffusion, and their consequences in unfolding time. Culture does not float amorphously; it is tied to its bearers, their predecessors, and successors. Thus, in my own study of Jim Jones's Peoples Temple as an apocalyptic religious social movement that ended in mass suicide, I traced a number of meaningful cultural elements (for example, the idea of a "promised land") not only in relation to their historical sources, but, more importantly, in relation to the specific conduits by which their meanings became transmuted as they were adopted within Peoples Temple. By contrast, extrinsic cultural history does not identify specific action conduits of cultural transmission and diffusion. Either lacking any identifiable intrinsic historical connections or lacking interest in them, it must employ some other device of plot, series, or analysis to arrange a discussion of cultural objects and practices (e.g., cultural histories of privacy in different historical epochs, sexuality over centuries, dieting in heterogeneous circumstances).[10]

The hallmark of specific history thus can be fixed precisely in its analysis of events held to be interconnected intrinsically – in unfolding historical time. Plot occupies the central place in narrative as the discourse whose regimen gives order to a coherent practice. In these terms, successfully addressing Lawrence Stone's questions of "what happened" and "how" yields at least preliminary understanding. Much debate about specific histories focuses precisely on Stone's questions. For example, if it were possible to identify European feudalism in its most significant features, controversies about why it was transformed or supplanted would be easier to resolve.[11] For more narrowly circumscribed intrinsic objects, the questions of what happened and how are just as salient and even more glaring when unresolved. Thus, important questions remain open to debate about how (and which) Nazis organized the "final solution" of genocide, and what role other Germans played in carrying out the policy. Similarly, for all that is documented about the assassination of John F. Kennedy, more precise information about Lee Harvey Oswald and other key figures might shed further light on the question of whether there was a conspiracy and, if so, what its social sources were. In short, the construction of narrative and its assertion of plot give overall shape to specific history. Yet narrated plot does not stand apart from either social theory or explanation and interpretation.

Theory comes into play by two different articulations. In the first place, it may inform the colligation that frames the intrinsic sociohistorical object. Thus concepts such as "the Renaissance," "English Methodism," "ragtime music," "American frontier expansion," and "Italian fascism" are formed by the juxtaposition of intrinsic historical developments with more general theoretical concepts and ideal types.[12] We are always in danger of becoming the prisoners of concepts along these lines. Second, social theory surfaces at particular junctures in specific history via narrative's invocation of models, generalizations, and rules of experience. Such application may occur in a variety of ways. Potentially, a social theory may provide an overall explanation or interpretation for a specific history. Thus, once the expansion of the American frontier is identified via an "epochal concept," a social theory, for instance about migration or ideology, might be put forward as a general account of plot development. Here, a theoretical model offers a way of subsuming unique events by describing them in terms of the operation of general processes under specific circumstances.[13] But such bold explanation of an intrinsic object runs a high risk of being labeled "reductionist." More typically, the uses of social theory in specific history are not so encompassing.

How else, then, does theory get invoked? One way, widely practiced, is to draw loosely upon theory for the conceptual vocabulary that organizes a detailed narrative, invoking such terms as class, mobility, bureaucracy, solidarity, and so forth. A more explicit use of theory was anticipated in chapter 3. There, I suggested that narrative is resilient in its capacity to juxtapose diverse events, processes, factors, and actions – the weather, transportation conditions, collective sentiments of a given social stratum, the psychological quirks of an individual, and so on. Within a narrative of specific history, theory helps distinguish features salient to a study that can be accounted on a general basis from those that seem unique. In my specific history of Jim Jones and Peoples Temple, for example, I found that the group's demise in murder and mass suicide at Jonestown, Guyana, in 1978 had spawned numerous popular histories that amounted to exposés of psychosis, brainwashing, and extortion. In the analysis, comparison with theoretical (and sometimes empirical) typifications helped locate Peoples Temple sociologically. Thus, following the *verstehende* method of Max Weber, a theoretical model of the "charlatan" as a meaningful ideal type offered a basis for hermeneutic analysis of whether Jones's actions could be subsumed under such a motive structure.[14] In a different way, typifying contemporary practice within the public relations industry in the United States yielded an empirical baseline with which to compare Temple PR practices. In general, analogical comparison with theoretical and empirical models helped ferret out the more general social and cultural dynamics at work in Peoples Temple and its conflicts with its detractors.

Theoretical concepts thus can help construct the "empirical" object of inquiry under discussion in a narrative's plot, and theoretical models can help account for specific events and processes. But these uses of theory still leave unexplained residuals: to attempt a more or less complete derivation of narrative from theory would amount to a universal history (described in chapter 7). When the power of both narrative and social theory are exhausted in a specific history, the core of explanatory and interpretive discourse – its concern with contingency and uniqueness – becomes especially salient. Here, analysis is especially directed to what can be called "break points," where the task is to clarify why plot unfolds in one direction or another according to situation, conjunctures, accidents, and the wills of individuals. To pursue the example of Peoples Temple, social theory established analogical continuities between Peoples Temple and other sociohistorical phenomena. But these shared features were hardly sufficient to account for the unique outcome – the murders and mass suicide at Jonestown. Narrative therefore depended upon adjudicating alternative theories of plot based on critical interpretive and explanatory questions about contingencies and sequences of unfolding events. To take a substantive issue, popular histories of Peoples Temple had assumed that a *correlation* between the timing of adverse publicity and a mass migration of Temple members from the United States to Guyana implied that the publicity had *caused* the migration. This depiction both flowed from and reinforced a plot that cast the Temple's opponents as heroes determined to liberate Jones's captives. More careful analysis showed, however, that the migration preparations began *before* the adverse publicity, thus could not be explained by them, and therefore required an alternative plot.[15]

In its typical practice, specific history centers on narrative that establishes plot in relation to theoretical discourse and contingent explanation and interpretation. But there are many possible variations in the approach, and these depend on the distinctive ways that narrative incorporates theory and accounts of contingency. In a strategy tipped in the direction of social theory, Mark Traugott offers detailed narrative and contextual explanation as a basis for evaluating alternative hypotheses about the 1848 political upheaval in France. Traugott's narrative seeks to explain why "armies of the poor" fought on both sides during the June insurrection. As I showed in chapter 5, the narrative is knit together by theoretical discourse that proposes class-based, age-cohort, and organizational hypotheses about the divergent actions of the Mobile Guard and the insurrectionists associated with the Parisian National Workshops. This analysis, however, rests not only on conventional tests of hypotheses, but also on the clarification of contingencies that shape the break points of narrative. As Traugott comments,

The problem of specifying just when, within a period of a few weeks, the change in workshops' loyalty occurred may at first glance seem of minor interest. Yet, fixing the approximate moment is actually of the greatest significance, for in order correctly to associate the shift in allegiance with the political events that motivated it, one must establish its timing with relative precision.[16]

Ultimately, Traugott accounts for the divergence of allegiances between the Mobile Guard and the workshops' insurgents by contingent explanation of events that are interpreted as reinforcing authority within one organization and leading to its collapse in the other.[17] Despite the differences, both Traugott's analysis of the June 1848 insurrection and my study of Peoples Temple clarify narratives by adjudicating among batteries of theories and contingent accounts that mediate alternative theories of plot. In ideal-typical terms, they are both specific histories ordered by their narratives.

Compared to these studies, Lynn Hunt's study of the French Revolution of 1789, *Politics, Culture, and Class in the French Revolution*, represents a transitional case. Basically, Hunt argues that the transformation of political culture during the French revolutionary period produced new, essentially ideological, ways of thinking and acting. As a cultural history of a revolutionary movement, the study describes widespread changes within a short time. But these changes are not narrated as a single coherent plot, even though there is good reason to suspect that the changes are intrinsically linked. Instead, Hunt uses a series of hermeneutic and structural analyses of specific materials, such as the writings of the marquis de Sade, to detail thematic shifts in rhetoric, symbols, images, and the social strata that became politically mobilized during the revolutionary period. In place of formulating a narrative that links diverse events, Hunt advances a theoretical metanarrative to link her various analyses of the revolutionary political unconscious and its social bearers.[18] Hunt's study thus is a demonstration that detailed event history can employ a metastructure of extrinsic analysis, even if the phenomena described might reasonably be asserted to have intrinsic linkages. Perhaps with richer data, Hunt would have pursued a specific history more concerned with intrinsic linkages. In any case, her study evidences a procedure that addresses a recurrent problem of specific history. Often, the historical record is too thin for inquiry to tell "what happened" through narrative, even though an intrinsically ordered plot could be constructed if adequate historical evidence were available. Under conditions of limited access to detailed information, a theoretical metanarrative offers an alternative narrative strategy that can maintain specific history's primacy of plot, but in a way that begins to approximate a different practice.[19]

Configurational history

The invocation of theoretical metanarrative in specific history marks a passage to configurational history, where the convergence of independent historical events is theorized in a way which transcends meaningful connections among events themselves. Sociohistorical models are constructed in relation to a particular epochal shift, transition, or transformation deemed culturally significant and therefore worthy of investigation.[20] Such models theorize phenomena in terms that range in scale from world-historical change, such as the consolidation of industrial capitalism, to more narrow shifts, such as the emergence of a particular constellation of gender roles in Brazil or the emergence of consumer culture in the United States. Consistent with the identification of configurational history as a methodological practice, the difference between it and specific history is not a matter of scale, but of approach. Whereas specific history proceeds by way of intrinsic narrative, configurational history is concerned with an extrinsic object of inquiry – one that may be theorized independently of the intentional actions of particular individuals and groups. The distinction is only a relative one, but it is significant. Whereas the balance of inquiry in specific history is tipped toward using narrative to analyze unfolding situations as they are meaningful to actors involved, by contrast, configurational history tilts analysis toward the interplay of diverse events and phenomena, and their unintended consequences.

As an ordered hybrid of discourses, configurational history is an exercise in theorizing history, and this is a project carved out in relation to a particular observer's lifeworldly or objective frame of reference (see table 1.1). Under this dispensation, meaningful social action may be relevant to analysis, but its relevance becomes established not on the basis of intrinsic connections among events, but in relation to an extrinsically defined analytic puzzle. The central task is to describe the salient features of an object of inquiry and decompose that object into a series of historically emergent components, each of which is held to be contributory or necessary, but not sufficient, for the phenomenon to emerge. The identification of the sociohistorical object and the component changes theorized as its basis yields an analytic framework for the causal or interpretive investigation of configurational change by throwing into relief issues that need to be pursued. Each component change identified can become the subject of its own subsidiary inquiry within the configurational inquiry. Logically, the practice involved in each of these subsidiary inquiries either approximates specific history (already discussed) or itself constitutes a configurational history subordinate to the thematic configurational history (thus, for example, a configurational history of the industrial revolution might be folded into a configurational history of modern capitalism). These subsidiary inquiries, along with contingent explanations or interpretations of their interplay, are synthesized through a metanarrative that links them to the more encompassing theorized history of configurational change.

Configurational history makes it possible to investigate broad features of social change without resorting to "evolutionary stage theories" or universal histories. It is on this basis that Max Weber offered his comprehensive analyses of both rationalization and capitalism.[21] Examining a controversy between Randall Collins and Wolfgang Schluchter about how to reconstruct Weber's analysis helps to clarify the range of configurational inquiry by revealing alternative strategies for analyzing configurational shifts. Collins's reconstruction challenges an "essentially idealist" thesis about the significance of the Protestant ethic (itself largely a product of Talcott Parsons's "normative" reading of Weber). What Collins calls Weber's "last theory of capitalism" amounts to a configurational framework in which there were "ultimate conditions," "background conditions," and "intermediate conditions"; the interaction and fulfillment of these conditions is theorized to have resulted in the "components of rationalized capitalism" – i.e., "unrestricted markets," a "free labor force," "rationalized technology," and "entrepreneurial organization of capital." The emergence of modern "rational" capitalism is derived from the concatenation of diverse changes in the ancient world and the medieval West – the emergence of double-entry bookkeeping, the rise of absolutism, the linkage of salvation with worldly duty, and so forth.[22]

Wolfgang Schluchter disputes Collins's claim of a "last" theory by arguing that Weber worked "within a conceptual framework that was beyond the alternatives of materialism and idealism." In contrast to Collins's account of the concatenation and interplay of a discrete set of historically specific factors (which included "idealist" factors),

Schluchter offers a more formal typological specification of successive historical configurations, by identifying typological shifts in dimensions such as domination, ethics, and law.[23] He describes the systematic underpinnings of Weber's analysis (in a way that Weber did not spell out) in order to emphasize that Weber's total project was concerned not just with explaining a discrete set of circumstances, but with constituting a historically oriented typological framework that could be used to compare capitalism both with prior historical configurations and with alternative patterns of development. In Schluchter's reconstruction, configurational history not only identifies a unique configuration and its antecedents; its typological social theory identifies the relevant range of structural possibilities. Configurational history thus becomes linked with a more general theoretical framework that can be employed in other inquiries. My point here is not to establish the "real" character of Weber's project, but to show that configurational analysis may be based on lesser or greater formalization of models.

Few studies match the temporal and developmental scale of Weber's practice, but the projects of Perry Anderson and Michael Mann do, and in ways that demonstrate its range of possibilities. In *Passages from Antiquity to Feudalism*, Anderson offered a configurational analysis of factors that transformed the Mediterranean and Europe in the wake of the Roman Empire's collapse. His explanation is quintessentially configurational: it depicts feudalism as a concatenation, specifically, a "balanced synthesis" of elements derived from Germanic communal social organization in conjunction with the social formation of Rome in decline. Like Weber, Anderson proceeds typologically, by identifying the salient features of the social formations in question, and, like Weber, he employs comparison, in his case, to demonstrate the deviations from the "balanced synthesis" – regions that failed to produce feudalism in its fullest sense.[24]

At a world-historical level, Michael Mann's *tour de force* on the history of power follows a similar configurational method. Mann decomposes power into a number of salient, historically contingent aspects such as "extensiveness" and "intensiveness" of power. In turn, and like Weber, he wields such distinctions in analysis of historically differentiated spheres, i.e., politics, the military, economics, and religion.[25] Because Mann is concerned with concrete developments of power, he does not deal in abstract "factors" and "forces." Instead, he ties his analysis to the realities of social situations as diverse as persecution of early Christians and the sixteenth-century erosion of the lord–vassal relation in England. Yet since the emergence of power has not involved its continuous exercise in time, power has no *specific* history, and Mann identifies an analytic framework of "stages" that amount to functionally specified "inventions" in the exercise of power. Mann's protestations to the contrary, in his analysis power becomes something of a functional abstraction. But this is not the intellectual sin that Mann believes it to be; abstraction is an inherent feature of any attempt to consolidate discontinuous events in an extrinsic history framed in theoretical terms. Precisely through configurational analysis, Mann is able to propose a multifactor explanation of power, rather than forcing diverse events and processes into a coherent theoretical matrix that subsumes history by tracing all explanations back to some putatively primal source.

Configurational history has several attractions. It can address the "big" questions of historical development without resorting to value-laden metaphysical schemes or teleological theories. A value interest informs inquiry at the outset, but once an object of cultural significance is defined, inquiry moves back and forth between empirically oriented theory and the historical record; thus configurations are "sociohistorical models" that "involve historical dynamics and are not just static descriptions of structural properties."[26] The absence of a propelling metaphysic – either of God or of history as totalized systemic process – accords with a philosophical commitment to the idea that history is open-ended. Mann's work, for example, leaves room for the possibility that significant historical changes are partly the result of "accidents." Beyond these value-based and "philosophical" considerations, there are pragmatic ones. In the face of manifold events and processes, configurational history offers an efficient strategy for streamlining analysis. Whereas in specific history, intrinsic narrative balances theory and contingent explanation and interpretation, in configurational history, the theoretically constructed object of inquiry orders how a metanarrative zeros in on "break points" – historical shifts that warrant intensive analysis. These break points in turn have to be investigated by nested narratives (either specific histories or narrower configurational histories) directed to the sequences, interactions, and accidents of interplay among multiple historical developments.

Optimally, configurational history is a practice directed to discerning culturally significant patterns of development on the basis of theoretically informed empirical reasoning. But the developmental elements linked by its analysis can be disparate, and, in any case, the object of inquiry has to be understood as a theoretical construction. Therefore the approach is particularly vulnerable to the deconstructionist charge that the object of inquiry results from "transcendent" staging devices imposed by the author.[27] Configurational history draws on more specific histories, but it is necessarily established on the terrain of metanarrative, where claims to test alternative plots are not particularly persuasive. The configurational enterprise thus injects into inquiry a dimension of explanation and interpretation that cannot be adjudicated solely by historical evidence. For this reason, arguments about the conjunctural, causal, or functional properties of configurational histories are (or should be) explicitly undertaken as contestations about the logic and adequacy of theoretical metanarratives.

Historicism

Weber and others of his generation consolidated their practices in response to the *Methodenstreit* – itself in part a critical reaction to Leopold von Ranke's "scientific history." Ranke's approach must be understood as "historicist" by anyone who, like Weber, seeks to establish a strong working relation between social theory and historical inquiry. To be sure, as Reinhard Bendix has argued, Weber himself was a historicist, but this is true only in the broad sense that Weber refused to subordinate history to natural science models of inquiry.[28] Ranke's solution exemplifies historicism more specifically defined – as a distinctive practice of inquiry that treats the origins, genesis, and unique character of specific sociohistorical phenomena in empiricist, self-referential, and seemingly antitheoretical terms. A central puzzle concerns how Ranke could embrace both a commitment to "scientific" history and a belief in a Guiding Hand that manifests itself in the currents of each epoch's history.[29] To address this question is to reflect on what "historicism" could mean.

Historicism is a rich term that has been subjected to multiple and highly contradictory definitions. The greatest confusion stems from Karl Popper's unfortunate use of the term in *The Poverty of Historicism*, a confusion exacerbated by his eminence. The target of Popper's dissatisfaction seems to have been any approach that *theorizes* history, most particularly Marxism. But this usage confuses historicism – in its range of meanings for historians – with universal history as a practice that totalizes history within an overarching theoretical framework.[30]

Popper aside, historicism can be understood by typologically locating Ranke's approach as a coherent practice of inquiry, specified as an approach grounded in explanation and interpretation, articulated in relation to the discourses of values, narrative, and social theory. Basically, Ranke sought an empirically clarified narrative, and he shunned theoretical generalizations. Nevertheless, he could not finesse value-based and theoretical issues: he simply tried to resolve these issues in ways that gave primacy of position to the trademark of historicism – the formulation of an explanatory and interpretive account that treats its sociohistorical object as unique.

Two different Rankes have their own histories – one German, the other American. As both Georg Iggers and Peter Novick have shown, American historians through the 1950s tended to embrace Ranke's creed of reconstructing what actually happened, *wie es eigentlich gewesen*, as the foundation of a scientific history that would avoid metaphysics. However, this was a creative misreading of Ranke's position, and one which avoids that post-Kantian puzzle of how the object of inquiry is to be constituted. It is worth recalling that Ranke reacted against eighteenth-century German Enlightenment theoretical models of historical process. He wanted to avoid any systematic theoretical scheme. Nevertheless, he understood that the writing of history required more than stringing together analytically established facts. For this reason, in contrast to the Americans, Ranke's German audience – both supporters and opponents – saw Ranke as seeking to uncover history's coherence. Sometimes understood as the Idea or Spirit that animates surface events, this coherence has more recently been dubbed by structuralist historian Christopher Lloyd as either an "idealist emanation" or "sociocultural evolution." Thus, for Friedrich Meinecke, German historicism of the nineteenth century offered the

idea of the inimitable, unique individuality which develops according to its own vital laws and which cannot be comprehended by means of logical thinking, let alone through the mechanical law of causation, but rather has to be grasped, viewed, and experienced or re-experienced with the totality of all spiritual powers.[31]

Much as the Americans liked to invoke Ranke as the founder of scientific archival research, Meinecke's depiction raises a troubling question for historicism as scientific history – how does it add up to something other than the accumulation of facts?

The two issues that most impeded Ranke's quest for scientific history are the problem of selection – which of myriad events to include in a history – and the relation of individual and unique events to a more general process of development. On the one hand, Ranke thought that all events great and small, of one era and of another, would be equal in the mind of God, and he rejected either teleological history or any assumption of progress. On the other hand, Ranke affirmed faith in God's purpose for this world, and he sought to discern the workings of God in the actions of individuals and the histories of groups. Paradoxically, Ranke wanted to be objective because he saw history as something of a sign of God, which should not be prejudged in terms of mere earthly conceptions of divine will or manifest, and which therefore required careful research to discover. Ranke's solution to the problems of selecting events and identifying the directions of history was to advance a single theory of historical coherence by connecting discrete events with ultimate process from the outset. By positing that society's institutional elites (the papacy, powerful political elites in national states) represent unique unfolding spiritual essences of history,[32] he finessed the need for any further invocation of social theory, and in the bargain solved the problem of selection by linking particular histories as the manifestations presumed to reveal general historical development. In Ranke's hegemonic historicism, history's larger pattern at the same stroke renders coherent the multitude of events and hints at God's ineffable mystery in the destinies of nations and the Church. In effect, Ranke posited contingent interpretation and explanation as the stuff of historical analysis, linking them through his resolution of the value problem to a general metaphysical ontology of elite history as History writ large. Such a move at the outset infuses inquiry with a general theory – of elites as bearers of history – that forecloses any need for more specific social theories and, by its emphasis on historical distinctiveness, precludes any "universal history."

During the twentieth century, various "new" histories have invoked Ranke's historicism as a negative exemplar, but they often have rejected his specific ontology rather than the practice of historicism itself. Reaction against event histories of elites inspired both the *Annales* program of social and ecological history as well as much of the recent interest in social and cultural history. Even so, the ordering logic of historicism looks to contingent interpretation and explanation of phenomena in their own terms, and this approach continues to have broad appeal. In conventional Rankean terms, Gertrude Himmelfarb affirms both the centrality of power and politics as well as the importance of narrative not just of one event, "but precisely of a series of events chronologically connected so as to tell a story over a significant span of time." However, the range of historicist practice is by now considerably broader than Ranke's (or Himmelfarb's) solution. When the kernel of historicist practice is separated from Ranke's specific historicist dispensation, it becomes clear that the focus on religious and political elites is not intrinsic to the approach that Ranke championed. What matters is the consolidation of unique History predicated upon an ontological metaphysic of historical connectedness. The ontological content of this consolidation remains open. Thus, like Ranke, Marxist historicism scorns any formal theoretical "laws" of development; it differs from Ranke by discerning the direction of history in concrete class conflicts rather than the interplay of institutional elites. And this is hardly the only alternative. More generally, historicism can be centered on the study of social movements as barometers of historical development.[33] In these terms, historicism retains a rich potential for ordering inquiry, despite the low esteem in which it is supposedly held.

Shorn of its theological trappings, Ranke's solution was to colligate carefully analyzed unique events into a history "of" something based on a philosophical commitment to a general social theory about the linkages between contingent events and a larger historical process. This is a conventional procedure that continues to be widely followed by historians of diverse persuasions, but the objectivity of the procedure has become widely questioned, most convincingly in the deconstructive assault on historical narrative by Sande Cohen. His critique is based on the general point that, insofar as historians try to establish their objects of inquiry objectively but without resort to theoretical formalization, they rely on one or another topical metaphysic that is extra-empirical (and therefore, in the present study's terms, a matter of valuation). In the extreme, the metaphysic may invoke the hand of God, as Ranke did. But the theological trappings are incidental. As Cohen shows, the signature feature is an overarching self-referential narrative "of" an object that is consolidated as "history."[34]

In philosophical terms, history is one or another bootstrapped construction. As Cohen so starkly demonstrates, the basis on which Historical coherence can be asserted remains a stumbling block. Hans-Georg Gadamer's reflections on historicism suggest two alternatives. In general, Gadamer points to the hermeneutic circle at work in historicism's understanding of particular historical events and episodes in relation to a larger whole, while the larger whole is understood in terms of particularities. As Gadamer observes, one version of this interpretive quest to recapture the past has a romantic inspiration that would restore the relevance of a past wiped out by Enlightenment reason. On the other hand, if historicism becomes legitimated as objective science, as Ranke wanted, Gadamer concludes that it universalizes the "discrediting of all prejudices" and thus eclipses the self-understandings of "traditions." This tension – between historicism as the recapture and self-understanding of "our" history versus scientific historicism – remains highly salient today, for it frames a basic struggle over the content of history as moral discourse. Employing explanation or interpretation, historicism consolidates a claim to account for the unique meaning of a given narrative by invoking larger moral stakes. But either Enlightenment or enduring (or invented) traditions can define the moral stakes. Thus, without ever venturing beyond historicism as a practice of inquiry, we can trace endemic struggles concerning whose agenda is to define the value discourse of historicism's history. Such, indeed, is a standard topic of historiography.[35]

Historicism offers moral drama on an unstable philosophical basis, in a hermeneutic circle open as to the source of its coherence. It thus should come as no surprise that the practice is subject to periodic reinvention as "new" history, and to manifold claims concerning what "real" history *is*. To survey the possibilities would amount to a historiography of grand narrative of the sort framed by Dorothy Ross.[36] That project is beyond the present scope, but examining several exemplars that Ross cites suggests the range of historicist practice today.

Eric Hobsbawm's *The Age of Extremes*, published in 1994, works self-consciously in the genre of a jeremiad. The book employs a solidly historicist device of thematic coherence – periodization – as a framework for sketching major geopolitical, social, economic, technological, cultural, and military developments of the twentieth century. Hobsbawm is thus able to analyze large-scale historical forces – the Great Depression as the catalyst for the rise of both fascism and Franklin D. Roosevelt, the importance of the Soviet Union's Red Army for allied victory over Germany, the consequences of agricultural biology and chemistry for the end of the peasantry as a world class. By mapping a complex web of forces and events, Hobsbawm consolidates a vision of a shared world in unfolding time. The result is a history of "the Short Twentieth Century from 1914 to 1991" – from an "age of catastrophe" beginning with the First World War and ending with the Second, through a "golden age" of economic and social change and political decolonization that ended in the 1970s, toward the end of the short century – "a new era of decomposition, uncertainty, and crisis" marked by demographic and ecological pressures, the destabilization of the Soviet bloc, and doubts concerning the salience of democracy as a political model for non-western states.[37]

A more conventionally upbeat historicist study, Gordon Wood's 1991 book *The Radicalism of the American Revolution* describes "a momentous upheaval that not only fundamentally altered the character of American society but decisively affected the course of subsequent history." Here, the sense of national history and its moral significance is palpable. Wood's account ranges widely into social, cultural, economic, and religious histories of North America, but his central agenda is to claim that the American Revolution as a social revolution was neither narrowly concerned with political independence nor conservative in its interests. At points Wood invokes population growth, migration, and commercial expansion as master trends, but he holds the diverse discussions of his narrative together by a strong thread that follows what amounts to a telos of change begetting revolutionary change. "In the end," he argues, "the disintegration of the traditional eighteenth-century monarchical society of paternal and dependent relationships prepared the way for the emergence of the liberal, democratic, capitalistic world of the early nineteenth century." Wood's telos is a human and social one, and it has an ironic denouement not unlike the story that Perry Miller once told of the Massachusetts pilgrims' "errand into the wilderness." In Wood's account of the eighteenth- and early nineteenth-century formation of an American national society, the revolutionaries aimed to consolidate republicanism over monarchy, but their success unleashed forces for democratization more radical than they intended, and these forces could not be contained.[38]

A quite different kind of study suggests both the resilience of historicism, as well as the malleability of "power" as an ontology of the social that can be used to constitute "history." *City of Dreadful Delight*, by Judith Walkowitz, is not a grand narrative at all in the tradition of Hobsbawm or Wood. Indeed, it is not even a developmental narrative. Nevertheless, Walkowitz is concerned with power, specifically in a feminist and Foucaldian sense, which she explores via discourses of sexuality in urban space. Although *City of Dreadful Delight* "observes chronological boundaries, it does not proceed in linear fashion." Instead, Walkowitz "maps out a dense cultural grid" by juxtaposing narratives of sexual danger in Victorian London (Jack the Ripper and the "Maiden Tribute" exposé of prostitution) and sexual exploration (the sexually liberated Eleanor Marx, Karl Pearson in the Men and Women's Club). These narratives do not completely coalesce either intrinsically via their connections on the ground nor extrinsically, on the basis of a theoretical argument concerning linkage. Instead, their juxtaposition establishes something of a poststructuralist tableau that displays how narratives in the social world rework both popular culture melodramas of narrated sexualities and practiced sexual sensibilities. If Hobsbawm offers an enlightenment jeremiad, if Wood offers an invented tradition of democratic enlightenment, Walkowitz works in a way like Gadamer's romantic historian, but with irony, to "recapture" something of the sexual anxieties and aspirations of Victorian London, so that we may experience something of that historical moment with all its ambiguous resonances for our own day.[39]

The diversity of these exemplars is suggestive of how idealist and scientific strands of Ranke's program coexist in many contemporary historians' practices. So long as inquiry refuses the value commitment of situational history or the theoretical totalization of universal history, and insofar as it resists specific and configurational practices, the alternative is a scientific historicism of contingent interpretation and explanation about a historical reality deemed to have an existence independent of the analytic practices that frame inquiry – events as they "actually" were. Ranke's philosophical solution oddly resonates with the critique of it by Sande Cohen: the claim to a historical reality ontologically prior to its investigation can be sustained only on a metaphysical basis. This convergence of views suggests three conclusions about realist assumptions and the historicism that they inform.

First, although idealism and science are often counterposed in debates among historians, they are two poles of a single overall practice, tied together by the shared interest in consolidating a topic beyond the intentionalities of individuals, but without resorting to thoroughgoing social theoretical constructionism. At one pole, idealist historicists like Meinecke will embrace an intuitionist grasp of historical individualities and deride science as impoverished in its capacity to understand the inner connections that give history its force. Conversely, scientific historians who want to use detailed empirical research to establish "what happened" will disdain obviously idealist narratives (in this, they are in the company of Ranke himself). These differences may seem striking, but they are dialectical ones: each depends for its existence on a secret embrace of the repressed other – idealism in its claim of objectivity, science in its metaphysical object – in a more encompassing logic of historicism that fuses the two of them in the pursuit of idiographic accounts.

Second, the metaphysical character of "History" (for example, "the" history of the United States) even at the "scientific" pole accounts in large measure for both the resilience and the intractable conflicts of historicist inquiry. Because the "aboutness" of realist history is established metaphysically, narrative is open to radical disputation about how the object of inquiry is to be constructed in the first place. Much historical argumentation concerns not facts or even historical sequences. It addresses the relation of facts and sequences to "historical reality," when that reality itself is a metaphysical construction open to contestations of inquiry. Especially when historicism is tilted toward its scientific pole, the metaphysical aspects are suppressed, with the result that metaphysical argumentation becomes transmuted into arguments for the superiority of one narrative over another. Such arguments are about which story is told, not which story is true.

Third, various proclamations of "new" histories over the years often amount to the old historicism applied to new topics. As I pointed out in chapter 3, Fernand Braudel's formulation of the *Annales* vision did not abandon objective temporality; instead, it broadened the canvas of conventional political history by including a diverse range of social, institutional, and ecological events within a multiscale yet realist framework of linear time. Like Braudel's, much other work within the *Annales* tradition and social histories inspired by it has been resolutely antitheoretical. In these practices, "new" history shares the historicist problematic. As with historicism more generally, arguments concern the metaphysical constitution of the object of inquiry or, in other words, the focus and style of narrative that emerges from the facts woven together, chosen in relation to manifold events. Ranke had hoped to establish an objective basis for inquiry about the unique. But once the metaphysical basis of scientific realism is acknowledged, historicist inquiry is relativized by social constructionist disputes over the "proper" realist metaphysic. The recurrent debates among historians about agendas of inquiry thus are the perverse product of thoroughgoing historicism.

These points suggest that historicism will be the site of continuing struggle. Indeed, the struggle is now renewed not only by the turn toward historicity in the social sciences, but also by the historicist turn in literary criticism – a convergent textual and material historicism represented here by *City of Dreadful Delight*. For literary critics, the "New Historicism" – which Stephen Greenblatt also called "cultural poetics" – may be understood in the general sense as a turn away from ahistorical and highly theorized textual literary criticism, and toward consideration of the historical context of literature and the literary and discursive contexts of history. More specifically, Greenblatt wants to displace the older historicized literary criticism, which "tends to be monological; that is, it is concerned with discovering a single political vision, usually identical to that said to be held by the entire literate class or indeed the entire population."[40] Such a formulation resurrects on a more "textual" basis the nineteenth-century reaction against Ranke's narrowly political history. As with the once "new" social histories, a multivocal and intertextual New Historicism displaces a previously canonical literary historicism.

But insofar as cultural poetics simply reinvents historicism under a new metaphysic, it comes head up against the problematics concerning values, narrative, social theory, and interpretation and explanation embodied in the contemporary *Methodenstreit* of sociohistorical inquiry – a conflict ironically fueled by the literary critical deconstruction of historical narrative. In the New Historicism, as Fredric Jameson has it, "extreme theoretical energy is captured and deployed, but repressed by a valorization of immanence and nominalism that can either look like a return to the 'thing itself' or a 'resistance to theory.'"[41] The humanistic journey to history as anything like a "natural" practice of inquiry arrives at a destination that has disappeared. As Brook Thomas has shown, the New Historicism is burdened with the same problems as the old historicism, problems that Thomas rightly identifies with its assertion of temporal continuity and its constitution of an "objective" reality.[42] Cultural poetics, and cultural studies more generally, carry an important potential for erasing disciplinary boundaries, partly by emphasizing the sociohistorical character of humanistic inquiry. Yet these moves do not resolve the methodological problems of humanistic inquiry. Instead, they draw it into the shared terrain of inquiry in a more encompassing frame. Once texts are historicized, their understanding requires analysis of how writing and reading are socially embedded. Humanistic inquiries thus rightly become enterprises of sociohistorical inquiry, facing the same problematics that confront other practices. What they all share is the status of a cultural enterprise that cannot be reduced to any naturalized metaphysic – even a "fragmented" and "postmodern" one.

9   The prospects for inquiry

Contemporary conflicts over knowledge have an unfortunate effect: they reinforce ideological divisions at the very time when there is an opportunity to better understand the complex web of uneven connections that structure the entire range of inquiry's practices. To map the connections has been the project of the present study. I have shown how inquiry's formative discourses become differentially intertwined in various generalizing and particularizing methodological practices that are widely deployed in research. These practices and their shared discursive sources reflect seldom recognized but deep affinities among seemingly alien projects. Despite the affinities, however, it is apparent that inquiry cannot be reduced to any single overarching logic. Even projects that share the same research agenda, discipline, interdisciplinary enterprise, or emancipatory endeavor may diverge from one another in their methodological practices and the character of knowledge produced. The overall domain of sociohistorical inquiry is thus considerably less than unified.

When inquiry is understood in these terms, what are its prospects? To begin with, the map is not the territory. I have sought to explore the connected sources of inquiry's practices, not to "represent" inquiry comprehensively. The diversity is obvious. The practices initially identified in table 6.1 encompass both particularizing and generalizing orientations, used for the investigation of one or many cases, and they admit to the possibilities of both qualitative and quantitative data.[1] In exploring examples, I have drawn on historically focused studies. However, ethnographic and cultural studies also employ practices of the particularizing orientation and, indeed, comparative practices of the generalizing orientation are not solely the province of social scientists. In short, the typology of inquiry's practices bears wide relevance. Substantive topics of research are diverse, yet practices of inquiry are shared across the humanities, history, and the social sciences.

In the 1950s C. P. Snow famously worried about the gulf between "two cultures" – one humanistic, the other scientific. Today, even with the crisis of positivism and the rise of social and historical studies of science, the ideological demarcation between science and other inquiry remains virtually intact. But ideology notwithstanding, actual practices of inquiry can no longer be so neatly divided. The present study shows that despite presumed antipathies, seemingly divergent practices of inquiry are actually connected to one another in specifiable ways. Even if it does not violate pure reason as such, any practice of inquiry is constructed through one or another cultural *bricolage* of reasonings drawn together from heterogeneous formative discourses – values, narrative, social theory, and explanation and interpretation – each with its distinctive problematics open to multiple resolutions. Thus, no practice can claim the epistemological superiority of an unalloyed logic based on isolation from the contaminated reasoning that plagues other practices. In any of multiple dispensations, sociohistorical inquiry is an exercise in impure reason. Most fundamentally, history is never an atheoretical enterprise, and science is infused with value influences that shape the character of its generalizations.

The impurity of reason, however, does not imply a relativism in which separate practices produce autonomous kinds of knowledge, completely sealed off from one another's substantive and discursive critiques. To the contrary, because any practice is tied to multiple formative discourses, and because these discourses are also embedded within alternative practices, sociohistorical inquiry has the property of "integrated disparity." This property reflects an encompassing, complexly differentiated, unevenly articulated *communicative field* – a pandisciplinary realm of inquiry that I initially sketched in chapter 6. Previously, the implications of this communicative field for inquiry remained largely unexplored, in part because advocates of research programs, theories, and disciplinary boundaries tended to glorify their own practices and mystify the relationship of those practices to the wider communicative field. But the present study suggests that these postures are untenable.

Scholars in the humanities alternately embrace and reject both history and theory. Yet because the sociohistorical world can be analyzed in textual terms, literary critics bearing textual methods enter into the unfamiliar terrain of cultural studies about history and society. In this region, they are greeted with some hostility and faced with a predicament: either mount a paradoxically totalistic and relativizing argument that privileges texts, or take on the vagaries of inquiry about the relation of texts to other phenomena – technology, social control over distribution of material goods, processes of cultural group formation, etc.

The story for historians is a parallel one. Seemingly, the discipline has undergone dramatic revolutions. The grand narratives are now regarded with great suspicion, and political history has been supplanted (more often, displaced) by cultural history, labor history, women's history, subaltern history. Yet the "new" histories often amount to ideological and topical shifts, rather than reconstructions of practice. Ironically, the new historians can end up resurrecting the dilemmas of their predecessors. Social historians and postmodern historians alike perpetuate the suspicion toward social theory long worn as a badge of honor by more traditional historians, and for much the same reason – the desire to submerge issues of theory through the consolidation of a topic of inquiry and a style of narration. New historians as well as old resist breaking loose from the twin horns of their dilemma – historicism and universal history. They thus find it difficult to come to terms with the relations of values and theory to their relatively unformalized methodological practices.

Researchers in the social sciences endure a similar predicament. In the face of poststructuralism, social epistemology, feminist theory, cultural studies, and the welter of new narrativities, social scientists often seem more interested in sustaining narrow disciplinary practices of "normal science" by some new, postpositivist legitimation (or ignoring the epistemological issues altogether), rather than taking up the task of determining how inquiry might be reformed through critique of its practices.[2]

For those who advocate objective knowledge – whatever their disciplines – "foundationless" inquiry portends a hopeless relativism. Their worst fears are manifested in their favorite protagonists: deconstructionists and theorists of rhetoric whom they charge with failing to account for how inquiry yields any knowledge at all, along with those practitioners of cultural studies who abjure issues of truth in their pursuit of knowledge. To salvage science in the face of such critiques, philosophers sometimes have gravitated toward ontological realism as a basis for inquiry after the demise of positivism. Yet like the broadly poststructuralist critiques it opposes, realism affirms a general account that nevertheless privileges a particular project of inquiry to the exclusion of others, yet on a different basis than pure reason or empirical validation.[3]

For all the supposed refusal of totalizing theory in deconstruction, for all the rejection of foundationalism in postpositivist epistemology, insofar as they tend toward essentialist arguments, neither could resolve the performative contradiction of asserting either relativity as the one truth or one truth that claims to escape its conditioned relativity. They thus pose unfounded impediments to informed participation in the communicative field of sociohistorical inquiry under the conditions of "integrated disparity" revealed by the present study.

The Third Path

The hermeneutic deconstruction of sociohistorical inquiry makes it possible to consider the prospects of inquiry under the very conditions of diversity that protagonists demonstrate by their conflicting practices. Knowledge – including that gained in the present inquiry – is necessarily the fruit of the cultural reason used to produce it. Yet to acknowledge this point does not result in a performative contradiction. The present inquiry does not transcend the conditions of knowledge production anticipated in its own lifeworldly account of inquiry. Nor is the account on offer here the comprehensive "view from nowhere" repudiated by postmodern critics of objective knowledge. Those critics take as their target a particular modernist attempt to warrant or deny knowledge on the basis of a "correspondence" model of concept formation. But once the socially constructed status of concepts is admitted, once concepts are no longer claimed as "representational," once any totalization of a sociohistorical object is understood as only a heuristic of inquiry rather than a system of correspondences, then, finally, knowledge produced through inquiry can be recognized as a fragile and hardfought achievement – limited by resources, values, and the play of political interests, neither warranted by philosophical foundationalism nor denied by the critique of representation.

Pursuit of knowledge in the historicized lifeworld follows a Third Path that winds beyond the disjuncture between the modernist quest for truth and the postmodern displacement of its foundations. This path reaches a clearing where inquiries can be understood as one or another historically emergent practice in the lifeworld. Like other lifeworldly action, the actions of inquiry are meaningful and hence discursive. This claim is hardly novel. Others – among them, Michel Foucault, Richard Rorty, Dorothy Smith, and Jean-François Lyotard – have made much the same point.[4] The present study has simply drawn on this general insight to examine the discursive relations in sociohistorical inquiry. This inquiry into inquiry has not resolved logical problems on some philosophical basis, but neither has it arrived at the dead end marked by the self-contradictory logical assertion of relativism. And it has not reduced inquiry to the judicious practice of rhetoric applied to ideas, any more than it consolidates inquiry via some "local" realist ontology. Nor, as I will show in greater detail below, does the Third Path reach a stopping point at an abyss that isolates local practices of inquiry from one another. Instead, the Third Path takes a route that was missed in both the modernist quest for objectivity and various postmodern critiques. This route was already suggested by Max Weber in response to the late nineteenth-century *Methodenstreit*. As Weber held, perspectivity is a condition of knowledge. This view was refused within the dominant modernist disciplines in favor of a quest for objectivity. But less than fifty years after Weber's death in 1920, developments in philosophy, the history of science, and literary criticism began to identify the path of procedurally founded objectivity as a dead end for sociohistorical inquiry. Now the so-called postmodern turn away from the grand narratives of modernism either ends in relativism or it can be followed back to the junction where Weber stood, nearly a century ago. There, we find, the supposedly postmodern blur of discourses and perspectives already figures strongly in modern thought. As Lyotard has remarked, postmodernism is "not modernism at its end but in the nascent state, and this state is constant."[5]

For our own *Methodenstreit*, a social epistemology along Weberian lines recognizes inquiry as a lifeworldly phenomenon in its historical emergences, the internal problematics of its discourses, the combinatory relations among discourses, and the institutional structures of inquiry in particular disciplines, research programs, and practices. In these terms, histories (or archeologies) and ethnographies reveal cultures of inquiry – rationales of investigation that cannot be derived from pure reason, but still have meaningful bases. These revelations do not imply that knowledge is pursued in the absence of standards for its evaluation. The cultural practices that I have identified amount to alternative pathways to knowledge, each subject to distinctive kinds of scrutiny that weigh alternative claims to truth within their domains.

How are these alternative practices and the relations among them to be understood? On the basis of the present study, it is possible to consider the communicative field of sociohistorical inquiry as a domain woven together by complex relations between practices of inquiry and three levels "below" and "above" those practices: (1) *regimens* that resolve problematics within forms of discourse (e.g., value-neutrality as a resolution of formative discourse on values), (2) *relations* of affinity and transition among alternative practices, and (3) *assemblages* of research methodology – practices that "nest" various other practices (e.g., a universal history that draws on various other practices of specific and configurational history). Implications for the uneven integration of the overall communicative field can be drawn by sketching the relation of inquiry's practices to each other "level."

Regimens of discourse and the articulations of practice

Conflicts over the practice of inquiry stem in the first instance from contending regimens that differentially resolve problematics *internal* to any given discourse – on values, narrative, social theory, and explanation and interpretation. Any particular solution to a problematic within a formative discourse is a refusal of alternative possibilities. For example, pursuing objective explanation may yield increased technical control over empirical phenomena, but this knowledge is of value only for certain purposes, and other value commitments may have their own attractions. On other fronts, narrative has its genres of emplotment and its choices concerning intrinsic versus extrinsic constitution of its object, and there are multiple explanatory and interpretive ways of accounting for sociohistorical phenomena.

Even within any given discourse, there does not seem to be any *a priori* basis to adjudicate among wholly alternative regimens. Thus, as chapter 4 showed, any social theory constructs an object of inquiry in one way (for example, by use of systemic-function concepts), even though other conceptualization strategies (e.g., ideal types) and admixtures remain equally viable as ways of bringing aspects of sociohistorical phenomena into focus. Different regimens of theory yield alternative crosscutting principles for organizing how we apprehend the sociohistorical world.

Absent the definitive consolidation of a regimen ordering a problematic issue within a given form of discourse, all practices of inquiry appropriate particular regimens that coexist with alternative ones. Given multiple ordering regimens (that indeed go well beyond the possibilities sketched in the present study), any one discourse can be articulated in divergent ways with other discourses. Value discourse can either consolidate a metaphysical telos around which narrative is draped or it can issue narrative a pressing demand for knowledge about a particular set of historical events. Narrative may either provide the core axis of analysis for social theory or it may serve as a rhetorical device for considering theoretically deviant cases. Relations among discourses, in short, are manifold rather than determinate.

Any practice of inquiry – including the present one – routinely spans heterogeneous forms of discourse.[6] Typically, the points of articulation and subsumption among discourses' regimens are institutionally conventionalized in ways that make a practice appear "natural." Nevertheless, all conventions of practice constrain inquiry's possibilities in relation to other viable alternatives, and in this sense they are culturally arbitrary. The consequence is a condition of pluralism and perspectivism. That is, competing practices of inquiry – and cultural constructions of sociohistorical objects – necessarily remain in play.[7] For instance, because narrative cannot be definitively validated either only as an intrinsic form of discourse or only as an extrinsic one, any practice that appropriates one approach or the other (or both) cannot warrant the superiority of its knowledge over knowledge based on practices that resolve the problematic differently. Thus, a practice of analytic generalization that uses extrinsic narrative has no logically based privilege over a practice of historicism based on intrinsic narrative. This suggests why any assumption about a representational correspondence between concepts and reality runs into difficulties. Given the alternative viable ways of constituting inquiry in relation to the "same" object, even formally specified and realist theories with substantial explanatory power depend on culturally constructed concepts that draw out aspects of a phenomenon of salience to a particular research agenda. Because this is the state of play among alternative regimens of discourse today, there is no *a priori* basis for according primacy to any particular perspective, including the present one. However, the absence of any single practice's primacy spells not the end of inquiry but the point of departure for understanding inquiry in a relational way.

Relations among practices

Given variability in discursive regimens, any practice of inquiry may be elaborated in more than one way. For example, the practice of "universal history" straddles both the totalizing projects of modernist social theory and the grand narratives of modernist historians; its actual character depends on how the value problem is resolved and what metatheory of history is proposed. Similarly, alternative practices approximating the "application of theory" depend on the operative model of explanation and interpretation – value-neutral, value-objective, or so forth. Generally speaking, more nuanced subtypes and hybrid practices of inquiry are open to development. Thus, one way to create new kinds of knowledge is to elaborate practices that resolve the problematics of discourses and relations among them in novel ways. For example, it should be possible to:

- draw social theories of texts into intrinsic narratives in order to deepen understandings of relationships between cultural meanings and historical agency;

- employ narrative in ways that more self-consciously theorize the temporalities of events and social processes; and,
- enhance the power of critical theory by bringing value-based criteria of explanation and interpretation into stronger relation with substantive projects of analysis.

Beyond opportunities for innovative elaboration of any given practice, it is also important to recognize that various practices are not necessarily isolated from one another; they are often connected via corridors of transition based on alternative resolutions to shared problematics. One example of such a transition can be found in Wolfgang Schluchter's *Rationalism, Religion, and Domination: A Weberian Perspective*. In the terms of the present study, Schluchter can be said to chart a configurational history of rationalism, but his account is based on a typology that is formal rather than substantive. It thus begins to take on the teleological features of stage theories, and this possibility underscores the thin line that divides configurational history from universal history.[8] Other affinities among practices can be similarly identified. For instance, universal history differs from alternative generalizing practices most notably by its totalization of history via theory. But if the totalizing assertion is relaxed, the substantive questions of universal history may be addressed through macro-analytic generalization, application of theory, or contrasting comparison. That is, when assertions derived from a totalizing theory are separated from the practice of universal history, they can be evaluated by practices of generalizing inquiry that sidestep the problem of a nondisprovable discourse. In these and other ways, the relations between practices can be both fluid and interactive.

Assemblages of inquiry

Beyond the differential implications of alternative regimens within discourses and the possibilities of elaborating closely related hybrid and subtype practices, there is a third point – that alternative practices are not autonomous and mutually exclusive. Instead, practices often become bound up with – and within – one another. Even in a single study, different "moments" of analysis may call for the development of contrasts at one point, for situational analysis at another. I have already noted one such relationship: specific history is typologically differentiated from configurational history by the way that its object of inquiry is established. Specific history typically involves an attempt to construct an "intrinsic" object based on the immanent meanings of events and situations for historical actors. By contrast, configurational history identifies an analytic puzzle or theorized explanation "extrinsically" – that is, independently of its meaning for historical actors. Yet research often will mix these two enterprises, moving back and forth between a *verstehende* narrative about social actors and an analysis of analytic issues that are identified by way of a theoretical model. Beyond any given study, generalizing practices – as well as the particularizing practice of configurational history – are often secondary analyses that draw upon other studies as primary analyses. As these examples suggest more generally, the overall practice of a given research project can "nest" other practices within its enterprise. This means that the diversity of inquiry ranges far beyond any map of practices as ideal types.

Almost paradoxically, however, ideal types are well suited to identify the constitutive discourses and practices at work in nested practices. For example, Leonard Hochberg has drawn on the typology of practices presented here to argue that conventional understandings of Alexis de Tocqueville as an exemplary historical sociologist require reconsideration. In *Democracy in America*, Tocqueville might seem like the contrast-oriented comparativist *par excellence*, just as Tocqueville's study of the French Revolution could be cited as a classic example of configurational history. But Hochberg argues that these "modern" projects of inquiry are enmeshed within a universal history. Tocqueville saw the progress of democracy as a force divinely decreed, yet infused with perverse tendencies toward despotism. It is this universal history that lends moral force and explanatory power to Tocqueville's writings. As Hochberg observes, Tocqueville remains important today precisely because he cast empirical inquiry within a larger, enduring drama. But for many who admire Tocqueville, his grand narrative and his universal history remain invisible, and thus unavailable to scrutiny of how they structure the rest of his arguments.[9]

Hochberg's consideration of Tocqueville suggests a more general point: as analytic benchmarks, ideal types can be brought to bear at diverse "levels" of inquiry. This property of ideal-type analysis is important because the same problematics that originate in inquiry's practices can also be found in more complex assemblages. Any practice of inquiry, even a nested one, still depends on the articulation of different formative discourses with one another. There is, in other words, a "fractal" quality to inquiry: problematics that must be addressed within a given practice resurface when that practice is folded within a more encompassing practice. This point already seems obvious for any generalizing practice – say, contrast-oriented comparison – that draws on primary research from specific or configurational histories. Not only must the generalizing practice somehow shape its analysis in relation to regimens (e.g. value-neutral explanation or interpretive narrative) of discourses already embedded within the nested studies, it also must resolve problems of its own practice – how to construe explanation and interpretation, what to constitute as the object of narrative, and so forth.

These considerations about regimens of discourse, relations among practices, and assemblages of inquiry suggest an irony. Ever new practices and ever new constructions of substantive problems will come to the horizon, if for no other reason, because the unfolding play of social and cultural forces yields historically unprecedented ways of life. Yet despite the virtual inevitability that inquiry will follow new practices, practitioners also will invoke old canons, established conventions, and persistent and invented traditions of inquiry. And certain lifeworldly conditions will endure: the differends among the discourses will continue to yield circumstances of impure reason in which inquiry is perspectival, encumbered by methodological problems open to alternative resolutions, and subject to Derrida's "supplementation" – the deconstructive effort to reveal what is elided by a practice of inquiry intended to produce knowledge.

Under these conditions, any innovative resolution of one constellation of problematics tends to move inquiry into confrontation with other problematics. "New" practices of inquiry can be promoted as correctives to previously conventional practices, but old problems (albeit "fresh" ones) are likely to surface. This is the case because the problematics are more general than any particular practice, since they derive from enduring contentions within and between multiple forms of discourse ordered by alternative regimens. Inquiry is like a kaleidoscope: each turning of the rim, each shaking of the pieces inside creates a new vision by way of a unique constellation among the elements. The possible practices of inquiry are infinite, but longstanding problematics tend to be revisited on any new approach. This is already evident in the "new historicism" that shifts from the internalist examination of bounded texts toward exploration of textual interplay in the sociohistorical world. The escape from the ahistorical and transcendent construction of texts as cultural objects is to be applauded, but it opens Pandora's box: the "new" historicism either carries the baggage of the "old" historicism, or it moves to an alternative practice of inquiry, itself with a distinctive resolution of the problem of values, the regimen of narrative, and so on. In short, any reconstructive practice of inquiry will confront new problems as it solves old ones.

Choices and developments of practice

Despite the perspectival character of inquiry, practices and assemblages of inquiry are not so idiosyncratic as to produce knowledge within totally relativistic cells in a tower of Babel. To make such a claim would be self-contradictory and essentialist. However, alternative practices do move the thread of inquiry in divergent directions. An important question thereby arises about what basis there might be for choosing one practice over another. Absent agreement about the ultimate purpose of inquiry, choosing a practice depends on affirming the power and relevance of the knowledge that can be obtained through it. But this begs the question – power and relevance for what and to whom? Alternative practices may each meet logical standards of pure reason, yet produce perspectival knowledge. Because perspectival practices are culturally arbitrary, the promotion of any one practice amounts to a kind of special pleading – sometimes not only for the practice itself, but for a research agenda elaborated through it. Each practice of inquiry has its own cultural standards of validation, and each is capable of producing knowledge, but all knowledge is not equally valued by all audiences. Here, the pragmatics and politics of inquiry are important.

Researchers who are eclectic in recognizing the potentials of various practices of inquiry may tailor their methodologies to the questions at hand. The practices of inquiry are cultural tools, and the choice among them is a matter of formulating a workable strategy of research. The practice of situational history, for example, can produce knowledge to help advance broadly political interests. By contrast, inquiry with less political stakes will focus on knowledge relevant to substantive and theoretical questions. Here, practices deemed suspect in some quarters may find their relevance in others. Historicism will always have its use when the task is to explore the distinctive character of a particular object of inquiry – especially when that object bears cultural or moral significance for a wide audience. Universal history has a different attraction: it can either formulate comprehensive social theory or propose a dynamic model of history. The nondisprovable and teleological tendencies of universal history notwithstanding, its practice can yield clearly formulated theories of historical change. Other approaches have their distinctive strengths. The application of theory can demonstrate a theory's power by its compelling analysis of diverse phenomena; specific histories will evaluate alternative accounts of a finite set of events; and contrast-oriented comparison can tease out the developmental pathways of similar cases under divergent conditions. Given these differential strengths, a researcher may have good reasons for using one practice rather than others to address particular questions at hand.

Nevertheless, certain practices have been especially prone to problematic usages, and they need to be approached with special caution. Despite the potential of universal history, it can easily become the province of an intellectual sect, and such sects tend to become sealed off from wider inquiry, thus diminishing the prospects for adjudication of their ideas vis-à-vis competing universal histories or any other formulations. The limitations of situational analysis are much the same, though the reasons are different: the practice depends for its salience upon an audience's shared value interest, and the significance of knowledge gained thus will depend on how widely the value interest is shared.

Historicism confronts a different challenge: the practice seems difficult to transcend. Even when the limitations of any given version of historicism become evident, if the critique of its historicist metaphysic only leads to the affirmation of a different one, the practice of historicism itself remains unchanged.[10] In diverse manifestations (in history, ethnography, and so on), the practice thus maintains the faith of a tradition that absorbs this or that critique by moving from one historicism to another – from political to cultural or literary historicism – without resolving the fundamental issues that generate the critique of the first historicism. Perhaps because historicism is averse to formal explication of presuppositions, it is not given to reconstruction of practice.

These criticisms of practices depend on a particular value criterion. It is one that opposes any insular and self-referential tendencies of inquiry, whether they arise in situational history, universal history, historicism, or anywhere else. Whatever local value the knowledge gained from these practices may have, if there is to be a broader communicative field, it will depend on practices of inquiry in which values are made explicit, where theoretical presuppositions – embedded in all inquiry – are spelled out, where narrative becomes more self-consciously employed in relation to its multiple modalities, where alternative interpretive and explanatory accounts are engaged on some common ground, and where the implications of evidence can be assessed. These preferences are general ones; they do not narrowly limit inquiry to a particular ontology, methodology, or theoretical framework. Instead, they promote the agones in which competing ideas are contested. How, then, do various practices advance these interests?

Aside from the universal history that depends on totalizing theory, all generalizing practices tend to promote contestation, because analysis of multiple cases raises questions about the adequacy of theories and the comparability of instances. However, it is also important to consider the stakes of contestation. Generalizing approaches sometimes theorize solely in terms of variables. When theories are formulated in statements like "as x increases, y decreases" or "wealth is a function of parents' occupations and education," they undermine the capacity to analyze lifeworldly meanings and contingencies. If generalizing practices are to come to terms with action, agency, and culture in emergent historicity, they must incorporate concept formation by use of case-pattern concepts. This suggests that central issues confronting generalizing inquiry in the near term ought to concern how to develop its practices in relation to theories and uses of narrative.

Along with generalizing practices, two particularizing practices of inquiry – specific and configurational history – are also well suited to promoting contestation of knowledge. Of course, like historicism, both specific and configurational histories can submerge their theoretical, explanatory, and interpretive aspects – by using narrative in a way that hides the roles of other discourses. But these two practices also can promote contestation, by making explicit use of social theory and the discourse of interpretation and explanation. For this potential to be realized in specific histories, social theory has to be brought to the foreground, and explanations and interpretations have to be spelled out, rather than remaining implicit components of narrative. As for configurational history, the central argument that undergirds it – about the consequences of various specific outcomes and conjunctures – ought to be constructed as an explicitly historically developmental social theory – what sometimes has been referred to as a "secular theory." By these devices, just as generalizing inquiry will benefit from a narrative turn, particularizing inquiry can come to better terms with social theory.

To favor generalizing and particularizing practices that encourage the agones of inquiry is to promote a particular value in inquiry, one that opens inquiry to disputation, directed toward forging agreement or clarifying grounds of disagreement. This commitment does not resolve questions about the ultimate value of inquiry. Yet, as I will demonstrate, it can be a central axis that helps connect the inevitably diverse practices of inquiry.

Commitments of value

Values of inquiry like the ones just described – disputation, narrativizing theory in generalizing practices, and theorizing narrative in particularizing ones – cannot be sealed off in some fortress of epistemology. They must hold their own in a war among gods and goddesses of the sort

Max Weber once described.[11] In this war, there are also other purposes to be served. Knowledge gained from some practices may empower individuals, social groups, and movements, or it may offer leverage for moral and ethical intervention in matters such as sexism, racism, economic inequality, war, and future patterns of social organization. The general interest in emancipatory knowledge has been advanced by Jürgen Habermas as a viewpoint beyond two others – technical and communicative – the three which Habermas identifies as the alternative possible standpoints by which social reality can be understood.[12]

Habermas himself has had relatively little to say about practices of inquiry, yet the emancipatory interest that he describes can be promoted by developing new ways of connecting moral social discourse with empirical critical inquiry. Nancy Fraser, for example, has subjected social-welfare discourses about "needs" to a feminist critique that shows the gendered construction of public life. Other scholars have pursued Habermas's lead by debating the theoretical definition and historical possibilities of a "public sphere" of civic discourse.[13] These and similar projects are important for their particular substantive knowledge, but they also have a more general import: they unveil a power of critical inquiry that goes far beyond "normal science" – the potential to help reconstruct public institutions and social life. As Craig Calhoun suggests, the role of critical theory in creation of knowledge is not a matter of establishing a "new foundationalism, but rather, an aspect of a knowledge-forming process."[14]

Critical empirical research of the sort that Fraser has conducted demonstrates that, although values cannot be founded epistemologically, they can have profound consequences for the sort of knowledge obtained and the cultural significance of inquiry. Yet the choice among values and purposes of inquiry cannot be reduced to any neat formula such as value-neutrality, bias, or value commitment. As I have pointed out at various junctures in the present study, problematics of values encompass considerably more than the choice of topic or theory: they saturate knowledge with significance. As Foucault held, value constructions are deeply embedded in inquiry, which can never be fully purged of them.[15]

However, the value saturations of inquiry are not all of a piece. They differ across practices. These differences can be identified by recalling the binary distinctions displayed in table 2.1, concerning (1) the ways that values shape *criteria* of adjudication among alternative accounts, and (2) how values figure in the constitution of either an "objective" or a "value- or theory-relative" *object* of inquiry. In the coda to chapter 2, I showed that crosstabulating these distinctions identifies four alternative projects of inquiry – *interpretive explanation, value-objective explanation, value-neutral explanation*, and *objective explanation*. Now that the eight methodological practices of inquiry have been described in chapters 7 and 8, it becomes important to locate them in relation to the four value-defined projects of inquiry. As figure 9.1 suggests, elective affinities obtain between the value-based projects of inquiry and the eight methodological practices.[16]

In figure 9.1, each of four value-based isomorphisms establishes an affinity between a generalizing practice and a particularizing practice as a pair. For example, in one isomorphism, contrast-oriented comparison and situational history both involve interpretive explanation – the way of accounting for sociohistorical phenomena that depends on both relative criteria of adjudication and value- or theory-relative construction of the object of inquiry. There are similar isomorphisms between the three other pairs of particularizing and generalizing practices. Thus, remaining on the "relative adjudication criteria" (left) side of the diagram, both universal history as a generalizing practice and historicism as an individualizing one posit an objective value/theory basis of the object of inquiry, and they both can be considered practices of value-objective explanation; that is, they are explanations that "count" for proponents of a particular value perspective who take it as beyond dispute. Parallel isomorphisms can be found on the "universal adjudication criteria" (right) side of the diagram. There, both the application of theory as a generalizing practice and the particularizing practice of specific history are framed as value-neutral explanation, on the basis of their "relative" construction of the object of inquiry. Finally, analytic generalization and configurational history both make claims to objective explanation on the basis of commitments to universal adjudication criteria and objective representation of inquiry's object.

If, however, we view figure 9.1 from the point of view of generalizing versus particularizing orientations (that is, the "rear" plane versus the "front" plane), it is evident that the four practices within the particularizing orientation, and similarly the four practices within the generalizing orientation, are marked precisely by their lack of value affinities with one another. The four practices of generalizing inquiry share common sources in the various formative discourses of inquiry, but their differential infusions of values inscribe fundamentally alternative projects of inquiry – interpretive versus objective explanation, for example. Thus, contrast-oriented comparison serves other values than those that animate analytic generalization. Starkly put, the differences among generalizing practices are informed by value preferences beyond empirical adjudication, and conflicts among generalizing practices therefore seem

Figure 9.1: Generalizing and particularizing practices of inquiry arrayed according to value/theory criteria of adjudication and value/theory basis of the construction of the object of inquiry

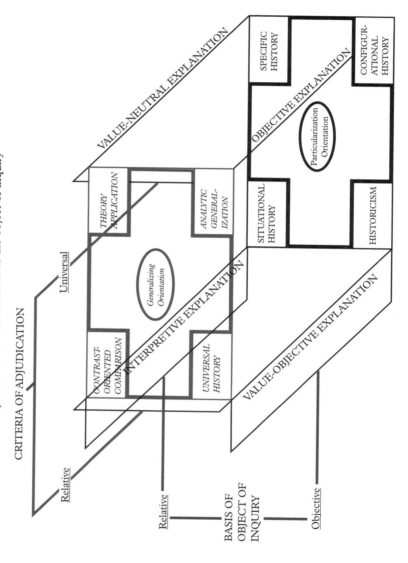

endemic. The same is the case with particularizing practices. Solely on the basis of value orientations, a given generalizing practice shares common cause with a particularizing practice more than with any other generalizing one, and particularizing practices are similarly divided from one another. Values saturate inquiry, and they both connect and partition inquiry's practices in unanticipated ways. The divergences, however, do not imply that the substance of findings produced under manifold value circumstances of inquiry lie beyond meaningful discussion.

From truth to knowledge

After Foucault, it is widely understood that knowledge is a historically variable form of power shaped by the political, institutional, moral, and strategic circumstances of its production. Knowledge is one or another cultural construction, something other than unequivocal truth. However, this dispensation is not the stopping point. Although no overarching monist account of knowledge seems sustainable, two broad possibilities of "bootstrapping" can help us to come to terms with evaluating heterologous kinds of knowledge in relation to one another. First, the identification of forms of discourse and practices of inquiry yields a basis for revisiting the widely debated issue of whether translation is possible among different types of knowledge. Second, practices of inquiry can be turned to examining the reflexive connections between historically emergent constructions of society and the socially constructed practices of inquiry.

The practice of translation

"Translation" is a basic metaphor relevant to communication in the world in general, to "reading" the world through inquiry, and to relations among diverse discourses and practices of inquiry.[17] The perspective of social phenomenology suggests certain instabilities both in the *intended* meanings of social action and in multiple *observed* meanings about intentional actions. Translation is not simply a philosophical problem; it is an ongoing problem of practice in the lifeworld. Translations may be judged good or bad by authors and their readers. But no matter what the substance of these judgments, translation will take place, and, when it does, there will be shifts among cultural symbols and contexts of interpretation. Here, I concentrate on the problems of translation for inquiry.

Given the multiple value interests and practices that can yield knowledge, the distinct possibility exists that more than one explanatory or interpretive account – each valid relative to its criteria – may be derived from inquiry into "the same" phenomenon. The question thus necessarily arises as to whether differences in perspectival knowledge achieved through alternative practices can be adjudicated. Here, postfoundationalist accounts of inquiry are open to elaboration. In *The Structure of Scientific Revolution*, Thomas Kuhn can be read as depicting a condition of relativism that has sources both in the divergence of objects of inquiry and in standards of evidence between competing paradigms. Kuhn regarded the prospect of a "neutral language of observation" as "hopeless," and he argued that the measurement activities of research are largely "paradigm-determined." Drawing on this analysis, he advanced the thesis of "incommensurability" between paradigms, based on (1) differences in problems they seek to address, (2) "misunderstanding" because they draw concepts and research into different relationships with one another, and (3) a basic condition of divergence in what might be called "worldview" or "gestalt" – a condition that Kuhn expressed difficulty in fully explicating, in which "the proponents of competing paradigms practice their trades in different worlds." Later, in a postscript, Kuhn emphasized that incommensurability need not be total, but divergences may result in a condition in which the parties to a dispute find that they do not share premises, and, under these conditions, each "must try, by persuasion, to convert the other." They may best do so when they "recognize each other as members of different language communities and then become translators." This activity, Kuhn suggested, happens in two ways, either as the translation from one language into another, or as the learning of another language to the point where one can "go native."[18]

Like Kuhn, others who have addressed issues of incommensurability suggest that different local logics or practices of inquiry may block any direct mediation among conflicting claims. For Richard Rorty, responding to these conditions suggests a hermeneutic task "of the informed dilettante, the polypragmatic, Socratic intermediary between various discourses. In his salon, so to speak, hermetic thinkers are charmed out of their self-enclosed practices. Disagreements between disciplines and discourses are compromised or transcended in the course of the conversation." Jean-François Lyotard seems less optimistic: discourses marked by differends cannot be linked by a transcendent discourse or a "table of correspondences."[19]

Other arguments suggest greater potential for translation. Charles Taylor, for example, suggests that the circularity of hermeneutics does not imply a hopeless relativism. Taylor recognizes the existence of limits to rational argument based in shared language and understanding, but nevertheless affirms the possibility of "hermeneutic explanation," and proposes an initial, albeit tenuous, criterion: "The superiority of one position over another will thus consist in this, that from the more adequate position one can understand one's own stand and that of one's opponent, but not the other way around. It goes without saying that this argument can only have weight for those in the superior position."[20] In a parallel way that explicitly connects Kuhn's problem of translation with the hermeneutic tradition, Richard Bernstein has concluded that Kuhn did not assert a radical relativism of knowledge under different paradigms. By following Kuhn's recognition of incommensurability, Bernstein argues, "we are not showing or suggesting that such comparison is irrational but opening up the types and varieties of practical reason involved in making such rational comparisons."[21]

The actual limits and possibilities of translation only emerge in focused inquiry. However, it is possible here to go further in specifying the alternative circumstances of practical reason and incommensurability under which attempts at translation occur. The point is not to reinvoke the general pragmatic ideal of a hermeneutic "conversation of mankind" that transcends incommensurate perspectives.[22] Instead, I propose a more differentiated understanding of communication about knowledge as it transpires among alternative practices of inquiry, construed as local epistemologies. An approach is suggested by Paul Roth's Kuhn-like idea that knowledge differences resulting from a condition of "methodological pluralism" can be subjected to efforts at reconciliation through a competition among translations.[23] What grounds might there be for such competition? This question can be addressed by recalling that sociohistorical inquiry is not about the unmediated world, but about sociohistorical objects constructed through inquiry in relation to phenomena that are themselves in part constructed through social action. Thus, the sociohistorical objects that inquiry analyzes are already second-order translations – about social activities that involve translation. Given this social circumstance of inquiry, it requires no great leap to engage in third-order translations among competing sociohistorical inquiries, themselves second-order translations. Indeed, synthetic reviews of previous research at the beginnings of new projects, sociologies of knowledge, historiographies, and the present study already operate along these lines. Such third-order translations are neither inherently less nor inherently more problematic than the translations that occur both in the world of everyday life and in direct research practices of inquiry. Nor, since translation is a craft practice of communication rather than a science, is there any reason to think that all translations in a given venue are equally good or bad.

Table 9.1: *Possibilities of translation according to whether practiced standards of evidence and objects of inquiry are shared by two or more projects of inquiry*

| | | Practiced Standards of Evidence | |
		SHARED	UNSHARED
Object of Sociohistorical Inquiry	SHARED	1. *Interchange* within a shared universe of discourse	3. *Shared object* as referent of contestable empirical expectations
	UNSHARED	2. *Shared practice* as incomplete basis for adjudication	4. *Differend* between divergent universes of discourse

The prospects for improving translation among seemingly incommensurate discourses and practices of inquiry can be clarified by formalizing Kuhn's distinction between (1) the shared versus disparate *objects of inquiry* constructed through concept formation and measurement, and (2) the shared versus disparate *standards of evidence* that guide particular practices of inquiry. Four ideal-typical circumstances of translation can be identified in these terms (see table 9.1). Translation may face circumstances of (1) *interchange*, in which research projects share both the same practiced standards of evidence and the "same" object (e.g., two accounts – both practices of specific history – that explore "Theodore Roosevelt's presidency"). Alternatively, (2) inquiry about *different* objects of inquiry – even in relation to the same broad empirical events ("the English Revolution" versus "the Long Parliament" or the "English Civil War") – might be undertaken within a *shared practice* of inquiry (e.g., configurational history). Or, (3) inquiries about a *shared object* (land settlement in nineteenth-century Chinese frontier consolidation) may be undertaken through divergent practices (e.g., one specific history, the other analytic generalization). Finally, (4) in a circumstance of completely divergent universes of discourse – a *differend* – neither the object nor the practice of inquiry would be shared, even if they share interests in some of "the same" events (e.g., a specific history of the Vietnam War versus a configurational history of the Cold War).[24] These four situations yield different prospects for translation, and it would thus be a mistake to affirm any "absolute" relativism whereby different "paradigms" exist as relatively discrete, equally incommensurate approaches to knowledge, available to mediation only through the hermeneutic "conversation of mankind." But it would be equally misguided to assert the privilege of any particular practice on the basis of its ideological legitimation as "science," and thereby claim a warrant for ignoring knowledge created through other practices. The prospects of translation are not dependent on staying within any single method. They are relational and, under certain conditions, they open up the potential for mediation of knowledge claims even across heterologous practices.

Clearly, translation is least difficult when both object and standards of evidence are shared, that is, in the interchange possible within a shared universe of discourse. In turn, there are different prospects for the two additional possibilities of translation that involve either shared standards or a shared object but not both. One involves exploiting shared standards of argumentation, and the other aligning evidence about a shared object of inquiry generated from divergent practices. Only beyond these three lies the differend.

First, let us consider interchange as a situation in which a shared practice (e.g., analytic generalization) juxtaposes contradictory assertions (e.g., from a rational-choice theory versus a network-theory analysis) about a shared object of inquiry such as solidarity within an array of social movements. Here, the shared practice may help adjudicate among alternative theoretical claims and yield knowledge transcendent to either one. Similarly, a practice of inquiry into one object may be open to extension to other objects of inquiry, so long as those objects are constructed in equivalent ways. Thus, within a shared practice of analytic generalization, the viability of rational-choice theory can be evaluated in relation to multiple objects of inquiry, varying both in subject matter (legislative politics, social movements) and empirical questions (free riders, optimization) because the objects are constructed on the basis of shared research strategies, and evidence is evaluated according to shared standards.

However, if the objects of inquiry themselves are constructed in different ways (i.e., on the basis of different values or theoretical frames), translation faces the second situation, in which even the standards of argumentation of a shared practice do not insure translation, because the objects of analysis about which to resolve controversies diverge. For the same broad range or class of empirical events, the initial debate is over the proper object (or, sometimes, "unit") of analysis. As I already noted, a central part of the debate about seventeenth-century English political history concerns whether it is colligated into "the English Civil War" or "the English Revolution" as an object of inquiry. Similarly, between Goffman's world of face-to-face interaction among patients on the ward of a mental hospital, a rational-choice account of ward interaction, and a Freudian analysis of the same patients' psychopathologies, there may be little basis of adjudication even if all three analyses are pursued within a shared practice of theory application, because they construct different objects out of empirical flux. All that translation can offer in this situation is the rather rhapsodic hope that bad ideas framed within one or another account will not survive the shared criteria of argumentation. But short of that, the differend of multiple constructions of the world will not succumb to direct translation.

The prospects for translation when different practices of inquiry yield knowledge about "a shared object" (e.g., practices of universal history and contrast-oriented comparison about the Portuguese colonization of Brazil) are more hopeful. Under these circumstances, it may be possible to practice "empirical" translation, by reference to disputed expectations about findings, even ones produced through different practices. However, there are tricky problems here too. Different practices often fit empirical evidence within different frames of relevance. Therefore, even if arguments about facts may be adjudicable in principle, there may be no apparent calculus by which to resolve the most important initial question – which facts are relevant? The task of translation is to tease out issues for which the alternative practices yield fundamentally different empirical expectations about the same events (e.g., whether the Portuguese settlement of Brazil was "feudal").[25] Under these conditions, comparison of expectations with findings may yield some implications about the relative viability of knowledge produced through heterologous practices. Otherwise, there is a strong possibility of slippage into the situation of completely divergent universes of discourse.

That situation, the differend, is marked by the use of different practices to investigate different objects of inquiry – even in relation to "the same" phenomenon. This circumstance severely constrains the possibilities of translation. The contestation of analyses can depend neither on any direct mediation by empirical evidence nor on the application of standards of inquiry within a shared practice. Instead, if there is to be any translation at all, the parties must work to "go native," as Kuhn put it, to think through how arguments of two radically different approaches make sense in their own terms, and to make their peace – if any – on some basis other than internal adjudication via shared objects or practices. Perhaps the best that can be hoped for under the condition of the absolute differend is "persuasion" (as Kuhn had it) during the conversation of mankind, held in the salon of Richard Rorty's Socratic intermediary.

One way to conduct discussions in the salon of the differend would be to identify a topic – whether a theoretical or empirical controversy –

that is the subject of the most diverse constructions of objects of inquiry and the most diverse practices of investigation. Focus on a theoretical controversy or empirical proto-object that even divergent universes of discourse share – for instance, seventeenth-century English history, the Dreyfus affair, the problem of altruism, land tenure in medieval France – may establish "traditions of controversy" in which inquiry confronts a relatively established set of conflicting arguments, formulated via different practices, about different objects of inquiry within a shared overall domain of controversy. Despite the ultimate differends entailed in this situation, the various inquiries share root discourses (i.e., value discourse, narrative, social theory, and explanation and interpretation), and these discourses may give grounds for argumentation, even when the practices and objects of larger projects diverge. In these terms, for example, it might be possible to "translate" various inquiries about the rise of Hitler into their social theoretical components, and evaluate these component theories relatively independently of the practices within which they are circumscribed. Similarly, narrative discourse can be brought to the service of a third-order translation that mediates among various accounts of the English Civil War. In this way, discourses and practices can feed on the knowledge produced through other practices. Inquiry in general thus has the same dialogic quality that Don Levine claims for social theory: at "higher" levels (actually, later times) of analysis, it may be possible to sort through and subsume debates that end in differends at "lower" levels (earlier times).[26] Indeed, much scholarship, both historical and analytic, depends on this process of sorting through and building up from previous inquiries. The success of such efforts can hardly be guaranteed in advance. But the hermeneutic potential within root discourses embedded in inquiry cannot be bounded, and, thus, even the differend does not become an absolute stopping point.

In sum, translation among inquiries is not a monolithic problem to be resolved generically; it depends in part on what points of articulation can be established among diverse inquiries, what next step can be taken, what further question can be addressed, under a given state of play among inquiries. Even under conditions of the differend, traditions of controversy and shared forms of discourse provide at least some fractal possibilities of translation in subsequent nested practices. Because there are differential possibilities of translation, the perspectivity of inquiries does not entail either solipsism or absolute relativism. On the other hand, so long as there are radically alternative ways of constructing objects of inquiry, neither would purity of (e.g., scientific) practice provide a monistic resolution to inquiry's condition of integrated disparity.

Instead, the ways in which inquiries may or may not share objects and standards of evidence give rise not only to barriers but also to complexly structured differential routes of translation.

Reflexive practice

The present inquiry into the cultural rationales by which inquiry is constructed is reflexive in a specific sense: it could not proceed outside inquiry, and thus employs value discourse, narrative, social theory, and explanation and interpretation in practices like those described herein. By this inquiry, I have focused a Foucauldian archeology of knowledge on culturally coherent practices of inquiry.[27] But this is not the end of reflexivity. As Foucault showed in his studies of madness and of prisons, knowledge disciplines have consequences wherever their practices arise: they spread panoptic power by disciplining the surveillance of the social realities they both construct and analyze. Just as "lunacy" and "personality disorder" are not only proto-objects of knowledge but in turn constructs that order the flux of reality and its apprehension, so sociohistorical inquiry does not simply observe and analyze. Its knowledge becomes cultural artifact. These conditions make inquiry something quite different than an autonomous enterprise, but they also present a reflexive opportunity to explore the implications of inquiry's constructions for the knowledge it yields.

To illustrate reflexive possibilities of inquiry, consider the uses of quantification. Typically, in mainstream social science, positivist or realist assumptions warrant quantitative modeling of social events, processes, and dynamics, even though early inventors of social indicators voiced skepticism about attributing meanings to numbers by any calculus of correspondence with social reality. Some theorists of quantification, like Herbert Blalock, concur with statistical theorist Karl Pearson in admitting to the socially constructed character of measurement.[28] Social reality, they in effect acknowledge, is manifold, and any categories used to depict it can always be deconstructed or reconstructed in ways that bring to the surface other aspects of a (socially real) phenomenon.

For the most part, acknowledgments by measurement theorists that measurement is socially constructed are only perfunctory. Practical quantitative strategies typically assume that the task is to improve measurement through some correspondence solution that purports to bring measured variables into closer, more predictable relations with reality – latent, theoretical, or empirical. These approaches take as their central problematic the refinement of measurement, and this problematic is typically approached within a rhetoric left over from the heyday of positivism or refurbished under realism. But there might be payoffs if practitioners of quantitative inquiry would now draw their enterprise into broader intellectual currents tied to the acknowledgment of perspectivism and the social construction of knowledge.

The problem of measurement shifts when inquiry is considered as a practiced constructive process. There is no general reason to doubt that measures can be more or less aligned with manifold analytically construed aspects of sociohistorical reality. But given the alternative procedures for constructing objects of inquiry even in relation to the same proto-object, it is questionable whether any given theoretical concept – gender, revolution, class – refers to some ontologically stable objects, events, or processes that can be ever more precisely approximated by measurement. Nor can constructed empirical statistical indices such as "gross domestic product" be assumed to reflect some enduring underlying reality. Instead, analytic constructs are historically and theoretically unstable referents to analytically identified realities that are themselves culturally and historically unstable (and increasingly constructed on the basis of quantitative measurement activities).

This constructionist understanding of measurement maintains a healthy skepticism, but it hardly implies that mainstream quantitative social science is a hopeless enterprise. Instead it suggests that research using quantitative measurement ought to come to terms with the reflexive, socially constructed, and historically embedded nature of quantitative inquiry as social action. Measurement can be understood, for example, as an instance of the more general problem of translation. A quantitative project in these terms would require sorting through the possible contradictory implications of alternative accounts by way of an "axial objectivity" of measurement that bridges the competing perspectives. Under conditions of axial objectivity, researchers operating within two alternative theoretical perspectives or research programs would expect the same constructed measurement to yield different results. This circumstance does not occur "in nature" or by "testing a hypothesis" *within* any given research program; it would happen because researchers puzzled through deductions from two *different* accounts and the divergent translated implications of those accounts for certain measurements. As this possibility suggests, the cultural rationales of quantitative methodologies could be substantially reformulated on the basis of reflexive practice.

The reformation of quantitative measurement (which I have elaborated elsewhere) parallels broader critical reflections on the constructed character of sociohistorical inquiry.[29] In recent years such reflections have been brought to bear on questions of how knowledge is produced.

To begin with, the concepts used in inquiry feed upon prior sociohistorical developments that they describe. As Charles Taylor has observed, the language we use when we talk about the rise of Puritanism was – and had to be – unavailable before the development itself.[30] In turn, this historicity of concepts can be shown to be reflexive insofar as categories of sociohistorical knowledge flow back into the worlds they describe. Foucault demonstrated this not only in his studies of madness, confinement, and sexuality, but also in his analyses of scholarly knowledge in *The Order of Things* and *The Archaeology of Knowledge*. He argued, for instance, that "the Analysis of Wealth played a role not only in the political and economic decisions of governments, but in the scarcely conceptualized, scarcely theoreticized, daily practice of emergent capitalism, and in the social and political struggles that characterized the Classical period [i.e., in particular the seventeenth and eighteenth centuries]."[31]

Other inquiries have described connections between categories of sociohistorical inquiry and wider cultural and ideological sensibilities in related ways. Notably, Margaret Somers has initiated an "historical epistemology" that unmasks deep cultural affinities between modern sociohistorical inquiry and Western market-capitalist, democratic ideology. In one project, Somers examines the reflexive relation between different discourses of citizenship. Her political and cultural history identifies the construct of "citizenship" as having countervailing communalist and individualist sources, and she identifies the historical circumstances under which the individualist trope began to narrow the usage in modern political inquiry of a potentially richer concept.[32] Somers's work does not stop at ideological critique or deconstruction; it offers grounds for the reconstruction of theoretical concepts central to inquiry about the social construction of civitas.

We are able to have knowledge at all because we construct sociohistorical objects and employ practices of inquiry. How, then, to avoid essentializing concepts that bear cultural and ideological content? How can they be used in a way that acknowledges socially constructed aspects of their referents? How, for example, might inquiry study gender identities in relation to industrialization in nineteenth-century Europe? A pragmatic perspectivism admits that social conventions are necessary to reference aspects of phenomena related to gender and to industrialization. As with social life more generally, such conventions make communication in inquiry possible.[33] But the constructions of inquiry are about social phenomena that themselves are socially constructed. Although both gender and industrialization depend upon naturally occurring phenomena (e.g., biological sex and reproduction, the change of water from liquid to steam), neither is a "natural" phenomenon. The myriad phenomena of social life that may be studied under the rubrics of either gender or industrialization have a "suchness" to them – they are rich in their existential specificity, but they could be otherwise. Until inquiry shows differently, there is no reason to assume some hidden mechanism or Grand Mover whereby the myriad phenomena relevant to analysis under the rubrics of gender and industrialization are all "of a piece." Considerable empirical diversity can be found, say, in gender-related employment activities within factories in Paris during the 1870s. And the socially operative categories of gender are themselves variable constructions: the salient distinctions are not the same from person to person, situation to situation, relationship to relationship, region to region, culture to culture, time to time, and so on. These conditions are not propitious ones for the consolidation of any objective-correspondence approach to conceptualization. Yet this does not mean that concepts bear no relation to their referents in the world. Precisely because there are nonrandom social worldly differences in how gender (industrialization, etc.) is constructed, meaningful distinctions can be made – in inquiry as much as in the social world more widely. To be sure, such distinctions single out aspects of the world on the basis of some value interest. But the patterned constructed coherences (e.g., of gender) in the social world are what make possible any of various coherences manifested in the constructions produced through inquiry. A relatively unpatterned world could not be well patterned by inquiry. But a patterned world can be represented in multiple patterned ways.

In turn, the patterns of inquiry's knowledge have properties similar to other forms of culture. Social science theories (e.g., using concepts such as system, network, and citizenship), historical readings of "the past," and critical interpretations of culture all contain embedded meanings that potentially become diffused into wider social worlds of understanding and action. These meanings are created through differentially distributed practices of inquiry that socially anchor production of different kinds of knowledge in diverse institutional fields (historicism is a central practice in departments of history, while mainstream sociology typically embraces analytic generalization as a practice). Inquiry is practice of a deeply cultural sort, which can become reflexive only by investigating these relationships through inquiry itself.

Between reason and the differend

In this inquiry into inquiry, I have shown that any research practice spans regimens from discourses foreign to one another in their enterprises. A practice of inquiry attains coherence, I have argued, as a cultural *bricolage*. Yet precisely because the particular discourses spanned *within* a practice are shared *across* practices, local "cultural" practices of reason are linked in complex relations with each other. This analysis is based upon my own favored tools of comparative research, namely, the analysis of substantive phenomena in relation to ideal types. Some social theorists once held high hopes for a sociohistorical theory of the totality. They criticized ideal types as empiricist hypostatizations of manifold reality.[34] I agree that ideal types – like concepts in general – never capture the complexity of sociohistorical phenomena. I therefore do not mistake my typifications for the activities by which inquiry is practiced. However, typification of inquiry has the great merit of bringing to light diverse interrelations among discourses and practices that have previously remained opaque to understanding, and it offers a meaningful basis for charting new practices of inquiry that have yet to emerge. Overall, this approach opens up ways to:

- explore discourses of inquiry and their regimens;
- map the affinities among alternative value orientations, strategies of narrative, social theories, and approaches to explanation and interpretation;
- identify how diverse practices of inquiry are consolidated as cultural ensembles of discourses;
- examine alternative practices of inquiry and the relations among them;
- deepen the specificity with which we approach the problem of translation; and,
- inform reflexive cultural histories concerned with the institutional consolidation of practices of inquiry and their objects.

These possibilities do not derive from any foundational Reason that claims to establish a totalization of inquiry's method through epistemology, but they do help us to understand and critique the culturally conventional forms of reason that operate in inquiries.

The controversy over Reason is, of course, the major divide that marks off postmodernist thinkers from modernist ones, most famously in the debate between Jean-François Lyotard and Jürgen Habermas. This debate is hardly less significant for its familiarity, nor have scholarly struggles over its stakes declined. To the contrary, the disjunctures between various binaries of modern Reason and postmodern decenterings of knowledge have become if anything more keenly felt in recent years. Within and across disciplines, scientists and objectivists disparage the "Others" who draw the legitimacy of their own knowledge into question. In transdisciplines, the commitments of practitioners to an enterprise are often matched by their profound ambivalence about method and theory, and, thus, by mercurial shifts between hubris and anxiety about the nature of the enterprise itself. These antagonisms and ambivalences permeate academia today. How they play out in higher education, graduate training, faculty appointments, and programs of research will structure the institutional conditions under which knowledge is produced in the twenty-first century. It is a central implication of the present study that a great opportunity will have been lost if the old divide persists between a hollow epistemology of pure Reason and shallow denials of the potential for reasoning. Neither Habermas nor Lyotard takes either of these positions, yet the divide is replicated in them. How can this divide be bridged?

When Habermas accepted the Theodor Adorno award in a 1980 speech in Frankfurt, he drew on Max Weber's analysis of the modernist differentiation among science, morality, and art, itself inspired by Kant's three critiques – of truth, ethics, and aesthetics. In the Habermasian reading of Weber's neo-Kantian analysis, the three spheres developed in autonomous directions, each increasingly staffed by a cadre of experts whose professional knowledge separated these spheres from the lifeworld of praxis. Against this modernizing tendency toward differentiation, Habermas argued for what might be called a higher, more transgressive modernity. "A reified everyday praxis," he maintained, "can be cured only by creating unconstrained interaction of the cognitive with the moral-practical and the aesthetic-expressive elements." In effect, Habermas called for blurring the boundaries among the three spheres. He emphatically denied that the Enlightenment project should be mistaken as a form of "terroristic reason," he refused any project of establishing an epistemological foundation for inquiry, and he underscored the historicity of communicative reason.[35]

Nevertheless, Jean-François Lyotard, Habermas's most energetic critic on these matters, subsumed Habermas's proposal under "the narrative of emancipation" – a grand narrative for which Lyotard could find no validation, particularly because "language games are heteromorphous, subject to heterogeneous sets of pragmatic rules."[36] For Lyotard, the quest for consensus cannot be a principle that enforces legitimacy of knowledge, and no pragmatic metalanguage that bridges the practices of inquiry can be codified. If Habermas would mix Kant's three spheres, Lyotard affirms their inevitable differends. In his dispensation, inquiry cannot achieve the very thing that Jeffrey Alexander regards as the aim of specifically theoretical discourse – "to gain provisional acceptance on the basis of universal argument."[37] Because theory cannot operate as a completely isolated discourse, agreement about the standards of argumentation remains elusive, and the arguments themselves remain less than universal.

By his own argument, Lyotard could never be sustained in his analysis, any more than his opponents could. However, the present study – which resonates with Lyotard in its exploration of discourses – shows that the domain of inquiry is crisscrossed by channels of translation. Thus, the condition of inquiry is something less than complete isolation of its practices. Lyotard explored the limits of translation in absolute differends. On the other hand, I have shown how translations can be facilitated in ways that are not reducible to the pure reason of a unified epistemology, yet offer channels connecting practices of local reason. These possibilities of translation are not as fully utilized in inquiry as they might be, for they transcend local research-program, disciplinary, and transdisciplinary practices that isolate the production of any particular kind of knowledge from alien critiques. But the concerted use of such translations would enlarge the domain of mutually engaged practices of inquiry. It would thus push back the frontier of the differend, beyond which translation occurs only by way of the "conversation of mankind" in the salon run by Rorty's Socratic intermediary. This possibility suggests that the differend is not some formal logical limit to adjudication about knowledge. Given Lyotard's own analysis, which centered on discourse, the differend must be construed as historically, socially, and culturally constituted, that is, defined in part by how the discourses of inquiry are developed and how they are articulated in practices, including practices of translation.

Habermas's project finds qualified support in the integrated disparity of inquiry that comes into view via a hermeneutic deconstruction of its discursive practices. As the present study shows, sociohistorical inquiry does not reflect the supposed modernist differentiation of reason into autonomous spheres of science, morality, and art. It is this division that, Habermas argues, has dialectically reinforced usurpation of reason by supposedly autonomous professionals disconnected from the lifeworld of praxis. But modernist professional usurpations of reason fail to account for how divergent practices are constituted as cultural *bricolages* via hybrid relationships among values, narrative, theory, and explanation and interpretation. The web of inquiry's discourses and practices is far more complex than the professional guardians of pure science, of history unadulterated by theory, of aesthetics untrammeled by life, would have had us believe. By the opposite token there are more specifiable possibilities of reasoning within and across practices than pragmatists and postmodernists have yet acknowledged. Recognizing both the alternative *bricolages* of ethical and empirical concerns as well as the contested yet shared terrains of aesthetic (broadly cultural) analyses and scientific ones erodes the modernist construction of pure autonomous spheres. It thus undercuts scientific claims for autonomous legitimacy. But it also belies critiques that would dismiss all knowledge as mere rhetorical accomplishment and it offers more tangible procedures of translation than those that would bridge local practices only via conversation.

Given that diverse practices share the general feature of dependence on culturally conventionalized ways of combining inquiry's constituent discourses, no practice can claim to operate completely within the bounds of pure reason and, thus, participants in contending camps within the domain of sociohistorical inquiry cannot so easily dismiss one another. They therefore ought to take each other more seriously. In practical terms, this means that proponents of social science in the strong sense of the term will need to become deeply critical of the boundaries that maintain institutional isolation of their disciplines and research agendas from approaches in humanistic, critical, and cultural studies concerned with meanings. On the other hand, proponents of transdisciplinary enterprises will no longer be able to deny the issues of theory and method that have been repressed during the postmodern wave of fascination with culture, representation, and memory, for knowledge about these issues is itself gained through practices of inquiry – explicit, reflexive, and self-conscious, or not.

Against both sides of the binary – universal method and the differend that leaves only conversation – the Third Path brings us to possibilities of articulation, subsumption, and translation among discourses and practices of inquiry. The possibilities help facilitate Habermas's project of seeking emancipatory consensus through communicative rationality, even given the heterology of practices. Projects of inquiry tied to emancipatory praxis have their channels, even if their pursuit does not encompass all inquiry or all praxis, and even though consensus, because unforced, will be less than universal.

In this accounting, neither the view of Lyotard nor that of Habermas can prevail. Intractable differends divide certain practices – in the instance at hand, those of Habermas and Lyotard. But their practices, like practices in general, are impure hybrids, and the dividing line of their differend thus no longer seems as absolute as it once did. In a similar way, the differends that marked the two cultures described by C. P. Snow have been historically constituted by the emergence of different disciplines and traditions of practice that are culturally arbitrary in the sense that they could be institutionally constituted on a different basis. If history is our teacher, in the course of creating new knowledge, those who conduct inquiry will institutionalize new practices that result in new differends. But the Third Path takes us beyond merely parochial assertions about the supposed superiority of any particular local method. By recognizing the hybrid discursive character of inquiry, those who practice it will be able to engage in more sophisticated adjudication, even about knowledge produced through strikingly different practices.

The great doctors of philosophy in the terrain where the discourses of inquiry meet know that their craft cannot be contained by any purely procedural formalization of practice.[38] Each in his own way, Max Weber and Fernand Braudel, to name two visionaries, offers a panoramic view that moves among diverse practices. The interpretive analysis of inquiry that I have presented in the present study does not guarantee such vision, nor ought it substitute narrow method for craft. Yet even the crafts of inquiry may be improved by understanding their practices.

The understanding presented here identifies limits to any quest for a single, objective social science, much less a "science of history" via social theory. The lifeworldly divergences in value rationales and grounds of explanation and interpretation permeate inquiry so thoroughly as to render moot any claims to a privileged or foundational approach based in ontology, epistemology, theory, or methodology. Multiple practices of sociohistorical inquiry will persist, each with its own distinctive rationale. Yet if foundationally warranted scientific knowledge is a lost cause, the alternative is something less than the total relativization of inquiry. The absence of foundations is the historical and existential circumstance in which contemporary inquiry proceeds. In this destabilized situation, no clarification of practices can reconcile the conflicted political, ethical, intellectual, and rhetorical stances that mark the differend described by Lyotard. It thus might seem that there is an affinity between Lyotard's differend and the endless war among gods and goddesses of values, famously depicted by Max Weber. But there is a difference. For Lyotard, the play of partial perspectives is inevitable, and the choice among them remains problematic. For Weber, precisely in the absence of a totalizing perspective, the ethical choice remains paramount.[39] An ultimate differend cannot be erased. However, in a provisional way, the hermeneutic consideration of inquiry's cultures of meaning-making moves beyond both general claims of relativism and the fruitless attempts to reach a general solution to the conduct of inquiry. The route of the Third Path opens out into an emergent network of communication, unevenly tied together by nodal connections among discourses, practices, and procedures of translation that push back the frontier of any absolute differend. Knowledge produced by way of culturally coherent practices of inquiry and their contestation can result in more than storytelling, even in the absence of an encompassing pure Reason.

Notes

PROLOGUE

1 In this feature, my account finds common cause with Steve Woolgar's
assertion that the embedded reflexivity of sociohistorical inquiry "need not
be conceived of as a 'problem'" (foreword to Ashmore 1989: xviii), but,
as Ashmore puts it, instead offers an "opportunity" to establish a more
self-critical basis of inquiry (1989: xxviii). The criterion of avoiding performative contradiction, when it is met, yields what is defined by Ashmore
as a "self-exemplary text" (1989: 76; see also ch. 3). Avoiding performative
contradiction is one of the few considerations that counts for both modernists and their critics: for example, for both Habermas (see Jay 1989) and
Derrida (1978: 286). As Jay points out, this consideration will not count
if contradictions are acceptable, or if all language cannot be held to standards of self-contradiction. But these assumptions are not the ones under
which arguments about perspectivity are subject to critique.

1 INTRODUCTION: THE THIRD PATH

1 Kiser and Hechter 1991; N. Z. Davis 1983, 1988.
2 For example, see the Gulbenkian Commission 1996.
3 Bendix 1984: 27.
4 Kant 1963; 1951: esp. 12–19. For a discussion of this problem, see Lyotard
1986.
5 Becker 1982.
6 Rorty 1979; Fuller 1988; Pels 1996: 42, emphasis in original.
7 Rorty 1979; Derrida 1978.
8 The term "postmodern" has been used in many different contexts – beginning in the late 1950s in literary criticism (Huyssen 1986: ch. 10), and
increasingly in the 1960s and especially the 1970s in architecture, film, art,
politics, and philosophy – most generally to describe cultural forms that blur
modern distinctions (e.g., between high and popular culture) and eschew
modernistic rationality in favor of innovations like architectural planning
through situated discourse. Postmodernists celebrate ambiguity and irony,
and it would be untoward to attempt a definition here. Suffice it to suggest
that, in intellectual terms, developments often described as postmodern are
bound up with disparate tendencies: the destabilization of meaning heralded

262

by the emergence of poststructuralist semiotics and Derrida's deconstruction; Michel Foucault's archaeological critique of Western institutions of professional knowledge and discipline; and the resurgence of subjectivist alternatives to objectivism in social phenomenology, social constructionism, and feminist-standpoint epistemology. There is nothing to be gained from trying to harmonize these developments: they move critically against modernism, but the currents are diverse. For mappings of the postmodern, see Lyotard 1984, Huyssen 1986, and my own account, in Hall and Neitz 1993: ch. 11.

9 E.g., Phillips 1973; Feyerabend 1975.

10 Hunt 1992; Greenblatt 1991.

11 I explore Weber's stance toward the *Methodenstreit* in greater detail in chapter 2.

12 Proctor 1991: ch. 12.

13 Ernest Gellner (1985) defended positivism as a special realm of discourse where no assertion can be privileged against the Hegelianist alternative in which privileged discourses of holism and realism establish a realm ruled by dogma that cannot be subjected to disproof. For an operational account of positivism, see J. Turner 1985.

14 The problems of positivism are reviewed by Adorno et al. 1976, Suppe 1977, and Halfpenny 1982.

15 For an example of Weber's institutional analysis of knowledge, see his famous (1946) essay, "Science as a vocation." His entire sociology of religion (1978: 399–634) is an essay in the sociology of knowledge. See Mannheim 1937, 1953.

16 Kuhn 1970. For social and historical studies of science and discussions of their implications, see Mullins 1980, Bourdieu 1975, Brannigan 1981, Barnes and Edge 1982, H. M. Collins 1983, Barnes 1985, Latour and Woolgar 1986, Latour 1987, 1993, Dant 1991, and Pels 1996. Further questions must be raised about the interests that scientific knowledge serves – a point made most strongly by critical theorists (e.g., Habermas 1973: 263–64) and feminists (e.g., Bleier 1986; Smith 1987; Harding 1991).

17 Latour 1993.

18 For feminist perspectives, see Groz 1988, Nicholson 1990, and Alcoff and Potter 1993; for anthropology, see Marcus and Fisher 1986 and Clifford 1988.

19 Derrida 1978; Margolis 1985: 150, brackets in original; Geertz 1988: 133.

20 Haraway 1988: 577, 588, 596; Harding 1991: ch. 11, p. 173.

21 For a modernist critique, see Searle 1993.

22 Lyotard 1988.

23 Lyotard 1984: xxiii–xxiv, 79; 1988. His list of metanarratives includes historical materialism and post-Keynesian economics; see Lyotard 1987b: 162.

24 Putnam 1981; R. Bernstein 1983; Alexander 1992; R. Collins 1989.

25 For a critique of one approach to textual analysis as self-privileging, see Smith's (1993) discussion of Patricia Clough's "feminist psychoanalytically oriented semiotics." Putnam (1990: 25) and Harding (1990: 99–100) have made the point that critics sometimes unwittingly adopt Enlightenment assumptions that they claim to be criticizing.

26 Latour 1993.
27 Snow 1959. For a discussion, see the Gulbenkian Commission 1996: 60–69.
28 Nietzsche 1957: 50.
29 Benhabib 1990: 125. It is reasonable to think that discourse is a feature of communities. For historical analysis of the Reformation, the Enlightenment, and socialism as "communities of discourse," see Wuthnow 1989. The scientific community as a guarantor of knowledge has been invoked previously within positivism. The difference today comes with the recognition of multiple communities rather than a monolithic model of science; see Longino 1993 and L. Nelson 1993 for feminist formulations of this approach.
30 Schutz and Luckmann 1973. The term has obtained a wider usage, in part through Habermas (1987b), who counterposes "lifeworld" and "system." Interestingly, a recent essay by Rawls (1996) suggests that the epistemology of Emile Durkheim can be traced to "enacted practice" in the social here-and-now, that is, within the lifeworld.
31 Giddens 1984b. On the subaltern character of inquiry, see Spivak 1988: 308. For feminist discussions locating inquiry in the everyday world, see P. H. Collins 1990, Grant 1987, Haraway 1988, Harding 1991, and Smith 1987. The image of "gazing back" is Harding's (1991: 161–63).
32 Various accounts of reflexivity are reviewed by Wacquant (quoted in Bourdieu and Wacquant 1992: 41); my approach differs from his by embracing contributions to reflexivity from the most diverse sources, including the phenomenological and ethnomethodological efforts that he discounts, as well as the vision he affirms.
33 Schutz 1967, 1970; Schutz and Luckmann 1973. Schutz differentiates three subtypes – the meaning connected with an "in-order-to motive," the meaning associated with a "because motive," and the "ambient" meaning of paying attention to the unfolding stream of events in the here-and-now. These distinctions become especially important for inquiry in the observer's lifeworldly frame of reference (Hall 1977).
34 For *verstehende* sociology, see Weber 1978 and the critique by Schutz 1967. On feminist-standpoint theory, see Smith 1987, and Harding 1991 for its relation to feminist postmodernism.
35 Mannheim 1937.
36 Putnam 1981; 1990: 21; Hacking 1982: 65.
37 McKeon 1951, 1987; see also Mitchell 1988. McKeon's approach has found philosophical elaboration in W. Watson 1985.
38 Derrida 1978: 279, 286.
39 Derrida 1978: 289, 292–93.
40 Dilthey 1976 (see also Makkreel 1975); Weber 1978: 422; Gadamer 1975; Taylor 1985; Ricoeur 1979, 1984, 1985, 1988; Geertz 1973. I discuss Habermas's objections to Gadamer in chapter 2. For reviews of hermeneutics, see Eagleton 1983: 61–90 and Calhoun 1995: 47–66.
41 I focus here only on the relevance of poststructuralism and phenomenology to the methodology of the present study. For a broader account, see Eagleton 1983: chs. 3 and 4. The pivotal anthropological study that turns against structuralism by offering a temporalized critique is Bourdieu 1977.

On the debate over sociohistorical phenomena as texts, see Brown 1987, Palmer 1990, and Eley 1996. Rosenau (1992: ch. 2) reviews claims about the death of the author. For a review of phenomenological and sociohistorical theorizations of reading, see Holub 1984. In brief, we cannot assume that a given text has any single objectively "real" meaning. Instead, potential instabilities and shifts in meaning derive not only from shifting intentions of an author or social actor, but also from how audiences apprehend and rework meanings in relation to their own contexts of interpretation.

42 Booth 1983; McCloskey 1985.
43 Gasché 1987.
44 Foucault 1970: 366, 371.
45 Foucault 1972: 15, 191, 21, 37.
46 Lyotard 1988: esp. 84, 129, 158, 160.
47 See, for example, Wagner-Pacifici 1994, Hall 1995, and Silverstein and Urban 1996.
48 Alexander 1982.
49 Lyotard 1988. The term "practice" is used in a related way by Foucault (1972: 46).
50 The approach taken here is "social constructionist," and on this point it parts company from Lyotard (1988: 41, 76), who affirms a "procedure for establishing the reality of a referent." Lyotard rejects "anthropological empiricism" and Wittgenstein, and seems to skirt questions about correspondence between concepts and their referents. My identification of practices of inquiry as ideal types thus differs from Lyotard in its concept formation.
51 Efforts at rationalization of inquiry's practices, in this sense, parallel rationalization in other social institutions – religion, law, and so forth. On Max Weber's analysis of rationalization, see Schluchter 1981 and G. Roth 1987.

2 VALUE DISCOURSE AND THE OBJECT OF INQUIRY

1 For an account of the crisis, see Marcus and Fisher 1986: ch. 1.
2 In discussing objects of inquiry, I take inspiration from Foucault (1972: 47), who takes as one goal, "To substitute for the enigmatic treasure of 'things' anterior to discourse, the regular formation of objects that emerge only in discourse."
3 Benjamin 1969: 254; Kant 1963: 24. On Christian sources of historical consciousness, see Patrides 1972 and Kemp 1991. On German idealism, historicism, and the *Methodenstreit*, see Unger 1971, Reill 1975, and Iggers 1983. For sketches in the philosophy of history, see Manuel 1965.
4 On Ranke, see L. Krieger 1977: 10–12; Georg Lukács (1971: 150–51) offered a critique relevant to Marxism as well. For a more recent reading of Ranke, see Gilbert 1990 (Ranke quote, 44–45).
5 Ranke's achievements as a historian exceed any warrant offered by his philosophy of history, and Marx (1978a) can be read in other ways. However, even a defense of Marx's position, by Kocka (1985), recognizes difficulties that stem from Marx's formulation of an "historical totality." Issues of

alienation considered in Marx's (1978b) essay on the Jewish question contain an important bridge toward the "later" formulations of *Capital*.

6   Callinicos 1995: 41.

7   Kant 1963: 24–26.

8   Lyotard 1986.

9   On neo-Kantianism, see Köhnke 1991.

10 Weber 1946: 147.

11 Oakes 1988; Rickert 1986: 105.

12 Oakes (1988: 40, 150–51) admits this. However, he thinks that Weber *should* have. Cf. Burger (1976: 87) on Weber's divergence from Rickert on this point.

13 For general accounts, see Giddens 1971: 138–41; Huff 1984; and Käsler 1988: 184–96.

14 Weber, in "The meaning of 'ethical neutrality,'" and "'Objectivity' in social science" (1949: 19–22, 21 [quote], 58, 77, 84 [quote], 81 [quote, emphasis in original]).

15 Weber 1949: 84 (quote); on Weber's recognition of his Eurocentric standpoint, see Schluchter 1989: 34. A slightly different position from Weber's is advanced by Arthur Danto (1985: 13). On Weber's turn to the sociology of religion for an empirical approach to the conflict of values, see Oakes 1988: 151.

16 Oakes 1985: 197, 183; cf. Schluchter 1979: 109, and Burger 1976: 91.

17 Weber 1949: 55, 9.

18 Schluchter 1979: 79; Weber 1946: 147, 152. In this light, Mommsen (1989: 3) sets up a straw person when he claims that a portrayal by Bendix and Roth of Weber bifurcates his politics and science; their discussions (e.g., 1971; G. Roth 1988–89) instead suggest two distinct, but methodologically and substantively connected, discourses. For Factor and Turner (1979), it would seem that, if all values are irreconcilable, no one can act with integrity toward more than one value. But this would be the case only if action is totalized, that is, if it were impossible for the individual to put aside scientific action and take up political action, that is, to act within different arenas (cf. Schluchter 1979: 103). This differs from Weber's substantive sociological conception, which includes, for example, the possibility that a given actor might face multiple class situations on the basis of diverse individual interests (Weber 1978: 926–31; cf. Goldman 1992: 76).

19 Gadamer 1975.

20 Oakes 1985: 183–95.

21 Simmel, quoted in Levine 1991a: 1048.

22 Levine 1985.

23 Weber 1978: 10–11, 18–19. On Weber's distinction between generalizing and individualizing inquiry, see especially Hekman 1983b: 20ff.

24 Miller (1987: 106–13) considers the value problem in such terms. However, he offers a somewhat confused discussion of Weber's position concerning value-neutrality (e.g., by ignoring Weber's and Rickert's admission of cultural significance).

25 For an itemization of how American sociologists appropriated the ethic of neutrality, see Sztompka 1979: 195–98.

26 Halfpenny 1982: 100–13. On the problems of theory-free measurement, see Hall 1996.

27 "Rationalism" in the form that entails abandoning the quest for absolute truth in favor of reasonable belief can be developed in both the realist and conventionalist directions; see Toulmin 1972, Newton-Smith 1981, and Foley 1987. Because rationalism is more modest than foundational "Reason," the central issue concerns realism versus conventionalism.

28 Popper 1979, 1983. Others, like Donald Campbell (1988) and David Papineau (1978), try to resolve the special problems of the social sciences within this sort of framework. Bhaskar's emergent position (1986; 1989: 76–77, 79, 81 [quote], 82 [quote]), on the other hand, rejects both positivism and hermeneutics. A well-known (but sociologically underdeveloped) realist proponent is Rom Harré, who confuses compelling sociological analyses, such as Erving Goffman's, with the social phenomena they describe. Insofar as Harré (1990: 350) posits "a species-wide and history-long Conversation, only partially available to individual human beings," he asserts as real the very thing that both Lyotard and Rorty find problematic – a monistic sphere of discourse.

29 Halfpenny 1982: 111.

30 The problem of multiple realities is largely ignored by Miller (1987), despite his interest in encompassing the social sciences within realism. An inconclusive attempt at a solution has been sketched by Outhwaite (1987), who proposes reconciling realism with the insights of hermeneutics and the emancipatory interest of critical theory. In a more programmatic way, Christopher Lloyd (1986, 1993) argues for the reality of social structures.

31 On the problems of realism, see O'Neill 1986.

32 On reality construction, see Berger and Luckmann 1966; on the general issue, see Spencer 1982, Layder 1985, and Feyerabend 1988; for a dialectical and materialist approach, see Sayers 1985. My argument concerning the trajectory of realism toward constructionist conceptualization is elaborated in Hall 1996. The most extensive recent effort to deal with the reality of the subjective while retaining an objective analysis is by Bourdieu (e.g., 1984); for a critique of totalizing elements in this analysis, see Hall 1992.

33 Outhwaite (1987: 105) describes Parsons's (1937) "analytical realism" in these terms, as ending up in "conventionalism."

34 Appleby, Hunt, and Jacob 1994: 250.

35 Weber 1949: 94 [quote]; 1978: 43–46, 348–49. The implications of this distinction between classificatory and ideal-typical concepts are pursued in chapter 4.

36 Outhwaite 1987: 57, emphasis in original.

37 Outhwaite 1987: 114; see also Halfpenny 1982: 112.

38 Polanyi 1967.

39 Harding 1991: 143, 159; Lakatos 1971: 99.

40 Becker 1982; Diesing 1991: 325. Sociological proponents of research programs include Wagner and Berger 1986 and Kiser and Hechter 1991, but cf. S. Turner 1990 and Diesing 1991.

41 Outhwaite 1987: 94.

42 Horkheimer 1972.

43 Adorno 1976: 56.
44 Habermas 1987b; Foucault 1988; Lyotard 1984; Harding 1991; P. H. Collins 1990. For general accounts of critical theory, see Buck-Morss 1977, Held 1980, Bottomore 1984, and Benhabib 1986. The distinction between fact and value is critiqued by Adorno 1976, but following Habermas (1976a: 145; 1976b; 1987b), it also may be accepted within the domain of science and rejected elsewhere.
45 Benhabib 1986.
46 Lukács 1971: 149–209; cf. Stewart 1978.
47 Horkheimer 1972; Adorno 1973, 1983: 88. Whether Adorno avoided the drift of dialectics toward a form of totalizing idealism is an open question; for a defense of critical theory on the issue of totalization, see D. Kellner 1990.
48 Benhabib 1986: 182.
49 A point made by Martin Jay (1973: 63).
50 Habermas 1989b. For recent work that pursues Habermas's problematic, see Calhoun 1992.
51 Habermas 1971: 311.
52 Habermas 1971: 311–14; 1987b.
53 Rickert 1986: 226. For analyses of Habermas's ontological basis for reconstructive science, see Held 1980: 325 and Alford 1985. Critiques of Habermas's concepts of an ideal speech situation and communicative reason are numerous, but see especially LaCapra 1977, van den Berg 1980, Keat 1981, and Benhabib 1986: 339–43, who suggests that communicative reason can be reshaped to create new and radical relations of self and other.
54 Habermas 1987a: 97.
55 Habermas 1988: 130–75, 170 (quote), 172 (quote); see also Hekman 1983a.
56 Rorty 1979: 379–86; Gadamer, quoted in Hekman 1983a: 222, and his autobiographical remarks (Gadamer 1985: 181).
57 Lyotard 1984: 39–41, 60, 63–65, 74.
58 Habermas 1988: xiv; see also 1984: xli; 1987b: 400; 1989a: 178–79; 1992: 117 (quote).
59 Lyotard 1984: 67; Benhabib 1986. Richard Bernstein (1991: 52 and *passim*) also points to interests in communication shared by Habermas and postmodernists like Lyotard, Foucault, and Derrida. A similar view is advanced by McCarthy (1991).
60 Benhabib 1995: 112; West 1989: 213. For other discussions of the pragmatist alternative, see Antonio 1989 and Shalin 1992.

CODA 2 HOW VALUES CONSOLIDATE PROJECTS OF EXPLANATION

1 Miller (1987: 18–24) reviews the covering-law model and its difficulties. Mandelbaum (1961) seeks to salvage the relevance of covering laws in historical explanation by rectifying problems with Hempel's account. On the other hand, Beauchamp and Rosenberg develop a Humean account of

causal explanation that they argue avoids the difficulties of Hempel's model. Their account (1981: 314–27), however, invokes a unity-of-science thesis that remains woefully underdeveloped when it comes to sociohistorical explanation.

2 Schutz 1967, 1970; Simmel 1950: xxxii; on accounts, see M. Scott and Lyman 1968.

3 It is a claim, however, supported by Garfinkel (1981), who shows how "explanatory relativity" holds because of the presuppositions brought to any given project of explanation, which science privileges on other than objective grounds.

4 On the problem that workers pose for Marxist theory, see Somers 1992a.

5 This example is described in probabilistic terms by Paul Humphreys (1989: 6); for a similar but nonprobabilistic example, see Miller 1987: 93–94.

6 Habermas 1987b. For discussion of the relations between value orientations and empirical research, see Bohman 1991, and, for examples of empirical research, see Calhoun 1992.

7 Harding 1991: 40, 147. My remarks do not preclude other ways in which contexts of discovery and justification might be related, but here I am concerned only with fields.

8 Miller 1987: 87, 93, emphasis added.

9 Miller 1987: 498–501.

10 Miller 1987: 498–501 (quote, 501).

11 Bohman (1991) makes a reasonable case that acceptance of multiple explanation patterns does not necessarily accede to a total relativization of knowledge.

12 It is perhaps for this reason that institutional economics has developed most substantially recently among sociologists; see Granovetter and Swedberg 1992.

13 Foucault 1972: 186.

3 NARRATIVE CULTURES AND INQUIRY

1 Parker 1979b: 71.

2 Stone 1979: 3–5; Veyne 1984.

3 I use Ankersmit's (1988) inclusive characterization of "representation" to underscore the problematic relation between events and their narration. For an effort to salvage narrative as "a fair representation of the fortunes of a central subject," see McCullagh 1987: 46.

4 For an exploration of the narrative qualities of social science, see Greimas 1990.

5 Affirmations of narrative, like its rejections, are diverse and sometimes contradictory. On the problems of non-narrative history, see, for example, Hexter 1972 and Stone 1979. For a defense of narrative against postmodern critiques, see Appleby, Hunt, and Jacob 1994: 231–37. For anthropological approaches to narrative, see Sahlins 1985, Clifford 1988, Trinh Minh-ha 1989, and Lavie 1990.

6 Lévi-Strauss 1966.

7 For discussions of historicity, see Hall 1980 and Aminzade 1992. See Jameson 1972 for a general consideration of linguistics and temporality, and D. Wood 1989 on deconstruction, phenomenology, and the textual construction of temporality.

8 Lyotard 1984: 27–37, quotations, 30, 31.

9 See Appleby, Hunt, and Jacob 1994: 232–37.

10 White 1973: 36–37 [quote], 276, 426–34; see also Callinicos (1995) who states that all history is theoretical, but still seeks to distinguish theoretical from philosophical history. Yet Callinicos's distinction, as I suggest in chapter 2, has to do with *how* theory is employed in philosophical history, not with *whether* it is used. This becomes more apparent in the comparison of "universal history" with other practices of inquiry, in chapters 7 and 8 in this volume.

11 White 1973: 49.

12 Lyotard 1988: 151.

13 White 1987: 23. On periodization, see Hall 1994 and Clemens 1996.

14 Barthes 1972: 128.

15 Ricoeur (1988: 214–16) specifically evokes Habermas in this formulation. For a discussion of White, Ricoeur, and other theorists of narrative after the poststructuralist turn, see H. Kellner 1987.

16 Morris 1980: 49.

17 Schudson (1978) makes this distinction.

18 Somers 1992a: 603.

19 *I Ching* 1967: 189.

20 Wilhelm, in *I Ching* 1967: liii.

21 On this issue, see Needham 1965.

22 Baudrillard 1983. On new directions in narrative, see Weimann 1987. The possibilities of feminist narrative have been explored by Carolyn Heilbrun (1988). The anthropological problem of crosscultural narratives is considered by Tyler 1985, Trinh Minh-ha 1989, and Rosaldo 1989: ch. 6.

23 Ricoeur 1988: 214–15, 217–19.

24 For discussions, see Jameson 1981: ch. 2; Norris 1985: ch. 1; and the critique of Jameson in Huhn 1989.

25 Booth 1983; McCloskey 1985. On rhetoric in inquiry, Ricoeur (1988: 160–66) provides a useful discussion for narrative; see also Hexter 1971a: ch. 2 and Gay 1974. For the social sciences, see Edmondson 1984, Rabinow 1985, S. Cohen 1986, M. Davis 1986, J. Nelson, Megill, and McCloskey 1987, and studies of particular authors by Overington 1981 and Green 1988.

26 Pratt 1977.

27 Schutz 1970.

28 Bloom, quoted in Holub 1984: 158.

29 Iser, quoted in Holub 1984: 82–106.

30 Gilbert 1990: 38. Booth (1983: 408, 424) notes the parallel issues of fictive and other kinds of narrative, distinguished most centrally by the reader's potential submission to simulated emotional reactions based on fictive events in the novel.

31 For critical readings of Jauss, see Holub 1984 and Ricoeur 1988. On the new historicism, see Greenblatt 1982 and Veeser 1989.
32 Paul Ricoeur (1985; 1988: ch. 5) suggests the relation of fictive poetic experimentation to the formulation of meaningful accounts about history.
33 Georg Simmel (1977: 149–55) alluded to similar possibilities when he distinguished between event-sequences of history versus the formulation of some external scheme, teleology, or theory that would assign historical importance to manifold topics and events.
34 See the discussion of Kant in chapter 2.
35 On the analysis of intrinsic historical objects in cultural history and religious history, see Hall 1990, 1991a, and forthcoming. The more disparate the elements combined in a cultural object, the more its narrative shades into an "extrinsic" form, discussed pp. 94–97 below.
36 Dilthey 1976; Foucault 1972.
37 On this point, see Foucault 1972, and, for Dilthey, Makkreel 1975: 26–31.
38 See Schutz's (1967) critique of Weber.
39 Bakhtin 1981: 38–40, 99 (see also Steinberg 1997); Ricoeur 1984, 1985, 1988; Hall 1978; D. Carr 1986.
40 Goffman 1959, 1974.
41 On this aspect of Dilthey's work, see Owensby 1994.
42 This argument, developed out of phenomenology (e.g., Schutz 1967), finds common cause with D. Carr (1986: 65) and Polkinghorne (1988).
43 These fragments of the story are drawn from the *Washington Post*, August 19, 20 (quote), 21 (quote), and 24, 1991.
44 The creation of history in history is a theme raised by Certeau 1988. For a general consideration of the social moments of narration, see Somers and Gibson 1994. On history, interpretation, and memory, see Henige 1974, Kammen 1991, Fentress and Wickham 1992, and D. Cohen 1994. See Steinberg 1995 for a discursive study of class conflict, and Hall 1995 for a study concerned with various actors' narratives in relation to unfolding events in the 1993 assault of the US Bureau of Alcohol, Tobacco, and Firearms against the Branch Davidian compound near Waco, Texas.
45 Stone 1979. On the assessment of sociohistorical plots, see Veyne 1984 and, for a more formal theory, Alker 1987. The classic work of Kenneth Burke (1969, 1984) is particularly important for the use of poetics in inquiry about plots, which offers an alternative to Hayden White's (1973) thesis of poetic structuration.
46 Lyotard 1988: 157–58. A similar point is made by Mink (1978: 143).
47 See Olafson 1979. The adequacy of this position is considered in the coda to this chapter.
48 S. Cohen 1986.
49 Lyotard 1988: 151.
50 For elaboration of this argument, see H. Kellner 1989: ch. 3.
51 In the 1960s, Richard Hofstadter offered a description of "analytic history" as different than conventional narrative; see Ross 1995: 661.
52 It is here that Callinicos's (1995) argument about the theoretical character of history becomes especially salient.
53 A point made by Hexter (1972), concerning Braudel (1972). On the

narrative figuration of even putatively non-narrative history, see Hobsbawm 1980 and Ricoeur 1984: chs. 4, 6, as well as Sande Cohen's (1986: ch. 5) consideration of Braudel.

54 Le Roy Ladurie 1978; Darnton 1984. On the new forms of narrative, see Stone 1979: 19; and, on the *Annales* relation to narrative, see Carrard 1992. Given the diversity of *Annales* plots, it seems misplaced to equate Braudel's *histoire événementielle* with political history, as is sometimes done.

55 Stone 1979: 5; see also Le Goff and Nora 1985.

56 Ricoeur 1988: 91.

CODA 3 THE EXPLANATORY AND INTERPRETIVE
POTENTIAL OF NARRATIVE ACCOUNTS

1 See, e.g., Veyne 1984, Martin 1977, and P. Roth 1988 and 1989.

2 Stone 1979. Olafson (1979) follows a path cleared by Oakeshott's (1966) denunciation of causal explanations in history; cf. Gallie 1964, Danto 1985, and D. Carr 1986. For efforts to develop new potentialities of narrative, see *Social Science History* 16, nos. 3 and 4 (1992), edited by William H. Sewell, Jr.

3 Olafson 1979: 36, 102.

4 An example from Dray 1985: 131.

5 Olafson 1979: 133–44; on this point, compare Veyne 1984, who refuses any analytic theoretical perspective such as sociology.

6 On this issue in relation to social theory, see chapter 4.

7 Olafson 1979: 143.

8 Apel 1984: 116.

9 Apel 1984: 204.

10 Von Wright 1971: 67.

11 For example, Callinicos (1995: 76–94) suggests that history is "theory all the way down."

4 THE CONCEPTUAL POSSIBILITIES OF SOCIAL
THEORETICAL DISCOURSE

1 On postmodern hostility, see Jameson 1991: 181–217. See Antonio and Kellner 1994 for a review of the criticisms and a defense of the project of social theory. Jay (1996) excavates ironies of anti-theory in its contemporary guises. Somers's (1995) issue of conceptual historicity is considered in its ramifications for critical theory by Calhoun 1995. Alexander (1992) makes the point about the accentuated need for theory that foundationlessness creates. See Gates 1994.

2 Alexander 1982.

3 Ragin and Zaret 1983; see also Ragin 1987. Here, I use terms consistent with the present study, not the terminology of Ragin and Zaret.

4 Parsons 1937: 753, 730. For reviews of the debates on Parsons, see Camic 1987, 1989.

5 Parsons 1937: 563–97, 634–35, 750–51, 583, 567 (quote, emphasis in original); Weber 1975.

6 The logical relationship between variable and case analysis has been detailed by Ragin (1987). The example of bureaucracy is taken from Weber (1978: 956–58). I have drawn a very simple example in which only the "pure" combinations (all 1s or all 0s) are defined as ideal types.

7 Parsons 1937: 640–86; on Weber's construction of types, see G. Roth 1971: 115.

8 Parsons's critique of Weber's incomplete formalization suggests the need to revise Bergner's argument that formalistic concern with internal consistency has its origins in neo-Kantian pluralism, exemplified in Weber. Bergner's (1981: 80) conditions of formalization turn out to be a poor description of Weber's analytic strategy, for Weber avoided the notion that formalizing relations among concepts would aid the search for knowledge.

9 Indeed, he would have been mistaken to do so. Formalized ideal types have become a central feature of recent German social theory, e.g., in Schluchter (1981; 1989: ch. 11) and Habermas (1987b: 153–97).

10 Parsons 1937: 607, 619, 621, 626, 631; for a later formulation of the critique, see Parsons 1967: 75–78. See Weber 1978: 20. The radical difference between Parsons's and Weber's approach is exemplified by Parsons's selective translation of Part I of *Wirtschaft und Gesellschaft* (Weber 1947).

11 Alexander 1978: 178.

12 On types of feudalism, see Weber 1978: 1070–73; on work-asceticism, see Weber 1958.

13 G. Roth 1971, 1976. For another example of Weber's subtype development, see his discussion of collegial authority (1978: 271–82). Concerning meaning adequacy, see especially Weber 1978: 20, and Parsons's n. 12 (in Weber 1978: 59); for a more extensive discussion of ideal types, see Weber 1949: 90–112. My description of meaning adequacy as a standard for the ideal type draws on Weber 1978: 11–12.

14 Parsons 1951: 151–67.

15 Abbott 1988b.

16 As Münch (1987) holds, this approach is implicit in *The Structure of Social Action*. There, Parsons (1937: 768) already defines sociology as "the science which attempts to develop an analytical theory of social action systems insofar as these systems can be understood in terms of the property of common value-integration."

17 Sewell 1992.

18 For this argument, see Hall 1977; the empirical examples are explored in Hall 1978.

19 On this point, see also Giddens 1979: 62.

20 It is true that certain AGIL functions – goal attainment, for example – could be fulfilled through rational action, in which means are temporally framed in relation to future goals (Gerstein 1975; cf. Parsons 1937: 750–51). But functionalist concepts specify only the importance of fulfillment of requirements for system persistence, not the temporally structured action whereby the function is or is not fulfilled. Indeed, functionalism provides the insight

that actions with different *meanings* (e.g., "rational" versus "affective") can have equivalent *functional* consequences.

The atemporal character of Parsons's categories is keyed to his identification with Edmund Husserl's early (1970b) atemporal essentialism, which contrasts with the emphasis Husserl (1931, 1964, 1970a) gave later to the essential temporal character of consciousness and its lifeworld setting.

21 Parsons 1937: 727; 1951; 1954: 212–19, esp. 218; 1978; cf. Münch 1987: 52. Parsons himself did not engage in the quantitative "operationalization" of analytic elements. But the displacement of *Verstehen* in analytic-element concepts is compatible with quantitative practice, in which all variables – analytic elements derived from decomposition of meaning complexes, along with functionalist and causal ones – are measured quantitatively and studied by examining relationships among variables across cases.

22 J. Turner 1988; Archer 1988; Blau 1989; Coleman 1990; Sewell 1992.

23 Münch 1987: 37–39.

24 Alexander, Giesen, Münch, and Smelser 1987.

25 For accounts of this development, see Alexander 1983: 110–18; Münch 1987: 76–108.

26 On Weber's theory of classes, see Hall 1997b. On cultural capital, see Bourdieu 1984; for a critique of the assumption of holism in Bourdieu's approach, see Hall 1992.

27 See also Münch 1989: 109.

28 Weber 1978: 4–7.

29 This constructionist distinction between "structure" and "system" roughly parallels Giddens's (1984a: 16) realist distinction between the same terms. From a constructionist viewpoint, however, the "same" phenomenon, e.g., a family, might be described either as a structure or a system. That is, the distinction does not hinge on real differences among phenomenon; the two terms may simply organize conceptualization of a given phenomenon in different ways.

30 Parsons, quoted in Levine 1980: xxx. For the text of the projected chapter, see Parsons 1993. On Parsons' failure to confront Simmel, see Levine 1989, Alexander 1989, and especially Levine 1985: 118–24, and Levine 1991b.

31 Parsons 1937: 716, 748, 772–73.

32 Effectively, Simmel (1959: esp. 314, 323, 325; 1950: 22) precipitated the interpretive problem out of his formal sociology by focusing not on meaningful contents, which are historically variable, but on enduring forms. This issue is considered on pp. 125–26 below.

33 On his resistance to theoretical integration based on a concept of "society 'as such,'" see Simmel 1959: 320. For the claim that sociology transcends social sciences based on "content" (such as political economy or political science), see Simmel 1959: 318. The gap between Simmel and Parsons is described in slightly different terms by Levine (1991b), who (1985: 99) also discusses Weber's views of Simmel.

34 Levine 1985: 100; Simmel 1959: 315; 1950: 22.

35 Simmel 1959: 319.

36 Weber 1978: 3–4; see also Weber 1972.

37 Parsons, quoted in Levine 1980: liii–liv. Despite Parsons's negative con-

clusion, in the unpublished *Structure* chapter, he (1993: 50–53) understood the construct of form in the sense of a "structure." This formulation accords with the present analysis, but Parsons did not fully pursue its implications.

38 For an interesting recent example in the symbolic interactionist tradition that amounts to formal sociology in these terms, see Perinbanayagam 1991. On the relation of Chicago School symbolic interactionists and Goffman to Simmel, see Levine 1989: 114–16.

39 Parsons 1993: 55.

40 Simmel 1959: 321.

41 Simmel 1959: 321–22; 1950.

42 I take the term "interchange" from Parsons both because it implies systemicity in a way that "exchange" does not, and because Parsons's conceptualization nicely bridges the multiple venues in which concrete interchanges have been analyzed, from economic markets to symbolic interaction.

43 For an even-handed survey of social theory, see R. Collins 1988. For a study of the history of social theory, see Levine 1995. Because the theories and theorists I discuss below are well known, and widely considered in these two and other works, I do not generally provide citations to works here.

44 Rubin 1975; R. Collins 1992.

45 J. Turner 1988; Giddens 1984a; Münch 1986; Habermas 1984, 1987b.

46 Levine 1995: 297.

47 Conversely, theory sometimes has been construed so narrowly as to dismiss it as inherently totalizing – a view that is contradicted both by resolutions of the value problem that yield nontotalizing approaches to inquiry (see coda 2), and by the ideal type as a basis of theory that offers analytic utility without assuming a "correspondence" theory of concept formation.

CODA 4 THE USES OF THEORY IN EXPLANATORY AND INTERPRETIVE ACCOUNTS

1 Kiser and Hechter 1991: 6. They embrace Beauchamp and Rosenberg's (1981) Humean specification of Hempel's model of explanation. But as Beauchamp and Rosenberg (1981: 320–21) acknowledge, their discussion is only programmatic.

2 As Humphreys (1989: 130) observes, the use of the disclaimer "carries the connotation that the assumption may well turn out to be untrue." In other words, other things may *not* be equal.

3 Von Wright 1971, Achinstein 1983, and Miller 1987.

4 Blau and Schwartz 1984; Hochberg forthcoming a.

5 A probabilistic explanation is thus inherently "an *incomplete description* of a case" (von Wright 1971: 163, emphasis in original). It may be argued, as Miller (1987: 39–47) has, that probabilistic explanation fails as an extension of a covering-law model of explanation. Yet this would seem to leave open the possibility of probabilistic explanation as incomplete explanation. It is this line of reasoning upon which Humphreys (1989) builds.

6 Olafson 1979: 185; see coda 3 in this volume.

7 Parsons 1937: 719. For an analysis of moral entrepreneurs taking on moral functions of a social order as their own goals, see Hall 1987: ch. 12.

8 It is possible that an empirical pattern would conform to theoretical expectations, but for different reasons than a theory suggests. Because of this possibility, conformity with predictions does not "confirm" a theory's hypotheses; according to Popper's (1968) model of falsification, failure to disconfirm despite a concerted search for negative evidence lends additional credence to a hypothesis and the theory from which it is derived. See also Achinstein 1983: 324 on the requirement that evidence in favor of a particular explanation not only be true, but be related to the thing to be explained in an explanatory fashion.

9 Goldstone 1997; the example I develop is my own. Goldstone (1990: 284–90) develops the construct of robust processes. For a more detailed exploration of the varieties of relations between different orders of social processes, see Stinchcombe 1968.

10 For phenomenological (and structuralist) discussions, see Gurvitch 1964, Schutz and Luckmann 1973, and Luckmann 1991. On deconstruction, see D. Wood 1989. On the relativity of social and historical time, see Needham 1965, Kracauer 1966, Leyden 1962, Hall 1978, 1980, 1994, Wilcox 1987, and Aminzade 1992. For discussions of time and narrative, see Ricoeur 1984, 1985, 1988, and D. Carr 1986.

11 Sewell 1996: 262.

12 Kiser 1994. My use of this and other rational-choice examples is not based on any assessment of their adequacy relative to other social theories.

13 On the frequent failure of functionalist theorists to specify explanatory mechanisms, see Kiser and Hechter 1991: 16, n. 34.

14 Lévi-Strauss 1969. For a recent study that pursues this analysis, see Bearman 1997.

15 Thompson 1978; Bourdieu 1977; Sewell 1990.

16 Weber 1978: 1121–23.

17 Brustein 1991.

18 See Tuma and Hannan 1984, Abbott 1984, 1992, Hall 1984a, 1988, Isaac and Griffin 1989, Mayer and Tuma 1990, and Griffin 1993. In general, these methodologies offer alternatives to causal analysis in experimental time, by providing either causal or interpretive analysis that potentially can be located in eventful time. In addition, Ragin's (1987) Boolean algebra method of Qualitative Comparative Analysis (QCA) is directly geared to the analysis of case patterns, and it can be adapted to eventful-time analysis by incorporating temporally defined variables. I discuss certain of these approaches in chapter 7, in the context of their use in actual practices of inquiry.

19 E.g., Abbott 1988a.

20 Lieberson 1992a: 8.

21 See Kiser and Hechter 1991: 6, n. 7.

22 Thus, Roger Gould's (1995) account of networks of mobilization in popular French uprisings during the Revolution of 1848 and the Paris Commune of 1871 organizes a narrative of intrinsic events by way of an objective theoretical model of network relationships.

23 By connecting narrative practices to types of theoretical concept formation,

these findings parallel the analysis of Hayden White (1973) concerning the genres of historical narrative and their ideological tropes.
24 Miller 1987: 262–63.

5 THE CORE OF EXPLANATION AND INTERPRETATION AS FORMATIVE DISCOURSE

1 Questions about the former communist states of the Soviet Union and the Eastern bloc occasioned a symposium on "prediction in the social sciences" in the *American Journal of Sociology* 100, 6 (May 1995).
2 Thus, Ernest Gellner (1973: 54) holds that no ontology – methodological individualism is his primary target – should dictate criteria of explanation.
3 On history, see Himmelfarb 1987; for an example of the new ethnography, see Lavie 1990; and on the turn toward cultural, case, and situational analysis in sociology, see Becker and McCall 1990, Ragin and Zaret 1983, Ragin 1987, Feagin, Orum, and Sjoberg 1991, and Ragin and Becker 1992.
4 Gallie 1964: 107–15. Hexter (1971b: 163) offers a similar contrast between the rhetoric of narrative and the rhetoric of historical analysis.
5 Conrad Russell, quoted in Dray 1984: 239.
6 Dray 1984; Goldstone 1991. Stone reviews Goldstone's book in Stone 1992; his quoted comment on *psi* is from an exchange with Goldstone, *New York Review of Books* April 22, 1993, p. 69.
7 Miller 1987: 163–77.
8 Traugott 1985: e.g., 86–113, 157, 190 (quote).
9 For critiques of the covering-law approach in sociohistorical explanation, see Mandelbaum 1961, Apel 1984, Danto 1985, and Miller 1987.
10 Miller 1987: 61.
11 Miller 1987: 60–61. Miller does not discuss explanation in terms of "negotiated orders" (Strauss et al. 1963), but his account of "standard causal patterns" (1987: 87) does not seem incompatible with such a depiction. Conventional acceptance of a standard causal pattern would seem to result in a conservative bias in inquiry. Whatever the empirical realities, settled knowledge is more readily accepted, and new knowledge more easily challenged. These circumstances can be lamented, but as Bourdieu (1975) and Lyotard (1984) argue, such circumstances can be changed only by an institutional culture which promotes both concerted challenges of received wisdom and concerted explorations beyond conventional boundaries.
12 Dray 1984: 244.
13 Stone 1972, discussed in Dray 1984: 249–50.
14 Sewell 1990.
15 Hawthorn 1991: 79. M. Bernstein (1994) similarly argues against treating outcomes as overdetermined by finding prior events that "foreshadow" them. In my study of Jonestown I critique the kind of foreshadowing Bernstein describes as a form of pseudoexplanation (Hall 1987: xvi–xvii).
16 Humphreys 1989: 20.
17 Humphreys 1989: 17.
18 In an alternative approach, as S. Turner (1984) has shown, Durkheim

sought to salvage a deterministic social causality by subsuming probabilistic elements into rates measuring the strength of deterministic force. But in the absence of specifying socially deterministic laws, Durkheim's project could not be sustained.

19 This example, similar to Humphreys's, is drawn from Miller (1987: 93–94), who adopts E. H. Carr's (1961: 137–41) standard of rejecting coincidents in explanation.

20 Compare D'Andrade 1986.

21 Parker 1979a: 13.

22 Miller 1987: 262–63; cf. coda 4 above.

23 Ragin 1987; Stinchcombe 1978; Tilly 1995.

24 Stinchcombe 1978: 4–7, 15–16, 117–21. A related account of explanation that similarly depends on comparison has been developed by Stephen Turner, who uses ordinary-language philosophy to describe explanation with "an intelligible character, a 'rationality,' so to speak, distinct from the rationality of scientific 'theory' that some sociologists take as a model." Turner envisions explanation as "translation." To suggest how this works, he compares it to the ways that people in everyday life explain different versions of games – bridge versus hearts, or football versus soccer – "by describing one as a variation of another – by describing them and *emphasizing* their differences and analogies" (S. Turner 1980: 5, 97 [emphasis in original]).

25 Cf. Sewell (1996) who discusses explanation under a slightly different rubric – of path dependence, causal heterogeneity, and contingency.

26 Hawthorn 1991: 80.

6 DISCURSIVE HYBRIDS OF PRACTICE: AN INTRODUCTORY SCHEMA

1 Seidman 1992.

2 Althusser and Balibar 1970; S. Cohen 1986.

3 McKeon 1951: 662; Foucault 1972: 46, 68; Certeau 1988: 92–99; Lyotard 1988: 84, 129. McKeon (1987: ch. 3) envisioned the variety of divergent philosophical positions as actualizations that derive from fundamental structures of meaning and cognitive acts. Actual debates among scholars sometimes acknowledge differences among discourses. Thus, in an exchange with William Sewell, Jr., James Coleman defends his use of abstraction with the comment, "Sewell's difference with me on this point is, I believe, due to a difference between his goal of historical explanation and my goal of developing social theory" (Coleman 1987: 175).

4 P. Burke 1993: 148; 1980; Abrams 1982.

5 Abbott 1991.

6 Burke 1993; Van den Braembussche 1989.

7 Skocpol and Somers 1980; Skocpol 1984a: esp. 363, quotation 388, n. 21).

8 Tilly 1984: 80–84. It seems that the "share-of-instances" axis differentiates uniqueness from science, whereas the "multiplicity-of-forms" axis moves between context- or phenomenon-specific propositions and exploration of propositions in relation to theoretical abstractions that have ever broader

ranges of application (that is, as opposed to single versus multiple cases in relation to a given abstraction). If this is so, the analysis in chapter 7 below suggests the following rough equivalencies obtain between Tilly's types and the "generalizing practices of inquiry": (1) individualizing = contrast-oriented, (2) encompassing = universal history, (3) universalizing = theory application, and (4) variation-finding = analytic generalization. If these equivalences hold, the discussion of "generalizing practices" can be understood as an elaboration of Tilly's strategies, while the practices of "particularizing inquiry" presents parallel approaches pursued within an alternative consolidation of inquiry.

9 On issues of identifying and analyzing cases, see Ragin 1987, Feagin, Orum, and Sjoberg 1991, Ragin and Becker 1992, and Stinchcombe 1978. On the historicity of conceptualizations, see Somers 1992a, 1995, 1996.

10 For invocations of this distinction, see Hamilton 1987 and Calhoun 1987.

11 The procedure used here identifies only practices elaborated fully in relation to all four forms of discourse. It is possible that a given study might not strongly employ all discursive forms, that a given study might approximate a given ideal type only weakly, and that a study might involve multiple practices (on the latter point, see chapter 9). Because of these possibilities, the cultural coherences of inquiry are open-ended.

7 GENERALIZING PRACTICES OF INQUIRY

1 See, for example, contributors to Skocpol 1984b.

2 Skocpol and Somers 1980; Skocpol 1984a.

3 On literature, see Eagleton 1983. Here, I do not make a concerted effort to locate either natural science or literary and other predominantly humanistic analyses in relation to generalizing practices, although I do not think there is any obstacle in principle to doing so. The case for the natural sciences' interest in generalization is obvious. As for humanistic inquiry, we can briefly note generalizing affinities for literary criticism as an exemplar. Literary inquiry is especially drawn to practices of: (1) the application of theory (of texts, authors, audiences, and the like) to cases; (2) universal history, where theory totalizes its object, as in certain psychoanalytic approaches; and (3) contrast-oriented comparison, where theory is relegated to a peripheral status. The practice of analytic generalization does not seem to hold much attraction for humanistic inquiry except in the quantitative analysis of texts.

4 Skocpol and Somers 1980: 176–78; Skocpol 1984a: 362.

5 For a discussion of the philosophy of history that describes universal history, see Danto 1985: ch. 1. On the German Enlightenment, see Reill 1975. Manuel's (1965) survey of philosophical history includes Hegel and Marx; Hobsbawm (1970) cites Marx's approach as revealing the "direction" of history; and Mink (1978: 137) identifies orthodox Marxism as the sole modern survival of universal history. Treatments by Jay (1984), A. Cook (1988: ch. 10), and Grumley (1989) document other, and more recent, approaches to the problem of totalizing history, including the ambiguous posture of Michel Foucault.

6 White 1987: 21, 61–64. On global integration, see, for example, Giddens 1990. On deconstructing historical writings, see S. Cohen 1986.

7 Parsons 1966; Wallerstein 1979: esp. ch. 9.

8 Wallerstein 1979: 35. Skocpol (1984a: 363) locates Wallerstein's project halfway between approaches that "apply a general model" and those which "use concepts to develop a meaningful . . . interpretation." See also Ragin and Chirot 1984.

9 See Freud's *Civilization and Its Discontents* (1962); Parsons 1966. For an attempt to develop a behavioristic social theory into totalizing history, see Homans 1987.

10 Burawoy (1990) uses Lakatos's idea of research programs to advance Marxism as a science. On a similar basis, Kiser and Hechter (1991) offer rational-choice theory as a framework for a theoretically robust historical sociology.

11 For a trenchant critique of the sort of "absolutist theory" that gives rise to universal history, see Gellner 1992: 89–93 on Freudian psychoanalysis.

12 The most sophisticated effort to resolve this problem, partly in response to teleological critiques, is that of McMichael (1990), who pulls back from the totalization involved in strong versions of world-system theory by reconstructing universal history as "incorporated comparison." Like the present study, his solution moves to identify a fourth type to fill out Skocpol and Somers's typology, and it does so by reworking the category of "encompassing comparison" used by Tilly (1984) to describe Wallerstein's work, i.e., what I am calling universal history. However, McMichael does not fully theorize the "generalizing"/"particularizing" distinction, and therefore ends up describing particularizing practice within a typology of generalizing practices. That is, he seeks to do away with universal history, substituting for it a practice that approximates what I describe in chapter 8 as a particularizing practice, namely, configurational history, using internal comparisons that approximate the contrast-oriented comparative generalizing practice. This "hybrid" combines typologically distinct practices in a fashion that I describe in chapter 9.

13 Skocpol 1984a; Smelser 1959: esp. 85–86, 408.

14 Calhoun 1982: 195.

15 Aronowitz 1981; Luhmann 1982. For substantive challenges to core assumptions of world-system theory, see Hall 1984b, 1991b, Stern 1988a, 1988b. Wallerstein (1988) offers a concerted defense to Stern's critique.

16 Skocpol and Somers 1980: 176–78; Skocpol 1984a: 362–68.

17 Paige 1975: 39 (quote), 40–71, 41 (quote).

18 Paige 1975: ix–x.

19 Paige 1975: 157.

20 Paige 1975: 166–80.

21 Goldstone 1986, 1991.

22 Goldstone 1991: ch. 2. For critical discussions, see R. Collins 1993 and Keddie 1995: Part II.

23 Weber 1978: 19. The method of analytic induction was developed by Lindesmith 1947. Ragin (1987) rightly notes the parallels between it and Mill's inductive method of agreement.

24 Calhoun 1982: viii.

25 Ragin 1987: 101; Skocpol 1984a: 375.
26 Kiser and Hechter 1991: 4. For a critique of Kiser and Hechter, see Quadagno and Knapp 1992.
27 Skocpol 1979: 41 (quote), 43, 47, and Part II.
28 For discussions of Mill, see Skocpol 1984a: 378–79 and Ragin 1987: 36–42.
29 Mill 1950: 216. Granted, as Ragin (1987: 39–40) observes, insofar as statistical analysis is probabilistic, it alters the assumption behind Mill's indirect method of difference, but the method's basic rationale nevertheless is reflected in the statistical comparison of subsamples in techniques such as the analysis of variance, and in what Mill (1950: 223–29) termed the "method of concomitant variations" that is relevant to correlation analysis.
30 Mill 1950: 221; Ragin 1987.
31 Lieberson 1992b; see also Kiser and Hechter 1991: 12–17.
32 Stinchcombe 1978: 21. This problem is not unique to the practice of analytic generalization; it is shared by any practice that engages in systematic classification or quantitative measurement; see the discussion in chapter 5.
33 On this point, see Miller 1987: 262.
34 Goldstone 1991.
35 Weber 1958. For Bloch's methodological commentary on comparison, see his 1967 essay; see also Sewell 1967.
36 Skocpol (1984a) terms this strategy "using concepts to interpret history." Because this practice encompasses explanation as well as interpretation, I employ the term used by Skocpol and Somers (1980).
37 Bendix 1978: 15; for an example of Bendix's culturalist argument, see pp. 265–72.
38 A point made by Skocpol 1984a: 371–74; see also Kiser and Hechter 1991.
39 Stinchcombe 1978: 117; S. Turner 1980: 97.
40 Pelikan 1985; Moore 1984.
41 The phrase "rules of experience" is from G. Roth (1976: 313).
42 Mill 1950: 216–18, 221.
43 Ragin 1987.
44 Skocpol and Somers 1980: 178.

8 PARTICULARIZING PRACTICES OF INQUIRY

1 G. Roth 1971, 1976, 1987.
2 G. Roth 1976: 310.
3 Lenin 1963: 192. The historical context is described in the introduction, by S. V. Utechin.
4 Richard Biernacki, personal communication, 1997.
5 Pateman 1988: 233.
6 White 1987: ch. 1. On nationalism, see Bhabha 1990.
7 Fogel and Engerman 1974. For one exploration of Columbus, see Greenblatt 1991.
8 Ginzburg 1980; Bonnell 1983; Thompson 1975; R. Scott 1985.
9 Duby 1968. Structural histories beyond the approach of specific history

typically take the form either of configurational history or historicism, discussed pp. 216–28 below, or universal history, discussed in chapter 7.

10 On Peoples Temple, see Hall 1987; on cultural history in these terms, see Hall 1990, forthcoming.

11 Stone 1979; Ashton and Philpin 1985.

12 Colligation is discussed by Dray (1989: ch. 2); it may be accomplished in relation to an "epochal concept" or "specific ideal type" (G. Roth 1976: 311). The example of ragtime music offers a cautionary tale for any such typification; see E. Berlin 1980.

13 Such an approach amounts to a single-case variant of "theory application" (see chapter 7).

14 See Weber 1978: 20 for his most accessible sketch of this logic.

15 Hall 1987.

16 Traugott 1985: 134.

17 Thus, embedded within Traugott's specific history is the generalizing practice of theory application, discussed pp. 188–92 above.

18 Hunt 1984: 219.

19 On the limits of historical knowledge, see Shiner 1969. Precisely the move to metanarrative gives rise to S. Cohen's (1986) critique of historical writing.

20 G. Roth 1976: 309–16.

21 The term "evolutionary stage theories" is that of Guenther Roth (1976: 309). For an argument that Weber's approach to rationalization did not involve evolutionary holism, see G. Roth 1987.

22 R. Collins 1980. The theorization is based on Weber 1981.

23 Schluchter 1989: 27. A succinct typological account is contained in Schluchter 1981.

24 Anderson 1974.

25 Mann 1986.

26 G. Roth 1976: 199.

27 S. Cohen 1986.

28 Bendix 1984: ch. 1.

29 L. Krieger 1977.

30 Popper 1961: 45. I agree with E. H. Carr's (1961: 119–20) assessment of Popper's confusions; see also Passmore 1975 and Lee and Beck 1954.

31 Iggers 1975; Novick 1988; Lloyd 1993: 164; Meinecke, quoted in Iggers 1975: 34.

32 For example, in Ranke 1973: 31–32.

33 Himmelfarb 1987: 9. For a Marxist defense of historicism, see Thompson 1978. For the possibilities linked to social movements see Touraine 1988: 63–74 and Hall 1991a.

34 S. Cohen 1986.

35 Gadamer 1975: Part II, esp. 244. White (1987: ch. 1) also explores the moral significance of narrative, as does Lyotard (1984).

36 Ross 1995.

37 Hobsbawm 1994.

38 G. Wood 1991: 6 (quote), 95 (quote); he summarizes trend analysis of population and commerce on p. 308, and makes claims for radicalness of revolution, e.g., pp. 231–32.

39 Walkowitz 1992: 5.
40 Greenblatt 1982: 5.
41 Jameson 1991: 190.
42 Thomas 1991.

9 THE PROSPECTS FOR INQUIRY

1 Though this is not the place to do so, it would be possible to locate experimental and quasi-experimental research designs (T. Cook and Campbell
  1979) and various parametric and nonparametric statistical techniques in
  relation to the typology of practices described here.
2 For an example of a defense of "mainstream" social science, see Huber and
  Morawska 1997; in my view, they seek to affirm a strong binary distinction
  between "facts" and "fables," yet do so, ironically, both by offering a fabled
  vision of science that fails to consider the problem inherent in multiple scientific perspectives, and by proceeding in an anti-intellectual fashion that refuses to engage the specifics of arguments raised by critics.
3 See chapter 2.
4 See chapter 1.
5 Lyotard 1984: 79.
6 On this point, see also Foucault 1972: 45–46; Lyotard 1988: 138, §189.
7 A point also argued by Paul Roth (1987).
8 Schluchter 1989.
9 Hochberg forthcoming b.
10 See chapter 8.
11 Weber 1946.
12 Habermas 1971: 311.
13 Fraser 1989; Calhoun 1992. The possibilities of critically informed empirical inquiry are considered in detail by Bohman (1991: ch. 5).
14 Calhoun 1995: 187.
15 Foucault 1972: 186.
16 In effect, this table uses the typology of projects of inquiry derived from the
   relation between analytic dimensions connected to two discourses – values
   and explanation/ interpretation – to array the alternative methodological
   practices that have value and explanatory/interpretive discourses embedded
   within them. This procedure was not used in the initial hermeneutic construction of the typology of practices, only to explore its coherence
   retrospectively.
17 The alternative possibilities of translation as described here parallel levels of
   discursive relations more generally, as described by Foucault (1972: 45).
18 Kuhn 1970: 126, 148–150, 198–204. For discussions, see R. Bernstein
   1983: 61–71 and Laudan 1987. I have used Laudan's terms to describe
   Kuhn's analysis – "object-level incommensurability" and "incompatibility
   of the standards" of alternative paradigms – and shifted them into alignment
   with terms used in the present study, i.e., objects of inquiry and practices
   of inquiry.
19 Rorty 1979: 317; Lyotard 1988: 135, 137.

20 Taylor 1985: 18, 52 (quote).
21 R. Bernstein 1983: 93.
22 Rorty (1979: 389) borrows this term from Michael Oakeshott to portray hermeneutic conversation as an alternative to foundational epistemology.
23 P. Roth 1987: 244; see also Stephen Turner's (1980) analysis of translation as a model of sociological explanation.
24 Here and below, some of the examples are from Dray 1984.
25 For this analysis of Brazilian colonization, see Hall 1984b.
26 Levine 1995.
27 Foucault 1972. The project of reflexive inquiry into inquiry has been promoted especially in the work of Pierre Bourdieu and Loïc Wacquant; in my view, however, Bourdieu's quest for objectivity (Bourdieu and Wacquant 1992: 214–15) is quixotically anti-Kantian if it exceeds an account of objectivity as socially constructed through the constitution of an object of inquiry by way of an observer's context of meaning (see chapters 2 and 3 of the present study); and, if it does acknowledge inquiry's dependence on its construction of its objects, it should do so explicitly.
28 Blalock 1982: 21–22; Pearson 1911.
29 See Hall 1996. Efforts in the direction of critiquing measurement include Lieberson 1985, Block and Burns 1986, Abbott 1988b, Desrosières 1992, and Donnelly 1997. A number of scholars – most notably Ragin (1987), Isaac and Griffin (1989), and Griffin and Isaac (1992) – have proposed specific strategies of measurement and analysis oriented to case-comparative and historical-developmental analyses. A major puzzle that must be faced by measurement and statistical theorists concerns the nature of abstraction (Sayer 1987). The most sustained reconstructive effort to date for statistics as a whole is the neo-realist program of Pawson (1989). For a critique of Pawson from the social interaction perspective, see Hall 1996.
30 Taylor 1985: 56.
31 Foucault 1970; 1972: 68 (quote).
32 Somers 1992b, 1995, 1996.
33 As Barry Barnes (1981) has argued.
34 See, for example, Parsons 1937 and Hindess 1977.
35 Habermas 1981: 8–9, 10 (quote), 11 (quote); his rejection of foundationalism can be found in 1984: xli, and 1987b: 400.
36 Lyotard 1984: 60, 65, 65 (quote), 43. For a useful review of Lyotard's engagement against Habermas, see S. Watson (1984), who points to the irony of how the modernist Kant's philosophy lends support to Lyotard's over Habermas's position. Later, Lyotard (1987a, 1988) himself elaborates what might be construed as a neo-Kantian account of the differend.
37 Alexander 1992: 361.
38 E.g., Bloch 1953. For a biography, see Fink 1989.
39 On this point, see C. Turner 1990.

Bibliography

Abbott, Andrew. 1984. "Event sequence and event duration: colligation and measurement." *Historical Methods* 17: 192–204.
1988a. *The System of Professions*. Chicago: University of Chicago Press.
1988b. "Transcending general linear reality." *Sociological Theory* 6: 169–86.
1991. "History and sociology: the lost synthesis." *Social Science History* 15: 201–38.
1992. "From causes to events: notes on narrative positivism." *Sociological Methods & Research* 20: 428–55.
Abrams, Philip. 1982. *Historical Sociology*. Ithaca, N.Y.: Cornell University Press.
Achinstein, Peter. 1983. *The Nature of Explanation*. New York: Oxford University Press.
Adorno, Theodor W. 1973. *Negative Dialectics*. New York: Seabury.
1976. "Introduction." Pp. 1–67 in Adorno et al. 1976.
1983 [1956]. *Against Epistemology*. Cambridge, Mass.: MIT Press.
Adorno, Theodor W., Hans Albert, Ralf Dahrendorf, Jürgen Habermas, Harald Pilot, and Karl R. Popper. 1976 [1969]. *The Positivist Dispute in German Sociology*. New York: Harper & Row.
Alcoff, Linda, and Elizabeth Potter, eds. 1993. *Feminist Epistemologies*. New York: Routledge.
Alexander, Jeffrey C. 1978. "Formal and substantive voluntarism in the work of Talcott Parsons." *American Sociological Review* 43: 177–98.
1982. *Theoretical Logic in Sociology, Vol. I: Positivism, Presuppositions, and Current Controversies*. Berkeley: University of California Press.
1983. *Theoretical Logic in Sociology, Vol. IV: The Modern Reconstruction of Classical Thought. Talcott Parsons*. Berkeley: University of California Press.
1989. "Against historicism/for theory: a reply to Levine." *Sociological Theory* 7: 118–20.
1992. "General theory in the postpositivist mode: the 'epistemological dilemma' and the search for present reason." Pp. 322–68 in Seidman and Wagner 1992.
Alexander, Jeffrey C., Bernhard Giesen, Richard Münch, and Neil J. Smelser, eds. 1987. *The Micro–Macro Link*. Berkeley: University of California Press.
Alford, C. Fred. 1985. "Is Jürgen Habermas's reconstructive science really science?" *Theory and Society* 14: 321–40.
Alker, Hayward R., Jr. 1987. "Fairy tales, tragedies and world histories: towards

interpretive story grammars as possibilist world models." *Behaviormetrika* 21: 1–28.

Althusser, Louis, and Etienne Balibar. 1970 [1968]. *Reading Capital.* London: NLB.

Aminzade, Ronald. 1992. "Historical sociology and time." *Sociological Methods & Research* 20: 456–80.

Anderson, Perry. 1974. *Passages from Antiquity to Feudalism.* London: NLB.

Ankersmit, F. R. 1988. "Historical representation." *History and Theory* 27: 205–28.

Antonio, Robert J. 1989. "The normative foundations of emancipatory theory: evolutionary versus pragmatic perspectives." *American Journal of Sociology* 94: 721–48.

Antonio, Robert J., and Douglas Kellner. 1994. "The limits of postmodern critique." Pp. 127–52 in David Dickens and Andrea Fontana, *Postmodernism and Social Inquiry.* New York: Guilford Press.

Apel, Karl-Otto. 1984 [1979]. *Understanding and Explanation: A Transcendental-Pragmatic Perspective.* Cambridge, Mass.: MIT Press.

Appleby, Joyce, Lynn Hunt, and Margaret Jacob. 1994. *Telling the Truth About History.* New York: Norton.

Archer, Margaret S. 1988. *Culture and Agency.* New York: Cambridge University Press.

Aronowitz, Stanley. 1981. "A metatheoretical critique of Immanuel Wallerstein's *The Modern World System.*" *Theory and Society* 19: 503–20.

Ashmore, Malcolm. 1989. *The Reflexive Thesis: Wrighting Sociology of Scientific Knowledge.* Foreword by Steve Woolgar. Chicago: University of Chicago Press.

Ashton, T. H., and C. H. E. Philpin. 1985. *The Brenner Debate: Agrarian Class Structure and Economic Development in Pre-Industrial Europe.* New York: Cambridge University Press.

Bakhtin, Mikhail M. 1981. *The Dialogic Imagination.* Austin: University of Texas Press.

Barnes, Barry. 1981. "On the conventional character of knowledge and cognition." *Philosophy of Social Science* 11: 303–33.

——— 1985. *About Science.* New York: B. Blackwell.

Barnes, Barry, and David Edge, eds. 1982. *Science in Context.* Cambridge, Mass.: MIT Press.

Barthes, Roland. 1972 [1957]. *Mythologies.* New York: Hill & Wang.

Baudrillard, Jean. 1983. *Simulations.* New York: Semiotext(e).

Bearman, Peter. 1997. "Generalized exchange." *American Journal of Sociology* 102: 1383–1415.

Beauchamp, Tom L., and Alexander Rosenberg. 1981. *Hume and the Problem of Causation.* New York: Oxford University Press.

Becker, Howard S. 1982. *Art Worlds.* Berkeley: University of California Press.

Becker, Howard S., and Michal McCall, eds. 1990. *Symbolic Interactionism and Cultural Studies.* Chicago: University of Chicago Press.

Bender, John, and David E. Wellbery. 1991. *Chronotypes: The Social Construction of Time.* Stanford, Calif.: Stanford University Press.

Bendix, Reinhard. 1978. *Kings or People*. Berkeley: University of California Press.

1984. *Force, Fate, and Freedom*. Berkeley: University of California Press.

Bendix, Reinhard, and Guenther Roth. 1971. *Scholarship and Partisanship: Essays on Max Weber*. Berkeley: University of California Press.

Benhabib, Seyla. 1986. *Critique, Norm, and Utopia*. New York: Columbia University Press.

1990. "Epistemologies of postmodernism: a reply to Jean-François Lyotard." Pp. 107–30 in Nicholson 1990.

1995. "Subjectivity, historiography, and politics: reflections on the 'feminism/postmodernism exchange.'" Pp. 107–25 in Seyla Benhabib, Judith Butler, Drucilla Cornell, and Nancy Fraser. *Feminist Contentions*. New York: Routledge.

Benjamin, Walter. 1969 [1955]. *Illuminations*, Hannah Arendt, ed. New York: Schocken.

Berger, Peter, and Thomas Luckmann. 1966. *The Social Construction of Reality*. New York: Doubleday.

Bergner, Jeffrey T. 1981. *The Origin of Formalism in Social Science*. Chicago: University of Chicago Press.

Berlin, Edward A. 1980. *Ragtime: A Musical and Cultural History*. Berkeley: University of California Press.

Berlin, Isaiah. 1970. *The Hedgehog and the Fox: An Essay on Tolstoy's View of History*. New York: Simon and Schuster.

Bernstein, Michael A. 1994. *Foregone Conclusions: Against Apocalyptic History*. Berkeley: University of California Press.

Bernstein, Richard J. 1983. *Beyond Objectivism and Relativism*. Philadelphia: University of Pennsylvania Press.

1991. *The New Constellation: The Ethical-Political Horizons of Modernity/Postmodernity*. Cambridge, UK: Polity Press.

Bhabha, Homi K., ed. 1990. *Nation and Narration*. New York: Routledge.

Bhaskar, Roy. 1986. *Scientific Realism and Human Emancipation*. London: Verso.

1989. *Reclaiming Reality*. London: Verso.

Blalock, Herbert. 1982. *Conceptualization and Measurement in the Social Sciences*. Beverly Hills, Calif.: Sage.

Blau, Peter M. 1989. "Structures of social positions and relations of social structures." Pp. 43–59 in Jonathan H. Turner 1989.

Blau, Peter M., and Joseph E. Schwartz. 1984. *Crosscutting Social Circles: Testing a Macrostructural Theory of Intergroup Relations*. Orlando: Academic Press.

Bleier, Ruth., ed. 1986. *Feminist Approaches to Science*. New York: Pergamon Press.

Bloch, Marc. 1953. *The Historian's Craft*. New York: Random House.

1967. "A contribution towards a comparative history of European societies." Pp. 44–81 in Bloch, *Land and Work in Mediaeval Europe*. Berkeley: University of California Press.

Block, Fred, and Gene Burns. 1986. "Productivity as a social problem: the uses and misuses of social indicators." *American Sociological Review* 51: 767–80.

Bohman, James. 1991. *New Philosophy of Social Science*. Cambridge, Mass.: MIT Press.

Bonnell, Victoria E. 1983. *Roots of Rebellion: Workers' Politics and Organizations in St. Petersburg and Moscow, 1900–1914*. Berkeley: University of California Press.

Booth, Wayne C. 1983 [1961]. *The Rhetoric of Fiction*, 2nd edn. Chicago: University of Chicago Press.

Bottomore, Tom. 1984. *The Frankfurt School*. New York: Tavistock.

Bourdieu, Pierre. 1975. "The specificity of the scientific field and the social conditions of the progress of reason." *Social Science Information* 14, no. 6: 19–47.

1977 [1972]. *Outline of a Theory of Practice*. New York: Cambridge University Press.

1984 [1979]. *Distinction: A Social Critique of the Judgement of Taste*. Cambridge, Mass.: Harvard University Press.

Bourdieu, Pierre, and Loïc J. D. Wacquant. 1992. *An Invitation to Reflexive Sociology*. Chicago: University of Chicago Press.

Brannigan, Augustine. 1981. *The Social Basis of Scientific Discoveries*. New York: Cambridge University Press.

Braudel, Fernand. 1972 [1966]. *The Mediterranean and the Mediterranean World in the Age of Philip the Second*, Sian Reynolds, transl. New York: Harper & Row.

Brown, Richard H. 1987. *Society as Text*. Chicago: University of Chicago Press.

Brustein, William. 1991. "The 'red menace' and the rise of Italian fascism." *American Sociological Review* 56: 652–64.

Buck-Morss, Susan. 1977. *The Origin of Negative Dialectics*. New York: Free Press.

Burawoy, Michael. 1990. "Marxism as science." *American Sociological Review* 55: 775–93.

Burger, Thomas. 1976. *Max Weber's Theory of Concept Formation*. Durham, N.C.: Duke University Press.

Burke, Kenneth. 1969 [1950]. *A Rhetoric of Motives*. Berkeley: University of California Press.

1984 [1937]. *Attitudes Toward History*. Berkeley: University of California Press.

Burke, Peter. 1980. *Sociology and History*. Boston: Allen & Unwin.

1993. *History and Social Theory*. Ithaca, N.Y.: Cornell University Press.

Calhoun, Craig J. 1982. *The Question of Class Struggle: Social Foundations of Popular Radicalism During the Industrial Revolution*. Chicago: University of Chicago Press.

1987. "History and sociology in Britain: a review article." *Comparative Studies in Society and History* 29: 615–25.

ed. 1992. *Habermas and the Public Sphere*. Cambridge, Mass.: MIT Press.

1995. *Critical Social Theory*. Cambridge, Mass.: Blackwell.

Callinicos, Alex. 1995. *Theories and Narratives: Reflections of the Philosophy of History*. Oxford, UK: Polity/Blackwell.

Camic, Charles. 1987. "The making of a method: a historical reinterpretation of the early Parsons." *American Sociological Review* 52: 421–39.

1989. "*Structure* after 50 years: the anatomy of a charter." *American Journal of Sociology* 95: 38–107.

Campbell, Donald T. 1988. *Methodology and Epistemology for Social Science.* Chicago: University of Chicago Press.

Carr, David. 1986. *Time, Narrative, and History.* Bloomington: Indiana University Press.

Carr, Edward H. 1961. *What Is History?* New York: Random House.

Carrard, Philippe. 1992. *Poetics of the New History.* Baltimore: Johns Hopkins University Press.

Certeau, Michel de. 1988 [1975]. *The Writing of History.* New York: Columbia University Press.

Clemens, Elisabeth S. 1996. "Continuity and coherence: periodization and the problem of change." Pp. 62–82 in Ragnvald Kalleberg and Fredrik Engelstad, eds., *Social Time and Social Change.* Oslo: Norwegian University Press.

Clifford, James. 1988. *The Predicament of Culture.* Cambridge, Mass.: Harvard University Press.

Cohen, David William. 1994. *The Combing of History.* Chicago: University of Chicago Press.

Cohen, Sande. 1986. *Historical Culture.* Berkeley: University of California Press.

Coleman, James S. 1987. "Actors and actions in social history and social theory: reply to Sewell." *American Journal of Sociology* 93: 172–75.

1990. *Foundations of Social Theory.* Cambridge, Mass.: Harvard University Press.

Collins, H. M. 1983. "The sociology of scientific knowledge." *Annual Review of Sociology* 9: 265–85.

Collins, Patricia Hill. 1990. *Black Feminist Thought.* Cambridge, Mass.: Allen & Unwin.

Collins, Randall. 1980. "Weber's last theory of capitalism: a systematization." *American Sociological Review* 45: 925–42.

1988. *Theoretical Sociology.* New York: Harcourt Brace Jovanovitch.

1989. "Sociology: proscience or antiscience?" *American Sociological Review* 54: 124–39.

1992. "Women and the production of status cultures." Pp. 213–31 in Lamont and Fournier 1992.

1993. "Review article: maturation of the state-centered theory of revolution and ideology." *Sociological Theory* 11: 117–28.

Cook, Albert. 1988. *History/Writing.* New York: Cambridge University Press.

Cook, Thomas D., and Donald T. Campbell. 1979. *Quasi-Experimentation: Design and Analysis Issues for Field Settings.* Boston: Houghton Mifflin.

D'Andrade, Roy. 1986. "Three scientific world views and the covering law model." Pp. 19–41 in Donald W. Fiske and Richard A. Shweder, eds., *Metatheory in Social Science: Pluralisms and Subjectivities.* Chicago: University of Chicago Press.

Dant, Tim. 1991. *Knowledge, Ideology and Discourse: A Sociological Perspective.* London: Routledge.

Danto, Arthur C. 1985. *Narration and Knowledge.* New York: Columbia University Press.

Darnton, Robert. 1984. *The Great Cat Massacre and Other Episodes in French Cultural History*. New York: Basic.

Davis, Murray S. 1986. "'that's classic!' The phenomenology and rhetoric of successful social theories." *Philosophy of the Social Sciences* 16: 285–301.

Davis, Natalie Zemon. 1983. *The Return of Martin Guerre*. Cambridge, Mass.: Harvard University Press.

1988. "On the lame." *American Historical Review* 93: 572–603.

Derrida, Jacques. 1978 [1967]. "Structure, sign, and play in the discourse of the human sciences." Pp. 278–93 in Derrida, *Writing and Difference*. Chicago: University of Chicago Press.

Desrosières, Alain. 1992. "How to make things which hold together: social science, statistics and the state." Paris: INSEE, unpublished manuscript.

Diesing, Paul. 1991. *How Does Social Science Work?* Pittsburgh, Pa.: University of Pittsburgh Press.

Dilthey, Wilhelm. 1976. *Selected Writings*, H. P. Rickman, ed. and transl. New York: Cambridge University Press.

Donnelly, Michael. 1997. "Statistical classifications and the salience of social class." Pp. 107–31 in Hall 1997a.

Dray, William H. 1984. "Conflicting interpretations in history: the case of the English Civil War." Pp. 239–57 in Shapiro and Sica 1984.

1985. "Narrative versus analysis in history." *Philosophy of the Social Sciences* 15: 125–45.

1989. *On History and Philosophers of History*. Leiden, Netherlands: E. J. Brill.

Duby, Georges. 1968 [1962]. *Rural Economy and Country Life in the Medieval West*. Columbia: University of South Carolina Press.

Eagleton, Terry. 1983. *Literary Theory*. Minneapolis: University of Minnesota Press.

Edmondson, Ricca. 1984. *Rhetoric in Sociology*. London: Macmillan.

Eley, Geoff. 1996. "Is all the world a text?" Pp. 193–243 in McDonald 1996.

Factor, Regis A., and Stephen P. Turner. 1979. "The limits of reason and some limitations of Weber's morality." *Human Studies* 2: 301–34.

Feagin, Joe R., Anthony M. Orum, and Gideon Sjoberg, eds. 1991. *A Case for the Case Study*. Chapel Hill: University of North Carolina Press.

Fentress, James, and Chris Wickham. 1992. *Social Memory*. Cambridge, Mass.: Blackwell.

Feyerabend, Paul. 1975. *Against Method*. London: New Left Books.

1988. "Knowledge and the role of theories." *Philosophy of the Social Sciences* 18: 157–78.

Fink, Carole. 1989. *Marc Bloch: A Life in History*. New York: Cambridge University Press.

Fogel, Robert William, and Stanley L. Engerman. 1974. *Time on the Cross: The Economics of American Negro Slavery*. Boston: Little, Brown.

Foley, Richard. 1987. *The Theory of Epistemic Rationality*. Cambridge, Mass.: Harvard University Press.

Foucault, Michel. 1970 [1966]. *The Order of Things*. New York: Random House.

1972 [1969]. *The Archaeology of Knowledge*. London: Tavistock.

1988. "The political technology of individuals." Pp. 145–62 in Luther H.

Martin, Huck Gutman, and Patrick H. Hutton, eds., *Technologies of the Self*. Amherst: University of Massachusetts Press.

Fraser, Nancy. 1989. *Unruly Practices: Power, Discourse and Gender in Contemporary Social Theory*. Minneapolis: University of Minnesota Press.

Freud, Sigmund. 1962 [1930]. *Civilization and Its Discontents*. New York: W. W. Norton.

Fuller, Steve. 1988. *Social Epistemology*. Bloomington: Indiana University Press.

Gadamer, Hans-Georg. 1975. *Truth and Method*. New York: Seabury Press.

1985. *Philosophical Apprenticeships*. Cambridge, Mass.: MIT Press.

Gallie, W. B. 1964. *Philosophy and the Historical Understanding*. London: Chatto & Windus.

Garfinkel, Alan. 1981. *Forms of Explanation*. New Haven, Conn.: Yale University Press.

Gasché, Rodolphe. 1987. "Infrastructures and systematicity." Pp. 1–20 in *Deconstruction and Philosophy: The Texts of Jacques Derrida*, John Sallis, ed. Chicago: University of Chicago Press.

Gates, Henry Louis. 1994 [1987]. "Authority, (white) power, and the (black) critic: it's all Greek to me." Pp. 247–68 in Nicholas B. Dirks, Geoff Eley, and Sherry B. Ortner, eds., *Culture/Power/History*. Princeton, N.J.: Princeton University Press.

Gay, Peter. 1974. *Style in History*. New York: Basic.

Geertz, Clifford. 1973. "Thick description: toward an interpretive theory of culture." Pp. 3–30 in Geertz, *The Interpretation of Cultures*. New York: Basic.

1988. *Works and Lives: The Anthropologist as Author*. Stanford, Calif.: Stanford University Press.

Gellner, Ernest. 1973. *Cause and Meaning in the Social Sciences*. London: Routledge & Kegan Paul.

1985. *Relativism and the Social Sciences*. New York: Cambridge University Press.

1992. *Reason and Culture*. Cambridge, Mass.: B. Blackwell.

Gerstein, Dean R. 1975. "A note on the continuity of Parsonian action theory." *Sociological Inquiry* 45: 11–15.

Giddens, Anthony. 1971. *Capitalism and Modern Social Theory*. New York: Cambridge University Press.

1979. *Central Problems in Social Theory*. Berkeley: University of California Press.

1984a. *The Constitution of Society*. Berkeley: University of California Press.

1984b. "Hermeneutics and social theory." Pp. 215–30 in Shapiro and Sica 1984.

1990. *The Consequences of Modernity*. Stanford, Calif.: Stanford University Press.

Gilbert, Felix. 1990. *History: Politics or Culture? Reflections on Ranke and Burckhardt*. Princeton, N.J.: Princeton University Press.

Ginzburg, Carlo. 1980 [1976]. *The Cheese and the Worms: The Cosmos of a Sixteenth-Century Miller*. Baltimore: Johns Hopkins University Press.

Goffman, Erving. 1959. *The Presentation of Self in Everyday Life*. Garden City, N.Y.: Doubleday.

1974. *Frame Analysis*. New York: Harper & Row.

Goldman, Harvey. 1992. *Politics, Death, and the Devil: Self and Power in Max Weber and Thomas Mann*. Berkeley: University of California Press.

Goldstone, Jack A. 1986. "State breakdown in the English Revolution: a new synthesis." *American Journal of Sociology* 92: 257–322.

1990. "Sociology and history: producing comparative history." Pp. 275–92 in Herbert Gans, ed., *Sociology in America*. Beverly Hills: Sage.

1991. *Revolution and Rebellion in the Early Modern World*. Berkeley: University of California Press.

1997. "Methodological issues in comparative macrosociology." *Comparative Social Research* 16: 107–20.

Gould, Roger. 1995. *Insurgent Identities: Class, Community, and Protest in Paris from 1848 to the Commune*. Chicago: University of Chicago Press.

Granovetter, Mark, and Richard Swedberg, eds. 1992. *The Sociology of Economic Life*. Boulder, Colo.: Westview Press.

Grant, Judith. 1987. "I feel therefore I am: a critique of female experience as the basis for a feminist epistemology." *Women and Politics* 7: 99–114.

Green, Bryan S. 1988. *Literary Methods and Sociological Theory*. Chicago: University of Chicago Press.

Greenblatt, Stephen. 1982. "Introduction" to *The Forms of Power and the Power of Forms in the Renaissance*, special issue. *Genre* 15: 3–6.

1991. *Marvelous Possessions*. Chicago: University of Chicago Press.

Greimas, Algirdas J. 1990. *The Social Sciences: A Semiotic View*. Minneapolis: University of Minnesota Press.

Griffin, Larry J. 1993. "Narrative, event-structure analysis, and causal interpretation in historical sociology." *American Journal of Sociology* 98: 1094–1133.

Griffin, Larry J., and Larry W. Isaac. 1992. "Recursive regression and the historical use of 'time' in time-series analysis of historical process." *Historical Methods* 25: 166–79.

Groz, E. A. 1988. "The in(ter)vention of feminist knowledges." Pp. 92–109 in Barbara Caine, Groz, and Marie de Lepervanche, eds., *Crossing Boundaries: Feminisms and the Critique of Knowledges*. Boston: Allen & Unwin.

Grumley, John E. 1989. *History and Totality*. New York: Routledge.

Gulbenkian Commission on the Restructuring of the Social Sciences. 1996. *Open the Social Sciences*. Stanford, Calif.: Stanford University Press.

Gurvitch, Georges. 1964. *The Spectrum of Social Time*. Dordrecht, Netherlands: D. Reidel.

Habermas, Jürgen. 1971 [1968]. *Knowledge and Human Interests*. Boston: Beacon Press.

1973. *Theory and Practice*. Boston: Beacon.

1976a. "The analytical theory of science and dialectics." Pp. 131–62 in Adorno et al. 1976.

1976b. "A positivistically bisected rationalism, a reply to a pamphlet." Pp. 198–225 in Adorno et. al. 1976.

1981. "Modernity versus postmodernity." *New German Critique* 22: 3–14.

1984 [1981]. *The Theory of Communicative Action, Vol. I: Reason and the Rationalization of Society*. Boston: Beacon.

1987a. *The Philosophical Discourse of Modernity.* Cambridge, Mass.: MIT Press.

1987b [1981]. *The Theory of Communicative Action, Vol. II: Lifeworld and System.* Boston: Beacon Press.

1988 [1967]. *On the Logic of the Social Sciences.* Cambridge, Mass.: MIT Press.

1989a. *The New Conservatism: Cultural Criticism and the Historians' Debate.* Cambridge, Mass.: MIT Press.

1989b [1962]. *The Structural Transformation of the Public Sphere.* Cambridge, Mass.: MIT Press.

1992. *Postmetaphysical Thinking: Philosophical Essays.* Cambridge, Mass.: MIT Press.

Hacking, Ian. 1982. "Language, truth and reason." Pp. 48–66 in Martin Hollis and Steven Lukes, eds., *Rationality and Relativism.* Oxford, UK: Blackwell.

Halfpenny, Peter. 1982. *Positivism and Sociology.* London: Allen & Unwin.

Hall, John R. 1977. "Alfred Schutz, his critics and applied phenomenology." *Cultural Hermeneutics* 4: 265–79.

1978. *The Ways Out: Utopian Communal Groups in an Age of Babylon.* Boston: Routledge & Kegan Paul.

1980. "The time of history and the history of times," *History and Theory* 19: 113–31.

1984a. "Temporality, social action, and the problem of quantification in historical analysis." *Historical Methods* 17: 206–18.

1984b. "World-system holism and colonial Brazilian agriculture: a critical case analysis." *Latin American Research Review* 19: 43–69.

1987. *Gone from the Promised Land: Jonestown in American Cultural History.* New Brunswick, N.J.: Transaction.

1988. "Social organization and pathways of commitment: types of communal groups, rational choice theory, and the Kanter thesis." *American Sociological Review* 53: 679–92.

1990. "Social interaction, culture, and historical studies." Pp. 16–45 in Becker and McCall 1990.

1991a. "Hermeneutics, social movements, and thematic religious history." Pp. 91–113 in David Bromley, ed., *Religion and the Social Order.* Greenwich, Conn.: JAI Press.

1991b. "World-system theory, Max Weber, and the patrimonial dynamic in colonial Brazil." Pp. 57–88 in Richard Graham, ed., *Brazil and the World System.* Austin: University of Texas Press.

1992. "The capital(s) of culture: a non-holistic theory of status situations, class, gender, and ethnicity." Pp. 257–85 in Lamont and Fournier 1992.

1994. "Periodization and sequences." Pp. 558–61 in Peter N. Stearns, ed., *Encyclopedia of Social History.* New York: Garland.

1995. "Public narratives and the apocalyptic sect: from Jonestown to Mount Carmel." Pp. 205–35 in Stuart A. Wright, ed., *Armageddon in Mount Carmel.* Chicago: University of Chicago Press.

1996. "Measurement and the two cultures of sociology." Pp. 181–208 in Stephen P. Turner, ed., *Social Theory and Sociology.* New York: Blackwell.

ed. 1997a. *Reworking Class*. Ithaca, N.Y.: Cornell University Press.

1997b. "The reworking of class analysis." Pp. 1–37 in Hall 1997a.

Forthcoming. "Theorizing hermeneutic cultural history." In Roger Friedland and John Mohr, eds., *The Cultural Turn*.

Hall, John R., and Mary Jo Neitz. 1993. *Culture: Sociological Perspectives*. Englewood Cliffs, N.J.: Prentice Hall.

Hamilton, Gary G. 1987. "The 'new history' in sociology." *Politics, Culture, and Society* 1: 89–114.

Haraway, Donna. 1988. "Situated knowledges: the science question in feminism and the privilege of partial perspective." *Feminist Studies* 14: 575–99.

Harding, Sandra. 1990. "Feminism, science, and the anti-Enlightenment critiques." Pp. 83–106 in Nicholson 1990.

1991. *Whose Science? Whose Knowledge?* Ithaca, N.Y.: Cornell University Press.

Harré, Rom. 1990. "Exploring the human umwelt." Pp. 297–364 in Roy Bhaskar, ed., *Harré and His Critics*. Cambridge, Mass.: B. Blackwell.

Hawthorn, Geoffrey. 1991. *Plausible Worlds: Possibility and Understanding in History and the Social Sciences*. New York: Cambridge University Press.

Heilbrun, Carolyn G. 1988. *Writing a Woman's Life*. New York: Norton.

Hekman, Susan J. 1983a. "From epistemology to ontology: Gadamer's hermeneutics and Wittgensteinian social science." *Human Studies* 6: 205–24.

1983b. *Weber, the Ideal Type, and Contemporary Social Theory*. Notre Dame, Ind.: University of Notre Dame Press.

Held, David. 1980. *Introduction to Critical Theory*. Berkeley: University of California Press.

Henige, David P. 1974. *The Chronology of Oral Tradition: Quest for a Chimera*. Oxford, UK: Clarendon Press.

Hexter, J. H. 1971a. *Doing History*. Bloomington: Indiana University Press.

1971b. *The History Primer*. New York: Basic.

1972. "Fernand Braudel and the *Monde Braudellien*." *Journal of Modern History* 44: 480–539.

Himmelfarb, Gertrude. 1987. *The New History and the Old*. Cambridge, Mass.: Harvard University Press.

Hindess, Barry. 1977. *Philosophy and Methodology in the Social Sciences*. Atlantic Highlands, N.J.: Humanities Press.

Hobsbawm, Eric J. 1970. "Karl Marx's contribution to historiography." *Diogenes* 64: 37–56.

1980. "The revival of narrative: some comments." *Past and Present* 86: 3–8.

1994. *The Age of Extremes*. New York: Pantheon.

Hochberg, Leonard. Forthcoming a. *Geography of Revolution: A Comparative Analysis of England, the United States, and France*. Palo Alto, Calif.: Stanford University Press.

Forthcoming b. "Reconciling history with sociology: analytical strategies in Tocqueville's *Democracy in America* and *The Old Regime and the French Revolution*."

Holub, Robert C. 1984. *Reception Theory: A Critical Introduction*. New York: Methuen.

Homans, George C. 1987. "Behaviorism and after." Pp. 58–81 in Anthony Giddens and Jonathan Turner, eds., *Social Theory Today*. Stanford, Calif.: Stanford University Press.

Horkheimer, Max. 1972. *Critical Theory*. New York: Herder & Herder.

Huber, Joan, and Ewa T. Morawska. 1997. "Of facts and fables: reply to Denzin." *American Journal of Sociology* 102: 1423–29.

Huff, Toby E. 1984. *Max Weber and the Methodology of the Social Sciences*. New Brunswick, N.J.: Transaction.

Huhn, Thomas. 1989. "The postmodern return, with a vengeance, of subjectivity." Pp. 228–48 in Douglas Kellner, ed., *Postmodernism/Jameson/Critique*. Washington, D.C.: Maisonneuve Press.

Humphreys, Paul. 1989. *The Chances of Explanation*. Princeton, N.J.: Princeton University Press.

Hunt, Lynn. 1984. *Politics, Culture, and Class in the French Revolution*. Berkeley: University of California Press.

  1992. *The Family Romance of the French Revolution*. Berkeley: University of California Press.

Husserl, Edmund. 1931 [1913]. *Ideas*. New York: Macmillan.

  1964 [1905]. *The Phenomenology of Internal Time Consciousness*, J. S. Churchill, transl. Bloomington: Indiana University Press.

  1970a [1954]. *The Crisis of European Sciences and Transcendental Phenomenology*, David Carr, transl. Evanston, Ill.: Northwestern University Press.

  1970b [1901]. *Logical Investigations*, J. N. Findlay, transl. New York: Humanities Press.

Huyssen, Andreas. 1986. *After the Great Divide: Modernism, Mass Culture, Postmodernism*. Bloomington: Indiana University Press.

I Ching, or Book of Changes. 1967. Richard Wilhelm, transl., rendered into English by Cary F. Baynes. Forward by C. J. Jung. Princeton, N.J.: Princeton University Press.

Iggers, Georg G. 1975. "The image of Ranke in American and German historical thought." *History and Theory* 2: 17–40.

  1983. *The German Conception of History*, rev. edn. Middletown, Conn.: Wesleyan University Press.

Isaac, Larry W., and Larry J. Griffin. 1989. "Ahistoricism in time-series analyses of historical process." *American Sociological Review* 54: 873–90.

James, William. 1908 [1907]. *Pragmatism*. London: Longmans, Green, and Co.

Jameson, Fredric. 1972. *The Prison-House of Language*. Princeton, N.J.: Princeton University Press.

  1981. *The Political Unconscious: Narrative as a Socially Symbolic Act*. Ithaca, N.Y.: Cornell University Press.

  1991. *Postmodernism, or the Cultural Logic of Late Capitalism*. Durham, N.C.: Duke University Press.

Jay, Martin. 1973. *The Dialectical Imagination*. Boston: Little, Brown.

  1984. *Marxism and Totality*. Berkeley: University of California Press.

  1989. "The debate over performative contradiction: Habermas vs. the poststructuralists." Pp. 171–89 in Axel Honneth, Thomas McCarthy, Claus Offe, and Albrecht Wellmer, eds., *Zwischenbetrachtungen: im Prozess der Auf-*

klarung. Jurgen Habermas zum 60. Geburtstag. Frankfurt, Germany: Suhr-kamp Verlag.

1996. "For theory." *Theory and Society* 25: 167–83.

Kammen, Michael. 1991. *Mystic Chords of Memory.* New York: Knopf.

Kant, Immanuel. 1951 [1790]. *Critique of Judgment,* J. H. Bernard, transl. New York: Hafner Publishing.

1963 [1784]. "Idea for a universal history from a cosmopolitan point of view." Pp. 11–26 in Kant, *On History,* Lewis W. Beck, ed. Indianapolis: Bobbs-Merrill.

Käsler, Dirk. 1988. *Max Weber: An Introduction to His Life and Work.* Chicago: University of Chicago Press.

Kauffman, Stuart. 1995. *At Home in the Universe.* New York: Oxford University Press.

Keat, Russell. 1981. *The Politics of Social Theory.* Oxford, UK: B. Blackwell.

Keddie, Nikki R., ed. 1995. *Debating Revolutions.* New York: New York University Press.

Kellner, Douglas. 1990. "Critical theory and the crisis of social theory." *Sociological Perspectives* 33: 11–33.

Kellner, Hans D. 1987. "Narrativity in history: post-structuralism and since." *History and Theory, Beiheft* 26: 1–29.

1989. *Language and Historical Representation.* Madison: University of Wisconsin Press.

Kemp, Anthony. 1991. *The Estrangement of the Past.* New York: Oxford University Press.

Kiser, Edgar. 1994. "Markets and hierarchies in early modern fiscal systems: a principal-agent analysis." *Politics & Society* 22: 284–315.

Kiser, Edgar, and Michael Hechter. 1991. "The role of general theory in comparative-historical sociology." *American Journal of Sociology* 97: 1–30.

Kocka, Jürgen. 1985. "The social sciences between dogmatism and decisionism: a comparison of Karl Marx and Max Weber." Pp. 134–66 in Robert J. Antonio and Ronald M. Glassman, eds., *A Weber–Marx Dialogue.* Lawrence: University Press of Kansas.

Köhnke, Klaus Christian. 1991. *The Rise of Neo-Kantianism: German Academic Philosophy Between Idealism and Positivism.* New York: Cambridge University Press.

Kracauer, Siegfried. 1966. "Time and history." *History and Theory, Beiheft* 6: 65–78.

Krieger, Leonard. 1977. *Ranke: The Meaning of History.* Chicago: University of Chicago Press.

Krieger, Murray, ed. 1987. *The Aims of Representation.* New York: Columbia University Press.

Kuhn, Thomas. 1970. *The Structure of Scientific Revolutions,* 2nd edn. Chicago: University of Chicago Press.

LaCapra, Dominik. 1977. "Habermas and the grounding of critical theory." *History and Theory* 16: 237–64.

Lakatos, Imre. 1971. "History of science and its rational reconstructions." *Boston Studies in the Philosophy of Science* 8: 91–136.

Lamont, Michèle, and Marcel Fournier, eds. 1992. *Cultivating Differences: Sym-*

bolic Boundaries and the Making of Inequality. Chicago: University of Chicago Press.

Latour, Bruno. 1987. *Science in Action: How to Follow Scientists and Engineers Through Society.* Cambridge, Mass.: Harvard University Press.

1993. *We Have Never Been Modern.* Cambridge, Mass.: Harvard University Press.

Latour, Bruno, and Steve Woolgar. 1986. *Laboratory Life: The Construction of Scientific Facts,* 2nd edn. Princeton, N.J.: Princeton University Press.

Laudan, Larry. 1987. "Relativism, naturalism reticulation." *Synthese* 71: 221–34.

Lavie, Smadar. 1990. *The Poetics of Military Occupation: Mzeina Allegories of Bedouin Identity Under Israeli and Egyptian Rule.* Berkeley: University of California Press.

Layder, Derek. 1985. "Beyond empiricism? The promise of realism." *Philosophy of the Social Sciences* 15: 255–74.

Le Goff, Jacques, and Pierre Nora. 1985 [1974]. *Constructing the Past: Essays in Historical Methodology.* Cambridge, UK: Cambridge University Press.

Le Roy Ladurie, Emmanuel. 1978. *Montaillou.* New York: G. Braziller.

Lee, Dwight E., and Robert N. Beck. 1954. "The meaning of 'historicism.'" *American Historical Review* 59: 568–77.

Lenin, V. I. 1963 [1902]. *What Is to Be Done?* Oxford, UK: Clarendon Press.

Lévi-Strauss, C. 1966 [1962]. *The Savage Mind.* London: Weidenfeld & Nicholson.

1969 [1949]. *The Elementary Structures of Kinship.* Boston: Beacon.

Levine, Donald N. 1980 [1957]. *Simmel and Parsons: Two Approaches to the Study of Society.* New York: Arno Press.

1985. *The Flight from Ambiguity.* Chicago: University of Chicago Press.

1989. "Parsons' *Structure* (and Simmel) revisited." *Sociological Theory* 7: 110–17.

1991a. "Review of *Literary Methods and Sociological Theory.*" *American Journal of Sociology* 96: 1047–49.

1991b. "Simmel and Parsons reconsidered." *American Journal of Sociology* 96: 1097–1116.

1995. *Visions of the Sociological Tradition.* Chicago: University of Chicago Press.

Leyden, W. von. 1962. "History and the concept of relative time." *History and Theory* 2: 263–85.

Lieberson, Stanley. 1985. *Making It Count.* Berkeley: University of California Press.

1992a. "Einstein, Renoir, and Greeley: some thoughts about evidence in sociology." *American Sociological Review* 57: 1–15.

1992b. "Small *N*'s and big conclusions: an examination of the reasoning in comparative studies based on a small number of cases." Pp. 105–18 in Ragin and Becker 1992.

Lindesmith, Alfred R. 1947. *Opiate Addiction.* Bloomington, Ind.: Principia Press.

Lloyd, Christopher. 1986. *Explanation in Social History.* New York: B. Blackwell.

1993. *The Structures of History*. Cambridge, Mass.: Blackwell.

Longino, Helen. 1993. "Subjects, power and knowledge: description and prescription in feminist philosophies of science." Pp. 101–20 in Alcoff and Potter 1993.

Luckmann, Thomas. 1991. "The constitution of human life in time." Pp. 151–66 in Bender and Wellbery 1991.

Luhmann, Niklas. 1982. *The Differentiation of Society*. New York: Columbia University Press.

Lukács, Georg. 1971 [1967]. *History and Class Consciousness*. Cambridge, Mass.: MIT Press.

Lyotard, Jean-François. 1984 [1979]. *The Postmodern Condition*. Minneapolis: University of Minnesota Press.

1986. *L'Enthousiasme: la critique kantienne de l'histoire*. Paris: Editions Galilée.

1987a. "Judiciousness in dispute, or Kant after Marx." Pp. 23–67 in M. Krieger 1987.

1987b. "The sign of history." Pp. 162–80 in Derek Attridge, Geoff Bennington, and Robert Young, eds., *Post-Structuralism and the Question of History*. New York: Cambridge University Press.

1988. *The Differend: Phrases in Dispute*. Minneapolis: University of Minnesota Press.

McCarthy, Thomas. 1991. *Ideals and Illusions: On Reconstruction and Deconstruction in Contemporary Critical Theory*. Cambridge, Mass.: MIT Press.

McCloskey, Donald. 1985. *The Rhetoric of Economics*. Madison: University of Wisconsin Press.

McCullagh, C. Behan. 1987. "The truth of historical narratives." *History and Theory*, Beiheft 26: 30–46.

McDonald, Terrence J., ed. 1996. *The Historic Turn in the Human Sciences*. Ann Arbor: University of Michigan Press.

McKeon, Richard. 1951. "Philosophy and method." *Journal of Philosophy* 48: 653–82.

1987. *Rhetoric: Essays in Invention and Discovery*. Woodbridge, Conn.: Ox Bow Press.

McMichael, Philip. 1990. "Incorporating comparison within a world-historical perspective." *American Sociological Review* 55: 385–97.

Makkreel, Rudolf A. 1975. *Dilthey: Philosopher of the Human Studies*. Princeton, N.J.: Princeton University Press.

Mandelbaum, Maurice. 1961. "Historical explanation: the problem of covering laws." *History and Theory* 1: 229–42.

Mann, Michael. 1986. *The Sources of Social Power, Vol. I: A History of Power from the Beginning to AD 1760*. New York: Cambridge University Press.

Mannheim, Karl. 1937. *Ideology and Utopia*. New York: Harcourt, Brace & World.

1953. "Conservative thought." Pp. 74–164 in Mannheim, *Essays on Sociology and Social Psychology*. London: Routledge & Kegan Paul.

Manuel, Frank E. 1965. *Shapes of Philosophic History*. Stanford, Calif.: Stanford University Press.

Marcus, George E., and Michael M. J. Fisher. 1986. *Anthropology as Cultural*

Critique: An Experimental Moment in the Human Sciences. Chicago: University of Chicago Press.

Margolis, Joseph. 1985. "Deconstruction: or the mystery of the mystery of the text." Pp. 138–51 in Hugh J. Silverman and Don Ihde, eds., *Hermeneutics and Deconstruction.* Albany: State University of New York Press.

Martin, Rex. 1977. *Historical Explanation.* Ithaca, N.Y.: Cornell University Press.

Marx, Karl. 1978a [1844]. "Economic and philosophic manuscripts of 1844." Pp. 66–125 in Tucker 1978.

1978b [1843]. "On the Jewish question." Pp. 26–52 in Tucker 1978.

Mayer, Karl, and Nancy Tuma, eds. 1990. *Event History Analysis in Life Course Research.* Madison: University of Wisconsin Press.

Mill, John Stuart. 1950 [1843]. *John Stuart Mill's Philosophy of Scientific Method.* New York: Hafner.

Miller, Richard W. 1987. *Fact and Method: Explanation, Confirmation and Reality in the Natural and the Social Sciences.* Princeton, N.J.: Princeton University Press.

Mink, Louis O. 1978. "Narrative form as a cognitive instrument." Pp. 129–49 in Robert H. Canary and Henry Kozicki, eds., *The Writing of History.* Madison: University of Wisconsin Press.

Mitchell, Douglas. 1988. "Special review essay: *Rhetoric: Essays in Invention and Understanding* by Richard McKeon." *Rhetorica* 6: 395–414.

Mommsen, Wolfgang J. 1989. *The Political and Social Theory of Max Weber: Collected Essays.* Chicago: University of Chicago Press.

Moore, Barrington. 1984. *Privacy: Studies in Social and Cultural History.* Armonk, N.Y.: M. E. Sharpe.

Morris, John, ed. 1980. *Nennius: British History and the Welsh Annals.* Totowa, N.J.: Rowman & Littlefield.

Mullins, Nicholas C. 1980 [1966]. *Social Networks Among Biological Scientists.* New York: Arno Press.

Münch, Richard. 1986. "The American creed in sociological theory: exchange, negotiated order, accommodated individualism, and contingency." *Sociological Theory* 4: 41–60.

1987. *Theory of Action: Towards a New Synthesis Going Beyond Parsons.* New York: Routledge & Kegan Paul.

1989. "Code, structure and action: building a theory of structuration from a Parsonian point of view." Pp. 101–17 in Jonathan H. Turner 1989.

Needham, Joseph. 1965. *Time and Eastern Man.* London: Royal Anthropological Institute of Great Britain and Ireland.

Nelson, Lynn Hankinson. 1993. "Epistemological communities." Pp. 121–59 in Alcoff and Potter 1993.

Nelson, John S., Allan Megill, and Donald N. McCloskey, eds. 1987. *The Rhetoric of the Human Sciences.* Madison: University of Wisconsin Press.

Newton-Smith, W. H. 1981. *The Rationality of Science.* Boston: Routledge & Kegan Paul.

Nicholson, Linda J., ed. 1990. *Feminism/Postmodernism.* New York: Routledge.

Nietzsche, Friedrich. 1957 [1874]. *The Use and Abuse of History,* Adrian Collins, transl. Indianapolis, Ind.: Bobbs-Merrill.

Norris, Christopher. 1985. *The Contest of Faculties*. New York: Methuen.

Novick, Peter. 1988. *That Noble Dream: The "Objectivity Question" and the American Historical Profession*. New York: Cambridge University Press.

Oakes, Guy. 1985. "Theoretical rationality and the problem of radical value conflicts: remarks on Simmel, Rickert, and Weber." *State, Culture and Society* 1: 175–99.

　1988. *Weber and Rickert: Concept Formation in the Cultural Sciences*. Cambridge, Mass.: MIT Press.

Oakeshott, Michael. 1966 [1933]. "Historical continuity and causal analysis." Pp. 193–212 in William H. Dray, ed., *Philosophical Analysis and History*. New York: Harper & Row.

Olafson, Frederick A. 1979. *The Dialectic of Action: A Philosophical Interpretation of History and the Humanities*. Chicago: University of Chicago Press.

O'Neill, John. 1986. "A realist model of knowledge: with a phenomenological deconstruction of its model of man." *Philosophy of the Social Sciences* 16: 1–19.

Outhwaite, William. 1987. *New Philosophies of Social Science: Realism, Hermeneutics, Critical Theory*. New York: St. Martin's Press.

Overington, Michael A. 1981. "A rhetorical appreciation of a sociological classic: Durkheim's *Suicide*." *Canadian Journal of Sociology* 6: 447–61.

Owensby, Jacob. 1994. *Dilthey and the Narrative of History*. Ithaca, N.Y.: Cornell University Press.

Paige, Jeffrey. 1975. *Agrarian Revolution: Social Movements and Export Agriculture in the Underdeveloped World*. New York: Free Press.

Palmer, Bryan D. 1990. *Descent into Discourse: The Reification of Language and the Writing of Social History*. Philadelphia: Temple University Press.

Papineau, David. 1978. *For Science in the Social Sciences*. New York: St. Martin's Press.

Parker, Geoffrey. 1979a. *Europe in Crisis, 1598–1648*. Ithaca, N.Y.: Cornell University Press.

　1979b. *Spain and the Netherlands, 1559–1659: Ten Studies*. London: William Collins Sons.

Parsons, Talcott. 1937. *The Structure of Social Action*. New York: Free Press.

　1951. *The Social System*. New York: Free Press.

　1954. *Essays in Sociological Theory*. New York: Free Press.

　1966. *Societies: Evolutionary and Comparative Perspectives*. Englewood Cliffs, N.J.: Prentice-Hall.

　1967. *Sociological Theory and Modern Society*. New York: Free Press.

　1978. *Action Theory and the Human Condition*. New York: Free Press.

　1993. "Georg Simmel and Ferdinand Tönnies: social relationships and the elements of action." *Teoria Sociologica* 1, 1 (Giuseppe Sciortine, ed.): 45–71.

Passmore, John. 1975. "*The Poverty of Historicism* revisited." *History and Theory*, Beiheft 14: 30–47.

Pateman, Carole. 1988. *The Sexual Contract*. Cambridge, UK: Polity Press/B. Blackwell.

Patrides, C. A. 1972. *The Grand Design of God*. London: Routledge & Kegan Paul.

Pawson, Ray. 1989. *A Measure for Measures*. New York: Routledge.

Pearson, Karl. 1911. *The Grammar of Science*, 3rd edn. New York: Macmillan.

Pelikan, Jaroslav. 1985. *Jesus Through the Centuries*. New Haven, Conn.: Yale University Press.

Pels, Dick. 1996. "Karl Mannheim and the sociology of scientific knowledge: toward a new agenda." *Sociological Theory* 14: 30–48.

Perinbanayagam, Robert S. 1991. *Discursive Acts*. New York: Aldine de Gruyter.

Phillips, Derek L. 1973. *Abandoning Method*. San Francisco: Jossey-Bass.

Polanyi, Michael. 1967. "Knowing and being." Pp. 123–37 in *Knowing and Being: Essays by Michael Polanyi*, M. Grene, ed. Chicago: University of Chicago Press, 1969.

Polkinghorne, Donald. 1988. *Narrative Knowing and the Human Sciences*. Albany: State University of New York Press.

Popper, Karl R. 1961 [1957]. *The Poverty of Historicism*. New York: Harper & Row.

   1968 [1959]. *The Logic of Scientific Discovery*. New York: Harper & Row.

   1979 [1972]. *Objective Knowledge: An Evolutionary Approach*, rev. edn. Oxford, UK: Clarendon Press.

   1983. *Realism and the Aim of Science*. Totowa, N.J.: Rowman & Littlefield.

Pratt, Mary Louise. 1977. *Toward a Speech Act Theory of Literary Discourse*. Bloomington: Indiana University Press.

Proctor, Robert N. 1991. *Value-Free Science? Purity and Power in Modern Knowledge*. Cambridge, Mass.: Harvard University Press.

Putnam, Hilary. 1981. *Reason, Truth and History*. Cambridge, UK: Cambridge University Press.

   1990. *Realism with a Human Face*, James Conant, ed. Cambridge, Mass.: Harvard University Press.

Quadagno, Jill, and Stan J. Knapp. 1992. "Have historical sociologists forsaken theory?" *Sociological Methods and Research* 20: 481–507.

Rabinow, Paul. 1985. "Discourse and power: on the limits of ethnographic texts." *Dialectical Anthropology* 10: 1–13.

Ragin, Charles C. 1987. *The Comparative Method*. Berkeley: University of California Press.

Ragin, Charles C., and Howard S. Becker, eds. 1992. *What Is a Case?* New York: Cambridge University Press.

Ragin, Charles, and Daniel Chirot. 1984. "The world system of Immanuel Wallerstein: sociology and politics as history." Pp. 276–312 in Skocpol 1984b.

Ragin, Charles C., and David Zaret. 1983. "Theory and method in comparative research: two strategies." *Social Forces* 61: 731–54.

Ranke, Leopold von. 1973 [c. 1830s]. "On the relations of history and philosophy." Pp. 29–32 in Georg G. Iggers and Konrad von Moltke, eds., *The Theory and Practice of History: Leopold von Ranke*. Indianapolis: Bobbs-Merrill.

Rawls, Anne W. 1996. "Durkheim's epistemology: the neglected argument." *American Journal of Sociology* 102: 430–82.

Reill, Peter H. 1975. *The German Enlightenment and the Rise of Historicism*. Berkeley: University of California Press.

Rickert, Heinrich. 1986 [1902]. *The Limits of Concept Formation in Natural Science: A Logical Introduction to the Historical Sciences.* New York: Cambridge University Press.

Ricoeur, Paul. 1979 [1971]. "The model of the text: meaningful action considered as a text." Pp. 73–101 in Paul Rabinow and William Sullivan, eds., *Interpretive Social Science.* Berkeley: University of California Press.

1984, 1985, 1988. *Time and Narrative,* 3 vols. Chicago: University of Chicago Press.

Rorty, Richard. 1979. *Philosophy and the Mirror of Nature.* Princeton, N.J.: Princeton University Press.

Rosaldo, Renato. 1989. *Culture and Truth.* Boston: Beacon Press.

Rosenau, Pauline M. 1992. *Post-Modernism and the Social Sciences.* Princeton, N.J.: Princeton University Press.

Ross, Dorothy. 1995. "Grand narrative in American historical writing: from romance to uncertainty." *American Historical Review* 100: 651–77.

Roth, Guenther. 1971. "Sociological typology and historical explanation." Pp. 109–28 in Bendix and Roth 1971.

1976. "History and sociology in the work of Max Weber." *British Journal of Sociology* 27: 306–18.

1987. "Rationalization in Max Weber's developmental history." Pp. 75–91 in Scott Lash and Sam Whimster, eds., *Max Weber, Rationality, and Modernity.* London: Allen & Unwin.

1988–89. "Weber's political failure." *Telos* 78 (Winter): 136–49.

Roth, Paul A. 1987. *Meaning and Method in the Social Sciences.* Ithaca, N.Y.: Cornell University Press.

1988. "Narrative explanations: the case of history." *History and Theory* 27: 1–13.

1989. "How narratives explain." *Social Research* 56: 449–78.

Rubin, Gayle. 1975. "The traffic in women: notes on the 'political economy' of sex." Pp. 157–210 in Reyna Reiter, ed., *Toward an Anthropology of Women.* New York: Monthly Review Press.

Sahlins, Marshall. 1985. *Islands of History.* Chicago: University of Chicago Press.

Sayer, Derek. 1987. *The Violence of Abstraction.* New York: B. Blackwell.

Sayers, Sean. 1985. *Reality and Reason.* New York: B. Blackwell.

Schluchter, Wolfgang. 1979. "Value-neutrality and the ethic of responsibility." Pp. 65–116 in Guenther Roth and Wolfgang Schlucter, *Max Weber's Vision of History: Ethics and Methods.* Berkeley: University of California Press.

1981. *The Rise of Western Rationalism: Max Weber's Developmental History.* Berkeley: University of California Press.

1989. *Rationalism, Religion, and Domination: A Weberian Perspective.* Berkeley: University of California Press.

Schudson, Michael. 1978. *Discovering the News: A Social History of American Newspapers.* New York: Basic.

Schutz, Alfred. 1967 [1932]. *The Phenomenology of the Social World.* Evanston, Ill.: Northwestern University Press.

1970. *Reflections on the Problem of Relevance.* New Haven, Conn.: Yale University Press.

Schutz, Alfred, and Thomas Luckmann. 1973. *The Structures of the Lifeworld.* Evanston, Ill.: Northwestern University Press.

Scott, Marvin, and Stanford Lyman. 1968. "Accounts." *American Sociological Review* 33: 46–62.

Scott, Rebecca J. 1985. *Slave Emancipation in Cuba: The Transition to Free Labor, 1860–1899.* Princeton, N.J.: Princeton University Press.

Searle, John. 1993. "Rationality and realism: what is at stake?" *Daedalus* 122, 4 (Fall): 55–83.

Seidman, Steven. 1992. "Postmodern social theory as narrative with a moral intent." Pp. 47–81 in Seidman and Wagner 1992.

Seidman, Steven, and David G. Wagner, eds. 1992. *Postmodernism and Modern Theory.* New York: B. Blackwell.

Sewell, William H., Jr. 1967. "Marc Bloch and the logic of comparative history." *History and Theory* 6: 208–18.

1990. "Collective violence and collective loyalties in France: why the French Revolution made a difference." *Politics & Society* 18: 527–52.

1992. "A theory of structure: duality, agency, and transformation." *American Journal of Sociology* 98: 1–29.

1996. "Three temporalities: toward an eventful sociology." Pp. 245–80 in McDonald 1996.

Shalin, Dmitri N. 1992. "Critical theory and the pragmatist challenge." *American Journal of Sociology* 98: 237–79.

Shapiro, Gary, and Alan Sica, eds. 1984. *Hermeneutics: Questions and Prospects,* Amherst: University of Massachusetts Press.

Shiner, Larry. 1969. "A phenomenological approach to historical knowledge." *History and Theory* 8: 260–74.

Silverstein, Michael, and Greg Urban, eds. 1996. *Natural Histories of Discourse.* Chicago: University of Chicago Press.

Simmel, Georg. 1950 [1908/1917]. *The Sociology of Georg Simmel.* New York: Free Press.

1959 [1908]. "The problem of sociology." Pp. 310–36 in Simmel, *Essays on Sociology, Philosophy and Aesthetics,* Kurt Wolff, ed. New York: Harper & Row.

1977 [1905]. *The Problems of the Philosophy of History.* New York: Free Press.

Skocpol, Theda. 1979. *States and Social Revolutions.* New York: Cambridge University Press.

1984a. "Emerging agendas and recurrent strategies in historical sociology." Pp. 356–91 in Skocpol 1984b.

ed. 1984b. *Vision and Method in Historical Sociology.* Cambridge, UK: Cambridge University Press.

Skocpol, Theda, and Margaret Somers. 1980. "The uses of comparative history in macrosocial inquiry." *Comparative Studies in Society and History* 22: 174–97.

Smelser, Neil. 1959. *Social Change in the Industrial Revolution: An Application of Theory to the British Cotton Industry.* Chicago: University of Chicago Press.

Smith, Dorothy E. 1987. *The Everyday World as Problematic: A Feminist Sociology.* Boston: Northeastern University Press.

1993. "High noon in textland: a critique of Clough." *Sociological Quarterly* 34: 183–92.

Snow, C. P. 1959. *The Two Cultures and the Scientific Revolution*. New York: Cambridge University Press.

Somers, Margaret R. 1992a. "Narrativity, narrative identity, and social action: rethinking English working-class formation." *Social Science History* 16: 591–630.

1992b. "The political culture concept: the empirical power of conceptual transformations." Presented at the annual meetings of the American Sociological Association, 1991. Working paper 88. Ann Arbor: University of Michigan Comparative Study of Social Transformations Working Papers.

1995. "Narrating and naturalizing civil society and citizenship theory: the place of political culture and the public sphere." *Sociological Theory* 13: 229–74.

1996. "Where is social theory after the historic turn? Historical epistemologies, narrative, and knowledge cultures." Pp. 53–89 in McDonald 1996.

Somers, Margaret R., and Gloria D. Gibson. 1994. "Reclaiming the epistemological 'other': narrative and the social constitution of identity." Pp. 37–99 in Craig Calhoun, ed., *Social Theory and the Politics of Identity*. Oxford, UK: Blackwell.

Spencer, Martin E. 1982. "The ontologies of social science." *Philosophy of the Social Sciences* 12: 121–41.

Spivak, Gayatri Chakravorty. 1988. "Can the subaltern speak?" Pp. 271–313 in Cary Nelson and Lawrence Grossberg, eds., *Marxism and the Interpretation of Culture*. Urbana: University of Illinois Press.

Steinberg, Marc W. 1995. "The roar of the crowd: repertories of discourse and collective action among the Spitalfields silk weavers in nineteenth-century London." Pp. 57–87 in Mark Traugott, ed., *Repertoires of Collective Action*. Durham, N.C.: Duke University Press.

1997. "Fence sitting for a better view: finding a middle ground between materialism and the linguistic turn in the epistemology of history." *Qualitative Sociology* 3: 26–52.

Stern, Steve J. 1988a. "Feudalism, capitalism, and the world-system in the perspective of Latin America and the Caribbean." *American Historical Review* 93: 829–72.

1988b. "Reply: ever more solitary." *American Historical Review* 93: 886–97.

Stewart, John. 1978. "*Verstehen* and dialectic: epistemology and methodology in Weber and Lukács." *Philosophy and Social Criticism* 5: 321–66.

Stinchcombe, Arthur L. 1968. *Constructing Social Theories*. New York: Harcourt, Brace & World.

1978. *Theoretical Methods in Social History*. New York: Academic Press.

Stone, Lawrence. 1972. *The Causes of the English Revolution 1529–1642*. London: Routledge & Kegan Paul.

1979. "The revival of narrative: reflections on a new old history." *Past and Present* 85 (November): 3–24.

1992. "The revolution over revolution." *New York Review of Books* June 11, 1992: 47–52.

Strauss, Anselm, Leonard Schatzman, Danata Erlich, Rue Bucher, and Melvin

Sabshin. 1963. "The hospital and its negotiated order." Pp. 147–69 in E. Freidson, ed., *The Hospital in Modern Society*. New York: Free Press.

Suppe, Frederick. 1977. "Afterword." Pp. 617–730 in Suppe, ed., *The Structure of Scientific Theories*, 2nd edn. Urbana: University of Illinois Press.

Sztompka, Piotr. 1979. *Sociological Dilemmas: Toward a Dialectical Paradigm.* New York: Academic Press.

Taylor, Charles. 1985 [1971]. "Interpretation and the sciences of man." Pp. 15–57 in Taylor, *Philosophy and the Human Sciences: Philosophical Papers*, vol. II. New York: Cambridge University Press.

Thomas, Brook. 1991. *The New Historicism and Other Old-Fashioned Topics.* Princeton, N.J.: Princeton University Press.

Thompson, E. P. 1975. *Whigs and Hunters: The Origin of the Black Act.* New York: Pantheon.

   1978. *"The Poverty of Theory" and Other Essays.* New York: Monthly Review Press.

Tilly, Charles. 1984. *Big Structures, Large Processes, Huge Comparisons.* New York: Russell Sage.

   1995. "To explain political processes." *American Journal of Sociology* 100: 1594–1610.

Toulmin, Stephen. 1972. *Human Understanding.* Princeton, N.J.: Princeton University Press.

Touraine, Alain. 1988 [1984]. *Return of the Actor.* Minneapolis: University of Minnesota Press.

Traugott, Mark. 1985. *Armies of the Poor: Determinants of Working-Class Participation in the Parisian Insurrection of June 1848.* Princeton, N.J.: Princeton University Press.

Trinh T. Minh-ha. 1989. *Woman, Native, Other.* Bloomington: Indiana University Press.

Tucker, Robert C., ed. 1978. *The Marx–Engels Reader*, 2nd edn. New York: Norton.

Tuma, Nancy B., and Michael T. Hannan. 1984. *Social Dynamics: Models and Methods.* Orlando: Academic Press.

Turner, Charles. 1990. "Lyotard and Weber: postmodern rules and neo-Kantian values." Pp. 108–16 in Bryan S. Turner, ed., *Theories of Modernity and Postmodernity.* Newbury Park, Calif.: Sage.

Turner, Jonathan H. 1985. "In defense of positivism." *Sociological Theory* 3: 24–30.

   1988. *A Theory of Social Interaction.* Stanford, Calif.: Stanford University Press.

   ed. 1989. *Theory Building in Sociology: Assessing Theoretical Cumulation.* Newbury Park, Calif.: Sage.

Turner, Stephen P. 1980. *Sociological Explanation as Translation.* New York: Cambridge University Press.

   1984. "Durkheim as a methodologist, part II – collective forces, causation, and probability." *Philosophy of Social Science* 14: 51–71.

   1990. "The strange life and hard times of the concept of general theory in sociology: a short history of hope." Pp. 101–33 in Seidman and Wagner 1992.

Tyler, Stephen A. 1985. "Ethnography, intertextuality and the end of description." *American Journal of Semiotics* 3: 83–98.

Unger, Rudolf. 1971 [1923]. "The problem of historical objectivity: a sketch of its development to the time of Hegel." *History and Theory, Beiheft* 11: 60–86.

Van den Berg, Alex. 1980. "Critical theory: is there still hope?" *American Journal of Sociology* 86: 449–78.

Van den Braembussche, A. A. 1989. "Historical explanation and comparative method: towards a theory of the history of society." *History and Theory* 28: 1–24.

Veeser, H. Aram, ed. 1989. *The New Historicism*. New York: Routledge.

Veyne, Paul. 1984 [1971]. *Writing History*. Middletown, Conn.: Wesleyan University Press.

Wagner, David G., and Joseph Berger. 1986. "Programs, theory, and metatheory." *American Journal of Sociology* 92: 168–82.

Wagner-Pacifici, Robin. 1994. *Discourse and Destruction: The City of Philadelphia Versus MOVE*. Chicago: University of Chicago Press.

Walkowitz, Judith R. 1992. *City of Dreadful Delight*. London: Virago Press.

Wallerstein, Immanuel. 1979. *The Capitalist World-Economy: Essays*. New York: Cambridge University Press.

———. 1988. "Comments on Stern's critical tests." *American Historical Review* 93: 873–85.

Watson, Stephen. 1984. "Jürgen Habermas and Jean-François Lyotard: postmodernism and the crisis of rationality." *Philosophy and Social Criticism* 10: 1–24.

Watson, Walter. 1985. *The Architectonics of Meaning: Foundations of the New Pluralism*. Albany: State University of New York Press.

Weber, Max. 1946 [1919]. "Science as a vocation." Pp. 129–56 in *From Max Weber: Essays in Sociology*, H. H. Gerth and C. Wright Mills, eds. New York: Oxford University Press.

———. 1947. *The Theory of Social and Economic Organization*, Talcott Parsons, ed. New York: Oxford University Press.

———. 1949. *The Methodology of the Social Sciences*. New York: Free Press.

———. 1958. *The Protestant Ethic and the Spirit of Capitalism*. New York: Scribner's.

———. 1972 [c. 1908]. "Georg Simmel as sociologist." *Social Research* 39: 155–63.

———. 1975. *Roscher and Knies: The Logical Problems of Historical Economics*, Guy Oakes, transl. New York: Free Press.

———. 1978. *Economy and Society*, Guenther Roth and Claus Wittich, eds. Berkeley: University of California Press.

———. 1981 [1927]. *General Economic History*. New Brunswick, N.J.: Transaction.

Weimann, Robert. 1987. "History, appropriation, and the uses of representation in modern narrative." Pp. 175–215 in M. Krieger 1987.

West, Cornell. 1989. *The American Evasion of Philosophy: A Genealogy of Pragmatism*. Madison: University of Wisconsin Press.

White, Hayden. 1973. *Metahistory: The Historical Imagination in Nineteenth-Century Europe*. Baltimore: Johns Hopkins University Press.

———. 1987. *The Content of the Form: Narrative Discourse and Historical Representation*. Baltimore: Johns Hopkins University Press.

Wilcox, Donald J. 1987. *The Measure of Times Past: Pre-Newtonian Chronologies and the Rhetoric of Relative Time.* Chicago: University of Chicago Press.

Wood, David. 1989. *The Deconstruction of Time.* Atlantic Highlands, N.J.: Humanities Press.

Wood, Gordon S. 1991. *The Radicalism of the American Revolution.* New York: Knopf.

Wright, Georg Henrik von. 1971. *Explanation and Understanding.* Ithaca, N.Y.: Cornell University Press.

Wuthnow, Robert. 1989. *Communities of Discourse: Ideology and Social Structure in the Reformation, the Enlightenment, and European Socialism.* Cambridge, Mass.: Harvard University Press.

Index